10/20

# The *The* Hunting *of* Hillary

THE FORTY-YEAR CAMPAIGN

TO DESTROY

HILLARY CLINTON

. . .

Michael D'Antonio

THOMAS DUNNE
BOOKS

NEW YORK

First published in the United States by Thomas Dunne Books,
an imprint of St. Martin's Publishing Group

THE HUNTING OF HILLARY. Copyright © 2020 by Michael D'Antonio.
All rights reserved. Printed in the United States of America.
For information, address St. Martin's Publishing Group,
120 Broadway, New York, NY 10271.

www.thomasdunnebooks.com

The Library of Congress Cataloging-in-Publication Data is available upon request.

ISBN 978-1-250-15460-6 (hardcover)
ISBN 978-1-250-15461-3 (ebook)

Our books may be purchased in bulk for promotional, educational, or business use.
Please contact your local bookseller or the Macmillan Corporate and
Premium Sales Department at 800-221-7945, extension 5442,
or by email at MacmillanSpecialMarkets@macmillan.com.

First Edition: May 2020

10  9  8  7  6  5  4  3  2  1

For the 50.8 percent

# Contents

It's not easy to be a woman in politics. That's an understatement. It can be excruciating, humiliating. The moment a woman steps forward and says, "I'm running for office," it begins: the analysis of her face, her body, her voice, her demeanor; the diminishment of her stature, her ideas, her accomplishments, her integrity. It can be unbelievably cruel.

—HILLARY RODHAM CLINTON

# The Hunting of
# Hillary

# Introduction

"There's not one shred of evidence that President Trump has done anything wrong." @GrahamLedger One America News. So true, a total Witch Hunt-All started illegally by Crooked Hillary Clinton.

—DONALD TRUMP, VIA TWITTER, MARCH 10, 2019

By March of 2019, two years into his first term, the forty-fifth president of the United States had issued more than two hundred social media attacks on the woman he had defeated in the 2016 election. His allies in Congress and across the country had joined in the vilification, barking Hillary Clinton's name every time events imperiled their man in the White House. Days after Trump's March 10 tweet, Senator Lindsey Graham of South Carolina took to the floor of the United States Senate to draw attention to Clinton's mishandling of emails years before. "Any American out there who did what Secretary Clinton did, you'd be in jail now," announced Graham. "The question I want to know is, does anybody other than me believe that?"[1]

The spur for Graham's question was not a groundswell of public demand for the former secretary of state to be imprisoned. Voters were little interested in this issue. Instead, Graham was seeking to deflect attention from the imminent completion of special counsel Robert Mueller's investigation of Russian meddling in the same election that had installed Trump in the Oval Office. Having joined a crowd of rabidly pro-Trump congressional Republicans, the senator uttered her name as if it were part of an evil-eye curse intended to save the president.

Graham, like Trump, had come to regard the Mueller probe as a destructive enterprise with little public purpose. The president went much further, bellowing the words *witch hunt* hundreds of times and castigating his critics in the crudest terms. Especially fixated on women who opposed him, Trump was venomous in his treatment of Representative Maxine Waters, Speaker of the House Nancy Pelosi, and upstart congressional newcomer Alexandria Ocasio-Cortez. However, time and again, he resurrected his favorite enemy, Hillary Clinton, as if she possessed powers that made her more (or less) than human and thus someone to be feared despite her retirement from politics.

The Hillary-as-enemy reflex was so much a part of Trumpism that true believers went to ridiculous extremes as they imitated the president. In the summer of 2019, when the wealthy sexual predator Jeffrey Epstein committed suicide in his jail cell, a Trump appointee at the Department of Housing and Urban Development suggested that somehow his death had been Hillary Clinton's fault. This theme circulated widely among conspiracy theorists who speculated that she was to blame for numerous deaths.

In truth, Clinton had always been regarded by her opponents as more monster than person, and they had devoted forty years to rendering her evil. Unprecedented in American history, this concerted and continuous attack had established her as a kind of devil in the hearts of millions who had been persuaded that she was the embodiment of every negative stereotype that could be mustered against a powerful woman. She was, in this calculus, not just a complex and flawed human being but, rather, scheming, untrustworthy, violent, greedy, cruel, and even murderous. As such, it wasn't enough for her to be defeated in an election. Instead, she had to be so humiliated and then obliterated that even history would forget her. Officials in Texas actually voted to remove her from history lessons taught in the state's schools but reinstated her after a public uproar.[2]

The Texas school board's decision was obviously intended to shape the minds of children who would not vote or even join adult society for years to come. By then, it would seem, Clinton and perhaps the whole notion of women asserting direct claims for power would be forgotten, at least in Texas. However, in the short term, the president and others needed her in the way that ancient peoples needed ghosts and goblins and devils. Demons are unconscious projections of the insecurities and negative impulses of their creators. "They" are heaped with sins and shortcomings so that "we" could feel pure.

As the least qualified major-party presidential candidate in modern times, Donald Trump's campaign depended on saddling his opponents with the traits that marked him—they were, in his words, crooked liars— and fomenting popular rage against them. When he learned that federal authorities were investigating links between his campaign and Russian operatives, he began saying he was the target of a "witch hunt." In just his first two years in office, Trump used the term more than one hundred times. As was so often the case with this president, his argument reduced a serious issue to an absurd and distracting slogan that was also a lie. Also true to form was the fact that with his complaint, Trump claimed to be victimized by an awful method that he himself had practiced to great effect.

During the 2016 campaign, Trump had used an arsenal of misogyny that included threats, rage, innuendo, smears, and lies against Hillary Clinton. As the Electoral College gave him the victory, despite a three-million-vote deficit at the ballot box, Trump completed the campaign of destruction that others had long waged. This effort, which is the most overlooked part of Clinton's biography, took place in the context of a backlash against the women's rights movement and a well-documented turn toward a more vitriolic politics practiced by hyper-partisans.[3]

Among the first of these extremists was a Republican congressman from Georgia named Newt Gingrich, who, beginning in the 1970s, mainstreamed the vilification of the opposition as "traitors" and "thugs" out to "destroy our country." In notes he made in the 1970s and 1980s, Gingrich showed himself to be a proto-Trump as he wrote that his side should "be willing to be unpopular, uncouth" and "have no shame." For example, he thought the GOP should try to exploit "anti-queer" senti-ment in the black community.

In addition to encouraging activists to "be nasty," Gingrich turned the old adage that says "all politics is local" on its head to make all politics national. This approach, which involved transforming the other side's leaders from opponents into enemies, made it easier for voters to form strong bonds with their political team and then join what Gingrich called "a war for power."

For a few years, Gingrich was regarded as a sideshow member of Congress, and his speeches reinforced this status. Among the choicest examples was his claim that under Democrats, "we in America could experience the joys of Soviet-style brutality and murdering of women and children." He said Speaker of the House Thomas P. "Tip" O'Neill "may not understand freedom versus slavery" and that in contesting the election results in one congressional district Democrats resembled Nazis. As he used this talk to claim the pure center of the GOP, Gingrich moved from the fringe to a place of influence. By 1985, he would lead a coterie of like-minded House members and declare, "I'm unavoidable. I represent real power."

Hillary Clinton was among the first big enemies Gingrich promoted. (He famously called her "a bitch.") Thus he applied his warfare method to the GOP's opponents and then to purge moderates from the party who were called *RINOs* for *Republicans in Name Only.* As Gingrich and others became even more rabid they attacked the very idea of verifiable facts like the science behind climate change and adapted to admit conspiracy theories about everything from vaccines to the assassination of John F. Kennedy. In some corners, a conservative's identity would depend on his or her willingness to embrace such extreme notions. The more feverish the thought—the Clintons order murders!—the more stalwart the believer.[4]

The swell of distortion and hatred had begun cresting after the election of Barack Obama in 2008. Even before he took office, Obama was accused of plotting to overthrow the United States on behalf of Muslim antagonists, secretly marrying a Pakistani man, and refusing to recite the Pledge of Allegiance. After his inauguration Obama was blamed for mass shootings and individual murders. One congressional Republican warned Obama would soon send young Americans to political reeducation camps. Faith in such outlandish ideas seemed to be part of

GOP identity. A year after Obama released his birth certificate in 2011, only 27 percent of Republicans believed he was native-born. By 2016, Hillary Clinton was the primary subject of GOP voters' fever dreams, which placed her in the middle of countless crimes and conspiracies, including of a pedophile ring operating in the basement of a pizzeria in Washington, D.C. There was no pedophile group, and the restaurant had no basement, but in a poll, nearly half of GOP voters said they either believed, or were open to accepting, the pizza pedophile story.[5]

Much of the energy behind the anti-fact extremism was generated by long-standing appeals to so-called culture war issues framed in apocalyptic terms. Beginning in the 1970s, right-wing activists and fundraisers sought to terrify voters with mass mailings and broadcasts that purported to reveal hidden forces of depravity and destruction. Urgent action was needed because, among other things, Democrats were trying to force parents to pay children minimum wage for chores; the United Nations was bent on destroying American families; schools were teaching children that "cannibalism, wife swapping, and the murder of infants and the elderly are acceptable behavior." Much of this harebrained propaganda emanated from television evangelists such as the Reverend Jerry Falwell, who, in 1981, told his flock that gay people were out to "recruit" their children into homosexuality, and the Reverend Pat Roberston, who, in 1986, called non-Christians "termites" worthy of "fumigation."

For years on end, Robertson, Falwell, and like-minded actors in religion and politics chased voters and raised tens of millions of dollars annually on the strength of dire warnings, conspiracy theories, lies, and appeals to primal emotions, especially about sexuality and gender, that made for a potent, fact-resistant political poison. Among the politicians, Gingrich was perhaps the most aggressive. Typical was his charge, in 1984, that "for a generation, the American people have allowed a liberal elite to impose radical values and flaunt deviant beliefs." By 1992, Robertson was saying that feminism "encourages women to leave their husbands, kill their children, practice witchcraft, destroy capitalism and become lesbians."[6]

Feminism in general, and some women specifically, agitated the Right in a special way. Of course, women have faced gender-based hostility in every era. Throughout history, major religions confined women to second-class status, and legal systems regarded them as chattel. The seventeenth-century pamphleteer Joseph Swetnam traced the problem to Eve and declared women "crooked by nature." Modernity hasn't erased the expectation that women would be weaker, less competent leaders, and are more suited to supporting roles in every realm outside childbearing. This belief is so ever present and ingrained that it is like the air we breathe and the ground beneath our feet. On a mass scale, it creates a hum of opposition to a woman's ambitions. The closer she gets to her goal, the louder the noise. One recent study done during an election in Oregon found that voters believed that political ambitions indicated a female candidate must be "uncaring." When told a female candidate was openly seeking power, they reported feeling "contempt, anger and/or disgust" toward her.[7]

With voters more inclined to pass harsh judgment on a strong female candidate, Hillary Clinton sought the presidency in an environment that was far more hostile to her than to her male opponent, despite her superior qualifications and his substantial and obvious flaws. She also brought to the campaign a lifetime of scars suffered at the hands of adversaries who had treated her with a level of animus so great that it seemed based on primitive instinct. She had, nevertheless, survived even as conditions in American politics worsened and set the stage for the most unhinged candidate in modern political history to oppose her. After the decades-long decline of political civility, Donald Trump used insult and fearmongering to defeat a large field of contenders for the Republican nomination and then gleefully amplified every lie and misogynistic slander ever used against Clinton to finally complete the destructive task. Trump said Clinton wasn't worthy of the presidency because "she can't satisfy her husband." During the campaign, he said she didn't have "the look" or the "stamina" to serve in the office.[8]

Just as ancient demonologists used magical words and methods to confront devils, Trump and his campaign used an array of techniques and mechanisms to carry out a political assassination. Like Joseph Swetnam, Trump used the word *crooked,* which he repeated at every opportunity, to stress the alleged deviance of his adversary. As he painted Clinton as physically weak, "erratic," and a criminal who should be imprisoned, campaign surrogates whispered about her sexuality, her religious faith, and her morals. During a nationally televised debate, Trump actually declared Clinton to be "the devil" and told her directly that were he president, "you'd be in jail." Out on the campaign trail, Trump beamed in appreciation as thousands chanted, "Lock her up! Lock her up!"[9]

The spectacle at Trump rallies, where arenas vibrated with rage, represented the ultimate expression of the fearmongering, distortion, and demonization that had been directed at Democrats in general, and Hillary Clinton specifically, for four decades. This phenomenon, which had no equal on the Left, exploited the well-established fact that messages of fear and loathing animate voters more powerfully than appeals to more benign emotions. With each election cycle, the rhetoric had become more extreme and emotional. By 2012, researchers found 43 percent of Republicans and 33 percent of Democrats felt angry at the other party's presidential candidate "just about always" or "most of the time," but it was left to Trump to cross the line that separates enthusiasm and fury. In speeches, social media posts, and interviews, he mocked his opponent and argued, without evidence, that she was a criminal who should be put on trial, convicted, and sentenced. This message, repeated and repeated, activated something so elemental in his supporters that they screamed obscene slogans, spat on journalists, and sometimes assaulted protesters.[10]

As Trump's crowds swelled with people wearing TRUMP THAT BITCH and LOCK HER UP! T-shirts and thousands roared approvingly at the idea that this woman who had dared to run for president be imprisoned, Clinton conducted a conventional campaign. She raised $1 billion, hired hundreds of staff, and logged 250,000 miles in an attempt to connect with voters. A cautious campaigner, she was not reliably exciting. However, her résumé was the best of any Democratic candidate to come along since Lyndon Johnson, and she offered popular ideas on dozens of issues from childcare to taxes. Her motto—"Stronger Together"—seemed blandly positive but likely exacerbated, if inadvertently, the fears felt by Trump's most rabid supporters. In her final campaign speech, she had encouraged Americans to vote for a "hopeful, inclusive, bighearted" future. She sounded optimistic and even busted a few moves when music signaled the end of the rally. However, a careful listener would note that she had urged her supporters to make one more day of effort because "none of us want to wake up Wednesday morning and wish we had done more. Right?"[11]

Like Fred Astaire's dance partner Ginger Rogers, who, it had been observed, had to perform her steps backward and in heels, Hillary Clinton had always been required to do more, because she was a woman. And like every woman who seeks to compete, she was expected to accept this extra burden without complaint, because complaining would only affirm the idea that she wasn't tough enough to lead. Of course, toughness was not to be shown in a way that could be mistaken as petty or mean. The tough / not tough bind was one of many paradoxes Clinton confronted in the campaign. The most vexing was the double standard applied to her words and Trump's. Her serious presentation prompted serious consideration, which meant that her truths were scrutinized more carefully than his lies.[12]

While Clinton's every utterance was parsed and analyzed for nuance, tone, and veracity, Trump was regarded more like a performer than a potential leader of the free world. When he was caught out by fact-checkers, his supporters didn't care, and some seemed to revel in the dissonance he created. Already prepared by decades of hype about conspiracies carried out by the mainstream media, the government, and other enemies, huge swaths of the electorate were either unable or unwilling to consider that he was lying to them. In their circular logic, which Trump encouraged, all information that confirmed their bias was reliable while anything that challenged it—"Fake news!" bellowed the candidate— was the product of a huge conspiracy involving the press, Democrats, moderate Republicans, academics, scientists, and a secret cabal within the government described as the "Deep State." Trump's stump-speech warning that "the fix is in" signaled that he was aware of the dark forces arrayed against him and was a call for his supporters to stand strong.

Conspiracy theories bring people into a community of believers who share a special knowledge that allows them to feel superior to ignorant others. They also bring a dramatic sense of urgency to life. Those who understand that evildoers are secretly undermining America and must be stopped do their part by refusing to consider any information that reflected negatively on their man. Trump's true believers rejected challenging information from the likes of *The New York Times, The Washington Post,* and CNN. They accepted, at face value, affirming messages on Facebook, where armies of Russian-backed trolls and automated helpers known as "bots" posted "news" that boosted their man, demonized his opponent, and cast doubt on the possibility that verifiable facts even existed. (The cleverest Russian posts, like one showing Satan fighting Jesus on Clinton's behalf, appealed to both religious and political beliefs and paid homage to messages made familiar by the likes of Robertson and Falwell.)

Russia's well-documented information war on Clinton was motivated by a general anti-Americanism and by President Vladimir Putin's dreaded fear of facing Clinton as an adversary in world affairs. He had become a Clinton hater during the Obama administration when, as secretary of state, she had called out his corruption. By the time he launched his effort to stop her campaign for president, his teams of online warriors could exploit all the rumors, innuendo, and insinuation that had been marshaled against her since the 1970s. Did Putin's minions produce the eighty thousand or so votes that gave Trump the Electoral College victory? No one will ever know. However, it was undoubtedly a factor in Trump's victory, which itself could be analyzed on two levels.[13]

First, and most obviously, Trump prevailed because he followed a long line of antagonists who had opposed Clinton with a remarkable virulence, and he was willing to campaign with a heedless disregard for the truth and, sometimes, public safety. Second the outcome could be seen as the product of a long fever dream of right-wing extremism that had burned away the very value of truth and prepared great numbers of people to *think* the very worst of Hillary Clinton and *accept* the very worst of Donald Trump.

More than anything, Trump's election showed the intensity of partisan feeling, especially religiously motivated partisan feeling, in voters isolated in an environment of like-minded people who were informed by biased media outlets and instructed by preachers who said God prefers Republicans. Having experienced and accepted the politicization of their religion, white conservative evangelicals ignored Trump's infidelities and divorces, his bankruptcies, profanity, and the many claims of sexual assault and harassment lodged by women who had encountered him in a variety of settings. They heard him say on videotape that he could "grab" women "by the pussy" and get away with it because he was a celebrity, and still favor him, according to the polls, by eight to one.

After running as a conventional candidate against a bizarre opponent in a carnival context, Clinton reached the end of the campaign fully exhausted and worried about the outcome. She hadn't slept in a day when she arrived to cast her vote—"It's a humbling feeling," she said—at the Douglas G. Grafflin Elementary School on King Street in the village of Chappaqua, New York. Tidy in a way that only a wealthy community can be, Chappaqua was where she and President Bill Clinton made their home after their White House years. With fewer than fifteen hundred residents, the village had more than a dozen sit-down restaurants, which offered cuisines ranging from Thai to French to Asian fusion. Chappaqua also was home to three yoga studios and one dessert "studio" where the owners sold giant s'mores—Girl Scout–style treats made of graham crackers, marshmallow, and chocolate—packed to ship around the world. They cost forty-nine dollars apiece.

Although easy to caricature, and Trump backers did sneer at it, Clinton's lifestyle in Chappaqua was actually *less* pretentious than Trump's existence, which was divided among various homes in wealthier precincts, including his Palm Beach club and a Fifth Avenue penthouse perched high above Tiffany & Co. However, Trump had never presented himself as anything other than a superrich businessman / heir to a family fortune, and with his crass, lifelong egomania, he had rarely asked to be regarded as anything but a braggart and a hedonist. Clinton had been an intellectual, moral, political, and later financial striver, and it was in her effort to achieve so many different things, especially as a *woman,* that she became vulnerable to those who would cast her as overly ambitious.

A presidential candidate who was born to wealth or married into it, like the Democrats' 2004 standard-bearer John Kerry, might get away with Chappaqua. Hillary Clinton of Park Ridge, Illinois, by way of Yale, Little Rock, and Washington, could not. For her, the pristine little place where she cast her vote could be seen as one more reason that she couldn't be trusted.

Throughout Election Day, Clinton backers in Rochester, New York, visited the grave of women's rights icon Susan B. Anthony at Mount Hope Cemetery, where hundreds placed on her headstone the "I Voted" stickers they got at the polls. At day's end, thousands of hope-filled Clinton supporters flocked to the Jacob K. Javits Convention Center in Manhattan. Twenty-five blocks away, a smaller crowd gathered on behalf of GOP candidate Trump in a ballroom at the New York Hilton hotel. Optimists could be found in this crowd, but many of the attendees expected defeat. At the Javits Center and the Hilton, surprise turned to astonishment as Trump accumulated electoral victories in the hotly contested swing states of Pennsylvania, Ohio, Florida, and North Carolina. The ten-dollar cash-bar beer at the Hilton began to taste better as the unlikely outcome became a reality.

Signs of Trump's victory came with a sense of unreality in part because on election night, Clinton gradually built a substantial lead in the popular vote. In the end, she would garner about three million more votes, for a 48.2–46.1 percent advantage. However, just after midnight, news agencies began declaring Trump the next president because he had captured enough individual states to win thanks to the Electoral College, which in 2000 had also made another Republican, George W. Bush, president despite his opponent, Al Gore, receiving nearly 550,000 more votes.[14]

Clinton absorbed the news of her defeat while ensconced in a suite on the top floor of the Peninsula hotel in Manhattan. She made a telephone call to offer Trump congratulations and told him she hoped for his success as a matter of "the country's success." After the call, Clinton met with her speechwriters, who were drafting an address for her to deliver in the morning. She then tried to sleep for a few hours.[15]

At 9:30 on the morning after the election, Hillary Clinton addressed a national television audience from a ballroom in the New Yorker hotel.

Standing in front of a row of American flags, Clinton wore a black suit with deep purple lapels, which matched her blouse. Her husband, who stood on her right side, wore a tie of the same purple, a color symbolizing the combination of red (Republican) and blue (Democratic) America. Determinedly dignified, Clinton said, "I'm hoping [Donald Trump] will be a successful president for all Americans. We owe him an open mind and a chance to lead." However, most of what she said was intended to encourage others. "You know," she said, "I believe we are stronger together and we will go forward together. . . . And you should never, ever regret fighting for that." Clinton then quoted the Bible, which was not something Trump could do. "You know," said Clinton, "scripture tells us, 'Let us not grow weary in doing good, for in due season, we shall reap if we do not lose heart.'"

Clinton's concession was remarkable for including one phrase—"I'm sorry"—which no other losing candidate for president had ever uttered on TV. Clearly, she recognized the peril posed by the election of a president with Trump's inexperience and temperament. The concession speech was also remarkable for what it did not include—namely, excuses and resentment. Instead, Clinton expressed gratitude for the support she received and encouragement for those who could take up the agenda her campaign had pressed. Clinton was, of course, responsible for her campaign's performance.

It would be left to others—political scientists, pollsters, journalists, and even social psychologists—to sift through the election process for the factors that determined the outcome. Early explanations focused on the notion that economic anxiety moved many to support Trump, but this idea was refuted by data that showed that in fact, Trump did not draw the votes of the unemployed, poor, or lower-middle-class voters who were concerned about the economy. Indeed, fully two-thirds of Trump voters came from families earning *above* the median income.

Deeper studies of the election, which took years to conduct, found that the main driver for Trump voters was what's termed *status anxiety* among white, male, conservative Christians. In a country where for centuries their group enjoyed unchallenged power, these voters felt that they were truer Americans than others. However, immigration and high birth rates among nonwhites were on track to push the white population below 50 percent by 2045. Conservative religion was in decline. Gender, sexual, racial, and ethnic equality were on the rise. All this change could be felt as loss and, worse, a threat. In response, older whites moved away from diverse cities to exurban and rural communities that became whiter and older as a result.

Anti-immigrant sentiment was a powerful motivator for Trump voters. Many also suspected that as white people they were themselves subject to discrimination. When Trump sounded his campaign slogan—"Make America Great Again"—they heard a promise to restore the old order.[16]

Identified by Professor Diana C. Mutz of the University of Pennsylvania, the status anxiety of Trump voters was as much about their sense of a dwindling social primacy as it was about economic concerns. Mutz's finding confirmed work by the Public Religion Research Institute (PRRI), which noted that Trump voters were upset by cultural changes and felt they were suffering from discrimination. This was the feeling that drove some to support the white nationalism common to the fringe of conservative politics and far more to feel they were losing some sort of competition that they were supposed to win. An older, extremely wealthy man rarely caught wearing anything other than an expensive suit and power tie, Trump not only promised a return to greatness but also guaranteed "winning" for his supporters. All they had to do was put their future in his paternal care. "Daddy," as his thirty-five-year-old daughter, a mother of three, called him, would make everything right.

Little noted by academics and other analysts was the fact that the cultural anxieties identified by Mutz and the PRRI had been deliberately cultivated and inflamed for decades by religious and political leaders aided by a somewhat recently established kind of partisan media that distributed extreme conservative views and conspiracy theories, all day, every day. From their pulpits, rally stages, microphones, and keyboards, these propagandists had turned Hillary Clinton into a threatening creature that had to be hunted and politically killed.[17]

The data and historical record show that the story of the 2016 election is the tale both of one woman's life and of a country that had been divided not by random events but by deliberate effort. Trump's personal misogyny and fearmongering were factors, but he did not pioneer the work of inflaming white Christian America against ambitious women and other perceived enemies. This effort had been under way for decades and had been carried out by a host of preachers, politicians, opportunists, and agitators. Like prophets of doom who must recalculate their predictions of every time Earth survives an appointment with apocalypse, they stayed relevant by continually raising the intensity of their appeals, veering further from the truth and from the respectful tradition of national politics.

As both the product and the exploiter of the derangement that had been festering for more than a generation, Trump gained the Oval Office thanks to all those who came before him. His election didn't mark the start of something new but rather the logical conclusion of something much bigger than one man. It also revealed a division so deep and wide that many reasonable observers feared for the future of American democracy. One way to understand how this happened is to consider candidate Clinton's life in the full context of her times. Her story is also the story of a people divided.

# 1

# What's in a Name?

As the wife of an ambitious young politician running for high office in 1970s Arkansas, Hillary Rodham didn't have the option of simply being herself. In every walk of life, women were expected to satisfy strict social standards. Deviate in the way you speak, act, dress, or style your hair and you will be judged. Break too many rules and you will be deemed an eccentric, a rebel, a failure, or even a danger. Woe to the woman who will not, or cannot, conform.

Conformity for a political wife meant being pleasant but not attention-seeking, concerned but not intrusive. Boosting your husband and his ideas was good. Offering your own insights was not. She could be pretty, but not sexy; well-spoken, but not opinionated. The path was narrow, and it led, inevitably, to a blank place where, no matter what she did, others would judge her according to their preexisting prejudices. This is the first obstacle every woman in politics encounters: Presentation is almost everything, and it's impossible to get it right.

The saving grace in the role required of a young Hillary Rodham was the fact that the public's interest in her was limited. As the wife of a politician who ran for Congress and lost and then was elected attorney general, Rodham didn't matter to most Arkansans. When Bill

Clinton then ran for governor, she mattered more, but for as long as he was merely a candidate, she was able to stay in the background. The press wasn't curious about her views on policy and generally ignored her biography. Then her husband won, becoming the youngest person elected governor, in any state, in forty years. Suddenly, Rodham was not the wife of a politician but the First Lady of Arkansas. Add the couple's youth and they could be considered actual, glamorous celebrities, and people wanted to know more about her.

The people of Arkansas finally got their first substantial exposure to Hillary Rodham, the actual person, in January 1979 as she sat for questions on a local TV program called *In Focus,* which was beamed across the state by a station in Jonesboro called KAIT. *In Focus* was recorded on a set that included a circle of bright green carpet on which were placed two straight-back chairs separated by a little white wicker table that had been decorated with a scraggly potted plant. It all looked like a parody of a small-market public affairs show, but it was, in 1979, where Arkansans turned for in-depth interviews with local people who mattered.

On this January morning, host Jack Hill sat opposite a young woman who wore big glasses that were stylish at the time but gave her an owlish look. As a woman in the public eye, Hillary Rodham would forever strive to communicate just the right message with her clothes, her glasses, her hair, her tone of voice, and even the expression on her face. (These were things most prominent men rarely considered.) On this day, Rodham sent the signal that she was a soft and feminine person. Her light brown hair fell just to her shoulders. A dusty-pink cardigan covered a white cowl-necked sweater. Her main concession to fashion was a pair of brown boots with three-inch heels.

Hill introduced Rodham to his viewers in the way that a ring announcer might present a boxer to the crowd at a prizefight, saying:

> *She's a native of Illinois and was raised in the Chicago area. She has an undergraduate degree from Wellesley University and a law degree from Yale University, and that's where she met her husband. Ms. Rodham is a former law professor at the University of Arkansas at Fayetteville and is a practicing attorney in Little Rock.*

Add her work on several high-profile political campaigns, as well as the House committee that initiated the impeachment of President Richard Nixon, and it would be easy to grasp why Rodham had been invited to be on the program. However, none of these accomplishments were noted by the host of *In Focus*. Instead, Hill stuck to Rodham's pedigree, stressing that she was "Arkansas's new First Lady and the wife of Governor Bill Clinton." Viewers who may have missed the point were helped by the message HILLARY RODHAM, ARK. GOVERNOR'S WIFE, which flashed on the screen. The label defined Hillary Rodham in a way that would surely irritate some version of herself, perhaps even the version that visited the Jonesboro TV station on that winter day. She might have been annoyed, too, by the hint of condescension in Hill's voice as he emphasized the word *Ms*. However, she didn't act annoyed or irritated. Instead, she smiled, and nodded, and waited for the questions to come.[1]

"Your husband won the governorship in a landslide," noted the talk show host. "But we're still led to believe that it possibly could have cost him a few votes because your name was not the same as his."

The "we" in the question was unclear, as was the identity of whoever led them to believe that Rodham had been a drag on her husband when, in fact, she was his most trusted advisor. Also, as a 63–36 winner who captured all but six of Arkansas' seventy-five counties, one would be hard-pressed to show how Bill Clinton could have received more votes than he got. Still, Hillary Rodham accepted the question as sincere and offered a sincere reply.

"I had practiced law," said Rodham. "I had worked in Washington and Boston. I had written several articles, had developed something of a specialization in the area of children and family law, and I knew that we were going to be undergoing a great deal of scrutiny and a great deal of attention if Bill continued in politics, which he intended to do in some form or another. And since I wanted to continue practicing law, I really did not want to mix my professional activities with his political activities.

"I didn't want anyone ever to think that I was either taking advantage of his position or in some way riding on it, and there aren't very many ways to persuade people of that. But I thought it essential that I try to keep as much of a distinction between my legal career and my obligations as Bill's wife as I could. Keeping my name was part of that, as well as the professional reputation that I'd already built up."

It should have been answer enough, but Hill wasn't satisfied. Instead, he stuck with this line of inquiry, offering a series of statements and questions that could be boiled down to an accusation. Among them were:

"You're not a native."

"You've been educated in liberal, Eastern universities."

"You are less than forty."

"You don't have any children."

"You don't use your husband's name."

"You practice law."

Rodham's face didn't register an emotion as basic elements of her biography, most of which would be unremarkable for any man, were listed like the elements of offense in a criminal indictment. Only a careful viewer would have noted the impatience betrayed as she bounced her foot a few times as Hill asked, "Does it concern you that maybe other people feel that you don't fit the image that we have created for the governor's wife in Arkansas?"

"I regret any reason for someone voting against Bill other than on the basis of an honest disagreement with the issues," replied Rodham. "People voted against him because of his youth, I think. Some people may have voted against him because he was born in Hope instead of Jonesboro. I mean," she said with a chuckle, "there are all sorts of reasons why a voter might vote against a politician. They aren't good reasons, in my mind."

This was the answer of a woman who was every bit as intelligent, experienced, and capable as her husband. She thought for herself and could not fully resist speaking her mind. Bright and thoughtful, she possessed a self-confidence borne of a life that had already brought her significant achievements and the respect of others. But according to the rules of gender and politics, showing this confidence was a risky thing to do

. . .

Although Jack Hill had inferred that Hillary Rodham was disconnected from the reality of ordinary voters' lives, she was not the product of multigenerational privilege or the advantages of wealth. Her mother, Dorothy Howell, had been raised in exceedingly bleak circumstances and left home at age fourteen to become a housekeeper and nanny. Howell married a salesman named Hugh Rodham, and in 1947, they had her first child, a girl they named Hillary.

At the time of their daughter's birth, the Rodhams lived in a one-bedroom apartment in the Edgewater neighborhood of Chicago. Hugh Rodham became successful enough as the owner of a small business to move his family to the suburb of Park Ridge, where they enjoyed a solidly middle-class lifestyle. Mr. Rodham was a Republican. Mrs. Rodham leaned toward the Democrats. They both were Methodists. Hillary would be followed by brothers Hugh in 1950 and Tony in 1954.

A classic big-sister achiever, Hillary was a school safety monitor and a top student whose experiences foreshadowed a life in which high performance didn't assure her the next opportunity. She dreamed of becoming an astronaut, but when she wrote to the National Aeronautics and Space Administration, the reply informed her that girls were not welcome to become space explorers. In high school, she was voted "Most Likely to Succeed," but when she ran for class president, she fell short. One of the two boys in the race told her, "You are really stupid if you think a girl can be elected president."

On the advice of teachers who thought she would be less affected by sexism at an all-women's college, Rodham applied to Wellesley, was accepted, and agreed to enroll in the fall of 1965 without ever seeing the place. When she got to the school, which is just outside Boston, Rodham was a politically engaged "Goldwater girl" at a moment when *Time* magazine could still report that female college students were mostly concerned about finding someone to marry. However, as so often happens, the journalists were behind the times. By 1965, the landmark feminist book *The Feminine Mystique* had been in print for two years, and one million copies had been sold. *Mystique* and Sylvia Plath's *The Bell Jar,* which was also published in 1963, had forced a consideration of the personal anguish caused by the unequal status of women. Add the civil rights movement, the assassination of President Kennedy, and the undeclared war in Vietnam, and college students were subject to dramatic events that made them question the status quo.

For Rodham, books, events, and people she met at college accelerated a political transformation that had actually started when she was in high school and the Reverend Donald Jones, the youth minister at her church, began to teach classes he called the *University of Life.* Field trips to poor Chicago neighborhoods and discussions of current events challenged her young Republican perspective. Her political reawakening continued at Wellesley until, by the time of the assassinations of Martin Luther King Jr. and Robert Kennedy in 1968, she was like millions of her peers—alarmed if not disillusioned by the acute and ongoing traumas in American politics.

Rodham was working as an intern in Washington, D.C., when Robert Kennedy was killed. Her assignment in the office of the House Republican leadership had begun with a handshake from then representative Gerald Ford on her first day of work. In July, her boss in the Capitol, a congressman from western New York named Charles Goodell, brought Rodham and a few other interns to the Republican National Convention in Miami. Goodell supported Nelson Rockefeller's bid for the presidential nomination, but neither he nor the other main hopefuls, Ronald Reagan and George Romney, stood a chance against Richard Nixon.

As he accepted the nomination, the man who lost to John F. Kennedy in 1960 pledged to "restore order and respect for law" and promised that "the long dark night for America is about to end." After the convention, Goodell would be named to serve what remained of Senator Kennedy's term. Rodham, her internship over, would go home to her parents' house in the Chicago suburbs with the memory of her first glimpse of big-time politics, which had included meeting Frank Sinatra and sharing an elevator with John Wayne.[2]

Chicago happened to be the site of the Democratic Party's nominating convention, which promised to be a far more tumultuous affair. As anti-war organizations called for protests, Chicago mayor Richard Daley had tried to make it impossible for them to disrupt the event. He ordered a steel fence topped by barbed wire installed around the convention site and denied the protesters permits to march near it. The glass in the doors at the hall were replaced with bulletproof plastic, and more than ten thousand police officers were equipped with riot gear and put on twelve-hour shifts. Daley requested, and received, more than five thousand Illinois National Guard soldiers to supplement them.

By the time the convention began, roughly ten thousand protesters had gathered in Grant Park, which was about five miles from the hall. They created little encampments, performed bits of political theater, and clambered all over a statue of Union Army general John A. Logan astride a horse. Learning of all this, Rodham was filled with the sense that something momentous was in the offing. Free to do as she wished, since her parents and brothers were away on vacation, she went downtown with a friend. They immediately ran into mayhem as the helmeted police had initiated a riot, beating protesters and chasing them into nearby streets. Pedestrians and bystanders were set upon by the officers. As one eyewitness testified to an investigating commission created by President Johnson:

> People who were not part of the demonstration were coming out of a tavern to see what the demonstration was . . . and the officers indiscriminately started beating everyone on the street who was not a policeman.[3]

An estimated fifty million people saw the TV broadcasts of officers in helmets wading into crowds and chasing those who fled into tear gas–filled streets. Rodham and her friend were among the brave few who witnessed it firsthand. They came upon a high school classmate who had gone into nursing and told them she had taken care of some of the injured. As this woman wondered aloud about the possibility of a revolution, Rodham and her friend quickly fled. Behind them, protesters hurled rocks and chunks of pavement. The bloody spectacle became a formative moment for Rodham and one more trauma for the country.

The violence and divisions in the party, which was displayed in the press, helped to give the White House to Richard Nixon.[4]

As a zealous convert to the Democratic Party, Rodham had been dismayed by Nixon's victory. However, she was not radicalized by what she had witnessed in the streets of Chicago or by the outcome of the November balloting. She was still committed to playing by the house rules, not burning it down. Back at Wellesley, she was chosen by her classmates to deliver the student commencement speech when she and her classmates were awarded their degree. In it, she defended the "indispensable task of constructive criticism and protest," but she was far more respectful than radical as she said she hoped for "politics as the art of making what appears to be impossible possible."

The comments her extended family heard about the Wellesley speech, which was covered broadly in the press, generally fell into two categories. One, Rodham would summarize as "Who does she think she is?" The other she called "She spoke for a generation." Neither of these reactions was nuanced enough to be fair. Rodham hadn't asked to speak, so she could hardly be painted as overweening or presumptuous. If she had spoken with less confidence, she would not have been heard. And she was too conventional in her thinking to have been a voice for the 1960s generation. Her undergraduate thesis, about the activist/organizer Saul Alinsky, was mainly a critique of his theory that positive change had to be imposed from outside the political system. She believed in advocating change from within. She disappointed Alinsky when she chose law school over an offer to work with him.

At Yale Law School, Rodham entered an even higher echelon of American society than she had encountered at Wellesley. Yale Law attracted sons and daughters of the elite and the superambitious children of more ordinary families. Among them were many who no doubt imagined themselves to be future presidents. The most charismatic of her fellow students was William Jefferson Clinton, whose Elvis-worshipping mother had filled him with dreams of the White House when he was just a boy. As a high schooler, he went to Washington on a trip sponsored by the American Legion and shook JFK's hand. Friends would recall that at about this time, he actually spoke aloud about running for president. He would eventually acknowledge that his commitment to politics had been made at this time, but it was not Kennedy but Rev. Martin Luther King Jr. who had been his inspiration. As a boy, Clinton had attended church alone, walking more than a mile each way in jacket and tie and with a Bible in hand. Politics was a religious calling—he termed it *ministry*—and he intended, like King, to make racial justice a central focus of this service. Not surprisingly, for a born-again Southern Baptist, he often quoted the Bible. He favorite passage, from Isaiah, reads, in part, "And he shall be called healer of the breach." (The Bible was hardly foreign to Rodham, but her Methodism was a cooler form of faith.)[5]

Scripture wasn't routinely quoted by students at Yale, but it would be a mistake to assume that the university was as godless as many in the Bible Belt believed. When Rodham and Clinton attended, Yale chaplain William Sloane Coffin Jr. preached religiously inspired activism against the Vietnam War. Religion courses were among the most popular on campus, and Yale Divinity School was among the most prestigious in the world. The Yale law faculty included top-rate scholars such as Robert Bork, Burke Marshall, and Jan Deutsch. The school contributed to the pipeline that provided clerks to federal courts, and it hosted visits by national leaders. Among the many whom Rodham met in New Haven was a lawyer named John Doar, who visited in 1973 to judge a mock trial competition. A Republican who had become famous as the top lawyer in the Civil Rights Division of the Department of Justice, Doar led the investigation of the murder of three student voting activists in Mississippi. He had also overseen James Meredith's arrival at the University of Mississippi, where federal intervention forced officials to accept him as the school's first black student. Doar had personally escorted Meredith to the campus on his first day in attendance. Yale students were aware of Doar's record and his courage. Rodham would describe him as an exemplar of "discreet, non-partisan professionalism."[6]

After earning her law degree, Rodham went to Arkansas to visit Clinton's family and then accepted a job with a new organization called the Children's Defense Fund. Rodham investigated the problems of juveniles held in adult jails in South Carolina and knocked on doors in New Bedford, Massachusetts, to locate children who weren't attending school because they were disabled or kept at home to care for brothers and sisters. The work led directly to the 1975 Education for All Handicapped Children Act, which required that schools educate disabled students or lose federal funds.

As Rodham was interviewing families in New Bedford, the nation was becoming transfixed by a scandal that began in June 1972 with the arrest of five would-be burglars at the Democratic National Committee's headquarters at the Watergate hotel / office complex in the Foggy Bottom neighborhood of Washington, D.C. The burglary had been ordered because Nixon wanted to find out if the Democrats or candidate George McGovern possessed documents related to money his campaign operatives had received from the reclusive Howard Hughes.[7]

With the help of an inside source at the FBI, Carl Bernstein and Bob Woodward of *The Washington Post* reported that Watergate had been just the tip of the iceberg. In fact, the White House had directed a broad campaign of political sabotage against Nixon's opponent, including possibly illegal activities.[8]

The legal proceedings against the burglars ensured the scandal would worsen. In the spring of 1973, White House counsel John Dean told investigators of the president's involvement in the scheme. In early 1974, the House Judiciary Committee, which was preparing to consider articles of impeachment against the president, hired John Doar to be one of two lawyers overseeing the work. Under pressure to hire a staff, Doar turned to a ready source of supply: the pool of recent graduates from the nation's top law schools. Hillary Rodham was one of the newly minted lawyers Doar called to offer a job. Rodham moved to Washington and reported to an office in a former hotel on Capitol Hill. She soon joined a small group assigned to listen to tapes of secretly recorded Oval Office conversations.

Among all the artifacts of the American presidency, few are more significant than the Nixon tapes. Profane, scheming, self-pitying, and paranoid, the president heard in the recordings challenged the assumptions any listener might have about the moral condition of the man or the dignity of the office he held. In one, he told his chief of staff, H. R. Haldeman, "We're up against an enemy, a conspiracy. They're using any means. We are going to use any means. Is that clear?" In another, Nixon said, "We're going to prosecute—got to prosecute everybody." The president then said, "Does that bother you as being repressive?" Haldeman replied, "We've got to be repressive."[9]

In other recordings, Nixon expressed racism, sexism, and homophobia. He mused about blowing up a safe in order to steal documents from the Brookings Institution. As insecure as he was paranoid, Nixon expected fawning attention from those who served him and he generally got it; when he asked Secretary of State Henry Kissinger if he agreed that courage—he used the term *guts*—had been the hallmark of his first years in office, his advisor answered, "Totally."[10]

The Nixon tapes provided an inside look at the presidency—or at least *one* presidency—that would disillusion millions. (Public trust in government plunged during Nixon's presidency.) Few would have been as quickly and immediately disturbed as Rodham and the other lawyers who were the first to hear Nixon scheme. They worked in secret and were barred from discussing what they heard. In July 1974, the House Judiciary Committee would approve articles of impeachment again. Nixon avoided trial by resigning on August 9. The images of him waving to weeping staffers as he departed the White House for the last time became an enduring emblem of political humiliation. He would be replaced by Gerald Ford, who had been appointed to the vice presidency when Spiro Agnew was forced to resign when it was revealed he had accepted bribes and illegally avoided taxes as governor of Maryland. (Agnew infamously told Nixon, "I apologize for lying to you. I promise I won't deceive you except in matters of this sort.") After taking the oath of office, Agnew's successor said, "This is an hour of history that troubles our minds and hurts our hearts."[11]

As the House Judiciary Committee finished work, twenty-six-year-old Hillary Rodham told her colleague Bernard Nussbaum she wanted him to meet her boyfriend, Bill Clinton, who was "going to be president of the United States." She left Washington, having experienced more history than most human beings witness in a lifetime. A straight line drawn from the moment she met Gerald Ford at the start of her Capitol Hill internship to his oath of office would pass through the GOP convention that nominated Nixon in '68, the Chicago police riot, and the Watergate crisis. At one level or another, Rodham was a participant in each of these events. And yet, when the House committee staff gathered for a farewell dinner, a senior attorney recommended she limit her ambitions. Rodham said that she wanted to become a litigator. He said that would be impossible because she wouldn't "have a wife" to take care of her. She decided to pursue the goal anyway and to do it in Arkansas, where she and Bill Clinton planned to start their life together.

In 1974, many Americans associated Arkansas politics with news film of enraged white citizens, some waving Confederate flags, screaming at nine black students who integrated into Little Rock Central High School under armed guard in 1957. The showdown at the school had been precipitated by Governor Orval Faubus, who responded to a federal court's integration order by shutting down Central High School. The governor made the crisis a states'-rights issue, a common tactic for segregationists, saying that with integration, "the good relations that existed heretofore between the races here will be gone forever." The standoff ended when federal troops escorted the black students into Central High as white segregationists lined the sidewalk and screamed in protest.

In time, Faubus's stand against integration would be seen as more an act of political pandering than personal racism. Standing up to the federal government made the governor seem strong while his comments on integration signaled to voters who were racists that he understood their resistance. This positioning was a function of Faubus's main ambition, which was to hold power. He was otherwise a rather liberal, anti-poverty crusader who brought roads, schools, sanitation, and electricity to isolated corners of the state. While little understood outside Arkansas, this blend helped Faubus win six terms in a state where no one had been elected more than twice in a century. He was defeated in 1966 by Republican Winthrop Rockefeller and was denied a comeback in 1970 by a relatively unknown candidate named Dale Bumpers, a lawyer/rancher who sold some cattle to raise money for his campaign. (After winning the Democratic primary, Bumpers easily defeated Rockefeller in the general election.)[12]

When Bumpers was elected governor, Arkansas was represented in Washington by a senator who might be regarded as the intellectual's

Orval Faubus. A Rhodes scholar and former president of the University of Arkansas, J. William Fulbright was a segregationist who was also an early opponent of the Vietnam War and a devoted advocate of international cooperation. By 1974, thirty years in office and an intense focus on foreign affairs—he chaired the United States Senate Committee on Foreign Relations for fifteen years—had made Fulbright vulnerable to the same candidate who knocked Faubus out of the governor's office. Possessed of vast amounts of country charm, Dale Bumpers applied a populist's skepticism to the power of the rich and corporations, and he spoke with what *The New York Times* called "sugar coated candor" that left people with the "feeling that he has genuinely listened to their problems." He beat Fulbright by almost two to one.[13]

Bumpers's success signaled that a new generation had seized power in Arkansas, bringing with it a more modern style and more open-minded values. By August, Bumpers was so far ahead in his reelection campaign that he could devote some of his time to young Bill Clinton's quixotic and ultimately doomed attempt to unseat four-term Republican congressman John Paul Hammerschmidt, whose district included Fayetteville and its surrounding area. Like so many campaigns, the Clinton for Congress operation was a small cult of personality dependent on the candidate's charisma. Perhaps inevitably, Clinton began a romantic relationship with one of the young women who provided much of the energy for the effort. Clinton and Marla Crider were unmarried, consenting adults, but she was only twenty years old and still a college student. Clinton was both an authority figure and a man in a committed relationship, which is something Rodham brought to his attention in a letter that noted "all your little girls" and reminded him of "the goals we set for ourselves."

The alliance that Clinton and Rodham had organized around his potential was something he would value throughout his life, even though he was reckless about it. "She makes me a better person," he would say. "She gets me started, kicks my butt, and makes me do the things I've got to do." In 1974, the things Clinton needed to do, and which she required of him, included bringing order to his congressional campaign and to his personal life.

As recounted by writer/psychologist John D. Gartner in his book *In Search of Bill Clinton,* the future president's affair with Crider and Hillary Rodham's response illustrated a dynamic that had been established early in his life and which would persist for decades. As Gartner saw it, Clinton's childhood had been dominated by his mother, Virginia, and grandmother Edith, who were rivals for his attention. A vivacious woman with big hair and big enthusiasms, Virginia left him in her mother's care for two years while she trained as a nurse anesthesiologist in New Orleans. After she returned, she poured much of her time and energy into her many relationships with men and her anesthesiology practice, which thrived. Edith was, in comparison, serious and reliable. Ever dependable, she also demanded much of the boy she had agreed to help raise. She was, in short, very much like Hillary Rodham.

The similarities were sensed by Clinton's mother, Virginia Kelley, who noted that Hillary cared little about her appearance and was disinterested in the kind of socializing she relished. Everything about Hillary—her refusal to wear makeup, her wardrobe, her hair—seemed an affront to Kelley. Eventually, she would confess that she resented Rodham for "being a lot smarter than I am," and though she would sometimes appear to be happy with her son's choice, the display was less than genuine.

Although some others were intimidated by Hillary Rodham, young Bill Clinton was not. By many accounts, in their early years he and Hillary demonstrated the kind of affection that couldn't be faked. Unique, as all pairings are, their relationship was based on so many shared values and interests that they were always more likely to stay together than to part. However, his affairs were betrayals and inflicted real pain. Perhaps, as Gartner suggests, Clinton would have treated her better if he understood himself more fully. Instead, he would, like so many others, regard Hillary through the lens of his own experiences and assumptions, many of them unacknowledged. She was not just a woman but also a representation of something, just as she was to Virginia, and this made her, in his eyes, both less than and more than her true self.[14]

Rodham was also a representational figure at the University of Arkansas School of Law, where she was known as the "new lady professor" who was also charged with creating a legal aid clinic to serve the poor. The work of overseeing dozens of students who were supposed to represent the poor in court gave her immediate and substantial trial experience. However, it was challenging work that included representing people accused of serious crimes. In one troubling case, which she tried to dodge, a judge asked her to represent a man accused of raping a twelve-year-old girl. The man passed a lie detector test, but Rodham still suspected he might be guilty. Her defense, and the victim's desire to avoid a trial, led to a plea bargain, which came with a five-year prison term.

Rodham and Clinton were married in October 1975. A month later, Jimmy Carter came to speak at the university, where he introduced himself with the words, "Hi, I'm Jimmy Carter, and I'm going to be president." Both Clinton and Rodham would commit to working in Carter's behalf even as they organized Bill's run for attorney general. Democrats so dominated statewide politics that when Clinton swamped two rivals in the spring primary, he was all but guaranteed victory in the November general election. Rodham went to run the Carter campaign's field operations in the heavily Republican state of Indiana, where she helped the Democrat do better than expected. With Carter's national victory, Rodham and Clinton became frequent guests at the White House, where it was possible for them to imagine themselves in residence one day.

Bill and Hillary moved one step closer to their shared goal when he announced he would run for governor in 1978. This was the moment when people close to Clinton began to worry about how voters in socially conservative Arkansas would respond to Hillary's appearance and persona. Bill was a true Southern charmer, with an uncanny ability to make every person he met feel that he was grateful to share a moment. Hillary was a midwesterner who had been educated in the Northeast and was so evidently not a local that there was no way that she could have passed for one. More remarkably, she insisted on calling herself Hillary Rodham, not Hillary Clinton.[15]

Preternaturally adept at combining values wherever he found them, even when they seemed to conflict, Bill Clinton attached no significance to his wife's decision to keep her name. He would eventually write that while others fretted about it, the choice "didn't mean a thing to me." She wanted to hang on to *Rodham*, he added, and "since I wanted to hang on to her, that was fine by me."

Clinton may have been more flexible on the matter because of his own experience with names and family identity. At birth, he was named William Jefferson Blythe III, after a father who had supposedly died in a car wreck three months before. However, some doubt clouds the matter of his paternity, since Blythe was not in the country when, according to Virginia, Bill was conceived. At fifteen, Clinton took the last name of his stepfather Roger Clinton, who was the kind of hard-drinking and hotheaded character who could, and did, fire a pistol shot into the wall to make a point.

Married five times (twice to Roger Clinton), Virginia would have just as many names during her lifetime. The changes occasioned by weddings and divorces complicated her life in a way that no man with the same experience would have to endure. Her financial and professional lives were also affected. Seen in this light, Hillary's desire to hang on to a name that was already attached to an impressive record—in politics, law, and academia—made sense in a way that was hard to refute. Besides, Clinton had no doubt that his wife loved him, and it was this love and not a willingness to adhere to tradition that mattered to him. What good had that tradition done where his mother's marriages were concerned?[16]

In 1975, roughly 17 percent of American brides made the choice to keep their names. (The number would rise to 30 percent in 2015.) Women with advanced academic degrees and those who waited longer to marry were more likely to make this choice. Rodham was nearly seven years older than the median age for women at the time of their first marriage. Add the fact that she had published several articles under her name and was off to a good start on her legal career, and she had ample reason to consider that her name had value.[17]

Rodham was so circumspect about her relationship that the Arkansas press seemed mostly oblivious to the fact that she was married to

Clinton even as he ran for attorney general—a race he won—in 1976. When the Fayetteville newspaper covered "Women's Week" at the University of Arkansas, they quoted a professor named Ms. Rodham, who addressed a symposium on rape and the legal system. The paper took pains to explain that she preferred "that designation [of Ms.]." A reader responded with a complaint, noting that people, even in Arkansas, were familiar with the honorific and that the editors didn't ever explain "the use of the words 'Miss, Mrs.' Or 'Mr.'"[18] The other "Ms." who was noted in the letter to the editor in the Fayetteville paper was Susan Brownmiller. Author of the recently published *Against Our Will,* which revealed the historical, social, political, and personal impact of sexual assaults, Brownmiller had addressed a big crowd at the university on the evening before Rodham participated in the panel on rape and the law. About five hundred people listened to her argue that because of rape, women were "the first subjugated people" on Earth. "Men who commit rape," she had written, "have served in effect as frontline masculine shock troops, terrorist guerrillas in the longest sustained battle the world has ever known."[19]

*Against Our Will* marked a turning point in society's response to sexual assault. Within a year of its publication, Nebraska would become the first state to make a husband's rape of his wife a crime. Within a decade, sexual assault was widely discussed as a problem in the law, in families, and in communities, and rape crisis centers were opened across the country. Brownmiller's book was also part of a wave of social activism that promoted the rights and equality of women. Their progress was so rapid that in 1976 the Republican National Convention, perhaps noting polls that said a majority of men and women supported it, endorsed the proposed Equal Rights Amendment to the U.S. Constitution. (The amendment said simply, "Equality of rights under the law shall not be denied or abridged by the United States or by any State on account of sex.") Before the year ended, the courts would outlaw the practice of excluding women from juries and bar states from withholding employment benefits from pregnant women on the notion that they were physically incapable of working.

In Arkansas, a year *after* her husband, Bill Clinton, won the office of attorney general, the *Hope Star* newspaper reported that a "Little Rock lawyer" named Hillary Rodham was being considered for a presidential appointment to the board of the Legal Services Corporation. It was, perhaps, a sign of the times that the paper didn't mention that her husband was the fourth-highest-ranking elected official in state government. It was also a sign of the times that the paper, in its second reference, called her "Miss Rodham."[20]

"Miss" Rodham surely knew that despite her accomplishment, some would always define her by her marital status. (In some states, landlords, banks, and employers were still permitted to discriminate against women, requiring they present male cosigners for some documents and paying them lower wages simply on the basis of their gender.) When her husband, Bill Clinton, won the race for governor in 1978, even he seemed incapable of talking about her in a modern way. In a post-election interview with the Associated Press, he talked about "my little wife," describing her as a "hard-working, no-nonsense, no-frills, intelligent girl." Surely Clinton spoke this way to signal the public that he was unaffected by the modern Eastern liberals he had encountered at law school and in national political circles. He may have even thought this way from time to time. But it strains credulity to think that in private he treated her as a "little wife" or a "girl."[21]

If her own husband wavered between the more sexist past and his wife's feminist present—in a conversation with a reporter, no less—then how could Hillary Rodham expect Jack Hill of KAIT-TV to treat her with any greater respect? So it was that she tolerated questions that would never have been asked of a man. This meant she sat patiently through many discussions of her status as a working woman, her decision to forgo having children, and her continued use of the name she had been given when she was born. She told Hill, "I think it's an understandable question, but for many of the things we've just been talking about, the decision to keep my own name, particularly in my professional work, was one that seemed a very natural kind of decision, because, as I said, I was older when I got married." Later, she would explain that she never wanted to make her husband's achievements the basis of her own identity. "I'm a lawyer," she would say. "If I met somebody at the airport, I wouldn't say, 'Oh, I'm the First Lady of Arkansas.'"

Rodham meant no disrespect to others, but no matter how she answered those who kept asking about her decision to live, as much as possible, by her own lights, she could never put to rest the feelings of suspicion and even anger she evoked in those who decided that she represented changes they couldn't abide. Born into a generation that pushed for greater equality for people of differing races, creeds, sexual orientation, and gender, she would be regarded as pushy and demanding just because she wanted a fair shot for people from all backgrounds, including herself. Civil rights activists had been deemed pushy for the same reason.

As of 1979, the Supreme Court had yet to overturn state laws that granted men "head and master" of a household and depriving wives of equal property rights. Women could still be denied partnerships in a law firm on the basis of gender, and schools could shortchange women students, in athletics and other areas of education, and still qualify for federal funds.[22]

In early 1980, Hillary Rodham earned a brief reprieve from critics who considered her too modern when she gave birth to her daughter, Chelsea, and began introducing herself as "Hillary, Governor Clinton's wife." However, her husband was running for reelection, and the Republican in the race, Frank White, pressed the issue of her nontraditional choices. He spoke of his own spouse as "Mrs. Frank White." Within a year, he was the new governor of Arkansas, and Mrs. White was the First Lady.[23]

Hillary Rodham had not been the determining factor in her husband's defeat. Voters were peeved by increased taxes on car registrations and by a mass escape by Cuban boat-lift refugees who had been held by the federal government at Fort Chaffee, an army base. Clinton had also been hurt by his youth and inexperience, which a local editorial cartoonist had stressed by drawing him on a tricycle. And then there were the inevitable missteps and failures that come with the job. Clinton had upset some people by recruiting out-of-staters for key jobs in his administration, and he had failed to shield utility customers from massive increases in the bills they paid to the local power company. Some were asked to pay for an out-of-state nuclear plant being built in Mississippi. (Questions about this scheme wound up in federal court, where Judge Robert Bork, once Clinton's professor at Yale, favored the utility over Arkansas consumers.)

As he wrote in a 2004 memoir called *My Life,* Clinton took the loss hard, descending into "self-pity and anger, mostly at myself." During a period of soul-searching, he asked just about everyone he met why he had lost. Some actually mentioned the fact that Hillary held on to her name, which was fine for a lawyer but not for the governor's wife. Most mentioned issues like the license plate tax. One voter said he recruited ten other people to switch from Clinton to White on account of the tax. When Clinton asked if he'd consider him for governor again, the man said he would because "we're even now."[24]

As he emerged from his doldrums Hillary Clinton encouraged her husband to believe he could be elected again, not just in Arkansas but someday in a national race for president. Thus she began calling herself Hillary Clinton. As he committed to a rematch with White, she decided to act as his top strategist. She helped him accept that he should apologize for letting the people of the state down in his first term as governor and played the staff disciplinarian to his cheerleader.

As she crisscrossed the state, greeting people as Mrs. Clinton, Hillary intended to spare her candidate spouse the complication of her earlier name choice. The trouble was that no one who cared about her name was likely to be persuaded and those who never cared might be alienated by the change. As an editorial in the *Blytheville Courier News* put it, "With either group it smacks of political expediency." The same editorial criticized another Democratic politician, Jim Guy Tucker, who went to an Ivy League college but enjoyed hunting and guitar picking. "The boys at the service station" wouldn't be fooled, declared the paper.

Bill Clinton won the race against White. Jim Guy Tucker would eventually occupy the governor's mansion too. But the judgment of the boys at the service station, and many who shared their perspective, would remain a problem for the woman who was Hillary Rodham and then Hillary Clinton. They might accept her highly educated husband, or Jim Guy Tucker, and let them play the good ol' boy when the situation called for it. The same option didn't exist for any woman, most especially one who, they suspected, considered herself any man's equal.[25]

## 2

## She's Ambitious

What is it about female ambition? In grade school, a smart girl might get away with striving for top grades. In high school, she is more likely than a male to be valedictorian. But once school is over, the real world will present a striving woman with special obstacles. Opportunities are fewer. Mentors are harder to come by. And as you begin to achieve, you can expect that others will wonder if, given your success, you are somehow lacking as a woman. No wonder that a recent study by Bain & Company found that while women begin their careers with high aspirations, after two years most had adjusted their hopes downward. Men do not lose hope in the same way.

In the 1970s, women faced longer career odds. Big cities did offer some chances for women to seek their ambition and find acceptance. The path was less clear in rural regions. With a population of about two million, Arkansas circa 1976 counted just a handful of major corporations—Walmart, Tyson Foods, J. B. Hunt freight—and a similarly small number of truly wealthy individuals. Like the local economy, the legal profession in the state was also a game for a small number of players. If you weren't fulfilled by divorce work, minor criminal matters, and small real estate projects, you went to the capital city of Little Rock and either hung a shingle or worked for one of a few old-line firms.

The most powerful attorney group in Little Rock, the Rose Law Firm, dated to 1820 and was also the oldest corporation in the state. One of the firm's founders, Robert Crittenden, served as secretary of the Arkansas Territory and negotiated a treaty with the Quapaw tribe of American Indians. In 1829, he challenged a political opponent to a duel and killed him. Five years later, at the age of thirty-seven, he suffered a heart attack in the middle of a trial and died. Another early partner, U. M. Rose, followed a more stately path. Erudite and multi-lingual, he was a founder of the American Bar Association and friend of the future Supreme Court justice Felix Frankfurter. Rose represented the United States at the Hague Convention, which drafted the first multi-national treaty on war crimes. He stands in marble in the U.S. Capitol's statuary hall.

Although they generally confine themselves to local and regional matters, firms like Rose, which can be found in every small state, ac-cumulate a wealth of knowledge and expertise that makes them hard to beat on their home field. However, their varied and seemingly conflict-ing relationships also made them ideal imaginary villains. Novelist John Grisham has sold more than three hundred million books by depending on the suspicions that arise when the rich and the powerful all use the same lawyers in proceedings before judges who may have once been their colleagues. Outsiders see the potential corruption in this dynamic. Bright young lawyers with ambition see the only game in town.

When Hillary Rodham settled in Arkansas and went looking for a job, Rose was the obvious option. The firm represented many of the state's most prominent people and entities, including food companies, media companies, and the burgeoning retail giant Walmart. The revenue flowing from these clients meant that partners and associates were likely the highest paid in the state. Unlike her husband, who never seemed much interested in money, Rodham's ambitions included financial se-curity, which Rose could provide. She also craved the opportunity to create her own place among powerful people engaged in work that mattered. Her education, experience with the Watergate committee, and appointment as a law professor made her unique among young lawyers in the state. On paper, she had sky's-the-limit potential.

Two factors complicated Rodham's effort to land a job. The first was the issue of her gender. In 1970, the American legal profession was 94 percent male. In 1976, when she reached out to Rose, the figure was 90 percent. At Rose, which employed no women attorneys at all, some of the men actually spoke out loud about how clients would reject a female lawyer and worried about what might happen if she became pregnant. Vincent Foster, a Rose partner who had been Bill Clinton's neighbor, kindergarten classmate, and lifelong friend, vouched for Rodham, and her confident, nearly perfect performance in her interview with his colleagues put their worries about gender to rest.[1]

The second complicating issue for Rodham and Rose was Bill Clinton. A young star of the Democratic Party, he intended to run for attorney general and was likely to win. Rose had been unable to identify any other attorney general in the entire country whose spouse worked in the law. A request for advice sent to the American Bar Association brought back a report indicating that Rodham could be employed if certain procedures were followed to limit conflicts of interest. With this semiofficial clearance, Rose could exploit the cachet and billing value of bringing her on board. No one would have to say a word to current or potential clients about the potential benefits of working with the legal group that employed the attorney general's wife. In fact, an understated approach to this connection, which allowed the imagination to run wild, could make Rose seem more powerful due to the connection. Less obvious were the complications the relationship could pose for her. For every benefit that might come from having a politically prominent spouse, there would be a price paid as his work inevitably provoked his political opponents and made some constituents unhappy.

When Rodham was hired, she was paid about the same as her husband, who earned a $25,378 state salary after he won the attorney general race. Soon, she was representing corporate clients and, with the help of Foster, found some acceptance. Foster and another partner, Webster "Webb" Hubbell, became her allies at the firm where many of the other women, who worked as office staff, regarded her as a bit of an oddity because she wore little makeup, peered at them through big glasses, and seemed to have no real jewelry. As one told biographer Carl Bernstein, "there wasn't one stereotypically womanly or feminine thing about her."[2]

There it was, the trump card that anyone could play, at any time, against any ambitious woman. No amount of achievement or intelligence could exempt Hillary Rodham from standards of femininity determined by society at large and enforced by anyone who chose to take on the job. The rules governing femininity—like the definition of "normal"—were widely accepted and enforced but difficult to describe. One of the first scientific efforts to define the norms was produced in 1977 by sociologist Erving Goffman, who observed that women are regarded as "precious, ornamental, and fragile" creatures who are expected to "display frailty, fear, and incompetence." Courtesies would be offered to women who conformed, especially if they are "young and pretty," but not to those who failed to comply to expectations.[3]

Of course, what constituted compliance, in behavior or ornamentation, varied from place to place. In 1970s New York City, fashions allowed for short hair and sleek clothes. In Little Rock, big hair was in. Sleek was out. Little Rock was also less flexible when it came to how women were supposed to behave. Women who sought power in realms previously reserved for men were regarded as unusual, challenging, even unnatural. In public forums across the South, defenders of the old order argued that women who wanted equal access to power were defying both God and nature. Typical was Christian Right activist Phyllis Schlafly, whose 1977 book, *The Power of the Positive Woman,* taught readers to accept that while men are "discursive, logical, abstract, or philosophical, woman tends to be emotional, personal, practical, or mystical." Women who defied these norms were not just wrong, they were trying, she said, "to repeal and restructure human nature."[4]

In her work, Rodham was sufficiently logical and abstract in her thinking to represent a range of clients, including corporations and children and families dealing with social service agencies and family law courts. The firm got a jolt of good publicity when she accepted President

Carter's appointment to the federal Legal Services Corporation board, which she came to chair, but this was not the kind of work that would make her locally famous. That status came when her husband ran for governor and won. Suddenly, she was recognized by constituents on the street and regarded by Democratic Party leaders as one half of a power couple.

The idea that a married couple would work together in the pursuit of a shared ambition was nothing new in American politics. From John and Abigail Adams to Ronald and Nancy Reagan, the historical record is full of examples. The main difference here was that Clinton and Rodham chose to be open about their effort and, more important, about her significance. Rodham was the woman *beside* the man, not *behind* him, and Clinton reinforced this notion. When he named her to lead a health care advisory committee, she used her own political connections, as well as his, to get increased federal funding for medical services in the rural parts of the state.

Rodham's personal success and her marriage to Bill Clinton brought her into contact with Arkansas's elite, which included more people of great wealth than one might expect in a place where people often said, "Thank God for Mississippi," as they contemplated the state's poverty. Key among them was a lawyer / investment advisor named Jim Blair, who was making huge sums in the arcane world of commodity futures. His performance was aided by the fact that his broker sometimes let him skirt the rules. When he opened accounts for family and friends— Rodham included—they, too, got the special treatment.

Even with the bending of rules, which spared her from making good on margin calls that would require her to pay large sums to cover investment losses, Rodham experienced significant ups and downs. In a little more than a year's time, she would rack up a profit of almost $100,000 and then stopped trading. This sum, equivalent to $390,000 in 2019, was a windfall for a couple who earned less than $60,000 per year and possessed few assets. In an effort to establish some wealth, they joined friends James and Susan McDougal to form a corporation called Whitewater Development, which purchased roughly 230 acres along the White River in the Ozarks. The area was rising as both a retirement community and a vacation destination as the city of Branson, Missouri, evolved into a country music mecca. The acreage would cost a little more than $200,000. Split into small parcels, the property could net many times that amount if buyers could be found.

A longtime Democratic Party operative, Jim McDougal had worked for William Fulbright and was well known across the state. He was in charge of the senator's Little Rock office in 1968 when Bill Clinton volunteered for Fulbright's reelection campaign. (Young Bill Clinton enjoyed the privilege of chauffeuring the senator around the state until he got lost, Fulbright called him "a damned egghead," and he was fired.) After Fulbright was defeated by Dale Bumpers in 1974, McDougal went into the real estate business. Clinton made a few thousand dollars by investing in one of his projects. When McDougal came around with the Whitewater idea, it appealed to him and his wife. The two couples formed a corporation to develop a vacation home subdivision. The land was promoted to would-be buyers with the phrase: "One weekend here and you'll never want to live anywhere else."

Real estate prices had been rising briskly for more than a decade. In much of the country, almost anyone could buy a property, hold on to it for a few years, and make a tidy profit. By 1978, with the trend accelerating, TV pitchmen were selling courses promising the secrets of getting rich quick. Books like *How You Can Become Financially Independent by Investing in Real Estate* landed on bestseller lists. Talk of real estate became as common as discussions about politics or sports. Homeowners borrowed against their houses to buy investment properties. Friends pooled their cash to make down payments on properties.

As a rule, investment booms generally end when, inspired by the press, great masses of people jump into the action. This is precisely what happened to the Whitewater group as a sharp increase in inflation raised prices and the Federal Reserve Bank responded with a series of interest rate hikes. The rate hikes were intended to make borrowing so expensive that investors and speculators would cease buying long enough for prices to cool. Mortgage lenders, following the Fed, raised their rates to the point where home buyers were charged, on average, more than 18 percent. Buyers retreated. As reduced demand pushed prices down, would-be developers like the Whitewater partners saw their investments wither.[5]

Whitewater failed so completely that the corporation couldn't make payments on the loan used to buy the acreage. With Clinton failing to win reelection, McDougal lost his job in state government. Eager to make money, he turned to a likely source, buying a little bank and then a savings and loan association in the county of Madison, population 11,373. The two institutions were rolled into a single entity called Madison Guaranty Savings and Loan Association.

Like the fictional Bailey Bros. Building and Loan in the film classic *It's a Wonderful Life,* S&Ls operated under government charters that stressed their obligation to support local communities and, especially, home ownership. S&Ls were backed by insurance systems that guaranteed depositors would get their money back in the event of insolvency. In exchange, they were put on a short leash, with authorities limiting the interest they could pay depositors or charge borrowers. The system got out of whack with the intense inflation of the early 1980s, and Washington responded by lifting many of the controls that had kept S&Ls in their traditional and boring areas of business. Suddenly, they could use federally guaranteed deposits to make risky, high-interest-rate loans. As money poured into S&Ls, Madison's assets grew from less than $7 million to more than $125 million in 1986.

What did Madison and the S&L boom have to do with Clinton and Rodham? For Jim McDougal, the answer would be nothing. However, in time, it would emerge that McDougal likely used Madison money to help pay off a Clinton campaign debt and to spare his friends Bill and Hillary from their full share of Whitewater's losses. (No evidence suggested that anyone asked him to do these things.) McDougal also turned to the Rose Law Firm as federal regulators swooped in to investigate its Madison operations and force him out of his management role. The feds discovered, among other things, that Madison had made so many bad loans that it was technically insolvent. However, so many S&Ls were in the same condition that the insurance system would not be able to cover the losses if they were forced into bankruptcy. Instead,

Madison and others were allowed to continue operating under a policy called *forbearance* in the hope that with time they could recover.

The folly of forbearance would be seen as S&Ls began to go bust. Several of these failures became political scandals because of the notable people involved. Neil Bush, son of then vice president George Bush, was on the board of Denver's Silverado S&L when its collapse cost taxpayers more than $1 billion. Two U.S. senators, Democrat John Glenn of Ohio and Republican John McCain of Arizona, were rebuked for intervening to help political donor Charles Keating manage the failed Lincoln Savings & Loan. Compared with Lincoln and Silverado, Madison was a small problem. However, it would eventually create political trouble for the couple, who, because of their mutually reinforcing ambition, had gotten so much so early in life that even their allies were suspicious of them.

Among the Democrats who harbored doubts about the Clintons was Dale Bumpers, who had been reelected to the U.S. Senate in the same election that saw the voters of Arkansas replace Bill Clinton with Frank White. Twenty years Bill Clinton's elder, Bumpers shared Clinton's goal, which, roughly stated, was an updated version of Franklin D. Roosevelt's New Deal. Bumpers recognized Clinton's energy, intelligence, and sincere desire to do well for the state. But he also found fault with him and his wife. In June of 1982, he wrote in his diary:

> Clinton ought to be most grateful to both of us, but he never is. You can never do quite enough for him and Hillary. I know that they blame [Senator] David Pryor and me both at least partially for their defeat in 1980. They are the most manic obsessed people I have ever known in my life, and perhaps even the most insensitive to everybody else's feelings. Everything centers around them and their ambitions. It is precisely the reason Bill got beat in 1980. People felt, and correctly, that they were being manipulated.[6]

Manipulation is inherent to politics. For example, Bumpers was a worldly wise and book-smart graduate of Northwestern University Law School, but he was known, at home, for the country wit and wisdom he offered to crowds at chicken dinner campaign stops. He would say that an opponent's ideas were "as thin as spit on a rock" or contained problems big enough "to choke a mule." These bits worked for Bumpers because he was a Marine Corps veteran of World War II who had entered bigtime politics when he was well into middle age. He was of the so-called greatest generation, and this status made it easy for people to trust him.

Among the first baby boom children born after the greatest generation returned from war, Bill Clinton was barely thirty when he won the statewide race for attorney general and two years later earned the nickname "the Boy Governor" as he became the youngest chief executive in the fifty states. Clinton's shaggy hair covered his ears, and though his Arkansas accent was genuine and ever present, he so loved the arcana of public policy that he sometimes lost his listeners on the way to making a point. The intermittent appearance of this Rhodes scholar–Yale Law School aspect of his identity could alienate voters who were sensitive to even the hint of a snub. Add a tendency to demonstrate empathy in a way that could seem too practiced and Clinton was vulnerable to being caricatured as insincere.

The first to identify this side of Clinton, and to give it a name—Slick Willie—was a local political columnist named Paul Greenberg. In 1980, Greenberg had watched as Clinton shifted his attitude toward the Cuban refugees housed in Arkansas. Prior to their attempt at mass escape, he stressed their desire to live free in the tradition of American immigration. After it, he complained about the federal government's decision to place substantial numbers of the boat-lift immigrants inside the state. This made Clinton a "dissembler" in Greenberg's eyes, and thus he dubbed him "Slick Willie."

The nickname helped defeat Clinton in 1980, but when Frank White used it in 1982, the label didn't work. By then, however, Greenberg was adding Hillary Clinton to his column, suggesting that it was up to her to control the governor's behavior. (This notion aligned with the stereotype that requires women to police their husbands' morality.) A case in point was her husband's appeal to the White House for help with an interstate dispute over who would pay for the Grand Gulf nuclear power station, which had been built in Mississippi but distributed power to several states, including Arkansas. Greenberg thought Clinton's out-reach was unseemly and asked, "Do you think the governor consulted Hillary Clinton before pulling this stunt?"[7,8]

Much as Greenberg may have wanted Mrs. Clinton to guide her hus-band, many in Arkansas worried that she was domineering to the point where she was emasculating him. With preconceived notions about what constituted proper behavior for a candidate's wife, critics were ready to hate Hillary simply because she deviated from their idea of the norm. Local journalist Meredith Oakley would declare her "a ball-busting feminist," and officials of the state teachers' union said she had no business helping to devise and promote her husband's education reform agenda.

By making Hillary the issue, the union could deflect attention from the sorry state of Arkansas's schools. In 1978, an independent study found that the state's children would have been better off attending school almost anywhere else in the country. Governor Clinton had as-signed his wife to lead a commission on school reform, which would hold meetings around the state to hear from educators, students, families, and taxpayers. This choice insulated the governor from the backlash that would invariably come out of this effort. It also ensured that the job would get done in a more efficient and orderly way. Where the governor was long-winded and incapable of leaving a room until he had spoken to every last person, Hillary was direct and purposeful. The panel visited every county in Arkansas and built support for higher classroom stan-dards, competency tests for teachers, and investments in school buildings, textbooks, and supplies. At the end of the tour, the commission wrote a plan for setting tougher standards for school and student performance while also increasing spending so that the goals might be met. The gov-ernor's wife was widely credited with the plan's approval by the state legislature, which came despite determined opposition from the teach-ers' union. By the end of Clinton's time as governor, the number of high schoolers going on to college would rise from 33 percent to 50 percent. Many attended on new, state-funded scholarships.[9]

Although teachers came to appreciate the education reforms (especially the pay hikes), no amount of service or success would persuade certain Arkansans that Hillary Clinton was to be trusted. Like KAIT-TV's Jack Hill, they were stuck on the bits of her biography that rendered her an outsider and perhaps a subversive. Her education could provoke feelings of resentment or insecurity. Her childlessness made her strange, or pitiable, or threatening. For them, she was a woman who was too eager to stand in the spotlight and wanted too much out of life. Her desire for a career, when every other First Lady of Arkansas was content to be a helpmeet, meant she must be up to no good. In 1986, Governor Clinton's regular opponent, Frank White, tried to make an issue out of the fact that she was a partner at Rose and that the firm did work for the Arkansas Public Service Commission. The commission, which set utility rates, retained the law firm when it became embroiled in lawsuits related to Grand Gulf.

In the political environment that existed after the 1979 accident and meltdown at the Three Mile Island plant in Pennsylvania, every nuclear project in the country was mired in controversy. Cost overruns made these plants expensive, and it wasn't unusual for regulators in one state to scrutinize plans to charge customers for construction of a facility in another. The PSC's decision to hire Rose, when Little Rock's other big firms represented other parties in the case, was approved by the state legislature and attorney general. The firm kept Hillary away from the case and cut her out of any share of the money paid to the firm.[10]

Utility regulations are boring, and even the general outline of the Grand Gulf dispute was hard to explain. Rather than try, the Clinton campaign chose instead to engage Frank White's criticism of Hillary. With a bit of their own sexism, the Clinton folks chided Frank White with the bumper sticker message FRANK FOR FIRST LADY. The inference, that to be a lady was somehow beneath a man, should have been beneath a candidate who considered women equal to men, but just as Clinton's critics used his wife to get at him, he exploited her to even the score.

In the same election, the governor's wife was drawn into a silly and demeaning stunt that was initiated by her husband. Candidates across the country were challenging one another to take tough positions on illegal drugs, and this posturing led to the brandishing of urine samples, or rather, reports on the results of testing done after samples were produced. In Arkansas, Bill Clinton was vulnerable on the drug issue because his brother, Roger, had been convicted on drug charges and served prison time. Also, Roger and Bill Clinton had been friends with a financier named Dan Lasater, who went to prison on drug charges. With these links in mind, White planned to use an upcoming debate to demand a candidate drug test. When the Clinton camp got wind of the plot, they had their man quietly submit to testing and revealed the negative results before White could raise the issue. A reporter also put the idea to Hillary, and thus cornered, she had no option. She and then Mrs. White were tested. Everyone passed.

Having endured the insult of being required to pee in a cup for a drug test, the results of which were released to the public, Hillary Clinton would be forgiven if she believed she had endured the worst of what might be possible for a political spouse. She had moved to a place where she knew no one and would have to fight to fit in. She had given up her name and done both the traditional things required of a First Lady and helped her husband with electioneering and governing. Although never perfect in this effort, she was many things to many people.

For his part, Bill Clinton generally showed her the respect and consideration due an equal. And he wasn't reluctant to demonstrate that he was a modern husband. A good example of this arose when she couldn't keep a date with a civic group in North Little Rock and he went in her stead. It was a touching gesture that got some attention in the press and suggested that Hillary might actually have in him the kind of husband who would give her a level of support approximating what she gave to him. She had taken risks in his behalf. He was taking lesser but nevertheless real risks for her as he welcomed her help on key issues and showed that he was the type of man who was happy to pinch-hit for her. Why wouldn't she think that life was coming together according to plan?

# 3

# Woman Trouble

Quick, name three famous scandals when husbands stood by their unfaithful but prominent wives to preserve their careers. Okay, it's difficult to name three. How about one? If you can't, it's because there is no betrayed-husband paradigm in American culture. On the other hand, the sight of a woman wronged standing beside her contrite spouse is so common that these public displays have become a cliché. This is the norm because the paucity of women leaders makes the odds of such a breach slight. But it's also the case that a woman is expected to forgive her powerful husband because he represents her access to status. The price she pays includes ridicule and questions—about her denial, her lack of self-regard, her willingness to compromise—that hang in the air long after the sinner has been rehabilitated.

The powerful husband's rehabilitation is possible, and indeed likely, because supremely ambitious men are assumed to be both voracious in their appetites and magnets for attention of all sorts. Bill Clinton was not an exception. He was tall and handsome, and his charm was a tool that could open a single heart at a dinner table or ten thousand at a political convention. It drew men and women into Clinton's orbit, where, circling him like planets around a star, they sought to both influence him and, perhaps, get something—power, money, fame—for themselves. His aim was to be president, and unlike others who eyed this goal, he possessed the political instincts and skills to make the fantasy real.

Clinton learned from his 1980 loss to Frank White that he had to match his charisma with middle-of-the-road stands on issues and a relatable style. Intelligence and worldliness were fine, but showing them off was a mistake. Better to be the fellow whom Republicans started calling *Bubba* with a sneer, but who was embraced by Arkansas voters who knew lots of men and boys—amiable, shrewd, and sometimes crude—who carried the same nickname. They generally liked Bubbas, and once they concluded that Bill Clinton was one, they stuck with him. For Hillary Clinton, who met and fell in love with a brilliant Yale Law School student, Bubba was her husband's troublesome alter ego. He was emotionally driven, dangerously overconfident, and self-indulgent.

Clinton valued Bubba for the ease he brought out in ordinary Arkansans who might otherwise feel shy around a governor. In his memoir, titled simply *My Life,* Clinton recalled a Bubba moment at the Arkansas State Fair, where he spent hours at the kind of booth where fairgoers might buy cotton candy or pay a quarter for the chance to win a prize by tossing a basketball through a too-small hoop. As was his habit, Clinton chatted with anyone and everyone who approached, and this included an older man in overalls who promised to vote for him in the next election but warned that despite his good record, "everybody else I know" was tired of him. Should he seek reelection in 1992, the voter warned, he might not win it.

Clinton had considered leaving the governor's mansion for the 1988 presidential race but had decided the time wasn't right. While he and the world watched, that campaign yielded one of the biggest scandals in political history—revelations that ended candidate Gary Hart's political career—and marked a profound shift in the unwritten rules that set the boundaries for the journalists who reported on elections. Suddenly, the private lives of candidates and officeholders, including their sexual relationships, were fair game. This shift also raised the stakes for the spouses and children of politicians and public officials.

Ten years older than Bill Clinton, Hart had a long record in national politics, which had begun in 1972 when he was the manager of George McGovern's campaign against Richard Nixon.

Intelligent, well-spoken, and blessed with movie-star looks, Hart had gained national fame as a member of the so-called Church Committee, which had produced investigative reports on the practices of American security agencies, including plots to assassinate foreign leaders. On this committee and in other work, Hart displayed such integrity that the archconservative senator Barry Goldwater of Arizona said, "You can disagree with him politically, but I have never met a man who is more honest and more moral."[1]

All that people believed about Hart, and all that he had accomplished, made him seem like an ideal candidate for the White House. However, some Democratic Party insiders were certain that like a rock star exploiting his groupies, Hart had been unfaithful to his wife. In the game of politics, as it had been practiced before 1987, infidelities had been private matters and were not regarded as disqualifying. This would all change with a *Newsweek* article about Hart's candidacy, which quoted former aide John McEvoy, who later insisted he was speaking off the record, saying, "He's always in jeopardy of having the sex issue raised if he can't keep his pants on."

Soon after the *Newsweek* story was published, an anonymous caller asked reporter Tom Fiedler of the *Miami Herald* if he would be interested in seeing some incriminating photos of Hart. Fiedler asked about the caller's motivation. She said that in light of the recent Iran-Contra scandal, in which the Reagan administration deceived Congress to fund anti-Communist rebels in Nicaragua, she was concerned about truthfulness in politics. "Gary Hart is having an affair with a friend of mine," the caller said, explaining they had all been together recently on a yacht called *Monkey Business*. "We don't need another president who lies like that." She also asked, "How much do you guys pay for pictures?"

The caller would eventually be identified as a bikini model named Dana Weems. Her "friend" was another model named Donna Rice, who had recently ended a relationship with rock star Don Henley. A former beauty pageant winner, Rice had lots of blond hair and a catalog of revealing swimsuit photos. She and Weems had sailed on the *Monkey*

*Business* with a third woman named Lynn Armandt, who owned the Too Hot Miami bikini shop. Armandt would recall that Rice didn't seem to know who Hart was and that the talk on the boat had included the sex scandal that was swirling around the famous television evangelist Jim Bakker. Bakker had had an affair with a church secretary who, perhaps not surprisingly, wound up posing nude for *Playboy*.[2]

*Herald* editors did not pay for the photos Dana Weems offered, but they did assign reporters to investigate. On May 2, 1987, they followed Rice to Hart's house in Washington, D.C. Eventually, five men, including a photographer, were positioned on a quiet street in the Georgetown neighborhood. When two of the journalists finally went to question Hart about the woman in his house, they found him in the alley behind his home. It was about 9:00 p.m. Hart stood in the darkness with his back literally up against a wall.

The *Herald*'s report on the not-yet-identified Donna Rice and what was said as the journalists confronted Gary Hart in the alley was spiced with suggestive notes. The icky term *womanizing* was attached to Hart in the first sentence of the article. The writers also observed that a woman in his company had "clung to his arm as they walked toward the car and he repeatedly scanned the neighborhood as they walked." They concluded with a nod to Hart's wife, Lee, who would be devastated by the news report and subsequent frenzy of press activity. One passage suggested a justification for the paper's dip into a brand of journalism commoner to supermarket tabloids:

> *The former senator has been dogged since announcing his candidacy by rumors that he has had relationships with other women during his 28-year marriage to Lee. He has insisted that the rumors have no basis in fact and, in an interview with* The New York Times, *challenged those who question his fidelity to follow him.*[3]

No political spouse could read about Lee Hart and not be chilled by the thought of winding up in a similar spot. Rumors of infidelity were so common in politics that it was the rare candidate who wasn't subject to whispers and innuendo. Journalists might justify breaking the old prohibition on investigating private matters by saying an affair would mark him as untrustworthy. Tom Fiedler would eventually cite this matter of character as a motivation. But he would also confess that competitive fervor—reporters love a scoop—was a big factor. As reporters raced to advance the story, Hart's poll numbers plummeted, and he soon dropped out of the race. A late attempt to restart his campaign failed, and he left politics for good in the hope that he might salvage his marriage, which he did. When tracked down by writer Matt Bai decades later, Dana Weems expressed a bit of regret, saying, "I'm sorry to ruin his life. I was young. I didn't know it would be that way."[4]

The end of Gary Hart's political life touched off debates that would persist for decades. To those who would say that it was a politician's policies that mattered, not his personal behavior, writer Gail Sheehy would reply, "Issues are today. Character is what was yesterday and what will be tomorrow." Thus Hart's apparent infidelities and attempts to cover them up became more important than his public service and politics. For the Clintons, the new norm meant that the press was bound to pursue longstanding rumors about the sexual behavior of a powerfully charismatic young governor who, like Hart, had his eye on the White House and a plan for getting there.[5]

The 1988 campaign also brought a new low in the practice of electioneering thanks to a racist attack ad focused on Massachusetts governor Michael Dukakis, who was the Democratic Party's nominee. The spot featured a frightening photo of a black prison inmate named Willie Horton, who had committed rape and assault while on furlough from a Massachusetts prison. The woman he raped was also depicted. She was white and blue-eyed. The message was clear: Michael Dukakis liked to free murderous black men to rape young white women.

As one of the most notorious racist episodes in political history, the Horton ad reflected a new level of viciousness devised by George H. W. Bush's campaign manager Lee Atwater. Atwater said of Dukakis that he "would strip the bark off the little bastard" and believed that "by the time we're finished, [voters] are going to wonder whether William Horton is Dukakis's running mate." However, Vice President Bush and his campaign would need some basis for denying direct involvement in such an inflammatory attack. Enter Larry McCarthy and Floyd G. Brown. Trained by TV producer and political consultant Roger Ailes, who was a Bush campaign advisor, McCarthy turned Horton into a terrifying bit of film, and its broadcast was arranged by a separate organization, Citizens United, which was run by Brown. (Opaquely named *political action committees,* or *PACs,* are routinely used to carry out all sorts of mischief on behalf of candidates.)[6]

The Horton ad worked so well that it was the beginning of the end of Dukakis's presidential hope. Bush won a landslide victory, and Lee Atwater became chairman of the Republican Party. In two years, Atwater would be diagnosed with a fatal form of brain cancer, which suddenly set him in pursuit of redemption. He apologized to Dukakis and to a congressional candidate who, he had once said, had been "hooked up to jumper cables" because as a teenager he had received electroconvulsive therapy for depression. Atwater also called Gary Hart's former campaign manager Raymond Strother and confessed that he had "set up" the episode that ruined Gary Hart's presidential campaign. He had planned the whole encounter, which involved no sex, so that photos could be snapped. To many, he expressed regret for his methods and declared his change of heart had been informed by a newfound faith that was reinforced by reading a modern translation called the Living Bible. (William "Willie" Horton would also publicly profess to have found God.) After Atwater's death, his colleague Mary Matalin said that the book, found among his possessions, had never been unwrapped.[7]

Matalin's quip was interpreted to mean that Atwater had continued to manipulate—in politics, this is called *spin*—right up to the moment of his death. The others involved in the Horton affair would go on to pioneer additional low-road methods in behalf of GOP candidates and against Democrats. Floyd Brown targeted Bill Clinton, hoping to gin up a scandal that would ruin his prospects for higher office. As part of this effort, he and two associates investigated the death of an Arkansas woman named Susan Coleman. They claimed to have been motivated by an anonymous letter, filled with gossip about Clinton, which had been faxed to news organizations around the country.

Coleman had been pregnant at the time of her suicide in 1977. Brown's colleagues David Bossie and Jim Murphy peered in the windows at the home of a family friend and pressed Coleman's husband for the details of her suicide note. They also followed her mother to the hospital, where her husband was recovering from a stroke, to question her. At the hospital, they barged into Mr. Coleman's room to question her. Brown himself called Susan's sister, who recorded the call. When she asked him to leave her family alone, he said, "You're making it so difficult for me to leave your family out of it. I want to have my lawyers approach Clinton's lawyers and tell him we want him out of the race because he's not morally qualified." When the recording of this conversation was made public, the Bush campaign team publicly declared Brown, Bossie, and Murphy "the lowest forms of life" and branded their tactics as "despicable." That they were also helpful to Bush's reelection effort went without saying.[8]

Gossip about Clinton stretched back to his first term as governor and sometimes revolved around a woman named Gennifer Flowers. Flowers's background was worthy of Hollywood. As a girl, she had set her sights on fame and did her best to sing her way to her goal. She recorded a couple of records under the names Gennie Flowers and Little Scooter, and when her parents brought her to New Orleans she sang "When the Saints Go Marching In" at a club on Bourbon Street. She had been a backup singer for country bands and a lounge performer around the South. (Her claim that she performed on the TV show *Hee Haw* was not true.) She briefly went by *Geannie* and finally settled on *Gennifer*. The capital letter G would distinguish her even if her singing did not.[9]

Although Flowers worked as a dental assistant and attended nursing school, musical stardom remained her true goal, and she tried to improve her chances by cultivating a certain big-hair, Southern sex appeal. She was distinctly feminine in the way the staff at the Rose Law Firm meant when they explained how Hillary Rodham failed at being womanly.[10]

Bill Clinton met Flowers in 1977 when he was attorney general and she worked, for a brief time, at a Little Rock TV station. In the ten years since, gossip about their relationship had not extended much beyond political insiders, but some who were close to the Clintons believed Hillary knew about his interest in other women and this had caused real strain in their marriage. It was a problem that, as documented later by writer Carl Bernstein, went back to the very beginning of their relationship. Longtime Clinton aide Betsey Wright would tell Bernstein that for twenty years, beginning in 1974, she devoted significant time and energy to limiting the damage done by her boss's sexual affairs. She did this to protect the prospects of a man she otherwise admired for his intelligence, politics, and potential. Eventually, she would turn self-critical about her failure to confront the issue directly, calling herself "chickenshit" because she might have averted endless controversy and scandal by revealing what she knew and pushing the Clintons to deal with it. This conclusion depended, of course, on her blaming herself, as so many women who care about wayward men do.[11]

Despite the pain and constant risk of revelation caused by what Wright would term "bimbo eruptions," the Clintons stayed together and maintained their commitment to his dream of the presidency. This made them much like his political idol, John F. Kennedy, and his wife, Jacqueline, who was born into the old-money Bouvier family of New York and East Hampton. JFK's infidelities were known by Mrs. Kennedy—and many in the couple's circle—and caused her enormous pain. However, she also believed in his talent, his mission, and his potential. The humiliation she suffered was, in a sense, a pain she endured as a service to the nation as well as her station. As a couple, the Kennedys were roughly equal in their desire for the power and status of the presidency and roughly equal in their belief that they deserved to occupy both the White House and a place in history.[12]

Although they came from a completely different caste from the Kennedys and the Bouviers, the Clintons also seemed driven by the absolute belief that they were supposed to lead and that they were qualified by their talents and education. They pursued this goal with a fiercely pragmatic, sometimes ruthless kind of politics, which they imagined would give them the power to enact policies they considered progressive, even idealistic. There was at times an ends-justify-the-means quality to this approach, but politics isn't for sissies, and winning seemed to require a willingness to play rough. Richard Nixon started his career by smearing Helen Gahagan Douglas in a U.S. Senate race. A charismatic and popular member of Congress, Douglas led Nixon until he began calling her the "Pink Lady" and a "fellow traveler" of Communists. On the other side of the political spectrum, LBJ ended Barry Goldwater's presidential hopes with the infamous "Daisy" ad that suggested he would bring nuclear war.[13]

Every candidate faces the possibility of a Nixon- or LBJ-caliber attack, which means that most begin their campaigns with a review of their own vulnerabilities. In Bill Clinton's case, everyone knew about his *woman* problem. For Hillary Clinton, the political implications of her husband's infidelities added to the personal burden they had imposed on her for years. Prior to the Gary Hart scandal, she suffered like any other spouse who had been repeatedly betrayed but who had reason to believe that her tolerance was in the service of a greater good. They were a team, and his success had brought her to ever-higher levels of political power, where she met important figures and could contribute to policy debates. Together, they had improved education and health care, and this work had been satisfying on many levels. The idea of playing a similar role in a Clinton administration in Washington had long been part of her thinking. In this, she was more obviously ambitious than other political spouses.

Compared with other political wives, Hillary Clinton put much less effort into deflecting attention, and her husband didn't seem to require it. Instead, he let it be known that she was the smartest person he knew and that he trusted her as both an advisor and an extension of his office. In a country where many churches still taught that men must head their families and lead their wives, there was some risk attached to a governor in a Bible Belt state who expressed such regard for his wife's abilities. For those who might be political critics or enemies, this attitude also smacked of hypocrisy. How much respect could a man have for his wife if he was so willing to betray her?

The enemy the Clintons feared would come along eventually arrived in the person of Larry Nichols, an odd character who had knocked around Arkansas Democratic Party politics and eventually landed a job with the state Development Finance Authority. Nichols was engulfed in scandal when the press discovered he spent much of his office time on personal and political interests. When Clinton fired him, Nichols went to work for Republican Sheffield Nelson, who intended to replace Clinton as governor. As the 1990 campaign neared an end, Nichols invited local reporters to a press conference on the steps of the state capitol. At the appointed time, Nichols distributed copies of the civil complaint he would file against the governor, in which he would seek $3 million in damages for wrongful dismissal and injury to his reputation. The papers alleged that the government abused the development authority by spending its funds to cover up affairs with five mistresses, among them a local TV reporter named Deborah Mathis, former Miss America Elizabeth Gracen, former Miss Arkansas Lencola Sullivan, and Gennifer Flowers. Nichols said he had been fired in connection with this supposed scandal. At the time of the filing, all five women disputed Nichols's claim—"Hell no" was how Mathis put it—and the suit was barely mentioned in the press.

For more than a year, the Nichols suit would be regarded as a gadfly event of the sort that occurs in every state capital. In Little Rock, for example, reporters routinely heard from a fellow named Robert McIntosh, who distributed crude flyers alleging all kinds of scandals from the sexual to the financial. His method resembled that of a fisherman who keeps throwing dynamite into the water on the chance that a fat carp might be killed and surfaced by an explosion. McIntosh exempted those who contributed to his annual Black Santa charity campaign. It was a worthy cause, but it was hard to ignore the signs that his troublemaking could be a shakedown scheme. Indeed, McIntosh seemingly admitted as much when he filed a lawsuit to obtain $25,000, which he said Clinton had agreed to pay him "to stem a wave of negative publicity about extramarital affairs." McIntosh also complained that the governor had failed to fulfill promises to free his son, a convicted drug dealer, from prison, *and* he was upset that Clinton had not arranged to get him into business selling a mix for sweet potato pie to the masses of Arkansas and beyond.[14]

With wild rumors and odd characters so common in politics, woe to the man or woman who seeks to sort the substance from the delusions. Two days prior to the election, which Clinton would win, Nichols said he would drop everything in exchange for $150,000 and a payment to clear the mortgage on his home. The demand, which Clinton's team made public, put the controversy to rest, but only temporarily.[15]

Although Nichols was publicly discredited and the suit would be dismissed in court, the threat that sexual innuendo posed to Clinton's aspirations, to his marriage, and therefore to his wife and daughter did not disappear. In December 1990, after he had won reelection, Clinton took a telephone call from Gennifer Flowers, who secretly tape-recorded the exchange. The two agreed that Sheffield Nelson had been behind the Nichols lawsuit, and Flowers said that the publicity had hurt her because she was "actively looking for a job, and I don't need that."

Nothing in the call, which would eventually be transcribed and made public, indicated any conflict between the two participants. If anything, Clinton's sign-off—"All right, my dear, I'll talk to you later. Keep your chin up"—suggested not anxiety but warmth. Flowers showed a similarly protective feeling toward Clinton by then directing her lawyer to threaten legal action against one of the few media outlets, a radio station, that had publicized Nichols's lawsuit. Flowers then began applying for jobs in state government. She was turned down for the first but hired for the second, which was a $17,500 clerical position. Soon after she started work, Bill Clinton declared he would run for his party's nomination to challenge incumbent president George Bush in 1992. With the economy souring into a mild recession, national polls showed the president's popularity in decline. These trends put Clinton, the front-runner among Democrats, in a good position. In public appearances, both he and Hillary drew big, enthusiastic crowds. He was still governor of Arkansas, and the problems of Little Rock remained.

Gennifer Flowers continued to telephone Clinton and record the conversations. In one of these recordings, which was eventually made public, she mentioned that reporters for tabloid TV programs, which were known to pay money for stories, were sniffing around. She said that a local Republican official named Ron Fuller had said he would pay her $50,000 to speak publicly about her relationship with Clinton and also offered her a job. (She didn't mention that she had worked on a Fuller campaign.)

That Bill Clinton would keep talking with Flowers, presumably believing he could manage the threat she posed to his family and his political future, suggests he was unable to tell himself the truth about the danger she posed. Flowers would report to him that she believed her home had been burglarized, but as far as she could tell, nothing had been taken, and she made no police report. Flowers told Clinton she hoped he would be elected and seemed to say she was troubled by the prospect of the national press hounding her. He counseled Flowers to simply deny having a sexual relationship, which, of course, would benefit him while solving her stated concern. In one call, he said, "I just think that if everybody's on record denying it, you've got no problem."

The problem began in January 1992, with the tabloid weekly *Star* cover headline about Clinton cheating on his wife with "Miss America and four beauties," which relied on the Nichols lawsuit and named all five women. Although the paper quoted Flowers saying she was afraid to talk, this was a lie. She had already agreed to speak in exchange for $150,000. This kind of arrangement, involving payments to sources who would make bombshell allegations, was forbidden in the mainstream press but routine for outlets like the *Star* and its stablemate at American Media, the *National Enquirer*. Seven days after the "beauties" story was published, the *Star* followed up with a report that said Flowers and Clinton had had a long-running affair.

At thousands of supermarkets across the country, Americans saw the headlines as they loaded their groceries onto the belts that delivered them to cashiers. Political scandals were less popular with its readers than Hollywood fodder, and the *Star* didn't sell more than its usual run of about one million copies. However, the article, which included quotes from Flowers's recordings, garnered such wide attention from the rest of the national press that the Clinton-for-president campaign was swamped by the story. The audio was also quickly monetized by none other than Floyd G. Brown, of Willie Horton fame, who advertised a telephone service that allowed people to pay to hear bits of the conversations. Brown also distributed an eighty-four-page pamphlet titled

*Slick Willie,* which argued that Bill Clinton was "sleazy," a "draft dodger," and a "radical" who was surrounded by "shady" characters. Hillary was, in Brown's booklet, a "Lady Macbeth" who was untrustworthy because she had dyed her hair.

With the New Hampshire presidential primary weeks away, the Gennifer Flowers allegations raised immediate comparisons to Gary Hart and Donna Rice. The difference was Hillary Clinton. Where Lee Hart had been a reluctant political wife, Hillary had always been interested in politics and power. The Harts met as undergraduates who attended tiny Bethany Nazarene College, and Lee worked as a teacher to support Gary when he studied at Yale. The Clintons had been two young people on the fast track to success when they met as law school equals. He had always solicited and generally followed her political advice.[16]

At a press conference immediately following the *Star*'s publication of the Flowers story, Hillary Clinton deflected the direct question of her husband's infidelities with nevertheless candid remarks about her marriage. "As with most married couples, we've had our good times and our bad times," she said. "We are more committed, more stable, and more in love now because when the tough times came, we didn't cut out. When people get to know us and talk to our friends in Arkansas, they won't give that story the time of day."

Friends weren't the point. It was the press that mattered, and as days passed, the pressure to sit down and answer questions grew. The Clintons decided to sit with a correspondent for the toughest TV news program in the country, *60 Minutes,* where they would defend his political future and their marriage. She would be required to play the supportive wife in the face of scandal, and he would enjoy—actually exploit—the shelter of her approval. Viewers would watch to see if the Clintons' bond seemed strong and genuine and if they could recognize anything of themselves in the candidate and his wife. In short, the Clintons needed to be likable and respectable, and the burden for doing this fell mainly to her.

Given the drama, the *60 Minutes* interview was bound to attract a huge audience. CBS added to the broadcast's drawing power by scheduling it to air immediately after the Super Bowl. Roughly eighty million

Americans watched the game. This number wasn't much below the total number of voters in recent elections. Huge numbers would stay tuned in for the exclusive interview with the accused candidate and his wife. His difficult job would be to answer the questions and demonstrate presidential caliber. Her assignment, to be a strong support without seeming too strong, may have been more challenging than his. No matter what she did, some viewers would reject her for sticking with an unfaithful man who was going to confess to betraying her, even though this was the choice that the majority of spouses make.[17]

The interview was recorded in a hotel room that the CBS News crew transformed into a TV studio. The space was lit with bright lights, and the furniture was arranged so the Clintons could sit on a cream-colored sofa facing reporter Steve Kroft and the cameras. Candidate Clinton was dressed in a blue suit, a pale blue shirt, and a tie the color of dusty eggplant. Hillary wore a light green turtleneck sweater and matching blazer. Her blond hair was held in place by a wide black headband, which would attract criticism because, as a woman, her fashion and grooming choices were subject to intense scrutiny. It would ever be thus.

Kroft, a square-jawed man with a direct, even forceful way of speaking, began with the understatement that "it's been quite a week for Arkansas governor Bill Clinton." He then recited recent events:

> On Monday, his picture was on the cover of Time magazine, anointed by the press as the front-runner for the Democratic presidential nomination. Six days later, he's trying to salvage his campaign.
>
> His problem? Long-rumored allegations of marital infidelity finally surfaced in a supermarket tabloid. Last week, they were picked up and printed, unsubstantiated, by the mainstream press. Since then, for better or worse, Governor Clinton's private life has become the overriding issue in the Democratic presidential campaign. Earlier today, Governor Clinton and his wife, Hillary, sat down with me to try to put the issue to rest.
>
> Keep in mind as we said earlier, all of the allegations are unsubstantiated. All have been denied by everyone involved. Except for the case of Gennifer Flowers. The former television reporter and cabaret singer

> *Gennifer Flowers, in a tabloid interview for which she was paid, says she carried on a long-term affair with Governor Clinton from the late 1970s to 1989.*

In 160 words, Kroft had described the stakes and the context with such precision that he could make the point about the allegations being "unsubstantiated" twice. This emphasis affirmed the shaky ground journalists occupied in this case. For the second time in as many election cycles, the Democratic Party's leading presidential candidate faced the prospect of disgrace due to a private sexual affair. This time, the candidate decided to respond assertively, while the claims were still unsubstantiated and journalists like Kroft might be receptive to hearing his side.

Kroft began with the obvious, asking, "Who is Gennifer Flowers? Do you know her?"

The Clintons both said they knew Flowers, but when it came to her claim about a twelve-year affair, he said, "That allegation is false."

Together, the Clintons noted they had been appalled by the *Star's* story and that they had been concerned for the feelings of the women named in the piece. "I felt terrible about what was happening to them," said Hillary as she described how her husband's concern was so genuine that he "talked to this woman [Gennifer Flowers] every time she called, distraught, saying her life was going to be ruined."

He interjected: "It was only when money came out, when the tabloid went down there offering people money to say that they had been involved with me, that she changed her story. There's a recession on." He added, "You can expect to hear more of these stories as long as they're down there handing out money." As he spoke, Hillary sat turned toward him, her left arm on the back of the sofa behind him. This body language indicated that she was attentive and even a bit protective.

Kroft said, "I'm assuming from your answer that you're categorically denying that you ever had an affair with Gennifer Flowers."

Clinton replied, "I said that before. And so has she."

Beyond the denials and the truthful description of how Flowers had changed her story, the Clintons admitted to an imperfect marriage. Kroft pressed the issue—"Help us break the code," he said—asking if they had been separated. Hillary shook her head and said, "No." Then Kroft asked the candidate, "Are you prepared tonight to say that you've never had an extramarital affair?" He pushed back. "I'm not prepared tonight to say that any married couple should ever discuss that with anyone but themselves. I'm not prepared to say that about anybody."

When the answer didn't satisfy the interviewer, Clinton elaborated, saying, "I have acknowledged wrongdoing, I have acknowledged causing pain in my marriage. I have said things to you, tonight, and to the American people from the beginning, that no American politician ever has. I think most Americans watching tonight will get it; they'll feel it that we have been more candid." For her part, Hillary said, "There isn't a person watching this who would feel comfortable sitting on this couch detailing everything that ever went on in their life or their marriage." She also argued for a "zone of privacy for everybody."

For a moment, as he said, "I couldn't agree with you more," Kroft seemed to relent. However, he had sole possession of one of the biggest political stories in history, and he wasn't going to let go so easily. He noted the obvious, that the Clintons hadn't offered a blunt denial of an affair, and said this would be the reason the controversy would persist. In response, Clinton offered a disarming admission that "of course" he had not given a categorical denial and then noted that the press would not be satisfied by an abject confession of infidelity because it would be followed by a frenzy of investigation to uncover the extent of his sins. Considering this, Clinton and his wife had decided to draw a line where they were comfortable.

Kroft said his questions were informed by a CBS News poll that found that 14 percent of Americans "wouldn't vote for a candidate who said he had an affair." Although Kroft called this number "sizable," it wasn't. Indeed, in other polls many more Americans would tell pollsters they believed interstellar visitors had come to Earth in spaceships. This point—that you might get some Americans to agree to almost anything—was not lost on Clinton. He noted the flip side of Kroft's statistic—that 86 percent who *wouldn't* consider an affair disqualifying—and said he would trust the voters. Hillary ended on a more personal note. "You know, I'm not sittin' here, some little woman standing by my man like Tammy Wynette," she said. "I'm sittin' here because I love him, and I respect him, and I honor what he's been through and what we've been through together. And you know, if that's not enough for people, then heck, don't vote for him."

The interview rendered high political drama in eleven minutes and nineteen seconds. Supporters like Democratic strategist Ted Van Dyk would proclaim that the Clintons had not just stemmed the tide that was running against them but reversed it. Critics would note the Tammy Wynette reference and hear Hillary Clinton violating the first commandment of politics by talking down to the American people. This was the point made by columnist William Safire, who combined the line about Wynette and an off-the-cuff remark about how she hadn't stayed "home and baked cookies and had teas" to declare the campaign had a "Hillary problem."

Safire neglected to note that decades before, his boss Richard Nixon's First Lady, Pat, had testily told photographers, "I think we've had enough of this kitchen thing, don't you?" when she tired of posing in an apron. No one then said anything about Nixon having a "Pat problem." It was possible that pundits in that time lacked Safire's wit and willingness to attack a politician's wife. Those days were gone, and Hillary Clinton would be subject to withering criticism from the *Times* columnist and others for the rest of her life.[18]

On the day after the *60 Minutes* interview, Gennifer Flowers, dressed in a hot-pink suit, stood behind a bank of microphones to speak to reporters in a meeting room at the Waldorf Astoria hotel in New York City. She explained that she was speaking publicly because she was "afraid" that she would somehow lose her job or club dates due to the uproar over her claims. "The pressure was so intense, I felt I might even have to leave Little Rock, which is my home," she also said. "When I heard Bill describe our relationship as an absolute, total lie, I knew what my decision should be, to tell my side of the story truthfully and as quickly as possible."

Flowers had moved quickly to get from Little Rock to Manhattan in less than twenty-four hours. The *Star* had apparently moved quickly, too, arranging to have huge blowups of the magazine's front page made to display and to get editor Dick Kaplan ready to introduce Flowers and her attorney, Blake Hendricks. Kaplan seemed to revel in the chaos prior to the start of the event, shouting at photographers to settle down as he stepped up to a podium wrapped in pink laminate. A lawyer for just six years, Hendricks had bushy brown hair that covered his ears and touched the back of his shirt collar. He wore big glasses and used words like *tendered* and *pursuant* and started out referring to the reporters as *ladies and gentlemen*. Soon, he would be barking at them like a father dealing with unruly children in the back of the family sedan. When a questioner asked if Clinton had used a condom, he threatened to end the meeting "if there are any further questions that are degrading in my opinion like that."

When reporters asked Flowers about how much she had been paid by the *Star,* she offered her own version of a nonanswer. Money hadn't been a motivating factor, she said. She decided to speak because "I cannot take the stress. I want to tell the truth. I want to be set free." Flowers said she had secretly recorded the calls with Clinton because "ninety percent of me wanted to believe that he would stand by me, and I still wanted to protect him at that point like I always had. Ten percent of me said that maybe my feelings wouldn't be as important to him as being the president of the United States."

Instead of freedom, Flowers got the kind of fame that she never could have earned with her singing talent. Appearing in print and on television across the country, she was probably better recognized than Tom Harkin, the senator from Iowa, who was actually challenging Bill Clinton for the Democratic Party's nomination for president. Political reporters returned to her claim over and over again, and long after the election she would remain a household name. Flowers would marry, move to Las Vegas, and then to New Orleans, where she wouldn't have to worry about getting booked to sing, because she and her husband opened their own club in the French Quarter.

In 1992, the Clintons continued to campaign, together and apart, and gradually regained the momentum lost when the scandal was at its height. Bill said he wasn't sure that his wife wouldn't make a better candidate. He wasn't alone in making this point. Many who knew the couple considered Hillary to be Bill's equal when it came to understanding politics and policy. And there were no "bimbos" in her past. Clinton friend and TV producer Linda Bloodworth-Thomason argued that her friends stayed together because they loved and admired each other. "Hillary doesn't have to stay with Bill Clinton," she said. "She could get to the Senate or possibly the White House on her own—and she knows it."

Bloodworth-Thomason may have been right about Hillary's potential, at least on paper, but in 1992 America even the most qualified women were disadvantaged as candidates. Glad-handing political seduction—wading into crowds, grasping shoulders, gleefully mocking opponents—was simply not an option for a female candidate. Similarly, men who were married with children were admired for campaigning day and night for weeks on end. A woman who adopted this pace would be asked how her children and/or spouse felt about her absence. Political reality meant that women of Hillary Clinton's generation were still more likely to reach the higher precincts of power as supportive wives than as candidates. Love had something to do with her decision to stay married, but in the end, her joint project with her husband the presidential aspirant succeeded because Hillary followed William Safire's admonition, expressed to her directly in a column, to "press your strength, which is not articulation but realism."

The Clinton ticket, which included vice presidential nominee Al Gore, stressed the economy at every turn, seeking to capitalize on the effects of a recent recession and President Bush's decision to raise taxes even though in 1988 he had promised that he wouldn't. (In a speech written by Peggy Noonan, he had declared, in 1988, "Read my lips, no new taxes!") Clinton and Gore called themselves New Democrats, which meant they balanced their preference for government action with proposed tax cuts for the middle class, restrictions on welfare, and greater support for law enforcement. These positions muted some of the usual GOP attacks made against Democrats, whom they painted as too free with taxpayer money and also soft on crime. To maintain their liberal bona fides, the candidates endorsed both abortion rights and affirmative action to redress the effects of slavery and discrimination against minorities. (The pro-choice position was especially important to Republican voters who disapproved when George H. W. Bush abandoned his previous position to court the Christian Right with a call for a constitutional ban on abortion.)

In the general election, the Bush team would try a variety of attacks, which were blocked by a group devoted to responding instantaneously for the Democrats. When they called Clinton "the failed governor of a small state," the Democrats immediately declared Bush to be "the failed president of a big country." By August 1992, President Bush was complaining about how he was swamped by the Clinton/Gore team's instant response: "Every time I tiptoe into the water . . ." Left with little else, the GOP settled on making targets of Hillary and the couple's family life.

At their annual convention, which was held at the Astrodome indoor football stadium in Houston, the Republicans talked about "family values" in ways that made it clear they thought the Clintons existed outside the American mainstream. This charge was expressed most forcefully by Patrick Buchanan, who had been the only one to challenge Bush's claim to be the GOP standard-bearer. A fiery speaker who had attracted lots of press attention without winning a single state primary, Buchanan was a right-wing populist who was critical of both the Democratic Party and moderate Republicans. Like Newt Gingrich, who had been tutoring fellow GOPers on how "to speak like Newt" (this involved calling opponents *sick, pathetic traitors*), Buchanan styled himself as a culture warrior who promoted the dominant white, male, Christian ethos in American life. His campaign slogan was "America First," which had previously been used by Charles Lindbergh to urge America to stay out of World War II. Lindbergh's America First campaign was pro-Nazi and notably anti-Semitic. William F. Buckley, the conservative intellectual who was Buchanan's hero, had judged some of Buchanan's rhetoric to be anti-Semitic too. "I find it impossible to defend Pat Buchanan against the charge," wrote Buckley in a forty-thousand-word essay called "In Search of Anti-Semitism."[19]

Buckley's essay cast a shadow that Buchanan's presidential campaign could not escape. No one who followed national politics would have failed to recognize that Buckley had, in a stroke, shown that Buchanan was unfit to represent the GOP in a national election. Nevertheless, Buchanan had always been able to animate a rabid element of the party—extreme social conservatives and resentful white males—and no Republican could win the White House without their enthusiastic support. And so it was that convention organizers and Bush campaign officials invited Buchanan to open the convention with a prime-time, first-night speech and did not ask him to submit his text for the usual review and editing. In the first place, the pugnacious Buchanan wasn't likely to accept any adjustments. But also, the militant Buchanan could say and do things that President Bush would not. He committed to this duty in the first sentences of his address, declaring, "The primaries are over, the heart is strong again, and the Buchanan brigades are enlisted— all the way to a great comeback victory in November."

Buchanan then launched into a full-throated attack that found both Clintons representing the "militant homosexual rights movement." He told the convention that Bill and Hillary Clinton were offering themselves as a two-for-one deal, which meant a lurch toward "radical feminism." By his definition, this meant "abortion on demand, a litmus test for the Supreme Court, homosexual rights, discrimination against religious schools, women in combat—that's change, all right. But it is not the kind of change America wants. It is not the kind of change America needs. And it is not the kind of change we can tolerate in a nation that we still call God's country." The crowd, which included some who had attended an earlier "God and Country" rally in the Sam Houston Ballroom of the nearby Sheraton Astrodome Hotel, responded warmly to Buchanan as he made certain to demonize Hillary along with her husband.

Setting aside the fact that God had never announced his feelings about America, Buchanan wasn't completely wrong. The Clintons had themselves spoken of her potential contribution to a new administration. Bill even quipped, "Buy one, get one free!" Hillary expected to work on issues affecting children and families, and she had ample experience in these areas. Buchanan considered her record, including a couple of published articles, and found much for Americans to fear. He made her a special target of his ire, as if she represented a threat to the nation's moral integrity.[20]

"And what does Hillary believe?" he asked the convention goers. "Well, Hillary believes that twelve-year-olds should have a right to sue their parents, and she has compared marriage as an institution to slavery—and life on an Indian reservation. Well, speak for yourself, Hillary. Friends, this is radical feminism."

Hillary Clinton had never actually written or said that children should be able to sue their parents. What she had, in fact, said was that the testimony of older children should be given more consideration in legal proceedings because they were more mature than little kids. This was common sense of the sort that might be voiced by any parent. Her reference to slavery, Indian reservations, and marriage was intended to show how, historically, some individuals were denied rights because they had "dependency relationships" that granted others custodial power. There was nothing controversial in these views, but with Bill Clinton seemingly immune to their criticisms, convention speakers seemed to agree that Hillary was the best alternative target. If voters couldn't be rallied to hate him, perhaps they would hate *her*. He spoke of the opposition as "Clinton & Clinton," and, after declaring America to be "God's country," he announced that in the "struggle for the soul of America, Clinton & Clinton are on the other side."

Later in the convention, television evangelist Pat Robertson made Hillary the issue by declaring, "No one can convince me that the American people are so blind that they would replace Barbara Bush as First Lady." Robertson's appearance at the convention affirmed the growing influence of conservative Christian activists in the GOP. Beginning with the Reverend Jerry Falwell's Moral Majority organization, which boosted Ronald Reagan, this Christian Right movement had supplied loyal voters to the Republican cause while demanding that candidates back ideas such as the restoration of prayer in public schools and a ban on abortion. Presidents Reagan and Bush did not take naturally to the likes of Robertson, who had recently said that Planned Parenthood advocates "every form of bestiality" and that mainline Protestants like them embraced "the spirit of the antichrist."[21]

When the First Lady herself finally appeared, she represented the model of American womanhood Pat Robertson evoked and which was presumably the opposite of Hillary Clinton. Old enough to be Hillary's mother—her son George was one year *older* than Hillary—Barbara Bush was descended from a blue-blooded New England family and counted President Franklin Pierce and Henry Wadsworth Longfellow among her distant relatives. As a young woman, she left college to marry. Though she did not pursue a profession, Barbara Bush was deeply ambitious for her family. She had been instrumental in her husband's career, and her nicknames included "the Enforcer." However, her power was expressed behind the scenes, which meant that she could still appeal to voters who regarded openly ambitious women with skepticism if not fear. They likely overlooked the modern sentiment expressed in her address— "However you define family, that's what we mean by family values"—in favor of the tableau the First Lady created at the end of her speech when she called her children and grandchildren to her side. Twenty-two in number, the younger Bushes were the epitome of a successful extended family. Each of the grown-up children came with a spouse, and each of these marriages had brought grandchildren. Together, they far out-numbered the voters in Dixville Notch, New Hampshire, who cast the first votes tallied in every presidential election.[22]

By the time the Republicans were finished, delegates were waving preprinted placards that read, IF HILLARY CAN'T TRUST HIM, HOW CAN WE? and various journalists were again comparing Mrs. Clinton to Lady Macbeth. However, the anti-Hillary tone had made President Bush so uncomfortable that he would later speak of the "attacks on Hillary" and note that he wouldn't speak this way himself, because he wanted to "stay out of the sleaze business." Across the country, voters who had taken in the convention were actually repulsed by the way Hillary—or, to be more specific, the kind of women she was made to represent—was treated. Kathleen Hall Jamieson, a professor of politics at the University of Pennsylvania, had detected a backlash, especially against Vice President Dan Quayle's wife, Marilyn.[23]

A former member of the pom-pom squad at Purdue, Mrs. Quayle was a lean woman with an angular face and the kind of flippy hairstyle

Mary Tyler Moore wore in the '70s. She had earned a law degree and worked for four years in a firm she'd founded with her husband. (He was an heir to a $2.6 billion newspaper company.) When he entered politics, she gave up her profession to be a full-time mother, wife, and political helpmeet. Protocol required she speak at the convention, and she used her time at the podium to make a thinly veiled attack on Hillary Clinton's approach to work and family. "Most women do not wish to be liberated from their essential natures as women," said Quayle. After she described her devotion to her children, she said, "There aren't many women who would have it any other way." And she added, pointedly, that "marriage and fidelity are not just arbitrary arrangements."[24]

In Professor Jamieson's interviews of voters who watched the convention on TV, she discovered that the critiques of Hillary, especially the one coming from Marilyn Quayle, backfired. "The level of hostility toward her in that speech was very high. I think there was some resentment at someone standing up and telling women what choices are and are not appropriate for them." A *Los Angeles Times* poll on the anti-Hillary notes sounded by Quayle and others found that 73 percent who had heard the comments disagreed with them. With most women employed outside the home, this response could have been anticipated by a strategist who should have understood that few who sought to balance work and family felt completely at ease with their choices. Only those with great resources made unfettered choices. The so-called Mommy Wars, which cast mothers who worked outside the home against those who didn't, wounded just about every parent.

Although Hillary Clinton had stumbled in February with her testy "I could have stayed home and baked cookies" remark, so much had happened in the ensuing months that many younger and middle-aged people could relate to her, and polls showed they rejected the effort to demonize her. They, too, were trying to figure out how to be married and raise families in a country where it was getting ever more difficult to follow their own parents' examples. Feminism and other social movements had contributed to this change, but it wasn't the only force at work. Equally significant were the economic trends that made the older model of marriage, which revolved around men whose jobs could support a family and women who stayed home to care for children, much more difficult to sustain. Global competition, rising health care costs, and tough bargaining by managers had depressed wages even as inflation made the cost of living higher. Women entered the workforce in droves, in large part to maintain their families' standard of living. In 1980, the number of families in which both parents worked passed the 50 percent mark. By 1992, roughly 60 percent fell into this group. This reality required new ways of thinking about everything from childcare to financial planning, and many couples found themselves functioning as teammates in ways their parents did not. To them, "Clinton & Clinton" made sense.[25]

The backlash noted by Jamieson killed much of the positive momentum the GOP should have gathered coming out of Houston. Soon, Marilyn Quayle, who generally resented the press, went to *The New York Times* seeking a do-over. Her op-ed article, titled "Workers Wives and Mothers," began with a reference to being misunderstood in a way that gave her a feeling "similar to looking in a fun-house mirror." (It was easy to imagine that Hillary Clinton had experienced this feeling too.) Quayle went on to offer a nuanced review of the challenges women faced, but this careful argument lacked emotional power. The GOP's convention had managed to generate more sympathy for Hillary than she could have generated on her own. By the time the voters went to the polls in 1992, whatever reticence they may have felt about her assertiveness or Bill Clinton's infidelity in light of Gennifer Flowers was so diminished that women voters supported him more strongly than men. With independent candidate Ross Perot siphoning votes from both the Democrat and the Republican, Clinton beat Bush in the popular count by 43–37 percent. His victory in the Electoral College, where most states followed a winner-take-all scheme, was 370–168. The president-elect began his victory speech by thanking "my family, my wife, without whom I would not be here tonight—[cheers]—and who I believe will be one of the greatest First Ladies in the history of this republic."

The Clintons had gained the White House, fulfilling a shared dream, but at a substantial cost. Here the argument could be made that she came out more scarred than he. In the course of the campaign, Bill Clinton had come into focus as a brilliant, gregarious, and passionate man whose charm included a significant amount of sex appeal. According to the same double standard that allowed for young men to sow wild oats, he was forgiven and perhaps even admired for the Gennifer Flowers scandal because it showed he was a red-blooded man. This outcome comported with the observations made by journalist Gail Sheehy in the wake of the scandal. She described him as "the eternal boy, a Jungian archetype, who remains stuck in an adolescent orientation toward life, often prompted by an exaggerated dependence on his mother. Seductive to men as well as women."[26]

The campaign worked out much differently for Hillary, who, in Sheehy's analysis, was stuck with playing the Valkyrie destined to lift up the stricken warrior and deliver him to Valhalla. As she performed this duty she was criticized to a degree never before experienced by a candidate's wife. (Eleanor Roosevelt didn't become the object of right-wing scorn until after her husband had been elected president.)

Hillary Clinton had been prepared for the rough treatment she received by twenty years of work in other campaigns, from McGovern in 1972 to Carter in 1976 and her husband's tenure in Little Rock. Politics is never a gentle sport, but in a relatively small and poor state like Arkansas, which offered few other diversions, it could be especially vicious. Experience had turned an already-strong woman into someone who could keep her own counsel and keep going, no matter what was being said about her, or her husband, or even her daughter. (Days after the election, Chelsea, age twelve, was mocked as unattractive by the political radio performer Rush Limbaugh.) Hillary coped with the onslaught by deciding that the opposition employed political hit men who would say or do anything to win and that the press wasn't much better. With this in mind, she became guarded in a way that could make her seem steelier and less knowable than her husband. In the campaign, he had promised, "If I get elected, we'll do things together like we always have," and this was one of the rewards she hoped to experience. But whether he could provide it was already in doubt.[27]

# 4

# Caricature

Powerful women aren't given much leeway. Express a little emotion—*any* emotion—and you risk being written off as unserious. Show too little and you're a bitch. The stereotypes are convenient for journalists and can be supported by selecting a few anecdotes or impressions and shading them just so. The same is true when it comes to couples. No one knows what happens inside a relationship, but outsiders still make guesses based on their own experiences and expectations.

After the 1992 election, *The New York Times* sent writer Michael Kelly to examine the Clintons. On the day before Clinton's first inauguration, Kelly published an article proposing that Bill and Hillary Clinton were like-minded people whose main problem, as a couple, might be that they were a little too close. They were "the man and woman who ran Arkansas," noted Kelly before he leaned on some loose clichés intended to capture them in essence. He was a liberal who made himself look more moderate. She was a "slightly hippieish, feminist lawyer," providing the hard work and practical strategy behind most of her husband's successes in Little Rock.[1]

Superficially flattering, the portrait of the First Couple was a setup where Hillary was concerned. Both the "hippieish feminist" and the woman-behind-the-man stereotypes were loaded with negatives. However, the Clintons were in public favor at the time, with polls indicating they were both well liked. As the president's first term began, they proceeded as if they truly intended to demonstrate a different kind of relationship from what Americans had seen before in the White House. As *Boston Globe* columnist Ellen Goodman explained it in a TV interview, the Clintons were confronting Americans with a new image for a married woman—namely, the "independent wife" who would be both a spouse and a professional power.

The independent wife of the president took space in the West Wing, close to the Oval Office. At thirty thousand square feet, much of it given over to hallways, meeting rooms, and waiting areas, the West Wing is the most precious office space in the world. (Up until 1977, not even vice presidents were welcome to establish themselves there.) The First Lady's second-floor office wasn't the most coveted, but she got "walk-in privileges," which meant she could roam the halls and talk with whoever was available, even in the Oval Office. Her aides would be known for their intense loyalty, which earned their domain the name *Hillaryland*. This community became a refuge from the critics who examined her so closely and the enemies who hunted her like she were a prey animal. The model citizen, who joined near the end of the first term, would be Michigan-born Huma Abedin. A daughter of two internationally known academics, she had lived much of her life abroad and spoke fluent Arabic and Urdu.

Five days into his presidency, Bill Clinton announced that the First Lady would lead the Task Force on National Health Care Reform, which would be given one hundred days to develop the outlines of legislation that would address the problem of rising costs, increasing insurance premiums, and a growing number of people without any coverage at all. In 1993, nearly forty million Americans lacked insurance, a circumstance that contributed to illness, poverty, and premature death. The patchwork system of employer-based, government, and individually purchased insurance plans offered wildly ranging benefits. On one side of the spectrum, people were covered only in the event of catastrophic illness or injury. On the opposite pole, some Americans enjoyed employer-paid plans that paid for everything from eyeglasses to psychotherapy. However, high-end plans were fading away as employers and companies sought to rein in costs by requiring workers to pay some of their premiums and more and more of their own medical costs. The system also handicapped corporations that faced foreign competitors based in countries with universal, state-funded health care.

Given the vast complexity of the system, which had defied previous efforts at reform, Clinton's charge—especially the one-hundred-day deadline—was obviously unrealistic. And in choosing his wife to lead the effort, he demonstrated a naïveté that was similarly notable. Hillary had undertaken big assignments for him in Arkansas, and she was, he said, "better at organizing and leading people from a complex beginning to a certain end than anybody I've ever worked with in my life." Add her education, her work for the Children's Defense Fund, and her experience talking with voters in the past eighteen months and the First Lady was quite qualified to lead a task force that would be staffed by professionals and filled with experts. However, Arkansas is to the United States what softball is to major-league baseball. She was also the president's wife, and some Americans were concerned about the First Spouse having a significant role in any area of policy. Nancy Reagan urged children to "Just Say No" to illegal drugs, and Barbara Bush had advocated for literacy.[2]

The president got firm data on this anxiety when he visited a TV studio in the Detroit suburbs for a town hall–style session with citizens. (Others gathered in cities around the country and were connected via satellite television.) It was his first trip away from Washington since the inauguration, and he reveled in the contact with people who asked questions, acknowledging the pain of one man whose son had been killed in a robbery and in another's frustration with long-term unemployment. The president's political team hired a panel of observers to view the event on TV screens and turn knobs connected to sensors to indicate how they felt about what they heard. Clinton earned approval as he spoke about his ideas for expanding availability and cutting costs, but when he spoke about the First Lady, the knobs were turned the other way.[3]

Despite the signals from the town hall gathering, Hillary pressed ahead with the health care task force, and she courted controversy by conducting two of the group's meetings in private, away from the press and public. The administration was promptly sued by a trio of conservative organizations led by the recently established National Legal and Policy Center. Operated by two longtime Republican activists, it was funded by Richard Mellon Scaife, the billionaire heir to the Mellon bank fortune and devoted funder of conservative political causes. The others were a "consumer" organization set up by a direct-mail fundraiser and a small doctors' group committed to the proposition, among others, that it is "immoral" for doctors to participate in government-based medical programs.

Although none of the plaintiffs were mainstream organizations and their lawyer wasn't a fixture in the federal courts in the District of Columbia, the claims had sufficient merit for Judge Royce Lamberth to put it on his docket. This is how the system is supposed to work. All are at least theoretically equal in the eyes of the law, including gadflies, provocateurs, and Potemkin organizations that create only the illusion of a public alarm about an issue. Ever since the grassroots protest movements of the '60s, big-money interests had organized and funded artificial groups to advocate their interests. With a nod to a famous brand of fake grass, this process was dubbed Astroturfing, and it typically involved conservative, pro-business interests attacking policies or politicians deemed a threat to profits. At the time of the suit challenging the First Lady's role in health care, the U.S. Chamber of Commerce had embarked on this kind of campaign against environmental protection rules and in support of the tobacco industry's long-running effort to create a groundswell of opposition to laws regulating smoking as a health hazard.[4]

Of particular interest to Judge Lamberth, who had been appointed to the bench by Ronald Reagan, was the matter of a person who wasn't a paid official—the First Lady—conducting government business behind closed doors. The Federal Advisory Committee Act of 1972 required presidential advisory groups to meet in public. (Proponents of this law had intended to limit the ways powerful interest groups or individuals could steer policy in secret.) The White House defended the private meetings with the claim that insurers, physicians, administrators, and others would not speak candidly in a public setting. Judge Lamberth disagreed and ordered that all the meetings be open to the public.

From a practical standpoint, the ruling made little difference to the work of the task force, but it underscored the risk associated with the Clintons' approach. It's possible that years of rough treatment in Arkansas and in the campaign had made Hillary Clinton wary of what could happen to her in Washington. Also, she seemed to crave the chance to get some work done out of the spotlight. However, as one Republican strategist said, "the whole world [was] watching" as Bill Clinton pursued his top priority through his wife. Health care was vital to every American's life, and a vast and powerful industry was determined to preserve the status quo. "The margin of error for her is zero."[5]

As she accepted the burden of the project, Hillary served as both a political buffer for her husband and a potential target for powerful lobbyists, donors, and their allies in Washington. A huge part of the economy, the health care system delivered top pay to doctors and executives and profits to drug companies and insurers. For years, the cost of care had risen faster than inflation, bringing a threefold increase between 1980 and 1992. However, those who were insured were accustomed to accessing whatever they deemed necessary at minimal personal cost. They may have felt compassion for the growing number of uninsured people—twenty-five million in 1980 became forty million by 1992—but they feared losing the sense of security and health benefits they got from the present system. Any attempt to address this problem, which devastated some but didn't touch most, would inevitably cause a furor. The president had acknowledged as much when appointing Hillary to the health care job, saying, "She'll be sharing some of the heat I expect to generate." In most instances, including a Capitol Hill blitz of representatives' and senators' offices, Hillary won high marks as someone who didn't need to consult note cards before entering a meeting, and she had absorbed, in prior study, information of the predisposition of every official she met.

By the end of the Clinton presidency, political concerns that an activist First Lady might pose problems for the man in the Oval Office would prove overblown. At almost every point in President Clinton's two terms, opinion polls would indicate the public felt better about her than it did about her husband. More remarkably, when the Roper Center for Public Opinion Research studied the popularity of First Ladies it would find that none ever notched a higher first-year score than Hillary Clinton. At 67 percent, her approval rating was ten points higher than Nancy Reagan's at the same point in their lives as First Ladies. She would also rank highest when Americans were asked which women in the world they admired most, eclipsing even the glamorous Princess Diana. Popular and therefore powerful in her own right, she had as much at stake as her husband.[6]

Although Hillary's poll numbers indicated her popularity, the picture was complicated by the fact that very few people were ambivalent about her. Where other presidents' wives often registered "no opinion" scores of 30 percent and higher, hers generally fell below 20 percent. At the end of February 1993, ABC News asked Americans how they felt about her. Sixty-one percent voiced a favorable view, 30 percent said they had a negative impression, and just 9 percent said they had no opinion. This polarization meant that with the right approach, political opponents could mobilize those who didn't like her to connect these feelings to the president and the Democratic Party. As social psychologists have found, beginning in the 1980s, loathing had begun to eclipse loyalty as a motivation for voters. In the same time period, negative political attacks had become commoner, with the most effective ones issued by groups that were not directly controlled by a candidate and therefore did not have to include the "I approve of this message" line required of official campaign spots. Negativity also worked better when coming from a third party, such as a trusted news media source or a credible individual. When it came to demolishing a political opponent, the culture war notes favored by Pat Buchanan would be most effective because they were personal, not political, and created a caricature powered by emotion.[7]

Many of the more effective culture war attacks on Hillary would play up the age-old trope of the weak husband and the controlling wife. Talk radio star Rush Limbaugh played "Hail to the Chief" every time

Hillary's name was mentioned on his program, and Reagan advisor Michael Deaver, a modern master of political manipulation, described her as the "person out-front, pulling the strings." In response, Clinton strategist James Carville argued that the likes of Deaver and Limbaugh were insecure males who feared competent women. "The world is full of weak men that have always been scared of strong women," he said. "I say the heck with 'em. Let 'em go wallow in their own insecurities."

Insecure as they were, the hyper-partisans who targeted the Clintons were more likely afraid of *his* political appeal than *her* position by his side. Bill Clinton, with the aid of Carville and his colleague Paul Begala, had cracked the code that had kept the White House in Republican hands for twenty of the previous twenty-four years. By moving toward the ideological center on issues like crime and welfare, they had taken away the GOP's advantage with many white voters outside of urban centers. With a sufficient number of these voters comforted by Clinton's positions and Arkansas roots, he had been able to win majorities in Georgia, Louisiana, Tennessee, Kentucky, and most of the Midwest. His personal appeal was so strong that Hillary represented the best alternative point of attack. She could be demonized in a way that hurt him indirectly and, given her own political potential, degraded her future prospects. This long-term project got some help when the *New York Times* writer who profiled the Clintons for the paper at the time of the inauguration, Michael Kelly, returned to develop a much longer assessment for the paper's Sunday magazine.

Kelly would interview Hillary shortly after the death of her father, Hugh Rodham, on April 7, 1993, in Little Rock. She had spent more than two weeks there with him and would confess to being unable to focus on much of anything outside the hospital room where her father was being kept alive after a massive stroke. She had left just once, to return her daughter to school and then give a speech to a crowd of fourteen thousand at the University of Texas. The event had been organized by Liz Carpenter, who had been Lady Bird Johnson's press secretary and was a woman to whom few people ever refused anything. The text, which Hillary wrote en route, was informed by a file of research items, which included an article by the late Lee Atwater, the reformed political attack dog, who wrote worriedly about the emptiness he felt in himself and saw in others. He said, "I don't know who will lead us through the '90s, but they must be made to speak to this spiritual vacuum at the heart of American society—this tumor of the soul."

Seizing Atwater's questions, which she quoted, Hillary declared, "The answer is all of us." She then offered a conventional call for a new ethos of individual responsibility and caring. "We need a new definition of civil society which answers the unanswerable questions posed by both the market forces and the governmental ones, as to how we can have a society that fills us up again and makes us feel that we are part of something bigger than ourselves." This combination of the conservative (individual responsibility) and the liberal (caring) that borrowed from her husband's politics could hardly alienate anyone.[8]

Hugh Rodham died within twenty-four hours of his daughter's speech in Austin. When she was interviewed a few weeks later by Kelly, Hillary spoke about spirituality and faith in the way people will after the death of a beloved parent. In Kelly's hands, this candor was combined with his own musing on so-called New Age religion to create an image of Hillary as self-important and clueless. Published under the cringeworthy title "Saint Hillary," the article opened with roughly eight hundred words in which Michael Kelly shared a personal evaluation that found Clinton ambitious, immune to irony, and "cocky" because, among other things, she noticed as a girl that the world was often cruel and, as the writer put it, she "would like to make things right." When he finally gave someone else a chance to speak, he reported that Clinton agreed with his suggestion that what she really sought was some sort of "unified field theory" for improving the world. But this wasn't her idea. It was his. (Borrowed from physics, the phrase *unified field theory* was often used in silly ways by New Agers who wanted to add a pseudoscientific sheen to their spiritual ideas.) "That's right, that's exactly right!" Hillary agreed as Kelly baited her with it. The exclamation mark was his addition, of course. It guaranteed that no reader would fail to notice her enthusiasm.

Despite Hillary's repeated insistence that she was open to others' views and unsure about her role, the clear purpose of the piece was to cast her as overly ambitious and dangerous in her certainty. This criticism could be made of anyone with high hopes and big plans, especially those who expressed them with great confidence. Hillary, on the other hand, told Kelly, "I don't know, I don't know," when an aspect of a problem stumped her, and she freely admitted, "It's not going to be easy," when pressed on just how she would address social problems. If this earnestness and ambition were worthy of mockery, what would Kelly have written of a First Lady who had no desire to do good in the world?

"Saint Hillary" was a good example of an indulgent journalistic style that cast a cynical eye on anyone who might be viewed as earnest or sincere. Although skepticism has always been a hallmark of the American press, magazine writing in the 1990s was marked by more than the usual amount of snark. The silliest venue for this attitude was *Spy* magazine, which depicted Hillary Clinton as a dominatrix on its February 1993 cover. But while *Spy* was a comic enterprise that made its points with slapstick, more traditional outlets did it with a combination of contrarian reflexes and snobbery. The pose became a profitable style for everyone from TV producers and advertising executives to ambitious writers. This was something the novelist and essayist David Foster Wallace saw as the corruption of a rebellious impulse. As he saw it, irony, irreverence, and rebellion had come to be "not liberating but enfeebling" because they had made sincerity impossible. Likewise, wrote Wallace, "anyone with the heretical gall to ask an ironist what he actually stands for ends up looking like an hysteric or a prig."

As Hillary Clinton recalled her girlhood for Michael Kelly and spoke of responsibility and caring in Austin, she made herself the perfect target for anyone who chose to depict her as self-inflated, naïve, and overbearing. All this culminated in his conclusion that she exhibited the worst flaw imaginable—earnestness. He wrote:

*What Mrs. Clinton seems—in all apparent sincerity—to have in mind is leading the way to something on the order of a Reformation: the remaking of the American way of politics, government, indeed life. A lot of people, contemplating such a task, might fall prey to self doubts. Mrs. Clinton does not blink.*

Arriving with the imprimatur of the most authoritative media outlet in the world, "Saint Hillary" supplied the rest of the press with a framework for reconsidering the First Lady. Editors and reporters across the media spectrum regularly consulted *The Times* to determine which stories mattered, and the paper's perspective invariably influenced what was seen in other publications and heard on broadcasts. (Internet news sources were in their infancy and not yet influential.) Journalists at other outlets felt comfortable following a particular narrative if *The Times* had blazed the trail first.

As a self-confessed "mad dog" of the political Right, David Brock did not need *The Times* to help set his agenda when he approached the rabidly political magazine *The American Spectator* about publishing hard-hitting articles on its supposed political enemies. After studying at the University of California, Brock had gone to work for the Heritage Foundation, which relied on donations from corporate interests to advocate for policies that favored business and right-wing Christianity. From there, he had gone to work for the Reverend Sun Myung Moon's *Insight* magazine, which supported conservative politicians and ideals. Moon, who claimed to be the second coming of Christ, also published the daily *Washington Times,* which had a similar slant. Brock worked there too.

At *The Washington Times,* Brock polished his identity as a rebellious archconservative who broke the constraints of so-called political correctness. This was a time when some academics, political conservatives, and entertainers had begun to push back against what they said was an oppressive effort to control speech. However, their complaints about what they called the PC movement may have been more significant than the movement itself. The term became a rallying cry for those on the Right who alleged a censorship effort for which little evidence could be found. By the time Brock placed himself in the vanguard of those fighting the PC menace, his side in the debate was bigger, stronger, and more outspoken. With cries of "PC!" powerful figures, many of whom were funded by corporations and right-wing organizations, painted themselves as victims. In time, this cause would be joined by those who wanted to promote execrable ideas without meeting resistance. The ultimate example of this would involve a candidate for Congress in Virginia who admitted he promoted white supremacy and legalizing pedophilia. "A lot of people are tired of political correctness and being constrained by it," said Nathan Larson. "People prefer when there's an outsider who doesn't have anything to lose and is willing to say what's on a lot of people's minds."[9]

Under the tutelage of *Washington Times* editor Arnaud de Borchgrave, who defined almost every other journalism outlet as part of a corrupt dominant media culture (DMC), Brock believed he was doing something rebellious as he undertook missions to advance that most mainstream of establishment institutions—the Republican Party. Along the way, he joined a coterie of like-minded propagandists who imagined themselves to be scrappy radicals even as their work was subsidized by deep-pocketed organizations representing wealthy individuals and corporations. (In this way, a writer could feel rebellious but live comfortably.) His circle included Ann Coulter and Laura Ingraham. Both women were given their start at Ivy League student newspapers funded by wealthy benefactors who wanted to groom a new generation of Christian Right advocates. At Dartmouth, Ingraham called members of a gay student association "cheerleaders for latent campus sodomites." (Later she would credit her gay brother for changing her mind about homosexuality.) With acidic personal attacks on Hillary Clinton and others, both Brock and Ingraham would become leading figures in archconservative media.[10]

As Brock would eventually explain, like the Hatfields or the McCoys, his crowd justified their animus by declaring that "*they* started it." The young provocateurs thought the original offense occurred when Democrats blocked Robert Bork's nomination to the Supreme Court by President Reagan. This theory ignored the fact that Bork had infamously fired Watergate special prosecutor Archibald Cox when Cox asked for secret recordings of Oval Office conversations.

Nixon had first ordered Attorney General Elliot Richardson to fire Cox, but Richardson resigned instead. Next, he told Deputy Attorney General William Ruckelshaus to do the dirty work. He, too, refused

and resigned. Third in line was Solicitor General Bork, who followed orders. According to Bork, Nixon promised him the next open seat on the Supreme Court if he complied. However, Nixon resigned before he could put his hatchet man on the bench. When Ronald Reagan tried, Democrats denied him the Senate's consent. Although two Democrats supported Bork and six Republicans voted against his nomination, the battle would be cited as a turning point by Republicans who believed the other side was responsible for the increasing partisanship in politics. When the Democrats later considered denying consent to President George H. W. Bush's nominee, Clarence Thomas, the Republicans were ready with their own tough methods.[11]

At *The Spectator,* Brock began his defense of Thomas by savaging law professor Anita Hill, who had told the Senate Judiciary Committee that Thomas had sexually harassed her when they worked together at the federal Equal Employment Opportunity Commission. Hill's shocking account of Thomas's behavior was supported when she voluntarily submitted to, and passed, a polygraph test. (Thomas would not participate in a test.) Thomas was confirmed, but this success was not enough for David Brock and other right-wing activists. As he later explained, he undertook "a demolition job" against her character, using private materials, including reports from the Federal Bureau of Investigation, slipped to him by Republican officials. Brock called Hill "a bit nutty and a bit slutty" and said she deserved this treatment because of "her uneven temperament, her underwhelming intellect, her political and sexual prejudices, her weird relations with men, her history of frivolously charging sexual harassment, and her petty dishonesty." Brock wrote that "Hill's behavior struck more than one of her colleagues not as feminism, but as plain sexism in reverse. Her flirtatiousness, her provocative manner of dress, was not sweet or sexy, it was sort of angry, almost a weapon."[12]

In time, Brock would experience a deep psychological crisis over his work as a character assassin. He would confess that his need for attention and acceptance inside a particularly rabid political community had driven him to lie, distort, and fabricate. (He even revealed that Coulter repeatedly pressed him to "convert" to heterosexuality.) But in the moment, he insisted that he, who had never been trained as a journalist, was

an investigative reporter, and he reveled in the way his provocative work had established him as a public figure. A high point came as the talk radio host Rush Limbaugh read his work to his nationwide audience for several days in a row.

The Spectator was the perfect platform for Brock's takedown of Hill. Its editors, who labored in the isolated subculture of right-wing advocacy, lacked significant experience in straight journalism and employed none of the usual safeguards, like fact-checking, that supported work done at actual newsmagazines. This nothing-to-lose approach was informed by the fact that as a magazine published by a nonprofit entity, The Spectator didn't have much to lose. Support from benefactors like Richard Mellon Scaife, who had funded the National Legal and Policy Center and its challenge to Hillary Clinton's health care task force, meant that The Spectator didn't rely on subscribers and advertisers in the way that a magazine published as a business enterprise did.

Scaife, who would soon declare, "We're going to get Clinton," couldn't fund legal action against every initiative launched by the new administration. However, The Spectator could send David Brock to collect dirt on the First Couple. Early in the process, he was aided by a Chicago millionaire and Republican benefactor named Peter W. Smith, who was a key ally of Congressman Newt Gingrich of Georgia, who would soon become Speaker of the House of Representatives. Smith would spend a reported $80,000 on investigations of Clinton in Arkansas, giving $5,000 of it directly to Brock. He wanted Brock to investigate the ludicrous "Bill Clinton has a secret black love child" story promoted by Little Rock gadfly Robert McIntosh.[13]

Smith connected Brock with sources in Arkansas, including state troopers who purported to have juicy stories to tell about both Bill and Hillary Clinton. In Little Rock, he was met at the airport by their leader, a lawyer named Cliff Jackson. A former Clinton friend, Jackson had his own political career end with a failed bid for country prosecutor in the same election that saw Clinton become governor for the first time. As Clinton soared, the relationship soured. By 1992, Jackson was, in Brock's words, "dedicated to destroying Clinton at all costs."

Jackson took Brock to a Holiday Inn and told him to wait as he went

to get the troopers. He returned with a quartet of large men who said they had been assigned to the governor's security details. Their names were Larry Patterson, Roger Perry, Ronnie Anderson, and Danny Ferguson. The fifth man present, Lynn Davis, had served as a police official but was not a badge-carrying officer. The group sat down and gushed with anecdotes and claims about both Clintons having sexual affairs. In the troopers' stories, the affairs were consensual; however, Brock would write that Cliff Jackson said they constituted "an abuse of women." Humor and a bit of grudging admiration seeped into the discussion of Bill's exploits. He was, to them, Bubba the good ol' boy. Hillary came in for extra venom as a professional woman whose feminism meant she deserved humiliation. Among themselves, the men speculated about the money they could make—the figure $2.5 million was mentioned—from book and television contracts. According to Brock, they were also in line to get money from Peter Smith.[14]

In modern America, where the mass media is regarded as a road to riches for those who have a brush with fame, thoughts of money occur to just about anyone with a story to tell, whether it's about alien abduction or political scandal. If Gennifer Flowers could get $150,000 from a tabloid newspaper, how much could the troopers earn with their lurid tales? Mainstream news reporters understand how dreams of a payday often lead to embellishment. However, a partisan with an agenda, which was where Brock stood at the time, might be willing to accept at face value the stories told by people with something to gain. If more than one source is involved, the money is likely to become an even bigger factor as everyone envisions the cash being divided into ever-more, and thus ever-smaller, portions. Here the need to make the tale grander, and the pot of book/TV/movie money richer, gets amplified and energized in a way that encourages storytellers to engage in a game of can-you-top-this?

As David Brock eventually confirmed, he was aware of the various motivations the troopers might harbor, but he was invested in what their stories would mean for his political cause and his career. In Washington, he sought reinforcement for his inclinations from his circle of friends and colleagues, who encouraged him to move forward. So it was that even though the troopers approached other media outlets with their stories and one—the *Los Angeles Times*—put serious effort into trying to verify them, Brock and *The Spectator* would be the first to publish in the January 1994 issue.

In his article, which was titled "His Cheatin' Heart," Brock painted the Clintons as a pair of monstrous climbers in a sham marriage devoted to their insatiable appetites for power. He noted "Bill and Hillary Clinton's loose sexual morals and their habitual foul language" and that their cat, Socks, often threw up. Brock explained that his sources were speaking out because "Clinton behaved ungratefully and even rudely toward them after Election Day." The troopers described Clinton as a "sexual predator and exploiter of women," [Brock's words] who had used them to facilitate his affairs. (Brock contradicted himself a bit further in the article, writing that "Clinton built relationships with each of the long-time girlfriends and treated them well.") According to the officers, Clinton confessed to them that he "never met a tax he didn't like," and they alleged that his table manners were atrocious. When he ate an apple, he devoured it, core and all. "He would pick up a baked potato with his hands and eat it in two bites," reported Brock.

Table manners weren't a problem for Hillary, in Brock's account, but he shared the troopers' reports that she was a profane and rage-filled woman who abused her position and was prone to wild outbursts. In a hyperventilating tone, Brock told readers that the troopers heard, from Hillary, "language that makes the Watergate tapes sound like a Sunday school lesson." He also shared shock and outrage over her referring to state troopers' guns as "phallic symbols." Truth be told, the gun-as-phallic-object idea is pretty well settled, and the fact that it was offered as proof that Hillary wanted to belittle men suggests that Brock and the troopers understood the symbolism well. They knew that guns were phallic objects, but they were so insecure—and therefore in need of their symbolic power—that they couldn't bear to hear about it.

In general, Brock and his sources were more offended by Hillary than they were by the president. They reported that she was both furious about her husband's infidelity and so eager for his attention that she loudly demanded more sex from him. Aside from describing his infidelities, Brock treated Bill Clinton well, writing that he was "personable and easy to be around." In contrast, the troopers and Brock took pains to squeeze every negative possibility out of what could be fact or fiction about Hillary. This included a report, from one of the troopers, that a cook identified only as "Miss Emma" once said of Hillary, "The devil's in that woman."[15]

Even friends would say Hillary Clinton was capable of anger and cutting words. No wallflower could have survived in the environments she mastered. But given the pettiness of Arkansas politics and the length of her career—from Watergate to the Rose Law Firm—no prior evidence existed to support the gutter behavior the troopers described. The absence of corroboration made their claims suspect. Even less believable was that someone who was at all aware of her vulnerability as a powerful woman in politics "liked to intimidate men" as the officers said. They even claimed that among her methods was the frequent request that the officers fetch feminine hygiene products from the governor's mansion and bring them to her law offices. The point of this anecdote, and others, was that Hillary was, like Anita Hill, a scheming woman who kept her bitchy wickedness concealed from everyone but eavesdropping security officers. What it revealed about the troopers, and Brock, was that they shared a bigoted grade schooler's view of women and, like children, they assumed that other people were just like they were.

By focusing on the Clintons' personal lives and manners, David Brock and his troopers bypassed the president and his policies to make them seem alien to American norms. With women still bearing the burden when it came to relationships and family, this emphasis made Hillary the frightening "other" who defied conventions and, obviously, neglected her duties as a mother. She and her husband were not responsible, caring people but power-mad radicals cravenly seeking to impose their will on America. Brock made this clear as he pronounced that their relationship was "an effective political partnership, more a business relationship than a marriage." (This he asserted even as he also said that Hillary desired more sex with her husband.) Consistent with the transactional nature of the relationship, Brock wrote, she had responded to Bill's affairs by having one with her law partner Vincent Foster, who had served briefly in the White House before committing suicide in July 1993.

With Foster no longer alive and Hillary Clinton unlikely to dignify his writings with a complaint, Brock could report the troopers' speculation about Foster and their anecdote about a public display of affection he made with Hillary at an event in Little Rock without much concern about being contradicted. The supposed relationship between Hillary and Vince Foster was offered as proof that the Clintons were both untrustworthy. In contrast, Brock granted others in the Clinton saga unnecessary courtesies. Gennifer Flowers, for example, had made herself a public figure, but she was not named by Brock as he indicted Clinton in print. In fact, out of the half-dozen women identified by the troopers, Brock would publish just one's first name—Paula. According to Brock, the troopers couldn't recall Paula's last name, which made checking their claims impossible. Nevertheless, Brock published a great many of the details they offered, without benefit of solid sourcing. Among them was that "Paula told him [Clinton] she was available to be Clinton's regular girlfriend if he so desired."

Promotion being the essence of career building, Brock took pains to have prepublication copies of his article delivered to more prominent press outlets, where editors and producers would be eager to report on his charges and analysis. The practice of disseminating stories on the grounds that their publication elsewhere automatically made them "news" was a relatively new phenomenon that permitted the press to sidestep the usual safeguards against journalistic malpractice. If one publisher or broadcaster went forward with a story, it became established in the public sphere and therefore a worthier subject. Similarly, after the experience of the Gary Hart scandal, which began with an unverified accusation and ended with his political demise, some journalists were more willing to indulge in speculation, which they justified by being open about the fact that they were not confirming a report as fact. In the case of the troopers' many accusations, which David Brock published without supporting evidence, editors and producers proceeded with a caveat emptor ethic that allowed them to spread all sorts of innuendo, distortions, and lies without a sense of responsibility.

With competitors already on the story, the editors of the *Los Angeles Times* finally published the work done by reporters they had sent to Arkansas. The *LA Times* withheld all the first and last names of women alleged to have had sex with Clinton and didn't mention Vince Foster. And unlike Brock, the paper gave ample space to Clinton aides, who refuted the allegations. Nevertheless, the report by one of the most respected press outlets in the country contained enough salacious material to confirm the idea that Bill Clinton was a reckless and sexually voracious philanderer, Hillary was at best unprincipled, and together the Clintons were an insincere, callous, and power-mad pair.

Following a predictable course for rumor-based stories, the circular media process next brought the authors of the various articles to TV studios, where they opined on uncertainties and mysteries in ways that made it seem as though they were engaged with actual facts. "Hey, Bill Clinton is a bizarre guy," said Brock on the TV show *Crossfire*.

Meanwhile, hewing to a tradition that began with Richard Nixon, quipsters named the matter Trooper*gate*. Comedians and talk show hosts began talking about President Bubba and his monstrous harpy wife in a way that would continue for decades. Likewise, the many stories told by the troopers and reported by Brock would be repeated in future articles, books, and videos as if they were as true as the date and place of her birth and the fact that she had a daughter named Chelsea.[16]

Some resisted the anti-Hillary tide. Frank Rich of *The New York Times* identified the contradictions in Brock's work, pointed to the inadequacy of his methods, and noted the viewpoint that ran through his writing on both Anita Hill and Hillary Clinton. "It's women, not liberals, who really get him going," wrote Rich. "The slightest sighting of female sexuality whips him into a frenzy of misogynist zeal. All women are the same to Mr. Brock: terrifying, gutter-tongued sexual omnivores."

As Rich analyzed Brock's tone, reporters from Long Island's *Newsday*, *The Boston Globe*, and local papers in Arkansas knocked down much of what the troopers said. In many cases, readily available facts proved the troopers' claims were false. For example, the social event where Hillary and Vince Foster supposedly displayed their affections never occurred and logs that had reportedly been destroyed to cover up Bill's infidelities had not existed in the first place. One trooper recanted his claim about Clinton offering jobs for silence, and a story about a sex scene supposedly witnessed by troopers watching images from a security camera turned out to be false. Based on the camera's position, it never could have captured what they claimed to have seen.

The trouble with the work done to refute the original stories was that it didn't get the same attention. This is typically the case with vivid reports of any famous person's supposed sins, especially if they involve some sort of conspiracy or are sexual in nature. For their part, there was little the Clintons could say themselves to address Troopergate. Anything short of categorical agreement would be regarded as self-serving. However, they both answered interviewers' questions about it. The president told a journalist for National Public Radio, "The American people gave me a four-year contract. In the political environment in which we're living today, we've seen repeatedly that painful, personal things can be alleged by anybody at any time. That's just, I guess, part of the deal." Mrs. Clinton told Reuters, "It also hurts. Even though you're a public figure, which means apparently in America anybody can say anything about you. Even public figures have feelings and families and reputations."

Hillary was right. As interpreted by the courts, the First Amendment to the Constitution gave wide latitude to those who would criticize public officials or speculate about them. The law did offer an opening for legal action if a speaker or author knowingly or recklessly spread a lie, but suing to prove such a claim could be costly, in terms of lawyers' fees, and bring the possibility that the original statement would get even more attention. Add the possibility of losing at trial, and public figures generally chose to ignore hurtful things that were said or published.

The First Amendment to the Constitution permits anyone to say anything about an American public official. Witness Robert McIntosh. Although other well-known figures like movie stars and businesspeople are also fair game, it's possible for them to file lawsuits based on misuse of their image or citing damage done to a reputation that has commercial value. Courts have denied public officials this option on the theory that the nation requires unfettered free speech in the realms of government and politics. Presidents are especially unprotected in this regard and have no practical recourse when smeared.[17] For media entrepreneurs who made politics their focus, the American legal landscape was a boon to the bottom line—the First Amendment could be quite profitable.

Rush Limbaugh built an audience in the millions by saying awful things about the Clintons and other political figures. A gifted storyteller and polemicist, Limbaugh could sound like a cult leader as he encouraged his audience to abandon newspapers, magazines, and TV news and trust him to deliver them the truth. "I will do all your reading," he assured them, "and I will tell you what to think about it." His most loyal fans embraced their status as followers, calling themselves "ditto heads."[18]

Limbaugh kept the ditto heads listening with a pitch-perfect appeal to their emotions and well-honed sense of drama. Two months after Hillary was depicted by Brock as an all-around awful woman, Limbaugh's voice boomed out of radios across America with the suggestion, which he credited to a small financial newsletter, that she was also a murderer. He said:

> OK, folks, I think I got enough information here to tell you about the contents of this fax that I got. Brace yourselves. This fax contains information that I have just been told will appear in a newsletter to Morgan Stanley sales personnel this afternoon. . . . What it is, is a bit of news which says . . . there's a Washington consulting firm that has scheduled the release of a report that will appear, it will be published, that claims that Vince Foster was murdered in an apartment owned by Hillary Clinton, and the body was then taken to Fort Marcy Park.[19]

Although Limbaugh would say he wasn't a news reporter, he called the item "news" and asserted his audience relied upon him not just for "information" but for the truth. Nothing in this report was true. It was more than deceitful to say that Hillary Clinton, the First Lady, kept a secret apartment in the suburbs—the love nest inference was obvious—when in fact public records showed she didn't own any property in greater Washington. Similarly, it was absurd to say that Foster died any-where other than in the park, and there was no evidence that his body had been moved after his death. Nevertheless, Limbaugh speculated freely, borrowing the credibility of Morgan Stanley to add credence to what he said. In the end, he had added a conspiracy theory to the trag-edy of a distraught man's suicide. Hillary's role, of course, was that of the black widow whose sexual immorality had fatal consequences. Often used against powerful women, it was a popular trope among insecure men who feared equality of the sexes.

After Limbaugh indulged in his Hillary-murdered-Foster fantasy, his executive producer, Roger Ailes, amplified the story on a New York–based, nationally broadcast morning radio show hosted by a shock jock named Don Imus. Ailes recommended that Imus's listeners consult arti-cles written by Christopher Ruddy, who had previously pushed the idea that Foster died as a result of "foul play." Said Ailes, "The guy who's been doing an excellent job for the *New York Post* . . . for the first time on the Rush Limbaugh show said that . . . he did not believe it was suicide. . . . Now, I don't have any evidence. . . . These people are very good at hid-ing or destroying evidence." (Ailes would also joke that Bill Clinton would soon visit New York to commit sexual harassment.)

Lack of evidence did not constrain Ailes or Christopher Ruddy, who reported in the *Post* the false notion that the gun found at the scene of Foster's death had not been tested by experts. He also quoted, as cred-ible, questions about the incident raised by two rescue workers who were neither investigators nor law enforcement officers. Ruddy allowed others to speculate on the possibility that Foster had died in one spot—namely, an apartment owned by Hillary Clinton—and was then moved to the park where his body was found. In a bit of typographic advocacy, the *Post* enclosed the word *suicide* with single quote marks, indicating doubt about the term as it applied to Foster's death. From the beginning, the speculation was taken up in other outlets, including the editorial page of *The Wall Street Journal*. The paper, urged by editorial page editor Rob-ert Bartley, then filed a lawsuit seeking documents related to the case.

Although the generally estimable *Journal* and others cast doubt on Foster's suicide, it wouldn't be long until Republicans in Congress joined the chorus who said his death was suspicious. Of particular note was Indiana congressman Dan Burton's hour-long speech in which he repeated the suggestion that the Clintons were responsible for Foster's death. Included in this diatribe was a recounting of an at-home forensic experiment Burton said he conducted. In this test, a melon was substituted for Foster's head, and the findings supposedly proved that someone should have heard a gunshot if Foster committed suicide. Burton said, "We, at my house, with a homicide detective, tried to re-create a head, and fired a .384-inch barrel into that, to see if the sound could be heard from a hundred yards away. Even though there was an earth-mover moving around in the background, making all kinds of racket—and you could hear the bullet clearly."[20]

All the conjecture and spectacle, including statements made by members of Congress in the ornate House chamber, pained Foster's grieving friends and family, who knew how he'd died. The ridiculous arguments required the assumption that a great many people who had no shared motivation—the police, Foster's doctor, his family, and others—conspired to create the false impression that a suicide had occurred. The speculation also defied the fact that nothing in Foster's death suggested foul play. On the contrary, before he died Foster was being treated for depression and had complained about the stress of his job, which required him to answer questions about the firing of staff in the White House travel office. (Though critics cried scandal, and once again Hillary became the main target, multiple independent investigations ended with no serious findings against her.) Foster's car was found parked near his body. The bullet that killed him had entered at his mouth and exited at the back of his head. His thumb was caught in the trigger of the gun that fired it, which was a family heirloom. A note found in Foster's briefcase, reconstructed from torn pieces, offered a list of things that distressed him, including, "The WSJ [*Wall Street Journal*] editors lie without consequence."

When he was alive and at the White House, *The Wall Street Journal* had worked hard to depict Foster as a shady character, even comparing him with convicted felon Oliver North of the Reagan administration's Iran-Contra scandal. Two days after the man's suicide, the paper declared,

"Those who knew him consider him an unlikely suicide," as it suggested his death was "mysterious" and "troubling." No effort was made to establish the identities of these people "who knew him" and questioned the cause of his death. Perhaps it was this kind of report that had caused Foster to write in his note, "I was not meant for the job or the spotlight of public life in Washington. Here, ruining people is considered sport."

The sport during Foster's time in Washington was all about the Whitewater real estate project, which had been considered and reconsidered in Arkansas for years. The failed development had been a debacle for both Clintons, which meant their antagonists could have an easy twofer (just as the president said the voters were getting) if they prevailed. Typical of real estate developments, Whitewater involved financial institutions and public agencies that dealt with land use. However, two factors made Whitewater irresistible for anyone hoping to find scandal. The first was that Bill Clinton was attorney general when he and Hillary joined the Whitewater partnership in 1978. (Although he soon lost his reelection bid and returned to private life, his political status remained high.) The second tantalizing element was Whitewater partner James McDougal's ruinous operation of the Arkansas-based S&L company called Madison Guaranty. The collapse of Madison and the 1990 prosecution of McDougal on fraud charges tantalized the Clintons' political opponents, but he was acquitted.

Given his background as a Clinton friend and Hillary's partner at the Rose firm, where she did some work for Madison Guaranty, Foster's suicide was regarded as ample reason for renewed partisan interest in all things Arkansas, including Whitewater. The conspiracy-minded could imagine that even if Foster wasn't murdered, he was driven to suicide by some Whitewater/Clinton secret. The key to destroying the political power of the president and his wife could thus be found by investigating his death. Their appetites for this outcome were increased when White House counsel Bernard Nussbaum separated the Clintons' personal papers from Foster's government files and turned only those he deemed relevant over to investigators looking into the suicide.

Where did the desire to demonize and then demolish the Clintons arise? David Brock, the only insider to ever reveal the inner workings of this campaign, credited both Republican ire over the loss of the White House, which the party had become accustomed to holding, and the destructive hyper-partisanship of politicians like Representative Newt Gingrich.

By the mid-1990s, Gingrich led a growing group that called themselves "young gun" political warriors devoted to both right-wing policies and a call to what Gingrich imagined would be "moral revival." None of the guns could outperform Gingrich, who was willing to say whatever was required to hold the public's attention. He tried to link terrifying moments in history to modern America and offered himself as a savior. As the 1996 election approached, he called Democrats "traitors" and declared, "People like me are what stand between us and Auschwitz. I see evil all around me every day."

Although they championed traditional family values represented by conservative Christianity—heterosexual-only marriage, a ban on abortion, opposition to feminism—many of these men were less than conservative in their personal lives. Gingrich, who had been unfaithful, infamously asked his first wife to negotiate a divorce when she was in the hospital recovering from cancer surgery. It was this kind of inconsistency that caused GOP senator Bob Dole to speak of them as "the young hypocrites."[21]

The young hypocrites were backed by a flood tide of money paid to activists and advocates like Brock, who competed to top one another with outrageous theories about the suicide. (This was part of a larger enterprise devoted to the task of proving that the Clintons were generally despicable human beings.) Christopher Ruddy left the *Post* in New York to work for Richard Mellon Scaife's Pittsburgh *Tribune-Review* and continued to add distortions to the record. Among them was suspicion he attached to the report that the pistol was found in Foster's right hand because he was supposedly left-handed. This was wrong. Foster was a righty. In one promotional letter sent to boost a book on the case, Ruddy said the Clintons' arrival in Washington represented a crisis more serious than the Civil War, which is why "I tremble for the future."[22]

Ruddy's work was related to a multimillion-dollar Scaife enterprise, informally called the Arkansas Project, which was pursued to take down both Bill and Hillary Clinton. The project was devoted mainly to promoting theories about Whitewater and often relied on testimony from an unlikely figure named Parker Dozhier. A professional fur trapper, Dozhier owned a lakeside bait shop in Hot Springs as well as a house in West Little Rock that was used for Arkansas Project meetings. Dozhier told Brock that he, too, had had a sexual relationship with Gennifer Flowers, and he had been a source for Michael Kelly's "Saint Hillary" article. Brock would write that the trapper was in frequent contact with Republican staffers on Capitol Hill, including the same David Bossie who had once tried to prove that a pregnant woman's suicide was linked to Bill Clinton. Although the Bush campaign had called him one of "the lowest forms of life," Bossie got a job as an investigator for GOP senator Lauch Faircloth of North Carolina.

Although Dozhier and his cronies took Scaife's money, funneled to them through *The Spectator,* much of their activity involved talking to one another at noisy gatherings where they kept guns close at hand because they assumed they were in mortal danger. As they fed reporters, the Arkansas talkers managed to aid the construction of a national political controversy. The results of all this effort included Attorney General Janet Reno's appointment of a special counsel named Robert Fiske, a moderate Republican who had been a federal prosecutor, then worked at a Wall Street law firm. (Special counsels are prosecutors who take up politically sensitive cases to assure the public that justice is blind in cases where a president or members of his administration could be targets.)

Fiske, who was supervised by three federal judges, was given a broad mandate to investigate Foster's death, Whitewater, and any crimes discovered in the course of his work. Of particular interest to those who suspected foul play, and hoped Fiske would uncover it, were files belonging to the Clintons, which Foster had held in his office. These were sent to the Clintons' personal lawyers. Here Hillary was targeted as the person who supposedly managed the files. Their transfer caused an alarm to sound in the minds of conspiracy theorists. When Fiske reported there was nothing sinister in how the papers were handled or in Foster's death, he didn't quite switch off the siren.[23]

Soon after Fiske made his report, Republican senators Jesse Helms and Lauch Faircloth, who was David Bossie's boss, shared lunch with one of the three judges who had supervised the special counsel. Notoriously mean-spirited, Helms was an expert at inflammatory rhetoric and fearmongering. Similar in manner, Faircloth was a man "D.C. loved to hate," according to *The Washington Post*. The senators were rabidly anti-Clinton and knew their guest, Judge David Sentelle, as a veteran of North Carolina politics. Within weeks of this lunch, the judges panel voted two to one along party lines to replace the special counsel. (The lunch companions denied that Whitewater had been a topic of conversation.) Sentelle would eventually explain that Fiske, a lifelong Republican, couldn't stay in the job, because he was "affiliated with the incumbent administration," which was Democratic. Of course, that affiliation depended solely on his selection to investigate the administration as an independent prosecutor.[24]

The new investigator chosen by the court to replace Fiske was former Bush administration solicitor general Kenneth Starr. Starr was a minister's son who had never worked as a prosecutor or even a trial lawyer. More conservative and openly moralistic than Fiske, he exuded both certainty and naïveté. Starr had recently gotten involved with a group of lawyers supporting a woman who had sued President Clinton for sexual harassment she said occurred when he was governor. His public statements in support of the suit, despite the established limits on lawsuits against sitting presidents, had prompted five former presidents of the American Bar Association to oppose his appointment. The plaintiff in this claim was David Brock's "Paula." Her last name was Jones.[25]

Of all people, Arthur Schlesinger Jr., the great liberal historian and friend to presidents, shouldn't have been wary of having dinner with Hillary Clinton. Nevertheless, Schlesinger had noted, from afar, something guarded about her, and this bothered him. On the day of the event, he confided in another First Lady, Jacqueline Kennedy Onassis, that he was worried that Hillary might be too reserved to be good company. She assured him, "She's great fun, she's got an excellent sense of humor, and you'll like her very much." As writer Henry Louis Gates reported in *The New Yorker,* Schlesinger found Hillary to be just as Onassis had described her, adding, "She's a charmer."

When he came upon the anecdote about Schlesinger and Onassis, Gates was preparing to write an article about a phenomenon he called "Hillary-hating," which was becoming a national pastime. The invisible but very real machine that reduced public figures to archetypes had cast her as a self-deluded do-gooder. This pasteboard image was no more accurate than the one that gave the world a gay Cary Grant as a lady-killer, but in a mass media era the cartoon is all that many people can recognize or absorb about a person they will see only on a TV screen or in magazines. When money and power are at stake, huge amounts of energy and capital may be devoted to creating or contesting an image, which often bears no resemblance to reality. Soda pop companies, brewers, and politicians do this by appealing to the same essential emotions—happiness, sadness, fear, anger, surprise, and disgust. With the exception of happiness and, in some cases, surprise, the base emotions tend to signal something or someone to be avoided. This makes sense if you consider human feeling to be about an organism's survival, but the disparity also means that it's much easier to make great masses of people shun a person than it is to get them to accept her. A scapegoating message can act like a virus, spreading through society and infecting vast numbers of people with a cartoonish image of the target.

The dynamic that turns people into caricatures for others to hate can also burden the minds of those who are scapegoated. As negative judgments pile up, defensiveness turns to fearfulness, and the victim can find herself filled with self-doubt and struggling to respond to the world in a natural way. For the not famous, who may be scapegoated inside a family, community, or workplace, the experience can ruin relationships and self-esteem. Politicians who endure a reputational attack can be brought low in the eyes of their constituents and lose the confidence they need to campaign for office and govern well. Often this process occurs at an almost imperceptible level. A trace of wariness infects a smile

flashed at an event. The spine stiffens during a press interview. Gradually, what is genuine and true about a person either is lost or becomes
beside the point. They become, at least in part, what "they" say they are.
This is made all the easier by the fact that there is little in human nature
that doesn't exist, in some measure, inside every individual. Selflessness,
equanimity, selfishness, and rage all wait to be expressed, invoked, or
accepted.

Hillary Clinton knew that many people would dismiss what she had
to say about her own public image, so when Gates asked her about it
she addressed not the personal part but the sociological aspect, noting, "I
apparently remind some people of their mother-in-law or their boss, or
something." She also observed that she was a stand-in for every woman
who ever sought to be heard in a society that still discounted them and
an emblem of the never-ending debate over gender roles, marriage, and
leadership.

In reality, Hillary *was* capable of displaying impatience, anger, and
arrogance. At health care hearings, she spoke about expert witnesses
who criticized without offering constructive ideas. When one physician
bemoaned the burden of paperwork he feared under a new system, she
asked "why the medical community in this country can't help us figure
out what will work . . . this is just one example of what really should
be solved by the medical community."

Coming from almost anyone else, this kind of display might not be
noted at all. For Hillary's critics, it was proof that she was disrespectful
and domineering. These judgments hurt, but after fifteen years in public
life and longer in the law, she had decided that since she couldn't please
everyone, she wasn't going to try. "Like all of us, Hillary would prefer
to be liked," explained a friend at the time, "but she's secure enough to
risk not being liked if that's what it takes."

Although she said she felt worn out after just six weeks on the job as
head of the health care effort, Hillary maintained a hectic pace. This included defending against a federal suit filed to contest her appointment
to lead the task force, which a court decided in her favor in the summer
of 1993. Her effort impressed even the top Senate Republican, Bob
Dole, who quashed rumors that he was miffed because she called him

Bob, saying, "Last time I checked, that was my name," and announced he would back a change in an anti-nepotism law if it were needed to permit her to continue her work. Asked to explain his fondness for Hillary, Dole cited the example of his wife, Elizabeth, who was president of the American Red Cross. "I'm used to smart women," he said. "At least Hillary doesn't ask for blood."[26]

Developed in eight months' time, the plan produced by the task force guaranteed health care for every U.S. citizen, including treatment for conditions they suffered when the law was proposed. This would be accomplished by requiring that major employers offer plans and that every person not covered at work obtain some type of insurance (the poor would receive subsidies for the premiums). The legislation needed to enact the plan was then developed inside the White House, where it was adjusted to accommodate promises made during the 1992 campaign. The president announced the hybrid proposal in an address to Congress.

With his own role in developing the plan partially obscured, Bill Clinton let his wife take the heat from opponents while he basked in the popularity suggested by his high poll numbers. Clinton felt confident about his chances for success, because earlier in the year more than twenty Republican senators had said they would support health care reforms like the ones Clinton proposed. However, he didn't anticipate the ferocious opposition that would come from the health insurance industry or the way his wife would be used by the political opposition who would dub the plan "Hillarycare" and make it possible for those voters who liked him to oppose the reforms because they were supposedly her idea.[27]

In time, the most memorable images of Bill Clinton's failed drive to achieve his main domestic policy goal were of a middle-aged couple seated at a kitchen table deciding that they hated the proposal. The "Harry and Louise" television ad campaign was unleashed by health insurance executives who defended the lucrative status quo by arguing that the change proposed would deprive most Americans of the care they wanted. The industry's public relations advisor Ben Goddard, who described this effort as a "war," had laid out the plan of attack just weeks after Inauguration Day, when the president's proposal wasn't even drafted.

Goddard selected the woman who played Louise because he considered her relatable. (This was certainly the case for him, as he would up marrying her.) He also made Louise "the smart one," because he estimated that women were more important players in health care decisions. When Harry says, "I'm glad the president's doing something about health care reform," Louise brings him up short by telling him, under the proposal, "the government caps how much the country can spend on all health care and says, 'That's it!'" This claim was never true, but it left the impression that a sick person could be denied treatment because others had soaked up all the resources.[28]

After the insurers came out against the reform plan and Clinton's postelection popularity faded, Republicans in Congress began to focus on simply killing it. The justification for this change came from William Kristol, who had been Vice President Dan Quayle's chief of staff. (Wags called him "Quayle's brain.") Kristol thought that if Democrats helped more Americans access health care, their party would get the credit for years to come and this would be trouble for his side. The only option, he announced, would be "an aggressive and uncompromising counterstrategy designed to delegitimize the proposal." The effort worked so well that when senators made a last-ditch effort at compromise, Kristol said they should reject it "sight unseen." They did.[29]

In the aftermath of health care reform's defeat, the Democrats faced a backlash in the 1994 congressional races, where many Republicans followed Newt Gingrich's playbook to attack their opponents with more heated rhetoric. A pamphlet on the Gingrich method suggested candidates use the following words as they talked about the other side:

*Decay. Failure. Collapse. Deeper. Crisis. Urgent. Destructive. Destroy. Sick. Pathetic. Lie. Liberal. They/them. Unionized bureaucracy. "Compassion" is not enough. Betray. Consequences. Limit(s). Shallow. Traitors. Sensationalists. Endanger. Coercion. Hypocrisy. Radical. Threaten. Devour. Waste. Corruption. Incompetent. Permissive attitude. Impose. Self-serving. Greed. Ideological. Insecure. Anti-(issue) flag, family, child, jobs.*[30]

The Gingrich method institutionalized a rancorous rhetoric that had previously been quite rare. Accusing an opponent of treason and pathology had long been beyond the pale. This was why the Willie Horton ad shocked people in 1988. As academic experts would show, the negativity polarized people who belonged to the parties and demoralized independents. It was also effective. In 1994, it helped Republicans swamp Democrats in congressional elections, but it wasn't the only factor in the outcome. Generally speaking, the party that wins the White House in one election will suffer losses in the next midterm. Also, Clinton's side was weighed down by presidential controversies. Gennifer Flowers, Whitewater, and the Paula Jones lawsuit had raised doubts about Clinton's character, and efforts to demonize Hillary had damaged him even further. In many ways, she suffered more in the public eye than her husband. He was a man with big appetites and passions, and this type was often forgiven for his transgressions. He was more suited, temperamentally, to the rough-and-tumble of politics. At times, he even seemed to thrive on the drama like a person addicted to risk.

Hillary, whose own dreams included the possibility of being president, too, wasn't so resilient, and she wouldn't get the benefit of the doubt afforded her husband. A woman in Hillary's position was damned if she stuck with her man—*What a fool!*—and damned if she left him—*How could she!* She tried to occupy a middle ground, as many betrayed wives do when they have a child and a long history to consider. And she attempted it in full public view. And she was far from finished with the challenge.[31]

# 5

# A Multifront Assault

With open-ended investigations of the president becoming the norm in Congress, the Republican wave that gave the GOP control of the House in 1994 guaranteed that Democrat Bill Clinton would be pursued as if he were a prey animal. Right-wing activists routinely made the First Lady a target too. Unlike previous presidential candidates, who disguised their wives' importance, Bill Clinton was transparent in his respect for, and reliance upon, his wife. As one half of the twofer offer candidate Clinton had made, Hillary was denied deference generally guaranteed to more traditional First Ladies. In declining to be content with the old role of the country's symbolic mother, she seemed to incite a carnal level of loathing.

The big fear was that Hillary would prove herself worthy. As writer Paul Johnson noted in the conservative journal *Commentary,* "They [Democrats] talk brazenly of a second term [new horror in administration] and, beyond that, of a Hillary presidency." This prospect turned the most labile right-wingers into hysterical, ravening wolves. "That is one of many reasons," wrote Johnson, "why the pack will never be called off the Clintons."[1]

Johnson, who had previously stood up for Richard Nixon, Augusto

Pinochet, and Francisco Franco, represented the intellectual apex of Hillary hating. However, like less literary partisans who loathed the Clintons, he was upset with the way the president and First Lady conducted their own relationship. The Clintons maintained a marriage of equals, and she played a full role in their life before Washington and in policy matters at the White House. More to the point were that her participation in the failed Whitewater development and her work at the Rose Law Firm, where Vince Foster was her partner and Madison Guaranty was a minor client, also made her relevant in the eyes of congressional Republicans.[2]

Americans who struggled to follow congressional probes of Whitewater and Madison found themselves lost in a record that mixed facts, lies, innuendos, and conspiracy theories that failed to show that crimes had been committed or the public trust had been abused. Journalists also labored to construct a helpful narrative that would show a governor and his wife manipulating S&L regulators, but they couldn't get the pieces to fit together inside a timeline that made any sense. Consider:

- The Whitewater development partnership with James and Susan McDougal began in 1978, *before* Clinton was governor.
- Jim McDougal's Madison S&L wasn't created until 1982, when Clinton was a *private citizen*.
- Madison's operation was ultimately overseen by federal and *not* state regulators.
- The Clintons' investment in Whitewater was always at risk, and they *lost* money.

In addition to the obvious misalignments, those working to fit the puzzle pieces into a picture of scandal had to account for the fact that the main peddlers of Whitewater theories were the same Clinton antagonists—Floyd Brown of Willie Horton fame, his partner David Bossie, Sheffield Nelson, and others—whom prosecutor Fiske already determined unreliable. For Bossie and Brown, hyping Whitewater/Madison had become a profitable endeavor. In fund-raising appeals, they highlighted their central role in the anti-Clinton cause, noting all the major newspapers, magazines, and TV networks that had used information they provided. In one year alone, this effort netted $3 million from 175,000 donors.

Journalists who relied on the likes of Bossie and Brown noted that they were the kinds of characters often found to be involved in scandalous issues. "You don't find swans in the sewer," was how NBC News producer Ira Silverman put it. And of course, reputable reporters tested every claim that emerged from the sewer. But as years passed and the hypesters failed to score a direct hit, it began to seem as though the journalists who continued to devote their energy to the cause were too eager for scoops and too reliant on flawed sources.

As reporters repeatedly tried and failed to confirm a Whitewater scandal, their effort—some might say obsession—became a story in and of itself. Journalist and Fulbright scholar Trudy Lieberman examined the work of the investigative reporters and came away with serious doubts about their judgment. In two hundred cases, she found journalists had aligned their reports with the "specific details" and the "omissions, spin, and implication" in materials provided by the likes of Bossie and Brown. Writing in the *Columbia Journalism Review,* she noted the absence of coherent narratives in Whitewater coverage and the repeated use of vague but incriminating terms, such as *questions persist* and *scandalous odors* and *ethically suspect* and *sweetheart deals.* These are not the phrases used by journalists who have the goods.

Where the Clintons were concerned, no sweetheart deals existed, and the questions and suspicions revealed in the press came in a remarkably circular fashion. At one point, the editors of *The Washington Post* actually printed allegations published in its crosstown rival, *The Washington Times,* only to knock down the charges in a correction printed in the next day's paper. Most dogged of all, *The Wall Street Journal* offered so many Whitewater articles and opinion columns—in just two years—that when they were gathered together in a book, it totaled 580 pages. On the back cover of this document, the book's authors asked, "Confused by Whitewater?" No one who read the book cover to cover would come away saying otherwise.[3]

Frustrated in the hunt for wrongdoing, critics made the Clintons themselves subjects for microscopic examination. In general, the affable president, who seemed able to charm even his opponents, glided through these inspections. For Hillary, who would be the first to admit she lacked her husband's charisma, the experience was like that of a frog undergoing dissection in a high school science lab. With every slice, the examiners exclaimed that they had found something startling when, in fact, they had discovered ordinary frog guts. In the case of Hillary Clinton, the feverish examinations revealed the ordinarily complex life of a woman who for more than twenty years had lived and worked at the top level of the legal profession and politics.

Deprived of facts, news reporters ceded the pursuit to opinion writers. William Safire of *The New York Times* was the most prominent of those who fixated on Hillary Clinton. Safire signaled his retrograde views of her in 1992, when he damned her with faint praise for using the Clinton name. This was, he wrote, a fitting rebuke to what he called "militant feminism." (To bolster his case, he quoted another writer's cringeworthy observation that this strand of feminism was associated "with overtones of lesbianism and man-hating.")

In his next examination of Hillary, Safire switched from passive-aggressive to merely aggressive as he called her "a political bumbler ... appearing to show contempt for women who work at home." Months later, Hillary was, in Safire's view, the president's wifely conscience who had "failed him." How she should be expected to be a wifely conscience, a woman contemptuous of homemakers, and political bumbler all at once he never explained.

Like many others, Safire sharpened his attacks after the death of Vincent Foster, which, he theorized, was not just a matter of a severely depressed man reaching the end of his ability to cope. In a January 1994 column ghoulishly titled "Foster's Ghost," Safire speculated, without proof of any sort, that Foster suffered from a guilty conscience because of something Hillary Clinton asked him to do. A week later, Safire misrepresented a plain-to-read document in service of his Vince Foster theory and swiped at Hillary, alleging she was trying to hide incompetence as a private practice lawyer. Two years later, after it was clear to all that a severely depressed Vince Foster had killed himself, Safire would still refer to his death as an "apparent suicide" and refer to a lawyer as both Clintons'"closest confidant since Foster's death and the cover-up coordinator." Safire opted to, in his words, "guess" and "deduce" to conclude:

> *A mysterious death; witnesses unbelievably forgetful about calls made in its aftermath; conflicts in sworn testimony about concealment of the dead man's files; now claims to a privilege of secrecy. Something is under that Whitewater rock.*[4]

The arguments against such a conclusion included the fact that Foster's death wasn't mysterious. His files were private. And in general, witnesses to any event are so likely to offer conflicting testimony that prosecutors become suspicious when they *don't* conflict. Of course, anyone who wanted to see intrigue could dismiss the mitigating facts in service to both their political and personal agendas. Here, again, Hillary's mere existence seemed to be a problem for certain people. Save for Eleanor Roosevelt, whom columnist Westbrook Pegler called "impudent, presumptuous and conspiratorial," no modern First Lady had ever been subject to such regular speculation and negative pronouncement. Others, including Nancy Reagan, had been close advisors to their husbands. All had, throughout years of marriage, been privy to all sorts of information on assets and investments made jointly with their spouses. Only Hillary had been cast as a scheming Lady Macbeth and subject to so much investigation and animus. Add the conditions of a media environment where the press was willing to give a platform to almost anyone willing to say something awful about her. After the 1994 election, CBS News reporter Connie Chung went to interview Representative Newt Gingrich's mother about her son—she called him Newty—and whatever else was on her mind. The result was a bizarre bit of video that found Chung coyly enticing Kathleen Gingrich to speak a secret. The two women sat across from each other in a cozy room in Mrs. Gingrich's home. Chung wore a broad-shouldered houndstooth jacket. Mrs. Gingrich propped one elbow on the table and held a lit cigarette. The scene evoked a couple of neighbors kibitzing at a kitchen table:

*"Mrs. Gingrich, what has Newt told you about President Clinton?"*
*asked Chung.*
*"Nothin'. And I can't tell you what he said about Hillary."*
*"You can't?"*
*"I can't."*
*"Why don't you just whisper it to me, just between you and me?"*
*Mrs. Gingrich leaned in and stage-whispered: "She's a bitch. About the*
*only thing he ever said about her."*

The interview became a minor sensation as the transcript was released
prior to the broadcast. Wire services and columnists jumped on the
story, and Representative Gingrich complained, not about what his
mother had said but about the way Chung posed her questions. CBS
News executives refused to grant him the apology he demanded, and
once the piece was aired, it got more attention, including a parody on
*Saturday Night Live.* When approached by journalists, Kathleen Gingrich wondered aloud, "What's all the fuss about?" As she explained, "I
said she's a bitch, and that's what all the [conservative political] pins are
saying." The bitch in question invited Mrs. Gingrich and her son to visit
the White House, and they took her up on the offer less than two weeks
after CBS presented the interview. Gingrich took the second of what
would be three wives along, and everyone was treated to tea, coffee, and
petits fours. When a reporter asked if any apology would be made to the
First Lady, Gingrich did not answer.[5]


If a woman who considered political campaign buttons good sources of
information was invited to trash her on national television and then the
media kept the story going, there was nothing Hillary Clinton could
do about it. Pat Buchanan had demonstrated that votes could be had
by braying about culture wars, and many others had shown they could
gain substantial fame by alleging, without evidence, that the Clintons
had done awful things. Under these circumstances, hatred of the sort
Mrs. Gingrich expressed would continue to circulate. More troubling
was the mischief done by those who possessed some official power and

were willing to use it recklessly. A case in point involved a low-level investigator who worked on the case of Madison Guaranty for the Resolution Trust Corporation. The RTC was a federal agency created to review the records of failed S&Ls and dispose of their assets for the benefit of taxpayers. Madison Guaranty was handled in the RTC's Tulsa office, where L. Jean Lewis recognized the political implications in the case of a bankrupt S&L operated by a man who had been the Clintons' partner in Whitewater.

Neither an accountant nor a lawyer, Lewis lacked experience and training relevant to investigating financial crimes. When she was hired, her main qualification for the job had been her work at the failed Western Savings and Loan of Phoenix, Arizona, where she had been a secretary and then custodian of the records the RTC scoured after its demise. In 1990, Bank of America took over Western. In 1991, Lewis went to work for the RTC. In March 1992, she was assigned to the Madison case and poured her attention into an archive of records, looking for proof of wrongdoing inside one of the smallest S&Ls to go bust during the crisis. In less than five months, she became certain that crimes had been committed to benefit the Clintons and that both the FBI and federal prosecutors should get involved.

The timing of Lewis's first referral for prosecution—late August 1992—meant that it could have created a so-called October Surprise that would have damaged challenger Bill Clinton's chances in the presidential election. At the time, Lewis told an FBI agent that her work could "alter history" and pestered prosecutors to act quickly so their moves in the Madison case would become public before the election. Although the White House, and thus the Justice Department, was in Republican hands, nonpartisan professionals considered the Lewis files and decided her findings did not justify action. (*Newsweek* quoted sources who said Lewis was inclined toward conspiracy theories, could reach conclusions based on meager evidence, and, according to one, "could make an incident out of just anything.")[6]

The election came. Bill Clinton won. But Lewis did not give up. In 1993, her case files were somehow leaked to the press. A flurry of newspaper reports based on the files set off a scramble to confirm that the

Clintons had somehow done something nefarious in Whitewater, but reporters never got beyond floating suggestions and rumors. However, Whitewater remained a hook on which political adversaries could hang suspicions about the Clintons.

By 1994, with midterm congressional elections at hand, Lewis returned to the political stage as GOP representative James Leach made public some of her work and then took to the House floor to praise her as "courageous" and declare that "Whitewater is about the arrogance of power—the Machiavellian machinations of single-party Government." Leach and fellow Republicans were unable to pursue an aggressive investigation of Whitewater because, as the minority party in the House and Senate, they didn't control committees and thus couldn't lead probes and issue subpoenas, which compelled testimony under the threat of prosecution should a witness lie. All this changed when they seized both the House and Senate in the 1994 elections. Representative Newt Gingrich, who would become Speaker of the House, said with delight, "Washington just can't imagine a world in which Republicans have subpoena power."

After the Republicans seized the House and Leach became chairman of the House Banking Committee, he brought Lewis to testify at a hearing, where she said she believed her efforts had been impeded by higher-ups. The only evidence she presented was a recording of a conversation with an RTC lawyer, which had been made without the other party's knowledge. The presentation was dramatic, but the content was open to interpretation. The RTC lawyer said she thought higher-ups wanted to be able to disconnect Whitewater and Madison, but she also insisted she wasn't expecting a particular outcome from Lewis's work. For her part, Lewis mentioned Mrs. Clinton by name, saying, "We are dealing with lawyers here. . . . You don't turn a blind eye to your business investments."[7]

Months later, Senator Alfonse D'Amato asked Lewis to answer questions before the upper chamber's Whitewater committee, which was about halfway into a probe that would consume thirteen months and roughly three hundred hours of broadcast time on the public affairs TV channel called the Cable-Satellite Public Affairs Network (C-SPAN).

The hearing had begun with a bang as Alaska Republican Frank Mur-kowski brandished Vince Foster's briefcase as he suggested that there had been something fishy in the discovery of a torn suicide note inside the case. Like so many others involving Hillary, this issue never went beyond the insinuation stage. Conspiracy theorists had promoted the idea that the note had been drafted in someone else's hand, but no real evidence for this notion, or any of the other supposed links between the First Lady and Foster's death, ever materialized.

By late November 1995, commercial TV networks had given up on the prospect of the investigation producing testimony that was either dra-matic or newsworthy. Whitewater and Madison Guaranty were minor episodes when compared with other busted developments and financial debacles revealed by the massive S&L crisis that began in the 1980s. Among the hundreds of S&Ls that collapsed were several that cost taxpayers more than $1 billion, including one in Denver that counted President Bush's son Neil among its board members. In comparison, Madison required a $60 million federal bailout, which, while conse-quential, was far from the costliest, even in Arkansas. (When FirstSouth Savings and Loan of Little Rock went under, this Madison competitor's collapse was the biggest S&L failure in history.)

Given the low stakes in the Madison bankruptcy, it never would have made national news but for the Clinton connection. At the same time, the people who testified before the committee were, for the most part, unremarkable figures who offered boring statements. The colorful and talkative Arkansas state troopers, who had had so much to say to the press about the Clintons, never appeared. Instead, lawmakers and the public were treated to a droning litany voiced by bureaucrats and lawyers. Surely Clinton critics prayed for a witness like John Dean, the White House lawyer who was key to the Watergate hearings. Instead, they got L. Jean Lewis.

When she spoke to D'Amato's committee, Lewis was aided by law-yers from the Richard Scaife–funded Landmark Legal Foundation. She did her best to maintain the tedium, presenting herself as a calm and de-voted bureaucrat motivated by the facts. A forty-year-old woman with short blond hair, Lewis wore big glasses of the type once favored by

Hillary Clinton and had dressed in a gray jacket with padded shoulders and a rust-colored blouse. She sat alone at a witness table with a few files set before her and addressed the senators as *sir* and *ma'am*. All went smoothly until committee counsel Richard Ben-Veniste called her attention a letter she had written about Bill Clinton in which she noted:

> *His ability to lie surpasses that of our most astute politicians. Gennifer Who?? I never slept with that woman . . .—quoth the illustrious Governor Bill Clinton! Everybody in Arkansas knows he did, the lying bastard, and then he puts her on the state payroll!*

Shaken by the revelation of the letter, Lewis said, "I'd like to know where you got that." Ben-Veniste told her that it had been found on her government computer. Lewis said that she believed that the letter had been deleted before she gave government investigators access to it and was surprised. Ben-Veniste replied, in deadpan, "I hate it when that happens, but there it is."

The same computer also contained communications about her plans to sell T-shirts and coffee mugs emblazoned with Hillary Clinton's likeness and the words PRESIDENTIAL BITCH. In one of the notes, she said she expected good sales "given the current political climate." The word BITCH, in her notes, stood for "Bill, I'm Taking Charge, Hillary."[8]

The BITCH marketing plan would have been a low but not an unprecedented one for someone involved in street-fight politics. In fact, a considerable and profitable industry had arisen to produce and distribute anti–Hillary Clinton materials. In writing it while at her job, Lewis showed a degree of partisanship and poor judgment rare among ordinary federal workers. Before the committee, Lewis struggled to explain that she considered the "bitch designation somehow not derogatory" and "there are a lot of women out there that would not take that particular comment as an offense."

Senator Barbara Boxer of California, who couldn't bring herself to utter the word *bitch,* did express offense. Another senator, Paul Sarbanes of Maryland, then began reading supervisors' negative evaluations of Lewis's reports, some of which had been written by Republican-appointed

r, if the issue remained open, it could justify expanding Starr's
into all matters Clinton. He wrote, "We are currently investigat-
ent Foster's death to determine, among other things, whether he
dered in violation of federal criminal law. [I]t necessarily follows
must have the authority to fully investigate Foster's death."[12]

both Kavanaugh and Ewing stressing the usefulness of the Fos-
le, nothing was done to tamp down the conspiracy theorists
pt rumors alive about Foster's supposed connections to Israeli
his responsibility for Waco, and the long blond hairs supposedly
on his body. No evidence supported these crazy notions, but they
ed unchallenged by Starr's team until Foster's name would be
nently stained by the speculation.

Starr team was familiar with the ways it could have made the press
of the facts in the Foster suicide without compromising its own
When Hickman Ewing failed to get the group's agreement to seek
ictment of Hillary Clinton, somehow his eagerness to indict her
he widely known in both Little Rock and Washington. In the fall of
Dick Morris, a political advisor to the president, told Hillary she was
to be indicted. He also said that "people close to Starr" thought she
d just ask her husband for a preemptive presidential pardon.

someone with strong links to Republicans, Morris could claim to
a line on Starr's thinking, but he was also a scheming sort of man
m Hillary regarded with great skepticism. (Within a year, Morris
ld be disgraced by a prostitution scandal.) Hillary offered a care-
considered reply to Morris, telling him she understood that grand
s could be persuaded to indict even "a ham sandwich" and that, if
ged, "I would never ask for a pardon. I will go to trial and show
r up for the fraud he is."

Astoundingly, the products of the anti-Hillary gossip mill became so
ely distributed that even the Arkansas bait shop owner–fur trapper
ker Dozhier told people that "they [the special prosecutor] had what
y needed to bring Hillary down." At this time, Dozhier was in reg-
r contact with Kenneth Starr's team and helped them deal with yet
ther odd Arkansas figure named David Hale. Almost a caricature of
heming hypocrite, Hale was a publicly pious Christian whose secre-

officials. One described her work as "junky" and "half baked." As Sarbanes read on, Lewis sat back in her chair and her eyelids began to
lower. She then removed her glasses and signaled she was in distress.
D'Amato declared the committee in recess, a doctor was summoned,
and Lewis was whisked away by ambulance to a nearby hospital.

Lewis would return to the committee to complete her testimony.
During this exercise, Democrats questioned her on a host of issues that
damaged her credibility and revealed that she had problems working
within the federal bureaucracy. Especially noteworthy was the committee's review of how she had recorded a conversation with a colleague
who had not been informed their meeting was being taped. Lewis said
the recording was done by mistake. The machine was old, she said, and
must have somehow switched itself on. Some senators asked, where was
the recorder now? She said she had disposed of it and purchased a new
one. Sales receipts actually showed the new machine was bought two
weeks *prior* to the taping incident. It was also revealed that coworkers
had complained to supervisors of her improperly disclosing confidential
information and moving documents from her office to her home. Lewis
left Washington with her credibility in tatters.[9]

As the press, special counsel Fiske, and committees in Congress failed
to find criminality in Whitewater and Vince Foster's death—and failed
to make it into a scandal the public could grasp—the cause remained
irresistible to those who detested Bill and Hillary Clinton. Presidents
enjoy certain legal protections, including immunity from lawsuits for
official acts. (This was established by the Supreme Court in 1982.) First
Ladies, who are not technically government officials, are much more
vulnerable. This condition became evident with 1995 news reports that
Hillary Clinton would soon be charged with breaking the law. The press
account hardly did justice to the intensity of the rumors that held that
a member of Kenneth Starr's team, an experienced prosecutor working
with a separate grand jury in Little Rock, had actually drafted an indictment in the spring of 1995.

Kenneth Starr's Arkansas-based prosecutor was the deeply religious

Hickman Ewing Jr. Ewing's early life was marked by the prosecution, conviction, and imprisonment of his father, a county official, for embezzlement. His subsequent career as a zealous prosecutor who identified those he deemed corrupt and labored to put them in prison was easy to recognize as a kind of psychodrama. Ewing would even comment, in the case of one man sentenced to twenty-one months for corruption, that his own father had gotten three years for stealing far less. He was also so confident in his own judgment that he once said, "After you've been doing this for ten, fifteen, twenty years, it doesn't take too long to determine whether somebody has committed a crime."

In the case of Hillary Clinton, Ewing determined she was guilty after reading depositions she gave to Robert Fiske in 1994 and interviewing her as part of the Ken Starr team in 1995. Starr, Ewing, and others had asked their questions in the White House residential quarters on Saturday, April 22, 1995. On that day, the country was reeling from the April 19 domestic terror attack on the federal building in Oklahoma City, where a truck bomb killed 168 people, among them children at a day care center. The Clintons were preparing to attend a memorial service the next day. Starr's team also interviewed the president, who, when finished, had one of his lawyers show them to the Lincoln Bedroom, where they could read the Gettysburg Address, written in Lincoln's hand. The First Lady thought her husband was too kind to his interrogators, whom she considered "hardcore Republican partisans." The difference in their approaches was evidence of their different experiences under examination. She had prepared diligently but nevertheless felt unsettled. "I seemed to be buffeted by every gust of wind," she would eventually note, "while Bill just sailed along."[10]

Hickman Ewing never offered a public evaluation of Hillary Clinton's demeanor on deposition day. However, his ear was tuned to detect the sound of criminality because, as he said, "when you're a prosecutor you always think about what laws are involved: perjury, bank fraud or whatever." Ewing drafted his indictment because, he said, "she was in conflict with a number of interviews" conducted with others. He showed the draft to one other lawyer, who declined the offer to read it, and didn't circulate it among his colleagues. Three years later, he would

make a final big effort to get Starr and t_____ Hillary.

Ewing presented his case against Hi_____ room, where every attendee was given a _____ rials to follow as he walked around the roo_____ He noted inconsistencies in her testimony _____ during questioning told him she had been _____ bothered by a document that he suspected _____ Foster. "Had he [Foster] been alive, he wo_____ witness for us, or a defendant," said Ewing _____ more to convey the idea that Foster's death _____ Clinton controversies.[11]

Beyond what was known about Vince _____ sion, no basis existed for anyone to speculat_____ suicide, and the physical evidence would sup_____ but that Foster had killed himself. Neverthe_____ alive by a young member of Starr's team name_____ was extremely active among politically motiva_____ Although Fiske's prior investigation had settle_____ persuaded Starr to revive it and would spend _____ $2 million on the effort to come up with so_____ received allegations that Mr. Foster's death was _____ Mrs. Clinton's involvement." The sources of th_____ Richard Mellon Scaife protégé Christopher R_____ theorist Ambrose Evans-Pritchard. Kavanaugh di_____ the accusations, but he thought they merited at_____ move forward.

Members of Foster's family, who were intervie_____ resented the interference, but Kavanaugh pressed _____ agents to collect a sample of Foster's daughter's ha_____ rists mused about carpet fibers supposedly found _____ Kavanagh looked for the fibers. Tantalized by the no_____ Hillary may have had an affair, he sent investigator_____ views about this theory and would even ask the Fir_____ a memo, Kavanaugh wrote that he believed Foster _____

tary was also his mistress. His business interests included a church-pew factory and a lending company. He was also a municipal-level judge who heard misdemeanor and traffic cases. Though often described as a warm and friendly man, Hale equipped his little courtroom with bulletproof glass and required those who entered to pass through two metal detectors. He was a frequent visitor to the bait shop where Dozhier kept bottles of champagne labeled with the names of the people Hale hoped to ruin either legally or politically, by telling what he knew to the press and prosecutors. One was marked with the name HILLARY RODHAM CLINTON.[13]

Hale had joined the Clinton hunt in earnest after the FBI raided his office and carted away files related to his business, which involved creating shell companies to take out federally insured loans. The companies went bankrupt and defaulted on the loans. He hired a lawyer who, since now everything that happened in Arkansas might implicate the Clintons, called the White House in hopes of provoking a response that might help his client. When this didn't work, the best Hale could get was a plea deal that required him to admit he'd committed both mail fraud and conspiracy to defraud the government. In the meantime, Hale embarked on a campaign to persuade the national press to report that the Clintons were somehow to blame for his troubles.[14]

Hale's accusations against the Clintons never bore out. However, he certainly did help to create an atmosphere of doubt and suspicion. And it was this atmosphere, as much as anything, that kept the controversy alive. In this effort, Hale got a hearing with Parker Dozhier's crowd and then with Kenneth Starr's lawyers and investigators. For a time, he was protected by federal agents and even spent time hiding out in a home paid for by the independent counsel's office. Ultimately, Hale would provide nothing significant about the Clintons, but Starr would ask that his sentence for fraud and conspiracy be reduced out of respect for the fact that he tried. The court ignored Starr's request.[15]

David Hale, L. Jean Lewis, the Arkansas troopers—one by one, the sources of anti-Hillary allegations ranging from the criminal to the absurd fired their best shots at her and missed. If these were Kenneth Starr's witnesses, and some were, then he would never capture his quarry and she would never get the chance to defend herself in court against what she deemed a fraudulent pursuit. However, this didn't mean she was finished defending herself.

At the end of 1995, as the Whitewater saga seemed to reach a sputtering end, the White House itself revived it by announcing the discovery of records related to the First Lady's Rose Law Firm work. The files, which Vince Foster held as the Clintons' private attorney, had been brought from Arkansas, with thousands of others, because they had no private home office in which to store them. After Foster's death, the papers were boxed and reportedly misplaced in a room that was otherwise used to store gifts sent to the White House. (The space was also beneath a roof where construction was under way, and protective drop cloths had covered much of what was in it.) Copies of billing forms already available elsewhere, the papers showed that Hillary Clinton may have done more legal work related to Jim McDougal's Madison Guaranty—sixty hours during a fifteen-month span—than she had previously indicated.

For Hillary Clinton's critics, who began referring to the investigation as Filegate, the evidence showed she had been more engaged with Madison Guaranty than she had said and thus couldn't be believed about anything. The cries of outrage reached a crescendo as opinion writer William Safire of *The New York Times* declared, "Americans of all political persuasions are coming to the sad realization that our First Lady—a woman of undoubted talents who was a role model for many in her generation—is a congenital liar." In response, her husband said that if he weren't president, he'd punch Safire in the nose.[16]

Soon, Hillary was required to appear before Starr's grand jury at U.S. District Court in the District of Columbia. She would testify as a witness and not the actual subject of the investigation. Nevertheless, the event provided the press with a rare and precious commodity: physical action in the context of high-level Washington politics. Except for committee chairpersons pounding gavels and the occasional protester, journalists were generally denied meaningful visuals for reports on controversies inside the Washington Beltway. But this time, they would get the political version of an old-fashioned "perp walk," the difference being that instead of a handcuffed criminal suspect being muscled out of a police station, the cameras would be trained on one of the most recognizable women in the world departing from the greatest seat of power in the world, the White House, and arriving at a courthouse.

As the government car she rode in pulled up to the curb at the U.S. District Court, Hillary emerged wearing a winter coat last seen during the inauguration celebrations of 1993. The long black wool coat was decorated on the back with an abstract design that resembled seashells. On the sidewalk, Hillary was greeted by two groups of demonstrators. One, gathered beneath signs that read, among other things, IT'S ETHICS, STUPID, had come to jeer her. The other, whose banners included one that read, WE LOVE YOU, HILLARY, was there to cheer her.

Inside the courthouse, Clinton and her lawyers went to the third floor, where the grand jury was meeting. As required by the rules, she would go in alone to participate in proceedings whose details she was bound to keep secret. At the door, she paused and, with a wave to her attorneys, said, "Cheerio! Off to the firing squad."

Emerging four hours later, the First Lady briefly spoke with journalists, who recorded her departure. The next day, *Washington Post* reporters who had been sent to cover an event that was entirely secret published accounts that focused on atmospherics. Under these conditions, the design on her coat was transformed from impressionistic seashells into "a gold dragon." Thus the First Lady was also a Dragon Lady, with all the conniving evil the term suggests.

Inference via wardrobe was not something men endured, but just as her hairstyles were regularly plumbed for meaning, Hillary's garments were reviewed as if they signaled the contents of her soul. Robin D. Givhan, *The Post*'s fashion writer, corrected the record on the coat and noted, "There probably are some folks who would swear they saw flames shooting out of the imaginary dragon's mouth." Clinton had been mocked previously for wearing pink because it meant she was trying to soften her image. With purple, she would have been called a royalist, and white would have signaled, to some, that she wanted to be seen as virtuous. Every color and every style provided critics with an opportunity, which meant that she should probably wear whatever she pleased.[17]

Wardrobe would remain under Mrs. Clinton's control, but events were often guided by antagonists such as Starr, who had been present at the grand jury session and who had consulted on the other big legal issue overshadowing the Clinton White House. Prior to accepting the Whitewater independent counsel job, he had talked with members of an anti-feminist group called Independent Women's Forum about supporting Paula Jones and her potential legal claims against Bill Clinton. (Despite using the word *independent* in its name, the IWF was founded by people who were Republican partisans and partially funded by the ever-present Richard Scaife through his Carthage Foundation.) Starr was then a lawyer at a prominent firm called Kirkland & Ellis. In addition to the IWF, he had offered advice directly to Paula Jones's attorneys, one of whom was a Kirkland & Ellis colleague named Richard Porter, who would stick with the case.[18]

Paula Jones had introduced herself to the national press in February 1994, when Clinton antagonist Cliff Jackson, Jones's local lawyer Daniel Traylor, and two of the Arkansas troopers who spoke to David Brock summoned reporters who were working at the annual Conservative Political Action Conference in Washington. Their claimed purpose—to clear Jones's name—seemed a bit off-kilter, as the American public had no idea who she was. Nevertheless, in pursuit of this goal, they said that when Jones was a state office worker, then governor Clinton summoned her to a hotel room and propositioned her for a sexual act, which she refused.[19]

The strange event on the sidelines at CPAC included Traylor's refusal to permit a full explication of the encounter "out of deference to the First Family" and a stomach-churning round of questioning by Reed Irvine, founder of one of the earliest organizations devoted to creating doubt about the honesty of news organizations such as *The Washington Post, The New York Times,* and major TV news programs. Funded by the ubiquitous Richard Scaife and other right-wing benefactors, Irvine's

Accuracy in Media (AIM) organization published newsletters and opinion columns that floated conspiracy theories and attacked journalists' work. Typical was AIM's long-running criticism of Raymond Bonner's reports on the massacre of civilians by troops of the U.S.-backed army of El Salvador. (The press was also criticized by Reagan administration officials.) Irvine said, "Mr. Bonner had been worth a division to the communists in Central America." Then, sixteen months before Irvine performed at the Paula Jones press conference, an independent commission confirmed Bonner's account, noting that among the civilians slaughtered in a place called El Mozote were dozens of children.

At CPAC, regular journalists who attended hoping to find political news groaned as Irvine pressed Traylor for salacious details. When asked whether Clinton had requested that Jones do "something that could have been performed without your taking your clothes off?" the question hung in the air, unanswered. In the end, the Jones press conference made barely a ripple in the mainstream press. Far more attention was devoted to David Brock, who also attended CPAC, and his recent revelation that he was gay. Brock was celebrated by some as a Clinton antagonist but scorned by others, including psychologist Paul Cameron (father of child actor Kirk Cameron), who said Brock should have kept his sexual identity secret. "Maybe there are fifteen hundred people here and three of them are child molesters," added Cameron. "As long as they don't try to push it, you know, get up and say, 'I've tried 8-year-old girls and it's good,' it's not really my problem."

As Cameron focused on a fellow conservative, he deviated from the main concern of the convention, which was to express outrage over the presence of Democrats in the White House. On a policy level, the activists were concerned with Bill Clinton's mastery of details and charming ways with both voters and members of Congress. On a gut level, they found it easier to get worked up over Mrs. Clinton than the president himself. Vendors did a brisk business in IMPEACH HILLARY bumper stickers while Todd Blodgett, a disciple of Lee Atwater, sold copies of a photo magazine he named *Slick Times,* which was filled with doctored photos showing Hillary Clinton's head on the bodies of women in sexual poses and various states of undress. Blodgett had worked in the Reagan White

House and then for the Republican National Committee. After CPAC, he would embark on a career of promoting racist and anti-Semitic causes and owning Resistance Records, distributor of Nazi-themed music known as "hatecore" and performed by bands with names such as Angry Aryans and Nordic Thunder.[20]

For someone like Blodgett, who had left the White House to exploit the business possibilities in political rage, *Slick Times* was a neat blend of profit-seeking and political advocacy. The same could be said for the members of the Paula Jones team, who had in mind a lawsuit that could make trouble for the Clintons and perhaps generate a payment in the form of either a settlement or a court award. Revenues from book, movie, or TV deals also hovered on the horizon, and in the meantime, the legal work would be funded by a right-wing Christian organization called the Rutherford Institute, which had been funded by, of course, Richard Mellon Scaife. The Jones group in Arkansas was aided by high-powered lawyers with national reputations, including George T. Conway III in New York, Jerome Marcus of Philadelphia, and Richard Porter of Chicago. Porter worked in the same firm Kenneth Starr left for the Whitewater investigations. Although Washington lawyers Gilbert K. Davis and Joseph Cammarata were attorneys of record for Paula Jones, they got substantial help with research, writing, and strategizing from Conway, Marcus, and Porter, who kept their participation in the case secret and called themselves the Elves.

The Elves were often led by Conway, who, like Kenneth Starr, counted cigarette-maker Philip Morris among his paying clients. (Starr would continue to represent tobacco interests in matters against the federal government while acting as independent counsel.) According to David Brock, Conway was so virulently anti-Clinton that he typically referred to the president not by name but by the term *scumbag* and literally jumped for joy as he saw a TV report on allegations of sexual misconduct against Clinton. Conway told Brock that the purpose of the Jones suit was not to win some sort of justice for Jones but to draw the president into a court-ordered deposition that could unveil all sorts of embarrassing information. The deposition would be conducted with

Clinton under oath, which also meant that any shaded truth or outright lie could be deemed perjury and even justification for impeachment.[21]

As an attorney, Clinton understood the peril. However, he was also a politician, a husband, and a father, and in these roles, he would be reluctant to speak candidly about any sexual activity outside of his marriage. This spot, between ruining his presidency with a criminal offense and humiliating himself and his family by confessing sexual betrayal, was precisely where the Elves wanted to put Clinton. Their motivations likely included a measure of moral outrage, a large element of political partisanship, and perhaps an interest in avenging Robert Bork. All three belonged to a legal fraternity called the Federalist Society, which Bork had helped create to support a politically conservative approach to law and promote like-minded candidates for the federal bench.

If Bork-related rage and partisanship were all that drove the Elves, they must have been truly afflicted by both. Writer Jeffrey Toobin, himself a former prosecutor, detected more than a little prurience in the Elves' pursuit of evidence of infidelities, which had no bearing on Clinton's work as president. Were they to speak for themselves, they might raise the Gary Hart argument, suggesting that adultery suggested poor character and bad judgment. Whatever their motivations, they prized their status as secret operators. Shortly after the Jones complaint was filed, Conway supported her cause in an opinion article he wrote for the *Los Angeles Times*. He noted Clinton's "high-powered lawyers" and predicted that he "will need all the legal firepower he can get." He didn't mention that Jones had her own high-powered team, which he had helped organize and supply with information, and that it was supported by wealthy Republican donors. Nor did he reveal that he had previously worked with Kenneth Starr.[22]

Two days prior to the moment when the statute of limitations would have barred a lawsuit, Paula Jones filed one against the president, seeking $700,000 in damages for intentional infliction of emotional pain by requesting sexual contact and exposing himself. This occurred, the complaint said, at about 2:30 p.m. at the Excelsior Hotel in Little Rock. (Clinton had been at the hotel to give a speech at 8:30 a.m., and he left soon after. At 2:30, he was at a gathering at the governor's mansion. In subsequent filings, Jones's attorneys would drop references to the timing of the alleged incident.)

The suit, which was brought in U.S. District Court in Little Rock, was based in part on a post–Civil War statute protecting former slaves from being mistreated by public officials. With an eye toward the Ku Klux Klan, Congress also targeted the law at private citizens who conspired with the public officials. Jones's lawyers theorized that when Clinton allegedly propositioned their client, he violated this statute and that anyone who stood in the way of her complaints was a coconspirator. Their filing noted that Jones could prove her claim by describing a distinguishing characteristic of Clinton's penis and reported that after she spurned the governor, Jones, a state worker, had been punished by her supervisors.[23]

Although experts noted that some claimants had used the same statute successfully, Jones's lawyers were stretching to connect her allegations to the anti-Klan act. They were also stretching to try to make any case at all. No evidence existed to show that Jones had suffered retaliation of any sort on her job. Instead, she had actually seen the classification of her position improved, which raised her status and her earning potential. Also, Clinton denied that the incident Jones said had occurred ever happened. And he asserted that as long as he was president, claims against him related to events prior to his election should be set aside until the end of his service. The question of whether a citizen can sue the president has been hotly contested. In 1982, the Supreme Court determined that the chief executive was immune from civil suits related to official actions, but this decision left open the possibility of a claim based on private behavior. The problem for Jones was that this ruling seemed to cancel out a complaint based on the Klan statute, since that had been written to deal with official acts.

For a layperson, the heart of the matter resided in the sober fact of a sexual harassment charge against a president by a woman who said he exposed himself to her. The daughter of a preacher, Jones came from the farm community of Lonoke, which, with the arrival of Interstate 40 in the 1960s, had become a suburb of Little Rock. (The place was supposed to have been named Lone Oak, after a solitary tree found on the landscape, but Lonoke stuck after a misspelling in a local paper.) A high school graduate with little life experience beyond Arkansas, Jones might be a sympathetic figure: the ordinary woman harmed by a powerful man. However, this image was refuted by an article in *Newsweek* that quoted coworkers who described her as an assertive Clinton "groupie" who spent much of her time at work engaged in "hours and hours of beauty-shop inane conversation." *Newsweek* also reported that Jones received a merit raise during the time she claimed to suffer repercussions for rebuffing Clinton.[24]

Jones did not offer a comment to *Newsweek*. When a reporter visited her home, no one came to the door, but her husband said, via an intercom, "Paula has no comment. You can print what you like. It looks like from what I read you haven't got the full story on anything." Surely many Americans who disliked Clinton felt similarly about *Newsweek* and other outlets they regarded as "mainstream" and thus deserving of suspicion. Clinton critics had begun to turn the word *mainstream* into a pejorative, which allowed them to turn away from *The New York Times*, *The Washington Post,* and others without considering their reports and embrace what they heard and read from sources that reinforced their assumptions. Thus politics became like sports, with citizens behaving like fans who reliably rooted for their side and complained about the refs. Just as umpires are always blind when your guy strikes out, the press was always biased when it reported on your candidate's failings and flaws. In the same vein, partisans relished media accounts that painted the other side in the worst possible shades. Those who wanted to delve into the allegations against both Clintons could consult a videotape of a new documentary called *The Clinton Chronicles: An Investigation into the Alleged Criminal Activities of Bill Clinton.*

Sold at forty-three dollars (shipping included) by the right-wing television evangelist Jerry Falwell, the video was produced by an organization called Citizens for Honest Government, which paid more than $200,000 to former Arkansas troopers Roger Perry and Larry Patterson and others who appeared in the film. The film's creator, Patrick Matrisciana, was also head of Citizens for Honest Government, which shared an address with his firm, Jeremiah Productions. He appeared in shadow with Falwell in a promotional video in which he posed as an unnamed investigative reporter, talked about mysterious deaths, and said he felt in danger. "Be assured, we will be praying for your safety," said Falwell.

Pat Matrisciana would eventually confess to being the man in the video and to lying about both his credentials and supposed fears. At the time he made these statements, his firm shared a joint bank account with Christopher Ruddy, the anti-Clinton journalist employed by Richard Scaife. The account held more than $3 million. Matrisciana would also reveal the culture-war aspect of producing the video, saying, "I don't think government should be involved in people's bedrooms, but let's just say he and Hillary had kind of a '60s kind of relationship. I could tell you stories for a very long time."[25]

*The Clinton Chronicles* opened with a slide informing viewers, in capital letters, ALL INFORMATION PRESENTED IN THIS PROGRAM IS DOCUMENTED AND TRUE, and then presented allegations that Bill and Hillary Clinton had been involved in everything from political corruption to drug dealing and murder. The same Larry Nichols who had helped David Brock meet Arkansas troopers appeared in the film to say, "Bill Clinton was hooked on cocaine and was a part of the system that was laundering millions of cocaine dollars." This claim involved a debunked theory about a pilot named Barry Seal, the Central Intelligence Agency, and an airport in Mena, Arkansas. He operated in Arkansas, noted one interview subject, because the state "had a sleazy governor hooked on cocaine," said the film.

Others in *The Clinton Chronicles* accused Clinton of attending sex parties and undergoing secret medical treatment related to drug use. Near the end of the film, Nichols declares, "Bill and Hillary Clinton have something to hide, and only through a congressional hearing does this nation have a snowball's chance of that truth coming to the light of day." Eventually congressional committees *that* look into many of the allegations in *The Clinton Chronicles* find none of them were true.

Truth would have little to do with how the American public regarded the Clintons or the allegations against them, many of which were repeated in a book published in the summer of 1996 as Clinton's reelection campaign against Senator Bob Dole, the GOP nominee, entered a critical period. *Unlimited Access* was authored by retired FBI agent Gary Aldrich, who was an advisor to Dole, and published by Regnery Publishing, which had been founded by a wealthy conservative activist who had been part of Charles Lindbergh's America First movement, which opposed U.S. involvement in World War II. Devoted to political warfare, Regnery was one of many media outlets energized by the notion that writers such as Aldrich were ignored by the nation's many large, regular publishers on the basis of ideology rather than merit.

Little of what Aldrich wrote would have been deemed fit for publication by a major publishing house. Filled with hearsay and innuendo, *Access* recycled claims made by others and developed a few new ones, including the charge that the Clintons secretly tried to "divide the powers of the presidency in a manner that is unconstitutional." Of course, this was a reference to Hillary Clinton and her husband's reliance on her for advice. This allegation, as well as a chapter titled "Mrs. President," was pitched perfectly to those who saw, in Hillary, a woman to fear and despise. She was somehow both the dominant harpy of anti-feminists' nightmares and a clueless victim of her husband's deceptions.

In Aldrich's account, an empty hallway indicated staffers feared encountering Hillary. He described her as a scheming woman who was so profane that in 1993 she arranged for the White House Christmas tree to be decorated with syringes and condoms. Although the tree was likely the most photographed one in the world and White House staff did the decorating, no photos with these ornaments were ever produced. The anecdote dovetailed with others depicting Clinton staffers as thieves, drug users, and slobs who had sex in the workplace. Aldrich pointedly reported that "homosexuals were present in the White House in large numbers" and said Hillary, who supposedly controlled all hiring, retained them. She "favored tough, minority, and lesbian women, as well as weak, minority, and gay men." (This would be affirmed by radio host Don Imus, who presented a song parody about Hillary with the lyric, "She goes to state dinners with her lesbian friends.")[26]

Aldrich's tales, reported without attribution, supported his paranoid declaration that "working at the Clinton White House could be *dangerous* [italics in original]." This "danger" justified the lack of attribution and a promotion scheme that gave journalists the impression that Aldrich was under threat. Interviews were arranged not by the publisher but by a political activist named Craig Shirley, who had helped with Paula Jones's coming out at CPAC, and by an editor at the anti-Clinton *Wall Street Journal* opinion section. Aldrich also got support from the Southeastern Legal Foundation, which had recently received $300,000 from foundations controlled by the ever-present Richard Scaife. Other Regnery authors, many also beholden to Scaife, would follow Aldrich to Regnery to create a canon of anti-Clinton titles, including:

> *Boy Clinton* by *Spectator* editor R. Emmett Tyrell (1996)
>
> *Partners in Power: The Clintons and Their America* by Roger Morris (1996)
>
> *The Secret Life of Bill Clinton: The Unreported Stories* by Ambrose Evans-Pritchard (1997)
>
> *Year of the Rat: How Bill Clinton Compromised U.S. Security for Chinese Cash* by Edward Timperlake and William C. Triplett II (1998)
>
> *High Crimes and Misdemeanors: The Case Against Bill Clinton* by Ann Coulter (1998)
>
> *Hell to Pay: The Unfolding Story of Hillary Rodham Clinton* by Barbara Olson (1999)
>
> *Betrayal: How the Clinton Administration Undermined American Security* by Bill Gertz (1999)[27]

Evans-Pritchard, to cite just one example of a Regnery star, confessed he wrote as a "Tory hooligan," and his sloppiness supported this admission. In Evans-Pritchard's account, Vince Foster arranged for those who did mysterious dirty work for the Clintons to be given cash payments so enormous they were handled with forklifts. He also quotes Foster speaking, a day or two before his death, of meeting Hillary at "the flat" to give her some files. Evans-Pritchard was alluding to the love nest supposedly owned by Clinton, where, conspiracy theories held, Foster actually killed himself. The flaw in Evans-Pritchard's reporting was his use of the word *flat* to reference an apartment. The writer, who was British, would reach for this word reflexively. Foster, an Arkansan through and through, would not. Putting it in his mouth rang about as true as the sound of a jackhammer emanating from a kitten.

The anti-Clinton books recycled anecdotes originally reported by David Brock, with varying emphasis and additions. Tyrell included imaginary scenes of Bill Clinton's drug use. Evans-Pritchard theorized about Clinton-controlled death squads loose in Arkansas. This made him one of the first to speculate that both Clintons arranged for the deaths of numerous people who had or could make trouble for them. In time, those who dabbled in this speculation would come to call it "Arkanicide," and the roster of deaths they found suspicious would exceed one hundred. Believers poured time and energy into finding supposed links between the Clintons and the deceased and suggesting that unexplained elements of their deaths could be explained by implicating the president and First Lady. All this activity ignored the fact that few deaths occur without some unanswered questions and that, with a little effort, it's possible to establish connections between any two people on Earth. In 1979, a political scientist named Ithiel de Sola Pool and a mathematician named Manfred Kochen published a paper that explained how in a country the size of the United States, most people could be connected with just two intermediaries.[28]

Despite the logical, literary, and journalistic shortcomings, the Regnery books sold well, as they were heavily promoted by right-wing radio hosts, columnists, and political book clubs. A shrink-wrapped collection of six anti-Clinton books, priced by Regnery at ninety-nine dollars, would also serve as a starter set for a library of affirmation for those who hated the Clintons. The genre was so successful that more mainstream publishers eventually began creating imprints to exploit the market for rabidly right-wing works. Crown Forum, Sentinel, Threshold, Broadside, All Points, and others lured Regnery writers and cultivated their own to reap the profits to be had in both Clinton-hating and liberal-bashing. In literary circles, their offerings garnered little respect, but publishers' accountants and shareholders appreciated what they did for balance sheets.

Regnery also served as a bridge to a developing netherworld of conspiracy theorists and political speculators who could be found on the internet. There, poorly researched books became authoritative sources of information for modern-day pamphleteers. Thus unscrupulous authors fed even less scrupulous keyboarders who needed fodder for their postings.

Perhaps the first to develop an online site devoted to allegations of Clinton crimes was a lawyer named Linda Thompson who created a Web-based bulletin board where she posted her theories about people whose deaths benefited the Clintons as well as various ideas about the construction of federal concentration camps. After getting arrested for trying to block a presidential motorcade in a car stocked with guns and ammunition, Thompson began to focus on the 1993 law enforcement assault on a compound in Waco, Texas, where a gunfight broke out at a religious sect's compound and more than eighty people were killed by gunshots, fire, and other injuries.

The Waco tragedy was prefaced by a raid on the compound, weeks before, by agents investigating the existence of a large cache of arms, including illegal machine guns. Residents killed four federal agents. A fifty-one-day standoff ensued. During this time, government officials tried to negotiate with the group's leader, who considered himself a prophet destined to die a martyr. After efforts at negotiation were exhausted, authorities began an assault with armed agents and a tank deployed as a battering ram. Almost everyone in the group's buildings died as the result of a fire set by the occupants.

Lawsuits and official inquiries into Waco concluded that residents armed with machine guns, which they used against law enforcement officers, had posed such a danger that the tactics finally deployed against them were appropriate. But what began as a legitimate police action ended in a tragedy that could not have been foreseen. However, these findings did nothing to dissuade the conspiracy theorists who imagined all sorts of wrongdoing and connected it to the president. Waco-related books and videos would sell for decades. Linda Thompson distributed a video called *Waco, the Big Lie,* which promoted, among other notions, the idea that the raid on the cult was conducted to cover the Clinton-ordered killing of federal agents. In other conspiracy scenarios, Hillary was the one who made the decisions. In a third category, the entire episode boiled down to a battle of Christian goodness versus satanic evil, with the compound residents who followed a prophet placed on the side of the angels. Timothy McVeigh, who two years later carried out the terrorist bombing of a federal building in Oklahoma City, which left 168 dead, acted to avenge Waco.[29]

Prior to the internet age, the dissemination of these kinds of ideas was limited by the cost of printing and stamps, which meant that even the most successful conspiracy theorists might reach, at best, a few hundred thousand people. (One of the most widely read mailers of this sort was distributed by the anti-Semite Willis Carto's *The Spotlight* reached three hundred thousand households monthly.) However, in the new media era, all anyone needed to reach a worldwide audience was a computer and access to the internet. Thompson was soon joined by younger and more engaged internet crusaders, including Preston Crow, a student at Northwest Nazarene of Nampa, Idaho. With an average of nearly ten thousand daily visitors, his site, which was devoted to all manner of Clinton conspiracy theories, was well trafficked for the Web circa 1994. In the era before Google made searching the internet easy, Crow's site appeared to newcomers like a found object of immense value. Much of what he posted found its way onto talk radio, where conservative hosts played a continuous game of one-upmanship, can-you-top-this. Nighttime talker Art Bell even let Linda Thompson, who dubbed herself acting adjutant general of a "citizens' militia," use his program to call for an armed insurrection against the U.S. government.

In the prior decade, Bell and others had come to dominate the AM radio band, which for technical reasons was better suited to talk than music. Their success made the medium a political echo chamber where facts were abused and the Clintons were upbraided on an almost continual basis. In this alternative universe extreme statements were justified as entertainment and habitual listeners tuned in expecting to hear something that would make them feel amused, or outraged or, perhaps, superior to whomever the host chose to attack. So it was that in the first six months of 1994 political talk show host Rush Limbaugh could and did say, among other things:

> "You know, the Clintons send Chelsea to the Sidwell Friends
> private school. . . . A recent eighth-grade class assignment re-
> quired students to write a paper on 'Why I Feel Guilty Being
> White.'"
> "Hillary and Bill Clinton cheating on their taxes was a protest
> against the Reagan-era tax breaks for the wealthy."
> "We have more acreage of forest land in the United States today
> than we did at the time the Constitution was written."
> "There are more American Indians alive today than there were
> when Columbus arrived or at any other time in history."
> "The larger the bra size, the smaller the IQ."
> "It has not been proven that nicotine is addictive, the same with
> cigarettes causing emphysema [and other diseases]."[30]

Although it hardly needs to be noted for the record, none of what Limbaugh said about Sidwell School, the Clintons cheating on their taxes,
U.S. forests, American Indians, bra sizes, and tobacco was true. However,
each of these statements would resonate with listeners who resented
Democrats and the social change that seemed to benefit women, or
racial minorities, as white males felt their power challenged. They liked
that Limbaugh frequently used the slur *feminazi* to disparage certain
women, and they enjoyed his punching-down diatribes about poor and
homeless people.

As writer Molly Ivins pointed out, Limbaugh provided scapegoats
for the white male listener who is "working harder, getting paid less
in constant dollars and falling further and further behind." He offered
feminists, schoolteachers, intellectuals, and Democrats as enemies, while
exempting Republicans, corporate chiefs, investors, global competitors,
and others whose actions affected wages, jobs, and other aspects of their
lives. Ivins wrote that Limbaugh was "addressing the resentments of
these folks [his listeners], and aiming their anger in the wrong direction."
A more factual critique would have taken aim at all the court rulings
and political arrangements that had amplified the power of campaign
donors and made the economy a predator's paradise, but this tale was
extremely complex and didn't include a cast of characters who could

be turned into villains. And the subtle moves made by political action committees and corporate lawyers just didn't raise the blood pressure like a false accusation against a feminazi.[31]

In the tradition of Nixon and Agnew, Limbaugh also railed against the mainstream press, as represented by the TV networks, *The New York Times*, and others. His success had been amplified by the demise of the Federal Communications Commission's Fairness Doctrine, which had been developed to give people with competing political viewpoints access to broadcasting frequencies, which were considered public properties. With the commission consisting entirely of members appointed by Republicans, the FCC abandoned the doctrine in 1987. President Ronald Reagan, also a Republican, vetoed legislation that would have restored it. With the Fairness Doctrine gone, broadcasters could air unbalanced political advocacy of any sort, and any volume, and those who long complained of unfairness on the airwaves seized the opportunity to indulge their own brand of unfairness. AM radio became a national platform for views that dovetailed perfectly with Republican orthodoxy. Pro-corporate, anti-regulation, and opposed to the Democratic Party, Limbaugh and his imitators also defended what they believed to be a traditionalist vision of American culture, which placed white men in charge of business and politics, urged women toward the home and child-rearing, and ignored the effects of both the legalized and informal racism and sexism that had shaped society.

However, as influential as Limbaugh and the other radio hosts were, their reach was limited by a medium that failed to attract vast swaths of the population. Limbaugh's show was on during the workday, which meant most people who held regular jobs couldn't listen. Although he tried to expand his reach to television, this effort fizzled. In the meantime, however, global media magnate Rupert Murdoch planned to launch a twenty-four-hour cable TV channel devoted to the same agenda of grievance against the Left and celebration of the Right.

A TV network would complete Murdoch's pursuit of an American media empire that could bring the down-market content of his tabloid *New York Post* and the aggressive conservative opinions of his recently created magazine *The Weekly Standard* to a massive national audience for both commercial and political purposes. At *The Weekly Standard,* the Clintons served as shooting gallery ducks for the magazine's writers, many of whom used its pages to share work originally sponsored by right-wing political think tanks. However, it was Hillary who would be regarded more cruelly. Typical was a piece published in the magazine's first year, which declared that she "embodies the zeitgeist of her generation." By this, the writer David Brooks meant she represented a caricature of baby boomers as pretentious, self-indulgent, and afflicted by "spiritual greed."

While Murdoch paid for writing that used words like *zeitgeist* from the likes of Brooks, he would put Fox News Channel in the hands of Roger Ailes, who had recently left NBC after a brief stint characterized by feuds, intrigue, and a fellow executive's charge of anti-Semitism. However, the distance between Ailes and the *Weekly Standard* crowd wasn't as great as one might assume. Although it featured many younger writers, *Standard* was remarkably cranky and reactionary. Its articles lamented Hollywood morals and rock music and declared with alarm a "crisis of manliness" caused by "public and educational institutions" intent on destroying "any psychological and emotional differences between men and women." One article, published in 1996, called for the reinstatement of anti-sodomy laws as part of a campaign to deny homosexuals the right to legal marriage.[32]

Ailes met with Murdoch in early 1996 and soon began working for him. In what his biographer Gabriel Sherman would note was his typical "doublespeak," Ailes claimed to have left politics behind and to be committed to "fine balanced journalism." In fact, the network would be devoted to full-throated attacks on Democrats—especially the Clintons—and ringing endorsements of Republicans. The Clintons were made into anti-American demons at the center of an endless stream of reports that innervated without enlightening. Fact and fiction flew at a pace that defied a viewer's effort to keep track of which developments were significant and which were the news equivalent of shadow puppets. All of this would be powered by Ailes's talent for addictive TV production and his perspective, which was amply spiced with paranoia. (Republican representative John Boehner would recall this part of Ailes's psyche while describing "the most bizarre" meeting of his political life. Ailes "had black helicopters flying all around his head that morning," said Boehner. "It was every conspiracy theory you've ever heard, and I'm throwing cold water on all this bullshit.")

At Fox, top executives were hired on the basis of loyalty as much as bona fides, and some worked in a space that was, without irony, called the War Room. A select few also consulted staff in a locked basement facility called the Brain Room. Ailes hired former American and foreign spies to conduct research and had bulletproof glass installed in his office. All this was justified by the belief that he was, as he declared, "a freedom fighter" waging war against everyone who didn't share his views.[33]

From the start, Ailes's Fox News subjected the Clintons to a continuous political and personal critique that made them the main representatives of everything that could irritate a conservative American who wished that the social change that began in the 1960s—civil rights, women's rights, the sexual revolution—had never happened. For Fox, the First Lady represented a nightmare version of feminists that imagined them as man-hating careerists who disdained women with different priorities. This chord resonated generally with anyone who wanted a reason to dislike her and more specifically with men who may have felt threatened by changing gender relations—in both their work and personal lives—and by women who had felt that they had been snubbed in the so-called Mommy Wars, which supposedly found women squaring off over parenting, work, and marriage. Debates raged over whether the war really existed, and Hillary Clinton readily acknowledged that she struggled to keep her roles in balance. With these confessions, she tried to reach out to all women. However, it was such an anxious time for so many families—median income had dropped sharply in the eight years prior to Fox News going on the air—that it was easy for many to resent a successful woman who encouraged more change—not less—for women, men, and families.

Gender was an essential political and economic factor for those who demonized Clinton to build an industry of outrage on the airwaves and the internet. Attacks on women, especially outspoken women, built high ratings for these outlets, many of which drew overwhelmingly male audiences. According to the Pew Research Center, 72 percent of Limbaugh's listeners were men. Other research would find the audience for all conservative media to be older than the general population and more oriented toward traditional gender roles. Attacks on powerful women sold well to this crowd, which pleased both advertisers and political operators who wanted to build a movement. This truth was made clear to David Brock during a hallway conversation when he worked for *The Spectator.* There he bumped into Ronald Burr, who was in charge of marketing and soliciting donations from the likes of Richard Scaife, who subsidized the magazine. Burr told him that with his attacks on Anita Hill and Hillary Clinton, Brock had hit upon a valuable formula. "Can't you find any more women to attack?" he asked.[34]

Hillary was such an inviting target for Ailes that producer David Shuster became one of the network's first hires after he told a Fox executive he knew "there's a fifty-fifty chance that the First Lady is going to get indicted" by a grand jury working with Kenneth Starr. Shuster had been a journalist, which made him different from many others who were recruited to Fox from the entertainment industry. Prime time on Fox was devoted to on-camera discussions, from a consistently conservative point of view, of scoops obtained by wire services, newspapers, and others. According to one early report on the network, Ailes operated on the thesis that "people don't want to be informed; they only want the illusion of being informed."[35]

Ailes's illusion was aided by the fact the many viewers brought so little information to the experience of watching Fox. This deficiency wasn't unique to the Fox audience. As literacy experts have discovered, 95 percent of Americans will fail a standard test that involves reading opposing newspaper editorials and evaluating their claims. However, in years to come, multiple studies would find Fox viewers even less well informed than those who relied on other news sources. In effect, Fox News made people who already struggled with information they received less knowledgeable.

With accuracy often an afterthought, Fox sought to establish its presenters and commentators as authorities who should be trusted to sort out facts. Generally, the authorities were much like Roger Ailes himself:

white, male, and middle-aged or older. Viewers were told little about their backgrounds or the basis for their views. Thus the sound and images that Fox transmitted to the nation were sometimes an outright charade. A case in point would be Dick Morris, the political consultant who had been, at the same time, both a Republican insider and a Clinton ally. After a scandal that revolved around his relationship with a prostitute he invited to listen to his calls with President Clinton, Morris would make his public comeback with the help of Fox. However, even he would need help determining just how to play the news-as-drama game. As Ailes biographer Gabriel Sherman would report, early in the life of Fox News Channel Morris would ask a producer to tell him what she wanted him to say. When she seemed puzzled, he added, "Well, which side am I?"

With Fox choosing sides for itself and its guests, the network and like-minded radio outlets would become, by 1997, the primary news sources for more than one-fifth of all Americans. Tens of thousands also subscribed to one of the earliest successful online newsletters, which was published by a politically conservative entrepreneur named Matt Drudge. A chatty young man who proudly confessed he had barely managed to earn a high school diploma, Drudge first distributed Hollywood gossip while working as a gift shop manager at CBS Studios in Los Angeles. He styled himself after Tinseltown columnists of the 1930s, right down to the fedora that seemed permanently fixed to his head, indoors and out. One of his early allies was the peripatetic Christopher Ruddy, who introduced Drudge to one of his longtime heroes, talk radio host George Putnam. Born in 1919, Putnam mixed Hollywood and politics in an idiosyncratic way that found him gushing over Lucille Ball one day and fulminating about pornography the next. His anti-gay crusading culminated in a documentary film in which he spoke of "perversion" and "misfits" and warned that gay men were inclined toward child molesting.

Among the first to turn a website into an influential force, young Drudge used the logic of drug cartels when he said the demand for his gossipmongering justified his effort at creating the supply. "Clearly there is a hunger for unedited information, absent corporate considerations," he said. "Every citizen can be a reporter." As a citizen reporter, one of Drudge's first big stories accused a Clinton aide of beating his wife. The story was false, and he quickly issued a retraction and an apology.

Drudge also expanded his media presence to include radio and, for a brief time in 1998/99, a weekly TV program on Fox News. Through trial and error, he evolved from an amateur citizen journalist into an information entrepreneur whose efforts drew advertising sponsors and generated enough income for him to actually hire employees. His success would increase steadily as openly conservative voices, who had long complained of a press they believed was aligned against them, drowned out liberal competitors and made traditional, middle-of-the-road journalism seem boring.[36]

# 6

# "I Love Dish!"

In the very long run, the world would discover that where Roger Ailes was concerned, it takes one to know one. However, during Bill Clinton's presidency, Ailes was known only as a media bully driven by the rabid bias he had expressed to radio host Don Imus in 1994. The producer, who got his start in politics with Richard Nixon, burned to see Bill Clinton's presidency end in a similar fashion. Gennifer Flowers's claims, followed by those made by Paula Jones, suggested the possibility of scandal to anyone with Ailes's sense of power and drama. So it was that Fox News made the pursuit of Clinton's sexual behavior, especially during the time he held high office, a top priority.

Hillary Clinton was rarely mentioned in the network's reports, but she was necessarily present in the minds of viewers. Depending on one's perspective, she would be the woman wronged, the failed wife, or the cynical schemer. Anything but a woman worthy of respect.

Ailes and others who were devoted to the Clintons' demise were interconnected in ways that could be imagined as an old-fashioned telephone switchboard with one row of jacks representing the press, another political activists, a third the courts, and a fourth Congress. People in these four groups spoke often, and information was also shared, indirectly, to avoid the appearance of collusion involving people like, say, judges and prosecutors, who were supposed to be nonpartisan. The way this all worked meant that one or two phone calls could establish a key connection. This is what happened when a White House secretary named Linda Tripp called a New York publishing agent named Lucianne Goldberg.

Although it strains belief, Lucianne Goldberg was yet another player in the drama who began in politics with Richard Nixon. An anti-feminist, she was upset about the presence of lesbians, whom she compared to Nazis and Communists, in the "women's lib movement." Goldberg believed these women's rights activists were promoting a "cult of ugliness" and that "raging hormonal imbalances" made women unfit for many jobs.

Despite her avowed anti-feminism, Goldberg was herself a modern, ambitious woman who pushed herself into worlds dominated by men. Like Hillary, who worked for the congressional team that confronted Nixon during Watergate, she had shown her talent at a young age, becoming the only female among the band that came to be known as the Dirty Tricksters of the Nixon reelection campaign. Her trick involved lying to Democratic challenger George McGovern's staff to get press credentials. Goldberg then traveled with the candidate, pretending to be a journalist, but the only reporting she did was to her Nixon handlers, who hoped she would discover sexual affairs and drug use in the Mc-Govern camp. Later she acted as a literary agent for conservative authors in sales to Regnery and other publishers. (She tried and failed to sell a book by the Arkansas troopers.) Politics mattered to her, but as she told *The New Yorker* in 1998, she was more interested in gossip. "I love dish!" she said. "I live for dish!"[1]


Goldberg's name was first mentioned to former White House secretary Linda Tripp by Fox News host Tony Snow. It was summer 1996, and Tripp had told Snow that she was interested in writing a tell-all book about her White House experience. Like her friend Gary Aldrich, the FBI agent who authored the salacious *Unlimited Access,* Tripp said she was appalled by the behavior and mores of Bill and Hillary and others in their orbit. The full truth of what went on in the White House was impossible to discern, but this was beside the point. Tripp had settled on her version of things, and like Aldrich, she was eager for a lucrative publishing deal. Snow reassured Tripp that Goldberg could be trusted as a member of his "rat pack" of friends.

At age sixty-one, Goldberg was a bit younger than the famous Hollywood Rat Pack—Frank Sinatra, Sammy Davis Jr., Peter Lawford, and others—but her demeanor was pitch-perfect. Her voice, made raspy by a lifetime of smoking, created an immediate sense of conspiracy. Her pose—fearless, egotistical, and self-serving—made her seem as worldly as the original rodents. Goldberg gave her woman-of-the-world persona free rein in her side hustle as the author of pulp novels like *Madame Cleo's Girls,* which told a tale of high-priced prostitution captured in tape-recorded interviews with a Parisian madam.[2]

With her keen interest in scandal, and a long-standing desire to see them driven out of politics, Goldberg had followed news of the Clintons closely. With telltale imprecision, she called Whitewater "Hillary's phony stock deal" and believed the press had failed in its duty to find something criminal in the busted real estate development. She wasn't impressed by Tripp's proposal, which lacked the juicy details required for a bestseller. Tripp set it aside. Then, a year later, Tripp used Snow as an intermediary to contact Goldberg again. She had more to tell. Goldberg, who had apparently developed a habit of taping telephone calls, switched on her machine while Tripp talked. On one call, Tripp spoke of a young friend who was "a quote 'girlfriend' of the Big Creep." The creep was Bill Clinton, and the woman, Monica Lewinsky, had been a White House intern.

Daughter of a doctor and a former writer for *The Hollywood Reporter,* Lewinsky had grown up in the exclusive Brentwood area of Los Angeles, which was made infamous when former football star O. J. Simpson was charged with killing his wife there. Lucianne Goldberg had served as the book agent for disgraced Simpson case detective Mark Fuhrman, whose racist speech had been revealed at trial and contributed to a not-guilty verdict. Goldberg knew the value of a scandalous story and listened attentively as Tripp said that Clinton and Lewinsky had conducted an off-and-on relationship for two years, but things had become difficult when "one of the female head honchos—not the Big One" discovered what was going on. The "Big One" was Hillary Clinton, who, it was generally believed, was supposed to keep the president in line.

Transcripts of Goldberg's recordings, which were eventually published, reveal that Tripp felt she knew what was best for Lewinsky and that it just happened to include a Linda Tripp tell-all book because "she needs to be going forward." Goldberg's outrage was focused on the fact that the affair occurred in the White House and she was eager to hear that Clinton was involved with many women and that people all over the White House must know. Tripp said she knew of no other affairs.

Tripp and Goldberg spoke as if they cared about Lewinsky, whose name Tripp would keep secret for some months. Goldberg speculated about what might happen "to this young woman . . . if someone goes public." Tripp replied in a tough love way, saying, "She has got to move on." In a matter of seconds, the women moved from considering the peril faced by Tripp's friend to ways in which she could be pressured to serve their literary, financial, and politic agendas.

GOLDBERG: Well, have you talked with her about going public?

TRIPP: She refuses.

GOLDBERG: Well, then, what can you do with it?

TRIPP: Well, because of all the dates and the times and the phones and the records.

GOLDBERG: Yeah, but you realize the press will destroy her.

TRIPP: (sigh)

GOLDBERG: The press will destroy her—you know—the press will destroy, you know, I mean, you know what [presidential counsel] Lanny Davis will do.

TRIPP: Do you really think, though, that they could destroy her?

GOLDBERG: Well, but no. The publicity might destroy her and you. I mean, I mean, I love the idea. I would run with it in a second, but do you want to be the instrument of the kid, really, um—

TRIPP: Well, let's . . . let me give you some history.

At this point in the conversation, Tripp began to offer reasons why the woman she would betray was no longer worthy of her protection. She described Lewinsky as a child of privilege raised in Beverly Hills, who was "definitely sophisticated" and "not a victim." Tripp added, "When this began, she was every bit a player." At hearing this, Goldberg chuckled. "She treats him and talks to him as though he were you or me," continued Tripp. "There's no reverence there."[3]

Goldberg steered the conversation toward the Paula Jones lawsuit, musing about whether Tripp's friend might work with Jones's lawyers. (Of course, she knew how to connect to them.) Tripp, who noted that her friend's "prime focus in life is not to expose" the affair, didn't think such an arrangement could be made.

Eventually, Tripp and Goldberg made a plan that could potentially ruin Monica Lewinsky's life and bring inestimable pain to Bill and Hillary Clinton. Tripp was to give just enough information to help *Newsweek* writer Michael Isikoff publicize the affair while preserving for herself the details that would go into a book. Dish, it seemed, should not be served all at once.

Goldberg suggested she could sell a book by Tripp to a publisher, and that it might fetch as much as $500,000. In the course of conversations that were punctuated with laughter and speculation that Clinton folks might poison Tripp, they mused about a purpose beyond financial reward. As the women talked, Lewinsky was transformed from an entitled sophisticated "player" into a "kid" who was "fresh out of college." Gradually, Tripp and Goldberg talked themselves into believing they were not just gossips heedless of the damage they would do. They were the ones who would awaken the world to the dangers facing innocent young women. With Goldberg's encouragement, and an incorrect assurance that the practice was legal in her home state of Maryland, Linda Tripp began secretly taping her phone calls with her distressed younger friend. She also followed through on the plan to share information with reporter Isikoff.[4]

Few reporters would have served Tripp's and Goldberg's interests better than Isikoff. He was as dogged as Drudge, but he hewed to mainstream standards. He also suspected that Bill Clinton was concealing behavior that revealed serious character flaws. Although he recognized that his colleagues were, as he would say, "queasy" about chasing the potential sex scandal, Isikoff was not. He had reported on Paula Jones and had recently begun investigating the tale of a White House volunteer named Kathleen Willey, who had talked about the president making unwanted advances that included groping her in a private hallway near the Oval Office. The first tip for this story had come from one of Jones's lawyers in January 1997. The attorney told him of a caller who hadn't given her name but offered enough details about her situation to allow Isikoff to identify her. During an interview with Willey, he asked if she had told anyone of the incident at the time it happened. She mentioned Linda Tripp.

Linda Tripp told Isikoff that Willey had been pursuing a relationship with Clinton and had eagerly sought a private meeting with him. She said that she had come upon Willey in the moments after her encounter with the president and noticed that she looked disheveled. According to Tripp, the two women went outside to sit at a picnic table and talk. Tripp reported that Willey was not upset and was hoping the president would help her with a serious problem. Her husband had been caught in an embezzlement scheme, and she wanted Clinton's help securing him a job. Ed Willey Jr. was so troubled that he actually committed suicide on the day his wife met with Clinton.[5]

Later, Willey would say that she had revealed to Tripp that Clinton had kissed her and touched her, but Willey was actually quite happy about what had occurred. Although Isikoff may have considered the conflicting tales a problem, Tripp urged him to consider a more substantial tale. It was about a woman in her twenties who had begun having an affair with Clinton when she was a White House intern.[6]

As perhaps the only reporter in the world who knew of Tripp, Willey, and the as-yet-unnamed intern, Isikoff was ready to spring into action when, in May 1997, the Supreme Court rejected President Clinton's claim of immunity from civil suits. This decision, which settled a legal issue that had been debated for decades, meant that the Jones suit could move forward. Isikoff interviewed Jones and wrote a cover story on the development. As the leader among journalists who were probing claims against Clinton, Isikoff was about to become part of the story himself. This happened on July 4, when Matt Drudge alerted readers that *Newsweek* was about to report that a second woman was making allegations against Clinton.

No regular reporter would do what Drudge did—making news out of an unpublished story—and no real publication would permit it. But Drudge operated with the usual standards and was writer, editor, and publisher rolled into one. A self-declared "information anarchist," Drudge was part of the Clinton-hating crowd of propagandists that included his friends Ann Coulter, Laura Ingraham, and David Brock (whom he had dated), who did not enjoy his level of independence. Drudge framed his half-truths and distortions as a form of protest. "Screw journalism," he said. "The whole thing's a fraud anyway." This self-justification leaned on the example set by the gutter-dwelling supermarket tabloids to demean the entire practice of seeking and reporting the news. According to this logic, honesty and fairness have no value, and nothing separates the sincere and the corrupt.[7]

Anarchist Drudge revealed Willey's name, which sent Paula Jones's lawyers scrambling to win her cooperation in her case. Monica Lewinsky, spooked by the publicity, pressed the president to help her find a job in New York. Linda Tripp tape-recorded conversations with the former intern. In one of these chats, she also persuaded Lewinsky to develop a spreadsheet showing all her encounters with Clinton. Tripp also encouraged Lewinsky to put in safekeeping a dress that had been stained by Clinton's semen. Lewinsky did.

Isikoff would one day realize that Tripp, Goldberg, and others were consistently sharing what they knew about Lewinsky and Kathleen Willey with the Paula Jones legal team. This information was extremely valuable to the lawyers, who dispatched private investigators to interview hundreds of women in hopes of finding someone else to testify about Clinton as a sexual predator. They would put Lewinsky's name on their list of potential witnesses for their case and eventually serve her with a subpoena requesting everything the president had ever given her. At roughly the same time, the self-described Elves told a member of Kenneth Starr's Office of the Independent Counsel team about Lewinsky and her taped conversations with Linda Tripp. With this outreach, the peril the president faced increased. The so-called Lewinsky affair, which was both a consensual relationship *and* personal/professional transgression on the part of the president, was added to the purview of Kenneth Starr's office because it was possible that in denying the affair, he had committed perjury.

As the world would come to know, what Clinton had denied was having a sexual relationship involving intercourse with Lewinsky. In fact, the encounter had involved her performing oral sex on him, and this fell out of the definition of "sexual relations" set at the start of the deposition. It was also the case that many people, especially younger adults, considered this kind of sex different from intercourse. As Lewinsky would later say, *she* also did not consider what had occurred "sex."

In commonsense terms, what Clinton said was a lie offered to deflect investigators. Legally speaking, it may not have constituted perjury, but it would be the basis for expanding the investigation, which had begun with Whitewater and was almost abandoned for lack of progress in February 1997. At that time, Starr had announced he would resign to take a job at Pepperdine University's law school. The position was to be funded in part by anti-Clinton zealot billionaire Richard Scaife (of course). However, after figures on the political Right criticized his decision, Starr reversed himself and announced he would remain on the job. "When I make a mistake," he said, "it's a beaut."[8]

Starr's approach to his work, which included maintaining his private practice while also serving the American people as independent counsel, was a tangle of oddities. When he took the job, he had absolutely no experience as a prosecutor, and yet he often posed as a tough-on-crime stalwart. Supposedly independent, he was very much a creature of the conservative legal establishment in Washington and Republican politics. Although he was guarded to the point of incoherence in his public statements, his office often leaked explosive information to the press.

Leaks are the lifeblood of journalism in Washington, where many stories would never be reported but for the secrets shared by insiders who harbored political or personal motivations. Starr's office, which was filled with ambitious conservative partisans, would be notorious for sharing information that might make the Clintons look bad or reflect well on them.

Taken together, the contradictions presented by Starr and his staffers created the impression that the investigation of the president and First Lady was a soap opera filled with intrigue that would have seemed comical—think of a legal Elmer Fudd chasing a political Bugs Bunny—if it hadn't threatened to cause a constitutional crisis. The trouble would inevitably involve Congress, where Newt Gingrich, having risen to Speaker of the House, stood to play a significant role. The razor-tongued man who had taught the GOP to use extreme partisanship to seize power would have been the Clintons' main tormentor if only he had been more virtuous himself. However, in early 1997 Gingrich had suffered a formal rebuke, the first ever endured by a Speaker, for violating tax regulations and lying about it to House investigators. The vote had been 395–28. Gingrich was also handicapped by his own problems with relationships. As a teen, he had married his high school teacher Jackie Battley. He told her he wanted a divorce during a visit to the hospital where she was being treated for uterine cancer, and he married his second wife, Marianne Ginther, with whom he had begun an affair, after the papers were signed. At the time of the Clinton scandals, Gingrich was betraying Marianne with a congressional staffer, Callista Bisek, who was twenty-three years his junior. (*The Washington Post* would note, ironically enough, that Bisek "bears a passing resemblance to Hillary Rodham Clinton.") Disqualified by his own behavior, Gingrich couldn't join the most important political battle of his time and resigned amid his GOP colleagues' complaints. Foreshadowing the extremism to come, which he had done much to create, he described fellow Republicans as "cannibals."[9]

Gingrich's disgrace meant that other congressional Republicans would have to take up the work of scourging the Clintons. Many, including Representatives Henry Hyde, Dan Burton, Robert Livingston, and Helen Chenoweth, would be handicapped by their own histories of sexual indiscretion. However, other voices would do the moralizing and make sure to keep the sordid aspects of the case front and center.

The investigation that eventually cornered Monica Lewinsky included a restaurant meeting with Linda Tripp, who was wired to secretly record their conversation for the federal prosecutors. In this chat, Lewinsky spoke as if she intended to lie if asked to testify about her relationship with the president. She also seemed to try to bribe Tripp to do the same. What she said was vague and open to interpretation, but it was the kind of talk that could make her vulnerable to prosecution on charges of obstruction of justice and perhaps suborning perjury. Soon, Tripp and the federal investigators hatched a scheme to lure Lewinsky to another meeting at a shopping mall in Virginia. There FBI agents swooped in, took her into custody, and spirited her up to a room in a hotel that was part of the mall. Members of Kenneth Starr's team waited there to question her and hoped to persuade her to become a witness against the president.

Having accompanied the group to the hotel room, Linda Tripp was forced to face her erstwhile friend, who, realizing how she had been betrayed, insisted Tripp be kept around because "I want that treacherous bitch to see what she has done to me."

Tripp chose to leave. As she departed, Starr's lawyers turned to pressuring Lewinsky with warnings that she faced prosecutions for crimes that came with long sentences. Included was the possibility of a perjury charge based on an affidavit she signed in the Jones case in which she denied having an affair with Clinton. She was also threatened with charges of obstruction of justice, witness tampering, and suborning perjury. If Lewinsky didn't understand the exact nature of these crimes, she surely grasped that she was in deep trouble that would change her life whether or not she was charged and convicted. To drive home the seriousness of the situation, the team showed her photos taken of her during the course of the investigation, which drove home the point that significant government resources had been devoted to the case over an extended period of time. They also mentioned the possibility of a prison term lasting twenty-seven years. When she talked about calling a lawyer, they encouraged her to delay. (She later reported she had often asked to call her attorney and was not permitted to do so.) When she mentioned calling her mother, she was told that at age twenty-four she should be able to handle facing the Starr team alone.

Over the course of many hours of talk, interrupted often by Lewinsky's crying, the questioners made little progress. Lewinsky would recall they suggested that her cooperation would require making phone calls that would be recorded and perhaps wearing a recording device on visits to people of interest. They also mentioned prosecuting her mother. When she finally did get to speak with her mother and then her father, Lewinsky put the brakes on her cooperation. Her mother arrived at the hotel. A lawyer located by her father stopped the interrogation, and both women were permitted to leave.

They left fearing that Monica was facing charges for filing a false statement in the Paula Jones case. They didn't know that this document had not been filed with the court in Little Rock and thus Lewinsky faced little peril. Nevertheless, she felt extremely vulnerable. This was yet another example of how, in this convoluted matter, the private Jones lawsuit, which was supported and promoted by Clinton's political enemies, supplied energy and ammunition for Kenneth Starr's criminal investigation. In this way, ordinary impulses to cover up a tawdry affair and escape political shame became an obsession for an independent counsel who would eventually spend four years and about $70 million investigating a president and his wife.

The self-reinforcing process that amplified the scandal and stirred public distrust of the news media also included reports by journalists who raced to be first with new details of a story that was salacious and politically significant. As the reckless Drudge floated theories and suggestions, more mainstream reporters repeated them on the theory that once a report was in the public domain, it was okay to repeat it. The process also worked in reverse. Drudge paid close attention to everything that was printed or included in broadcasts and issued alerts about the juiciest bits. Thus Drudge made reporting on reporters, including references about what they were *not* publishing, part of his mission. In this way, he could float speculative, half-tested ideas and prompt others to react.

All of what Drudge did was presented in a campy style stolen from the 1928 Broadway farce called *The Front Page,* which sends up the duplicitous and cynical tabloid press. This method gave readers the impression that they were reading something old-fashioned, if not homemade, which also made it believable to those who cast a skeptical eye on slick mass media outlets. Work that looked professionally polished was suspect. Amateur efforts, or at least the stuff presented to *look* amateurish, were deemed more authentic. Audiences prefer reports that align with their preconceived political and cultural biases. If Drudge was your favorite source, it was because he confirmed what you already suspected was true. If he did it crudely, it was because he wasn't one of those slick media manipulators. The idea that a crude-looking website may be purposely designed to *look* unsophisticated might never occur to a typical reader.

Whenever Drudge reported something titillating, he went all in with his esthetic. His first dispatch on Clinton-Lewinsky, for example, was packaged with all the tricks of his trade:

### BLOCKBUSTER REPORT:
### 23-YEAR OLD, FORMER WHITE HOUSE INTERN,
### SEX RELATIONSHIP WITH PRESIDENT

### **World Exclusive**

### **Must Credit the DRUDGE REPORT**

At the last minute, at 6 p.m. on Saturday evening, NEWSWEEK magazine killed a story that was destined to shake official Washington to its foundation: A White House intern carried on a sexual affair with the President of the United States!

The rest of the breathless prose addressed how the young woman in question "claims to have indulged the president's sexual preference" and portrayed Michael Isikoff's arguments with his editors as if the fate of the world had hung in the balance. In the ensuing hours and days, Drudge parceled out titillating details, and mainstream journalists quickly published their versions of the same information. Supplied by Goldberg and Elves Conway and Porter, Drudge and others would name Lewinsky and add details to make the story more vivid.

Soon, legitimate (non-Drudge) news outlets were reporting that Clinton and his longtime advisor Vernon Jordan were encouraging Lewinsky to lie to Kenneth Starr. If the charges were true, both men had committed felonies. Drudge advanced the story with a new lurid detail: Lewinsky had preserved a dress stained with Clinton's semen. This, too, was picked up by the mainstream press. Amid the whirlwind of publicity, Lucianne Goldberg, Linda Tripp's book agent, was ecstatic over what she and Tripp had helped to create. Early one morning, she called her son Jonah, a conservative journalist who lived in Washington, and exclaimed, "It's breaking! It's breaking! We've done it."[10]

What Tripp and the others had accomplished included providing key information to help the lawyers for Paula Jones frame the questions they would ask in a deposition conducted hours before Drudge touched off the media frenzy. (The questioning was done by a lawyer who later explained that "as a Christian," he was disturbed by Clinton's conduct.) Although ostensibly about one woman's claim against Bill Clinton as a private citizen, the interview was really about forcing him to consider questions about Lewinsky and Willey, questions that necessarily threatened his relationship with Hillary, in the hope that he would lie to protect his marriage and in the process commit perjury. He did by denying that he had sexual relations with Monica Lewinsky.

As Clinton lied, the lawyers for both sides assumed that his testimony about other women would almost certainly be barred by the judge hearing the Paula Jones case. Lewinsky and Willey did not enter Clinton's life until after he left Arkansas, which made them peripheral, if not irrelevant, figures in the Jones case. However, Paula Jones's lawyers also knew that Kenneth Starr, the independent counsel named in 1994 to probe Whitewater, had recently begun a criminal investigation of Clinton's behavior in the Paula Jones matter. Starr might be able to use the deposition to charge him with perjury.[11]

The threat to Clinton's presidency was great and became evident to his aides as the week wore on and news outlets delivered a stream of new information. Clinton kept insisting to them and to his wife that he had not engaged in sex of any sort with Lewinsky. He told the truth only to his pollster Dick Morris, who conducted a quick survey, which discovered that the American people could forgive adultery but not perjury. "If you get anywhere near lying under oath, you're cooked," Morris told the president.[12]

Old friends who knew the Clintons well worried about how all of this would inevitably affect Hillary and the Clintons' daughter, Chelsea. At age seventeen, Chelsea Clinton had never known a time when her parents were not public figures under intense scrutiny and subject to terrible accusations. In this rare family atmosphere, she had been taught to expect and to hear and read all kinds of statements about her family. As her parents, they would help her decide what to accept and what to reject, but they could not filter every input.

Anyone who would say that Bill Clinton bore a heavy responsibility for any pain that was to come would be correct. His need for approval, power, and the adrenaline high that comes with risk-taking had propelled him to the presidency, but this drive also presented grave danger. Obliged to preserve both his family and the stability of his government, Clinton would not be excused for deception and deceit. And more than anyone, he had to know that in the climate of hyper-partisanship and reckless publishing presented by the likes of Matt Drudge, he was under continuous threat.

No one in this whole drama, from the president to Monica Lewinsky, Linda Tripp, Lucianne Goldberg, or Matt Drudge, seemed much interested in how Hillary Clinton would suffer as the reports of her husband's alleged betrayals accumulated. Every player, save for the president, could claim to be serving a higher purpose in promoting the truth—freedom of the press!—or defending some concept of the White House as sacred ground. But in fact, those who had long harbored hatred for Hillary Clinton saw in the scandal a way to wound her both personally and politically. Others merely feasted on the scandal to make money, score political points, or gain the public's attention. Even Donald Trump, real estate huckster and future president, would weigh in during a TV interview.

"He certainly could have picked a better candidate," Trump offered in his smarmy style. "And I mean that, and you mean that, and everybody means that . . . somebody said to me that if he would have had the affair with a supermodel he would have been everybody's hero. But of course I would never say anything like that."[13]

# 7

# Almost Numb to It

As the storm gathered, the president and the First Lady were still obligated to fulfill their obligations and satisfy their commitments. Under normal circumstances, this work would require all a man or woman could muster. Now the Clintons bore the additional burden of accusation and investigation, which had begun almost as soon as they moved into the White House. Foreign travel, done together and separately, became one duty that was also an escape from domestic political pressure. With few exceptions, when they traveled abroad they were met by enthusiastic crowds and achieved real success.

Hillary Clinton had already established herself as an influential international figure of more substance than most previous First Ladies. In 1995, she used the United Nations' Fourth World Conference on Women to sharply criticize host China's "one-child" policy and failure to address violence and discrimination against women. Ranked by many historians as one of the most important addresses of the twentieth century, her speech in Beijing galvanized women's rights organizations around the world. It made the phrase *Women's rights are human rights* a rallying cry that echoed for decades and established Hillary Clinton as an international figure with a purpose beyond the usual First Lady's good works and appeals for friendship.

On his foreign missions, the president pushed to expand global trade and American power. With the dissolution of the Soviet Union just prior to Bill Clinton's election, the United States stood as the sole super-power in the world, and offered the opportunity for the expansion of Western-style democracy. Clinton focused much of his attention on the emergence of a new Russian state, which was led by a boisterous, unpredictable, and often-drunk Boris Yeltsin.

As the nation's former Cold Warriors seethed, the once-powerful Soviet empire disintegrated. Economic output declined by more than 50 percent, and by most measures, life for everyday Russians worsened. Yeltsin's struggle to create a new country often led to chaos. In one two-year stretch, for example, he appointed five different men to the post of prime minister, which is roughly analogous to the vice presi-dency in the United States. The last would be Vladimir Putin, a former officer of the Soviet spy agency whose worldview was organized around anti-Americanism. When Bill Clinton spoke to Yeltsin about Putin, he warned, "He doesn't have democracy in his heart." Putin would prove the point. He became president in 2000 and began cracking down on the free press and consolidating power in the presidency.[1]

At home, Clinton pursued the middle-of-the-road agenda that had won him the presidency, creating welfare-to-work programs, investing in charter schools, and establishing the Children's Health Insurance Pro-gram to provide care for millions of poorer kids. In early 1998, he gave his annual State of the Union address to Congress as the press reports were increasing in volume and pitch. Ever the performer, he made a cheering section out of the Democrats in the House of Representatives as he proposed using federal surpluses to shore up the Social Security retirement program, to pay teachers, and to improve health care for the elderly. In one and a quarter hours, Clinton was interrupted by applause ninety times. Those who kept track of these things noted it was his highest score in four years.[2]

Among the millions of Americans who watched the speech on

television were many drawn to the spectacle of a charismatic president caught in the middle of a sex scandal attempting to function with
some dignity. Viewers' verdicts would naturally align with preestablished
opinions. Those who believed that Clinton's sexual sins were nobody's
business cheered his resilience. Those who hated everything about Clinton heard a despicable, abusive man who was being propped up by a
crowd of power-mad enablers led by his wife. In Washington, people
who considered politics a sport organized State of the Union parties
where they behaved like fans gathered together to view the Super Bowl.
Clinton antagonist David Brock viewed the speech with a crowd that
included Brett Kavanaugh, who was Kenneth Starr's protégé. At one
point during the broadcast, when Hillary Clinton was shown watching
from the House Gallery, Kavanaugh turned toward Brock and mouthed
the word *bitch*.[3]

With the White House struggling to maintain business as usual, Hillary Clinton was scheduled to be interviewed on television the morning
after the State of the Union address. The venue was the most popular
national morning TV program in the country, NBC's *Today*. The topic
was supposed to be policies related to helping families deal with childcare in a time when more mothers and fathers worked, but the supply
of quality care was being overwhelmed by the demand, which drove up
prices and put families under stress.

Few political figures knew as much about this problem as Hillary
Clinton, who had worked with the Children's Defense Fund, written
on the needs of children, and made policies related to families a focus
of her service in Little Rock and Washington. Of course, none of this
history and preparation mattered in this moment. The childcare issue
was almost entirely eclipsed by *Today* host Matt Lauer's effort to use his
access to the First Lady to discuss the scandal. In the future, this moment
of television would be cast in a much different light—as Lauer would be
forced out of NBC in a storm of scandal related to many allegations of
his own sexual misconduct. But in January 1998, he enjoyed the public
trust as a calm and sober journalist who was willing to put the powerful
on the spot.[4]

In the video recording of the interview, Hillary speaks in a markedly unemotional way—a tone that could be called lawyerly—which may have been her only option given the excruciating circumstances. She began by expressing condolences for the recent death, due to cancer, of *Today* cohost Katie Couric's husband. After noting his colleague's loss, Lauer immediately pressed Hillary on the matter of Monica Lewinsky. He wanted to know if Hillary had ever met Monica Lewinsky (she didn't think she had) and whether her husband had given the young woman gifts. ("I think it's possible," said Hillary.) Lauer also asked if the president had "described the relationship in detail to you." She replied:

> *Well, we've talked at great length. And I think as this matter unfolds, the entire country will have more information. But we're right in the middle of a rather vigorous feeding frenzy right now, and people are saying all kinds of things and putting out rumor and innuendo. And I have learned over the last many years, being involved in politics, and especially since my husband first started running for president, that the best thing to do in these cases is just to be patient, take a deep breath, and the truth will come out. But there's nothing we can do to fight this firestorm of allegations that are out there.*

As television, the *Today* interview was almost as riveting as the one Hillary and Bill Clinton had done with *60 Minutes* in 1992. As a personal experience, it must have been equally difficult. Once again, Hillary Clinton was being asked to speak to things no one would ever want to address with a stranger, let alone on a national broadcast. The difference was that she had gone through five years of her husband's administration and a second successful election campaign, and these experiences had apparently made her steadier. Lauer read this as something else, asking, "Are you saying, though, that you're no longer—that this doesn't upset you anymore? You're almost numb to it?" She replied:

> *It's not being numb so much as just being very experienced in the unfortunate mean-spirited give-and-take of American politics right now. So having seen so many of these accusations come and go, having seen people profit, you know, like Jerry Falwell with videos accusing my husband of*

*murder, of drug running, seeing some of the things that are written and said about him, my attitude is, you know, we've been there before. We have seen this before. And I am just going to wait patiently until the truth comes out.*

Mention of the drug running and murder libels did not capture Matt Lauer's attention. He was focused on Lewinsky and, besides, there were so many accusations echoed by multiple voices that anyone who edged close to the topic of Clinton conspiracy theories risked falling into a rabbit hole with no end. Thus it was easier, and inevitable, that Lauer would bring up Gennifer Flowers and remind Hillary that "you said at that time, in an interview, a very famous quote: 'I'm not some Tammy Wynette standing by my man.'"

The phrase, uttered six years in the past, had caused Hillary Clinton no end of trouble as people across the country clucked about whether she should or should not have supported her husband and if she had insulted the First Lady of Country Music. Lauer, having resurrected the moment, asked, "Six years later, you are still standing by this man, your husband, through some difficult charges. If he were to be asked today, Mrs. Clinton, do you think he would admit that he again has caused pain in this marriage?" (Bill Clinton had said so back in 1992.)

Again put in an untenable position by her husband and the press, Hillary had listened, her face practically expressionless, as the question was framed. Her reply—"No, and he shouldn't"—was the only realistic option at her disposal. Decades of experience in politics and in marriage to Bill Clinton had taught her to be cautious and that she couldn't imagine how events would unfold. But whenever a marriage is hit by sudden turbulence, spouses must brace themselves first. The united front may break later, but in the emergency phase of a crisis loyal husbands, wives, and partners reflexively offer the person whom they love full support. Hillary Clinton, who had suffered through the stand-by-your-man fiasco in 1992, responded decisively. However, she also sought to draw attention to the context, which included the long-running effort that found a certain cast of characters—conspiracy theorists, provocateurs, wealthy donors, and political actors—waging a kind of war against both her and her husband. Dirty tricksters and provocateurs are common in politics, but Hillary was talking about opposition of a greater magnitude. She said:

> I mean, look at the very people who are involved in this. They have popped up in other settings. This is—the great story here for anybody willing to find it and write about it and explain it is this vast right-wing conspiracy that has been conspiring against my husband since the day he announced for president. A few journalists have kind of caught on to it and explained it, but it has not yet been fully revealed to the American public. And actually, you know, in a bizarre sort of way, this may do it.[5]

In the same interview, Hillary agreed that if the charges against her husband were true they would be serious but added that she believed they were "not going to be proven true."

Reaction to the interview fell along partisan lines, with Republicans gleeful about the discomfort Hillary surely felt and Democrats outraged. As opponents mocked Clinton as paranoid because of her quip about a vast conspiracy, in fact millions of dollars were being spent to dig up and in some cases manufacture negative information about the Clintons. Richard Mellon Scaife's various foundations financed much of this activity. Some of it, like the $4.2 million sent over a twenty-year span to a former John Birch Society activist for "research," was little more than charity for the like-minded. However, a comparable sum granted over seven years to a group called Judicial Watch produced eighteen lawsuits against the Clinton administration and supported publicity campaigns about the death of Vince Foster.

Years later, the man who provided much of the impetus for the persistent fever dreams about the Clintons confessed that, in fact, the vast right-wing campaign against the Clintons was real. In an interview with Chris Wallace of Fox News, David Bossie would confess, "No, it was true, Chris. There was an effort by the conservative movement to undermine President Clinton." Bossie knew the depths to which his side would sink in their attacks on Clinton. In May 1998, he would be fired from his House job for releasing documents edited to suggest

Hillary Clinton had committed crimes. Caught in the act, he brought such shame upon his boss, Representative Dan Burton, that even Newt Gingrich criticized him for the "circus" in his office.[6]

Looking on from the sideline, columnist Frank Rich of *The New York Times* placed all of it—the Clintons, the media, Kenneth Starr, Drudge, Lewinsky, Tripp, Goldberg—in the "squalid realm of lowest common denominator entertainment." For decades, the growth of cable television and then the internet had expanded the demand for content this false while driving producers to offer more extreme videos and articles. Game shows had given way to camera crews chasing real police officers in *Cops* and then the intimate voyeurism of *The Real World: San Francisco.* With so much effort being invested in turning life itself into amusement, it was hard to imagine anything that would be off-limits. At the end of January 1998, Rich noted that thanks to a compelling cast of characters led by a beautiful young woman and a plot filled with sex and power, TV news had become "All Monica All the Time," and there was no end in sight.

In retrospect, the most remarkable aspect of the Clinton-Lewinsky scandal was the speed of the developments that occurred once her story was revealed. The highlights would include a dramatic presidential press conference in late January at which he declared, "I did not have sexual relations with that woman, Miss Lewinsky."

In March, Kathleen Willey would tell a national TV audience on *60 Minutes* that the president had groped her, but a friend whom she offered as a cooperating source contradicted her. According to Julie Hiatt Steele, Willey had asked her to lie. Prior to speaking to *60 Minutes,* Willey had contacted a literary agent about selling her tale to a book publisher. It would later emerge that Linda Tripp told the FBI that Willey had pursued a sexual relationship with the president and would have welcomed any attention he may have given her.[7]

In April, the judge hearing the Paula Jones suit dismissed it. However, the Jones civil suit, and his own response to every development around it, had given Kenneth Starr new life as independent counsel. After three and a half years, which had resulted in just one person being sent to prison for crimes related to Whitewater, Starr had his prey cornered. He also enjoyed more outspoken support from House Republicans. Speaker Newt Gingrich, who himself was secretly engaged in an illicit affair with a House staffer, defended Starr in an article he wrote for the journal *Human Events.* In the piece, which was published in May 1998, he attacked Clinton for "a level of disrespect and decadence that should appall every American." Rarely had a man who occupied a glass house thrown such a big stone.

The independent counsel's office brought a new group of witnesses to the federal courthouse in Washington, where a grand jury heard Linda Tripp justify her avid record-keeping regarding Monica Lewinsky by citing conspiracy theories about the supposed murders committed by the Clintons. In the middle of this process, Starr wanted to end the work, send a report to Congress, and let the Americans' elected representatives sort out the president's future, but his team opposed the idea, and he kept moving forward. A subpoena was sent to the president demanding his testimony for the grand jury, and the group set about determining its strategy for questioning him. Brett Kavanaugh, the eager young lawyer whose reopening of the Vince Foster matter had led to a dead end, wanted Clinton to be tormented with questions because "it is our job to make his pattern of revolting behavior clear—piece by painful piece."

Kavanaugh suggested Clinton be asked ten specific questions about the details of his sexual encounters with Lewinsky, including requests for descriptions of particular sex acts and whether he or Lewinsky experienced an orgasm during certain encounters. The young lawyer made it clear he was appalled by Clinton's "callous and disgusting behavior," which he believed had made a "shambles" of a young woman's life. Starr's attorneys would not ask all the questions Kavanaugh recommended, but their interest in the prurient details, especially as they related to the possibility that Clinton committed perjury in the Jones case by denying having sexual relations with Lewinsky, was steadfast. This would be a major focus when they went to the White House to question Clinton during a session that would be transmitted, via video, directly to the grand jury.

Sex, and lying about sex, became the only topic of Clinton's testimony, because after multiple investigations into many supposed scandals the Office of the Independent Counsel had reached dead ends on White-water, the Vince Foster suicide, and the ancillary issue of firings in the office that handled travel arrangements for the White House press corps. Partisans who referred to this controversy as Travelgate believed that both the president and First Lady had tried to help their friends by diverting travel business to them. Both were exonerated.

Just prior to the interview, Bill Clinton finally told his wife that "the situation was much more serious" than she knew. As she struggled to breathe, he confessed to "inappropriate intimacy" with Monica Lewinsky. Like so many husbands before and after, he said he had lied to protect his family. This was part of the truth, but certainly not all of it. Obviously, Bill Clinton had intended to also spare himself the shame and humiliation of being found out and all that it would have implied for him personally and for his presidency. And though cynics would insist that Hillary must have been complicit in the evasion, those who knew the couple well would say she was not. Here she may have been like so many wives of serial adulterers who choose to believe that their husbands have reformed out of love.

In this moment of revelation, Hillary Clinton felt both privately and publicly betrayed. For decades, she had been required to consider what her husband and his aides, and the press, and the voters expected. She had worked to be smart but not overbearing, assertive but not aggressive, supportive but not subservient, and on and on. Along the way, she had been subjected to more open derision and innuendo than any First Lady in modern times. Despite all this, she had gone on television to defend her husband from the "vast right-wing conspiracy" and thus made herself vulnerable to critics who would depict her as a doormat. She would remain publicly loyal through the crisis, but as her husband sat down with Ken Starr and his team in the Map Room at the White House, she was burdened by the knowledge that he had misled her more directly than he had misled the country.

It was around this time, after so many betrayals and attacks on her person, that Hillary Clinton's friend Diane Blair noted a shift in her. "Sometimes, I am saddened by her understandable loss of spontaneity,"

Blair told *Time* magazine. "It was one of her most endearing qualities. But in public now, she filters out her first response, and sometimes her second one, and that contributes to the sense that she is aloof and haughty. She has learned to be careful about what she says." In personal papers made public after her death, Blair's diary of her friendship with Hillary attributed the First Lady's wariness to the "ugly forces . . . making up hateful things about them, pounding on them."

This caution was part of a strategy that Bill and Hillary Clinton had adopted to preserve themselves and their family during their years in the White House. Little considered, the human experience of First Families is marked by the same emotional ups and downs, with the added element of continual press scrutiny and political opposition that can range from the usual contest of ideas to the worst mudslinging. The Clintons decided that whenever possible, they would present a calm, united front in public no matter how they felt. As Hillary would reveal to a friend, this meant that a rapid series of personal losses—Vince Foster's suicide, her father's death, that mother's passing—took a toll on her husband was hidden from others but caused emotional damage.

As Hillary talked through the Lewinsky crisis with her friend, she placed the blame squarely on her husband, but added the context of personal loss and his isolation. *She* had confidants she could trust. Everything *he* said was eventually leaked to the press. She considered the relationship with Lewinsky a "lapse" that was consensual and became impossible for him to manage, in part because she was a "narcissistic loony tune." A psychotherapist had helped her understand how Bill's chaotic upbringing by a mother and grandmother who hated each other contributed to his infidelity even if it didn't excuse it. In the end, like many spouses who have been betrayed, Hillary weighed decades of marriage and a life built on shared commitments, and refused to give up. The result would be a stubborn effort to preserve and protect herself and her marriage, which would require a stronger defense against personal attacks, which would inevitably cause some people to judge her to be standoffish, calculating, and insincere.[8]

Who wouldn't steel themselves against the kind of insult that the First Lady had endured and would face in the days to come as the truth emerged? With Starr, as with Hillary, the president admitted to a physical relationship with Monica Lewinsky but insisted he had believed these contacts did not constitute "sexual relations" in the "strange" way defined by the lawyers in the Paula Jones case. Thus it was *their fault* that he appeared to lie and not his. In the ensuing four hours, he gave a bravura performance of deflecting, stalling, grandstanding, and hairsplitting. The spectacle was enhanced by ground rules that kept questioners off camera and allowed Clinton to loom presidentially on the screen viewed by the grand jury. With his trademark charm, he confessed that he didn't want the truth to come out but denied encouraging anyone to lie.

With Clinton seeming to outfox them, the interrogators took up the tack suggested by Brett Kavanaugh, asking specific questions about alleged sex acts, including, "Did Monica Lewinsky perform oral sex on you?" The question wasn't really about what Lewinsky did or did not do, since oral sex wasn't a crime. Instead, it was about whether Clinton had lied in the Paula Jones case, which would be a felony. Here he said what he had said before: "I had intimate contact with her that was inappropriate. I do not believe any of the contacts I had with her violated the definition I was given. Therefore, I believe I did not do anything but testify truthfully on these matters."[9]

Coming as a capper to the proceedings, this denial left the interrogators generally exasperated. With one exception—Brett Kavanaugh—the lawyers for the Office of the Independent Counsel felt dejected after their four hours with the president. Kavanaugh had pushed the group to press Clinton for sexual details. "You got what you needed to get," he told his discouraged colleague Solomon Wisenberg. Others, including Starr and the president himself, were less certain about the state of play. Clinton's side had decided to end the day with a presidential TV address, which was supposed to bolster his standing with the American people, who knew the testimony had taken place. Remarkably, the speech had not been finalized during the day, so after his Map Room ordeal, Clinton angrily revised a speech that some advisors said should be conciliatory, and others urged him to postpone or perhaps cancel the address altogether.

As he set about this work, the president would have to do without the aid of the woman who had long been his most trusted advisor and friend. Having been deceived and publicly humiliated, Hillary Clinton had nothing left to give her husband. Years later, author Ken Gormley would report that shortly before the speech, which Clinton would deliver from the same chair and desk he had occupied during the Starr interview, she refused to offer input. "Bill, it's your speech. You have to decide," she said. "You're the president of the United States, I guess."

The president of the United States did take responsibility for his role in the crisis, admitting, "I misled people, including even my wife," but he also insisted that the matter of Monica Lewinsky should, going forward, be "between me, the two people I love most—my wife and our daughter—and our God. I must put it right, and I am prepared to do whatever it takes to do so." On a personal level, Clinton was correct, but on the political and legal level, he was wrong. Worse, his short talk included complaints about the special counsel and the suggestion that the country "turn away from the spectacle of the past seven months." This was not an option for anyone, and by offering anything other than contrition, the president was unnecessarily provocative.

Ultimately, Kenneth Starr wrote a 250-page report to Congress that included a narrative that read, in certain passages, like pornography. Page after page offered specific dates when zippers were unzipped, breasts were caressed, and "passionate" kisses were exchanged. Starr reported that Lewinsky had purchased an ad in *The Washington Post* to publish a few lines from *Romeo and Juliet* on Valentine's Day. The report quoted other romantic messages Lewinsky sent to the president and her effort to obtain a "Christmas kiss." At many points in the story, the authors noted that Hillary Clinton was either out of town or not accompanying her husband on trips where he and Lewinsky saw each other or spoke by phone. The implication was that she had been a poor monitor of her husband's behavior and was thus a deficient wife.

Starr's narrative, which he considered vital to his argument, supposedly supported eleven grounds for impeachment. Five of the counts related to alleged perjury in the forms of lies told under oath to spare himself and his family embarrassment. Five additional counts charged that he had tried to obstruct justice by concealing evidence or trying to influence others' testimony. The eleventh charge alleged that, in general, the president had failed to "faithfully execute" the laws of the nation. This phrase echoed the oath presidents swear as they take office but did not refer to a specific impeachable offense, which the Constitution listed as "Treason, Bribery, or other high Crimes and Misdemeanors." Although scholars could argue the meaning of "high Crimes and Misdemeanors," in practice it was a political term that the Republican-controlled House of Representatives could define at will to have Clinton tried in the Senate. A conviction there would remove him from office.

The politics would be driven in large part by the public response to the Starr report, which was sent to Congress as a confidential document. Witnesses who testified for the grand jury, including Monica Lewinsky, understood that such testimony is almost always kept secret. Her mother begged Starr to honor this practice. Instead, he would enable the release of nearly every document obtained and interview conducted by his team. This included the transcript of a Lewinsky interview conducted by Starr associate Karin Immergut, who, like Brett Kavanaugh, was deeply interested in the details of her subject's sexual encounters with the president. For two hours, she asked about who touched whom, where, and when each of them experienced orgasm. Immergut's questions included, "Did he touch your breast with his mouth?" and "Did he touch your genital area at all that day?" and "Did he bring you to orgasm?"

After nearly two hours of such questioning, aided by a chart listing the sexual encounters, Immergut had produced a remarkable number of details on everything from Lewinsky's underwear to her recollections of her own sexually assertive behavior. No link was made to Whitewater, the death of Vince Foster, the White House travel office, or any controversy other than the affair. The testimony could be used to back the charge that the president had lied about it and to humiliate Bill and Hillary Clinton. It also revealed Starr, Immergut, and the Office of the Independent Counsel to be the political equivalent of an old-fashioned vice squad, hell-bent on policing sexual behavior.[10]

Although Starr would claim he didn't intend for his work to be rapidly loosed on the world, he had sent Congress a computer file version of the document, which allowed House leaders to make it available almost immediately on the internet. He also delivered boxes of files to the House. Inside them were statements from a woman named Juanita Broaddrick, who had both claimed and denied that Bill Clinton had raped her in the 1970s. When first interviewed by lawyers for Paula Jones, Broaddrick said the attack had never occurred. When Starr sent FBI agents to question her, she then said the rape had taken place. Whatever the truth may have been, the case fell outside Starr's charge, and he did not pursue it further. But as the file was included in the papers sent out for members of Congress to review, it quickly became a topic for gossip, and a stream of representatives trooped across Capitol Hill to the office building where they could pore over the file. The accusation never became part of the formal impeachment process, but Broaddrick would grant press interviews, which made the allegation a matter of public record.

In the meantime, the House of Representatives moved quickly to make vast amounts of Starr's work available for public consumption. Although grand jury testimony is almost always kept secret, in this case the video recording and transcript of Clinton's four hours with the OIC's lawyers were released. The House also made public audio recordings Linda Tripp had created of her conversations with Monica Lewinsky. Broadcast on television and radio, the testimony and phone calls could be combined with the Starr text to make a multiformat display of a president and a White House intern who had committed shameful personal acts and then tried to keep them private.

For Hillary Clinton, the Starr report and release of additional material meant the world could know about her husband's sexual betrayal, in great detail, and learn that Monica Lewinsky had been talking about whether the Clintons might divorce. Hillary had already become a magnet for criticism, even (perhaps especially) among women who would be her natural allies. Feminist writer Letty Cottin Pogrebin was appalled that Hillary had been photographed holding her husband's hand as they returned from a vacation. (Her refusal to take his outstretched hand on their departure had been widely reported.) Pogrebin fumed, "I have respected Hillary enormously—up until yesterday. It was the hand holding, the 'We love each other.'" She wanted the First Lady to evidence more anger. *Time* magazine speculated about the "enablers" who aided the president's deceptions, and political science professor Barbara Kellerman took to the pages of *Presidential Studies Quarterly* to do the same, but with an academic tone. Kellerman noted that generally Hillary was no more powerful than many other First Ladies, but she had failed as a spouse because she "aided and abetted the persistence of his [the president's] risky behavior."[11]

The term *enabler* had been borrowed from the realms of psychology and addiction treatment. Professionals used it to describe how others may play a role, usually unwitting, in a person's pattern of destructive behavior. This dynamic could deliver a gain of some sort to the person who is not identified as the one suffering from addiction or mental illness, and it was not a task for amateurs. Nevertheless, it had been added to the American lexicon, along with many other therapeutic concepts that could blur the concept of an individual's responsibility for his own behavior. In the case of the president, it allowed critics to shift blame from him to Mrs. Clinton, which meant that his betrayal damaged her in yet one more way.

If Hillary's haters found it convenient to blame her, the American people in general did not. As the Gallup Poll documented throughout the crisis, Hillary's approval ratings actually rose sharply from 50 percent to a high of 67 percent at the crest of the scandal. Her husband's job approval was a bit lower, at 60 percent, but when Gallup surveyed voters on the notion that the president should resign, even more, 66 percent, said no. Nevertheless, House Republican leaders Newt Gingrich, Bob Livingston, Henry Hyde, and Tom DeLay pressed ahead. Revelations of their own infidelities soon prompted Gingrich and Livingston to announce their retirements. Hyde's long-ago extramarital affair was disclosed by his paramour's former husband in an article that bore the headline THIS HYPOCRITE BROKE UP MY FAMILY. The Illinois congressman survived politically, but his family was devastated. Considered together, the revelations marked a moment when politics became even more personally destructive, as some Democrats were no doubt thrilled to see their rivals, who had so avidly pursued the president, subject to their own scandals.[12]

Despite the turmoil, the GOP leadership won a party-line vote on two articles of impeachment on December 19, 1998, making Clinton only the second president ever to be referred to the Senate for trial. (The other, Andrew Johnson, was acquitted by the Senate and remained in office until his term ended in 1869.)

After the impeachment vote, congressional Democrats went to the White House and gathered on the lawn behind a lectern decorated with the presidential seal. When Bill Clinton emerged, Hillary was at his side with her hand on his arm. The representatives applauded as the couple walked to address members of the press gathered for the occasion. In their last few steps, they clasped hands, which signaled to the world that the First Lady's loyalty was intact and she would fight alongside him as she had for decades. Others, like Letty Cottin Pogrebin, might be exasperated by her choice or question her sincerity because, after all, she had made that Tammy Wynette crack in 1992.

Having concluded that the House had acted as a partisan mob, Hillary went to Capitol Hill to declare herself "a wife who loves and supports her husband" and to rally Democrats. Even those who were angry with the president welcomed her, and by the end of the session the representatives and senators had taken to their feet six separate times to applaud her speech. New Yorkers had begun to talk of Hillary as the person to replace Senator Daniel Patrick Moynihan when he retired in 2000. Representative Eliot Engel, whose district included areas of Westchester County and the Bronx, gushed that Hillary was "probably the most popular person in the country with Democrats, period."[13]

When the impeachment process moved to the Senate, the chief justice of the Supreme Court presided over what was essentially a trial with one hundred senator/jurors proceeding with a wary eye on public sentiment. Ultimately a political process, the trial required every senator to consider his or her constituents and the fate of the institution in which they served. Entrusted to function as the deliberative counterweight to the more fractious House of Representatives, senators generally understood the fragile quality of the credibility they enjoyed. To contain the emotion, they agreed to seek new testimony from just three witnesses, the most relevant being Monica Lewinsky. Nothing in what they said would prove decisive, so the entirety of the prosecution boiled down to allegations and evidence produced by Starr's investigation, and the result depended as much on oratory as evidence.

Remarkably, speakers on both sides made sure to pull the First Lady into the process. (Andrew Johnson's First Lady, Eliza, wasn't mentioned during *his* trial even though she, too, was a prominent advisor to the president.) Republican senator Frank Murkowski of Alaska, who had used Vince Foster's briefcase as a prop in the dead-end Whitewater hearings conducted by Alfonse D'Amato in 1995, was the first. "The president refuses to be held accountable," complained Murkowski, "and I have a problem with the repeated reference from the First Lady that the president ministers to troubled people, suggesting that Monica Lewinsky was such a person. What has been happening, not just here in Washington but all around the country, is something far more disturbing than the trial of a president. What we have been witnessing is a contest for the very moral soul of the United States of America—and that the great casualty so far of the national scandal is the notion of truth. Truth has been shown to us as an elastic commodity."

The truth has been elastic since the moment human beings developed speech, and the fear that morality was in retreat was just about as old. And historically, monarchs, clerics, and politicians have expressed alarm about this kind of moral crisis whenever it could be blamed on a convenient enemy. Equally ancient and variable is the human tendency to use high-mindedness to mask a prurient interest in sex. In the Clinton scandal, prurience and moralizing mingled with more straightforward concerns about a powerful older man's relationship with a naïve intern to present serious challenges for those who supported the Clintons and their political agenda. Democrats, especially feminists, understood that the president had been on their side when it came to policy, and many felt personal affection for him. However, he had also betrayed his wife and daughter and taken advantage of a young woman who was, while technically an adult, vulnerable to a man of his status.

Finally, there was the whole problem of public versus private behavior and how partisanship had played an enormous part in the pursuit of the president and his wife.

In fact, the moment when the president's lawyers believed he was in the clear came as Dale Bumpers, who had just retired as senator from Arkansas, offered a closing argument on their behalf. The president's lawyers, noting that Bumpers was popular with his former colleagues, had recruited him for this task. He opened with a folksy anecdote about attending a racoon supper back home in Arkansas and quipped about how he was working as a volunteer, "and when I'm finished, you'll probably think the White House got their money's worth." He recounted Ken Starr's failure to bring any criminal charges despite "maybe the most intense investigation not only of a president but of anybody, ever." And he challenged the notion that the trial was about anything other than shaming Clinton for his sexual behavior. Added Bumpers, "When you hear somebody say, 'This is not about sex,' it's about sex."

The chuckles that greeted Bumpers's quip signaled that he had his audience where he wanted them. He then evoked Hillary and Chelsea Clinton to make an appeal based on humanity. "The president and Hillary and Chelsea are human beings," he announced. And though he would say Bill Clinton's behavior had been "indefensible, outrageous, unforgivable, shameless," he also believed that the pursuit of the president had gone too far. Referring to Clinton's evasive response to questioners, he said, "Put yourself in his position—and you have already had this big moral lapse—as to what you would do. We are, none of us, perfect."

Throughout the impeachment crisis, polls had shown that Americans did not expect perfection in their president. In fact, the more Bill Clinton and Hillary were hounded by prosecutors and political opponents, the higher both of their numbers rose. Right after the House voted to bring charges against him, Clinton's approval rating reached its zenith, at 73 percent. No president had been so popular since Dwight Eisenhower in the 1950s. The First Lady was not quite so popular, but she soared far above the House of Representatives, which languished below 30 percent. No doubt senators considered these numbers as they cast their votes. With the Constitution requiring 67 votes to convict, the

GOP couldn't even muster a simple majority, despite the fact that the party outnumbered the opposition 54–46. One article of impeachment garnered 45 votes; the other 50.

In the aftermath of Clinton's acquittal, the independent counsel would come under scrutiny for not honoring Monica Lewinsky's request for an attorney during her first interview with investigators. Jo Ann Harris, the investigator for the Justice Department Office of Professional Responsibility, found the Starr team had crossed a line that should separate a fair prosecution from a personally motivated drive to make any sort of allegation stick. Harris faulted Starr's hands-off leadership more than malice, noting that though he was widely respected, Starr had no experience in criminal matters and was thus a gifted man placed "in the wrong job." In the style of a corporate lawyer, he allowed his office to be run by committee, and the committee had become persuaded that Clinton was "a low life" and they "would have done virtually anything to get him." As Starr's team strayed from the usual process followed by prosecution groups, the result was "poor judgment" that left the impression that the whole enterprise had been a "seat-of-the-pants" operation. A subsequent investigation of the Starr team's contacts with the press showed that, contrary to their claims, the prosecutors were in regular contact with reporters, who revealed the workings of the Office of the Independent Counsel. The inquiry showed that in many instances, the lawyers in Starr's office either confirmed or contested items reported in the press even as they worked under a court-imposed ban on press contacts.[14]

The official inquiries into Starr's performance confirmed what many Americans had believed all along: that Whitewater was a minor concern and the pursuit of Bill and Hillary Clinton had been a partisan affair run amok. As Starr became personally identified with the investigation, survey subjects asked to describe him as either a "prosecutor" or a "persecutor" chose the latter by a margin of 53–30. The public reacted negatively to the release of the salacious elements in the Starr report, and a majority felt Starr was more interested in inflicting political damage on Clinton than fact-finding.

After the Senate chose to reject the impeachment charges, the Gallup poll reported that 73 percent of Americans deemed Starr to be a "loser" in the controversy. Mixed in with all the survey data was ample evidence that most people believed that the president had lied about his relationship with Monica Lewinsky, and a minority also believed Clinton had tried to obstruct Starr's investigation. However, like Dale Bumpers, they saw it all as a matter of moral failure, and like most senators, they rejected the notion that Clinton should be removed from office.[15]

Public sentiment suggested that Americans recognized that both Clintons were human beings with their flaws but also worthy of something better than what they had gotten from their political opponents. Bill continued to attract big crowds wherever he went, and Hillary became the subject of a groundswell of support within the Democratic Party for a run at the U.S. Senate seat that retiring Daniel Patrick Moynihan was leaving open. The GOP was already considering New York City mayor Rudolph Giuliani, whose national profile and downstate popularity, rare for a Republican, gave him distinct appeal in a state where a certain level of star power was almost expected of candidates for statewide office.

On the day of the impeachment vote, Senator Robert Torricelli of New Jersey waited mere hours before he announced he would support the First Lady's candidacy for the Senate. "Hillary Clinton asked that she did not want to deal with the issue of her candidacy for United States Senate until after impeachment," said Torricelli. "That moment has now arrived."

On the same day, Bill Clinton had briefly joined a meeting between his wife and advisor Harold Ickes, who were discussing her prospects in New York. He shared what he knew about the state, including an accurate recollection of his vote totals in various counties. No debate was joined over whether she should entertain the ambition of becoming a senator. Although she had delayed them, her personal aspirations had always mattered, and she had done so well as a campaigner in the 1998 election that it was clear the president wasn't the only member of the family possessed of political skills and acumen. And though voters in other states might look askance at anyone who moved there to run for office, New Yorkers were not so provincial that a newcomer couldn't be accepted. Robert F. Kennedy moved to Glen Cove on Long Island in August 1964. Ten weeks later, he unseated incumbent senator Kenneth Keating.

Few would doubt that the First Lady could mount a credible effort to capture the state Democratic Party's nomination to run for Moynihan's spot. However, she would then have to carry both the benefits and the burdens of her husband's presidency into the race against her Republican opponent. This penalty came as part of the twofer arrangement that the Clintons had made when they made themselves into the model power couple of American politics. It meant that his personal failings, her response to them, and every policy failure in his administration could be used in negative advertisements and debates and fed into the rumor mill. The health care proposal Congress rejected? Surely that was her fault. His infidelity? It must have happened because she had failed as a wife.

Hillary Clinton would have to carry into the election her own record, her husband's record, and public opinion about a marriage that had become the subject of a massive federal investigation, decades of partisan ridicule, and raving-mad accusations from conspiracy theorists who found sizable audiences on the internet. With this history, it was hardly surprising that as Hillary Clinton merely considered running for office herself, at long last, the propagandists who had failed to defeat her husband turned their attention to her.

# 8

# Unstoppable

By the time she set her sights on Hillary Clinton, Peggy Noonan had created for herself a public persona that was a mix of modern assertiveness and gal-Friday deference to sexist convention. Modern Noonan cultivated an image of a glamorous woman who could thrive in the male-dominated world of the White House speechwriter, circa 1985. Deferential Noonan, a child of the 1950s, raised in a conservative Long Island suburb, retreated to the pronoun *he* when describing the speech-writer's craft—*her* craft—and confessed, when she was in her thirties, that she had wanted to be admired for her virtue. A child of the middle class who had set her sights high and diligently pursued success, she was quite like Hillary Clinton, but her politics and her old-fashioned ideas about men and women seemed to blind her to this fact.[1]

Noonan just knew that an American leader should look like Ronald Reagan, not Hillary Clinton, and should speak the kind of words she had written for him. During her White House days, she made sure to signal to the press that she was the woman behind the man and responsible for many of Reagan's memorable speeches, including his address at Normandy in 1984 and his remarks following the space shuttle *Challenger* disaster. After Reagan, Noonan wrote speeches for George H.W.

Bush, two memoirs, a book about language, and columns for *The Wall Street Journal*'s editorial page. That she detested Hillary Clinton was well established before she set out to prevent her from becoming a U.S. senator. That she would try with a weird little book that mixed heaps of fantasy with reportage and argument was a surprise.

At just 181 pages, *The Case Against Hillary Clinton* opened with seven and a half pages of make-believe about election night 2000, complete with six long passages about what Hillary Clinton was thinking as she offered a victory speech. According to Noonan, she was thinking, "This is my night. This time it's me in the lights. . . . Now I've won and I've beaten more than Rudy [Giuliani], I've beaten Bill. He got it and he blew it. Now I'll show him how it's done." A second imaginary scene, described in sixteen pages, depicted a gathering, just after the Columbine High School shooting tragedy, where two students killed thirteen people and then committed suicide. (Columbine would come to represent the moment school shootings became a national problem.)

Writing within months of the school shooting, Noonan was among the first to fictionalize the Columbine tragedy for political effect. In her fantasy, which included her attending with a tape recorder, Hillary Clinton gathered media moguls to criticize their products—especially those depicting "premarital sex" and "pornography"—and demand change. Noonan couldn't resist including some digs about the Hamptons estates and private jets of the liberal elite, and she even reported that Hillary criticized Jane Fonda for strident activism against the Vietnam War. For Noonan, who came of age in the 1960s, phenomena like the sexual revolution, the anti-war movement, and feminism remained sore points that could be soothed by fantasy Hillary's talk. The trouble was, it never happened, and the fact of it *not happening* formed the central attack Noonan made on Hillary's character. Voters should reject Hillary's candidacy because she wasn't the woman Noonan preferred her to be. Evoking Reagan, she declared Hillary was not "towering and generous but squat and grasping" and ultimately undeserving. (Gross as this criticism was, it was more delicate than polemicist Ann Coulter's evaluation of Hillary in the pages of the journal *Human Events,* where she called her "pond scum" and "white trash.")[2]

If Noonan's case was a brief and occasionally writerly effort intended to persuade, a voluminous work called *Hell to Pay: The Unfolding Story of Hillary Rodham Clinton* was a kitchen-sink screed that targeted the appetites of Clinton haters who couldn't get enough of the conspiracy theories and unsubstantiated charges that had already informed dozens of books. First-time author Barbara Olson had worked for the congressional Republicans who had investigated the firings at the White House travel office. Olson interpreted every element of that investigation, from the First Lady's consistency to her sentimentality or resolve, in the most negative terms. She wasn't loyal to facts but a nimble liar. She wasn't protective of her family; she was "a master manipulator" whose "hidden hands" guided everything her husband did.

An energetic and devoted partisan, Barbara Olson was a Washington lobbyist who lived in the center of the moneyed conservative movement that had come to prominence in the 1980s. She had helped the team that pushed Clarence Thomas's Supreme Court nomination through the U.S. Senate despite Anita Hill's allegations of sexual harassment. Olson also participated in moot court sessions conducted to aid the Paula Jones legal team. Her publisher, Regnery, got financial support from Richard Mellon Scaife. Olson was a regular on television talk shows, where she offered caustic commentary from a conservative perspective. The party organized to celebrate the publication of *Hell to Pay* was hosted at the twenty-two-acre Virginia horse country estate called Tulip Hill by Richard Carlson, whose son Tucker was on the verge of becoming a right-wing media star. Among the guests were Kenneth Starr, fresh off his pursuit of Bill Clinton and Monica Lewinsky, and Jeanne Theisman, a former Miss America contestant whose recent divorce from a pro football quarterback had received ample coverage in the local press.[3] Although the book-party crowd was filled with the mainstream conservative elite and *Hell to Pay* sounded all the right notes about Hillary's supposed sins—from socialism to mob ties—the book was generally ignored by serious journalists and critics. Those who did treat it with seriousness were likely motivated by a desire to show fairness to conservative partisans. For decades, Republicans had hectored the press over its alleged bias in favor of liberals and Democrats. As GOP chairman Rich

Bond admitted in 1992, this was largely a matter of "working the refs," which is what coaches do when they scream at the officials who over-see basketball games. A coach wants to make the refs self-conscious in the hope that they will go easy on his or her team. In politics, partisans complain in hopes that the press might indulge fringe arguments to demonstrate fairness. In the case of *Hell to Pay,* one of the few to offer serious attention was Andrea Ahles of Knight Ridder newspapers, who credited Olson's effort to examine Hillary's ambition but couldn't find anything original in the text. It was obviously intended "for those will-ing to hate the First Lady, anytime, anywhere," wrote Ahles.[4]

Hatred was the main selling point for the book, which, thanks to the alternative marketing network established to sell right-wing titles, climbed onto the bestseller list of *The New York Times* and stayed there for weeks. Regnery, which was fully part of the effort to discredit main-stream media, respected the *stature* of *The Times* enough to trade on it by adding a banner declaring *Hell to Pay* a "*New York Times* BESTSELLER!" to its cover. In the echo chamber of conservative media, Olson got boosts from the likes of Rush Limbaugh, and even before Hillary declared her candidacy, Olson's readers in upstate New York were sending letters to the editors of local papers, urging people to read it before considering. "Don't be fooled by the image of Hillary Clinton on the David Letter-man Show," wrote Charles H. Quick in the Binghamton *Press & Sun Bulletin.* "The facts are out there, documented for all to read."[5]

The documentation was scant and relied frequently on deeply flawed and biased sources, including pollster Dick Morris, a sampling of Reg-nery propagandists, and lots of material from Scaife-funded writers and publications. Olson added her own decorations, of course. In her hands, Hillary Clinton's work on the House Judiciary Committee investigation of Richard Nixon became a "jihad" and staff at the White House func-tioned as her "secret police." Vince Foster had been, in Olson's telling, "depressed by Hillary's lack of attention to him," and she had actually offered heartfelt appreciation for sexual services another woman had supposedly provided to her husband. Also, her angry response to her husband's infidelity had actually been a cynically manufactured display intended to cast the scandal as a matter of sexual betrayal and herself as a victim. How either of these facts could be true was not explained. Instead, readers who had, by this point in the book, waded through three hundred pages of similar argument were, apparently, expected to accept the assertions.[6]

In its recycling of anecdotes from convenient sources, including the Arkansas police officers who made a cottage industry out of their Clinton tales, Olson's work resembled mass market books about celebrities. Like Matt Drudge, she exploited the fact that in many ways politics was becoming entertainment, with Washington evolving into Hollywood on the Potomac. John F. Kennedy's youth and glamorous wife made him a celebrity-style president, but it was Ronald Reagan who joined the two realms in both cities, using his performance skills to advance his candidacies and policies. It helped that as an actor, Reagan had rarely been asked to express much more than his own sunny personality. Thus it was easy for voters to square political Reagan with actor Reagan. His presidency was noted for its style, which blended old Hollywood with the power elite to make the White House a paparazzo's dream setting.

After Reagan, Americans were more inclined to look for flashes of celebrity brio in politicians. George and Barbara Bush got a pass, due to the fact that they predated the Reagans in Washington and were firmly old-school. However, the Clintons were new to the national stage and young when compared with other First Couples. (Bill Clinton was the third-youngest president in history, and Hillary was the fourth-youngest First Lady.) Despite what detractors might say, they were a handsome couple, and press of all sorts, from *People* magazine to *The New York Times,* pressed the White House for access. For Hillary, meeting this demand required being photographed thousands of times. As a woman, she was required to reveal herself as First Lady, mother, wife, daughter, and more, *and* be beautiful without alienating anyone or appearing to put real effort into her appearance.

One of the first photographers to make a portrait of Clinton as First Lady was Deborah Feingold, whose cover photo for *Redbook* made Clinton seem like everyone's next-door neighbor. One of the last portraits was made for *New York* by Mary Ellen Mark, whose black-and-white photo, made in 2000, showed Hillary at a window overlooking a Manhattan street, looking over her shoulder at the camera with an expression of utter confidence.

Eight years had made Clinton into the woman she projected in that photo shoot, and she looked far more beautiful than she had on the cover of *Redbook*. Fame and beauty both confer power. However, they also come with predictable downsides, as anyone in the public eye knows. The supermarket tabloids that publish glamorous images of movie stars on the red carpet also traffic in "stars without makeup" features. For Hillary Clinton, celebrity prompted attacks on her for looking too good and for not looking good enough. Sometimes these conflicting ideas were raised by a single critic, in almost the same breath. In 1993, syndicated writer Debbie M. Price made fun of the First Lady's "Betty Crocker helmet" hair and a few paragraphs later in the same column wrote admiringly of her "metamorphosis" from an ugly duckling into a beautiful woman.[7]

In addition to the photo shoots, Clinton used carefully chosen media appearances to define her own political identity. As the 2000 election approached in New York, the trickiest element of her public profile was her marriage, which remained both an advantage—her husband possessed astounding political knowledge and instincts—and a burden. Months after the president escaped impeachment, she sat for a series of interviews with writer Lucinda Franks, who would produce the first cover story for editor Tina Brown's new *Talk* magazine. Both Franks and Brown were friendly to the Clintons, and Hillary used the interview to deal with the notion that she had not evidenced enough genuine emotion about her husband's betrayals. Some of what Clinton revealed, about feeling "a great relief" to be making her own decisions and how she yearned to be judged on her own merits, was routine. However, she also spoke in a way that made her appear more human and emotionally accessible. She said she was often asked to "talk about things no one else in politics does." And she said of her relationship with her husband, "There has been enormous pain, enormous anger, but I have been with him half my life, and he is a very, very good man."

The frustration, pain, and forgiveness Hillary Clinton expressed would have been familiar to many married people. Long relationships—by this point, the Clintons had been married almost twenty-five years—inevitably face periods of crisis. The difference for the Clintons was that their crisis was also a global political concern. Gone were the days when a president's sexual sins would be ignored or quietly noted and excused. Instead, Bill Clinton's abuses of power and his betrayals were turned into a constitutional showdown and a lasting torment for his wife. When she broke her silence, it was after she had decided to run for the Senate and faced the reality that she had to explain herself how and why she remained married. "I don't believe in denying things," she said, "I believe in working through it."

For the most part, Hillary's answers—"He's responsible for his own behavior"—were not controversial. A reader might argue with her choices, but her explanations were reasonable. Many would find her reference to the difference between "sins of weakness and sins of malice" a familiar bit of theology. However, she took a risky step further into candor when she offered her assessment of her husband's weaknesses and their cause. The president's mother, having published a memoir of her chaotic life that recalled how she and her own mother had fought over young Bill Clinton, had already revealed the abuse perpetrated on the family by her second husband. With Franks, Hillary evoked this experience and noted her husband had been "scarred." He had "become more aware of his past," she added, "and what was causing this behavior."[8]

No one with a passing acquaintance with psychology or a basic understanding of human development would find much to quibble with in Hillary Clinton's assessment of her husband. Few people raised in similar circumstances would rise to the heights he achieved without being morally distorted in the process. His wife's effort to understand him and help him understand himself was reasonable in every way, but sharing it with Lucinda Franks would give anyone who was willing to suspend fairness in order to be politically cruel an opportunity. Rupert Murdoch's *New York Post* published a news report saying, "Democrats and Republicans alike expressed shock that the first lady blabbed," but didn't name or quote one of them. (The paper also criticized her for posing as the victim of a cheating husband, as if this weren't true.) Two days later, a *Post* columnist declared the interview with Franks "boneheaded" and expressed the hope that it "will finally explode the myth of Hillary Clinton's brilliance." Others piled on. "His mother? His grandmother?" wrote Cokie and Steve Roberts. "They're the ones responsible for Bill Clinton's bad behavior? Please!" In *Observer,* Richard Brookhiser lashed her for being, at heart, "a mosh pit screamer" besotted with her rock star husband, and at *The Weekly Standard,* Christopher Caldwell declared that Hillary had managed to "scare the country out of its wits" by suggesting in the article that her husband was a sex addict. (In fact, she explicitly rejected the addiction idea, preferring the term "weakness.")[9]

The vitriol and distortions that greeted the First Lady's candid comments overwhelmed the substance of what she had said. And given *Talk* magazine's limited circulation, *the stories about the story* were more widely read than the original report. This outcome could have led Hillary to conclude that cooperating with Franks had been a big mistake. However, New York voters understood that the *Post* was unreliable and deeply partisan. At the same time, the critiques of Hillary from more highbrow sources dwelled so much on insider politics that they were irrelevant. Remarkably, the more she was criticized by unfair propagandists and pundits, the more her stock rose. This was the silver lining effect that sometimes redounds to those who are vilified too often and too long.

Hillary Clinton's stock actually rose by ten points in the independent Zogby poll in the weeks after the interview appeared. The pollster, John Zogby, suggested his findings reflected an ongoing conflict between the views of political experts and voters who were generally more supportive of both Clintons. "It could very well be that the pundits and the public have a different viewpoint on this," said Zogby, "just as they seemed to differ during all of 1998 on the president." He also noted that Clinton seemed to rise in the estimation of other women when she showed herself to be more open about her feelings. Overall, he saw in her decision to participate in the interviews a well-calculated choice, not a blunder.

If Zogby was right, the *Talk* article erased a lead held by the presumed GOP nominee, New York mayor Rudy Giuliani. The mayor's ambition for national office was well established, and Republicans across the state and around the country were urging him to run. However, he would spend many months wavering on the edge of a decision, trying to decide whether his image as a law-and-order tough guy would give upstate voters who resented New York City enough reason to get excited about his candidacy.

Giuliani's indecision was inconsistent with his public persona. Public Rudy had a pugnacious streak that led him to rush into conflicts when they existed and create them when they didn't. But when asked whether he would run for the Senate, Giuliani offered an answer that suggested he would be guided by the Democratic Party's selection of its candidate. He said he'd be more likely to become a candidate if Hillary Clinton were his opponent. Her presence would make the contest "the most focused-on race in the country." He would try to win by seeking Jewish votes with criticism of her support for a Palestinian state to be created as part of a peace plan in the Middle East.

The size of the Jewish electorate in New York made Israel an important topic in every election. The Middle East would also matter should the mayor ever run for president. Giuliani's advisors had begun looking for ways to move in the direction of the White House, and some believed that beating Hillary in a Senate contest would be a big step forward. A victory over some lesser opponent would evoke a "So what?" reaction, explained one Giuliani partisan, "but beating Hillary Clinton . . . that's a big deal."[10]

Giuliani's advantage in the race would be his deep experience in local politics, where, especially in New York City, ethnic and racial signaling were important factors. In addition to fishing for Jewish votes, Giuliani practiced a bit of race-baiting, which he had done previously as a vocal critic of the city's black leaders and a reliable defender of the city's police force. In many cases where the police were alleged to have used unnecessary force against black or Hispanic men, the mayor rushed to defend the officers. In three instances, his administration revealed sealed juvenile records to discredit criticism of the police after officers had shot young men. This practice of demonizing the victims of police violence was not unique to New York. However, Giuliani was especially consistent and visible in his use of the technique, and despite the thousands of police misconduct complaints made every year, few officers faced serious consequences. A complaint review board investigated only 42 percent of complaints, and only 5.2 percent were deemed substantiated. Almost a third of those findings were overruled by the police department. In the meantime, the number of complaints rose steadily.

In March 2000, Mayor Giuliani cited prior misdemeanors charges— not convictions—to smear Patrick Dorismond, who was killed by officers. The tragedy began when an undercover officer approached Dorismond on the street asking to buy drugs. As the two men exchanged blows, other police officers arrived, and one of them shot Dorismond dead. Amid the controversy that ensued, Giuliani repeatedly described Dorismond as a violent man. "He spent a good deal of his adult life punching people," said the mayor. In fact, Dorismond had just one prior simple assault charge—for punching another young man—on his record. However, the mayor's statement let New Yorkers know where he stood. A few weeks later, he underlined the politics of his position by calling Hillary Clinton an "Al Sharpton Democrat."[11]

A black preacher who was among the most outspoken and controversial leaders in the state, Sharpton had become the Dorismond family's most visible advisor in the days after Dorismond's death. In this role, he showed he had rebuilt his reputation from a low point he reached in 1988, when he became a vocal advocate for a teenager who alleged that a police officer and a prosecutor assaulted her. Tawana Brawley's charges proved to be false, and both she and Sharpton were widely ridiculed. In the years since, however, Sharpton had rebuilt his reputation. By the time Giuliani tried to use him as a weapon against Hillary Clinton, many political activists, including some Republicans, considered this a losing tactic. However, it was a bit of rhetoric that let Giuliani, who was regarded as a bigot by many black residents, signal where he stood.

Few missed Giuliani's meaning, least of all the many New Yorkers who had long since concluded that the mayor had permitted the city's police force to abuse black citizens almost at will. Giuliani had chosen to side with racist police officers in 1992, when ten thousand of them marched on city hall to protest Mayor David Dinkins's call for the creation of an independent board to review allegations of police misconduct. Giuliani, who had decided to run against Dinkins, went to the protest, seized a microphone, and proceeded to curse and lead the angry officers in chants and jeers. The word *nigger* filled the air (Dinkins was the city's first black mayor), and then a riot broke out. Bystanders were assaulted, city hall was occupied, and thousands of officers streamed onto the Brooklyn Bridge, closing traffic in both directions. In the aftermath, the dean of the city's journalists, Jimmy Breslin, reported that an officer said to him, "Now you got a nigger right inside City Hall. How do you like that? A nigger mayor." Breslin concluded, "We have a police force that is openly racist."[12]

Though controversial with many of the city's voters, Giuliani's rabid pro-police posture placed him squarely in the mainstream of the national Republican Party, which had emphasized so-called law-and-order issues since the civil unrest of the 1960s. As he prepared to run for the Senate, Giuliani tried to make himself appealing to conservatives in other ways. Once an ardent environmentalist who fought to protect the city's upstate reservoir, he announced that developers should be allowed to build in the watershed. Never one to wear religion on his sleeve, he suddenly wanted to put prayer back into public schools and post the Ten Commandments in classrooms. He then sought to paint Clinton as a radical who harbored "hostility toward America's religious traditions" and alleged that she had waged a "relentless 30-year war" against the nation's "religious heritage."[13]

No evidence supported the idea that Hillary Clinton had conducted a "30-year war" against religious heritage. Although she favored a Christianity of action over words, she had been open about her own Methodist faith and had shown a far greater familiarity with the Bible and Christian theology than many other politicians, including Giuliani. But like the "Al Sharpton Democrat" line, the crack about religious heritage was not a rational criticism but a quip intended to make her into a frightening *other* whom regular Americans should cast out like a witch. Later in the campaign, when an art exhibit featured a profane depiction of the Virgin Mary, Giuliani threatened to withdraw all city funds from the Brooklyn Museum, where it was installed. Courts had ruled against this kind of unilateral action on free speech grounds, and Giuliani would be barred from doing it. However, as Clinton pointed out the mayor's grandstanding folly and supported the museum, he used her stand on free speech to create a controversy and paint his opponent as radically anti-Catholic.

Anti-religion. Anti-police. Racially divisive. These were the smears Giuliani would apply to an opponent who was a lifelong (and active) Methodist with ties to every racial and ethnic group and a supporter of a historically tough federal anti-crime bill that had expanded the death penalty and lengthened sentences for convicted criminals. She was also committed to marriage in a way Giuliani was not. These facts wouldn't matter to a candidate intent on ginning up some issues, but for Giuliani to succeed by casting Clinton as radical, he would have to present himself as a credible conservative in every way. Here he ran up against a series of problems that made him a dismal alternative, including his own record as a desultory Catholic, press reports of an affair with a young city hall staffer, and ample evidence that his marriage to Donna Hanover—she was his second wife—was falling apart.

As the mayor attacked Hillary Clinton as an enemy of religion, the press reported that he was building a deep relationship with a woman named Judith Nathan, who was seen with him at New York restaurants and events around the state. Twice divorced, Nathan was a drug sales manager who was eleven years Giuliani's junior. As he carried on this affair, inviting her to join him on New Year's Eve and at St. Patrick's Day celebrations, Giuliani made little effort to spare his family embarrassment. At times, reporters were offered the lie that Nathan, a nurse, was a security officer. An offended Donna Hanover, in a move widely regarded as a jab at her husband, announced she would play the lead role in a new feminist play called The Vagina Monologues, which had been written by Eve Ensler, who was an outspoken Hillary Clinton supporter. (The Post announced the news with the headline GYNO-MITE!)[14]

Finally, as the Republican Party prepared for its nominating convention, Giuliani embarked on one of the most tumultuous four weeks in the history of city politics. He began with a press conference announcing he had been diagnosed with a treatable form of prostate cancer. Six days later, the *New York Post* published a picture of the mayor and Judith Nathan leaving a restaurant together. Next came an emotional press conference where Giuliani announced to reporters that he was separating from his wife. This came as a complete surprise to her and their children. Having learned of her husband's plans via the press, Hanover summoned reporters to say, in a wavering voice, that she had worked to repair the marriage "for several years," but the effort failed "because of his relationship with one staff member." As Hanover filed for divorce, the mayor retained a pit bull lawyer who smeared her in the press as a careerist who "doesn't care what happens to the children" and was "howling like a stuck pig."[15]

In the middle of his bizarre month, the funeral of New York's Catholic archbishop, Cardinal John O'Connor, provided a startling visual of Giuliani's own shortcomings. Inside St. Patrick's Cathedral, where mourners who had come from around the world filled the pews, Bill and Hillary Clinton sat together in a group that included George and Laura Bush, Al and Tipper Gore, and New York governor George Pataki and his wife, Libby. Seated behind the president and next to the governor, both of whom towered over him, Giuliani appeared so forlorn that the press actually reported on his lonely appearance. He looked as if his own mother, who was alive and well, had suddenly died.

In fact, Giuliani was suffering from the sudden collapse of his own reputation, which left him in no position to continue attacking Clinton. (For her part, Clinton had busily raised money and conducted a "listening tour" that would take her to every county in the state and blunt critics who said she was an aloof carpetbagger.) The mayor's strange month culminated in his decision to drop out of the Senate contest and claim that the reason was his health. At the time, the five-year survival rate for men with prostate cancer was almost 100 percent, and many men lived for decades after the initial diagnosis. Treatment rarely sidelined patients for more than a month, and many top executives and politicians had undergone treatment while remaining on the job. However, the diagnosis gave Giuliani cover for withdrawal, and he used it. In a dramatic appearance, he explained that with a cancer diagnosis, "you confront your limits, you confront your mortality; you realize you are not a Superman and you are just a human being."

The opening Giuliani created was filled immediately by a forty-two-year-old congressman from Long Island named Rick Lazio. Regarded as a political moderate and a milquetoast campaigner, Lazio had a nice-guy image that made him appealing to his constituents but had made him obscure to most voters in a state where only larger-than-life personalities attracted consistent press attention. He tried to correct this when he went on a radio program hosted by rising right-wing media star Sean Hannity to say Clinton's "character is an issue." Next, a Lazio fund-raising letter sent to New Yorkers said the Clintons had "embarrassed our country and disgraced their powerful posts." It sought to depict her as an alien creature who "covets power and control and thinks she should be dictating how other people run their lives." It also asked, "How on earth does Hillary Rodham Clinton expect to truly represent people like you?" When the letter became public, a somewhat chagrined Lazio announced that he had not, in fact, written it. "I'm not disavowing it," he said, "but they're not written by me." A week later, one of his aides bashed Hillary with classic sexist stereotypes, including the claim that she was "calculating" and "scheming" and "annoying."[16]

The buttons Lazio and his campaign pushed were wired to the old critiques, voiced first in Arkansas in the 1970s, that described Hillary Clinton as alien to mainstream America. He may have been a bit embarrassed at being caught, but whoever wrote the letter knew what he or she was doing. Clinton's campaign had already discovered that after years of being depicted as unfeminine, overly ambitious, and ruthless, this was how many people saw her. Voter interviews, conducted by the campaign and later revealed by writer Michael Tomasky in his book *Hillary's Turn*, revealed often-contradictory judgments that coalesced around themes that male candidates rarely had to address with much sophistication. One interview subject applied to Clinton six different descriptors—*gutsy, smart, strong, cutthroat, calculating, evasive*—without any recognition that the first three positive qualities were contradicted by the following three negative ones. "She smart, savvy, cold, pushy," said another woman.

Many faulted her for not showing enough emotion, especially when her husband had betrayed her. One said:

> *I couldn't imagine what she's gone through, and I feel for her. But if she's not going to ask for it, show us that she's sad, then why should I give it to her? It's almost like I'm angry at her for that. . . . I admire people who can be strong, but people who can be strong can also be emotional.*

The interviews showed that many women applied a challenging standard to Clinton. It wouldn't be enough for Hillary to be capable and committed to the policies they preferred. She also had to display her emotions in a way these women found familiar. This would require "showing a weakness to us," explained one, who added that if she did, "we're going to look at her as a woman, as a wife, and as a woman."[17]

Surely the critiques involved some sort of gender penalty. Volumes of research had shown that women in politics were subject to both hostile reactions and benevolent rejection from those who feel men are better suited to public office. In part, these views were a matter of persistent norms. For the first 128 years of its existence, the U.S. Congress had not seated a single woman. Jeannette Rankin, elected by the state of Montana, broke the barrier in the House in 1916. Eighty-two years later, during the election of 2000, fewer than 13 percent of the House were female. Things were worse in the Senate. Hattie Caraway of Arkansas was elected in 1932 and reelected once in 1938. The high point for women in the upper chamber—nine out of one hundred—would be reached in 1997. With this history, it was easy to understand why some Americans imagined their leaders to be male and felt there might be something wrong with a woman who aspired to power.

Over the years, the idea that there was something wrong with Hillary was offered in political cartoons that depicted her as deviant and dangerous. Political cartoonists generally distill popular sentiments in ways that, while crude, nevertheless reflect something widely felt. When University of Indianapolis professor Charlotte Templin analyzed more than four hundred cartoons about Hillary Clinton, she recognized that nearly half leaned on the "Hillary's taking charge" theme exploited by the BITCH merchandiser L. Jean Lewis. Variously a puppeteer, a self-promoter, and a Queen of Hearts bully, in these drawings, she was ever the power directing the president. Emasculation was another popular trope, with cartoonists showing Bill Clinton in a dress or his wife rejecting his sexual advances in favor of books and reports. (In one of these, the title of her book, *The Lorena Bobbitt Story,* referenced the famous case of a woman who literally cut off her husband's penis.) Finally, Templin saw a category of cartoons that relied on the Alexandre Dumas axiom *cherchez la femme* (look for the woman) to blame Hillary for every problem. A classic in this genre showed two workers upset about layoffs and pay cuts. "So, we're angry at corporations?" asked one. "No," replied the other, "Hillary Clinton."[18]

The caricatures drawn by the cartoonists—castrating, domineering, malevolent—aligned perfectly with the opinions women voters offered to Hillary Clinton's campaign consultants. As Charlotte Templin observed, cartoonists may like to provoke, but they "also share fundamental biases with the societies they critique." In Hillary's case, the idea was that she was "not doing gender right," and this unsettled many people. However, the women who were surveyed and found it so easy to find fault with her were also willing to reconsider. Told about a campaign advertisement that would show Hillary saying she didn't regret that she had made enemies in the health insurance industry, nearly every one said she would respond favorably. "That's a strong person," said one. "This is her," said another.

In the end, the same cautious streak that made it difficult for Hillary Clinton to show her feelings led her to refrain from advertisements that confronted the issue of her image head-on. Instead, she continued to crisscross the state—two dozen visits to Buffalo alone—to shake every outstretched hand at every rally. During this retail politicking, many voters greeted Clinton as an admired celebrity, not a carpetbagger, and her persistence turned her into a familiar presence. Often overlooked by journalists and her opponents was the fact that after all of her husband's scandals and despite efforts to demonize and diminish her, Hillary Clinton was enormously popular. In Gallup's annual poll, she had been named the country's most admired woman for six of the previous eight years. (In the other two, she finished second to Mother Teresa of Calcutta, whose ultimate canonization would mean that at the time she was, in fact, a living saint of the Catholic Church.) In New York State, ten thousand people had called her U.S. Senate campaign offering to volunteer.[19]

Of course, public admiration didn't exempt Clinton from normal political skirmishes, and in these the other side would get the chance to challenge her policy positions and, perhaps more importantly, try to define her as a human being. Rick Lazio tried to paint her as a Washington insider, but as a member of Congress, he was one too. He was a bit more successful when he used Hillary's warm meeting with Suha Arafat, wife of Palestinian leader Yasser Arafat, to suggest she was insufficiently supportive of Israel. Then Clinton countered with a photo of Lazio shaking hands with Arafat himself. The picture showed Lazio grinning and grasping Arafat's shoulder as he shook his hand.

The press didn't fare much better than Lazio as it sought gaps in Hillary's armor, but then came the first televised candidates' debate, which was conducted by Tim Russert, Buffalo's native son turned national TV newsman. As host of the Sunday political talk show *Meet the Press,* Russert had refined the practice of finding video recordings of a guest's prior statements, which he then played to support a tough question about a current concern. At the debate, he showed a pro-Lazio TV commercial, which used clever editing to put him and outgoing senator Daniel Patrick Moynihan, a Democrat, together in the same place when they were not. The ad was not run by Lazio's official campaign, and he easily parried the question that followed. Hillary, on the other hand, was hit by video from the TV interview where she looked distraught and exhausted as she spoke of of the "vast right-wing conspiracy" and said that the allegations against her husband were not true. In the wake of the impeachment trial, Russert said, "Do you regret misleading the American people?"

The question did not surprise Clinton. Having never taken part in a candidates' debate, let alone one that would be televised, she had poured herself into preparation. She was expecting to be asked to accept greater responsibility for the crisis created by the Lewinsky scandal. What she did not expect was to be shown a video clip of one of the most trying moments of her life. Clearly rattled, she paused and looked away from Russert and the cameras. She didn't look back at him until she was well into a meandering answer that began with squishy generalizations—obviously she was seeking her bearings—but then became more direct and more specific. "Obviously, I didn't mislead anyone," she eventually said. "I didn't know the truth. And there's a great deal of pain associated with that, and my husband has certainly acknowledged that and made it clear that he did mislead the country as well as his family."

It was the kind of answer that any wife who had defended an unfaithful husband might give to friends after she found out she had been made to play the fool, and surely many women empathized with her experience. When he got the chance to speak, Lazio, not sensing how Clinton's answer might play outside the studio, tried to blame his opponent for her efforts to help her husband. "Blaming others every time you have responsibility?" he asked mockingly. "Unfortunately, that's become a pattern, I think, for my opponent. And it's something that I reject and I believe that New Yorkers reject. We can do well better."

The line sounded as if it had been devised during Lazio's own pre-debate preparations. What he did near the end of the debate certainly was plotted in advance. When the subject of campaign financing was raised and Clinton spoke, he nervously reached to his inside coat pocket, pulled his hand away, smiled knowingly, and then, when he was speaking, reached in again to pull out a piece of paper. He announced that it was an agreement to ban outside spending in the election and challenged Clinton to sign it. When she hesitated, he crossed the stage holding out the paper. As she backed up from him, he began jabbing his finger at her and saying:

> *"Right here, sign it right now!"*
>
> *"Well—well, we'll shake—we'll shake on this," said Clinton.*
>
> *"No, no, I want your signature. Because I think that everybody wants to see you signing something that you said you were for. I'm for it. I haven't done it. You've been violating it. Why don't you stand up and*

*do something—do something important for America? While America is*
*looking at New York, why don't you show some leadership because it goes*
*to trust and character."*

A unique moment in the history of televised debates in New York, Lazio's gambit was followed by the candidates' closing remarks and would be the moment everyone remembered. A *New York Times* report on voter reactions offered a tepid headline: LAZIO AND HILLARY CLINTON CLASH ON DONATIONS, TAXES AND TRUST. Both city tabloids declared Lazio the winner. (The *Daily News* went with a bold front-page headline IN HER FACE under a photo showing him walking toward Clinton with his finger pointed.)

The news media's first impressions came as the papers rushed to print and were likely based on the drama witnessed by reporters in the room and the post-debate spin offered by partisans. In those moments, much was said about how Lazio had himself plunged into the crowd of reporters gathered moments after the debate to declare himself the winner. Clinton had retreated from view, leaving the boasting to her advisors and campaign staff, which likely contributed to the notion that if anyone had prevailed, it was her opponent.

In the light of the following day, cooler heads had the chance to note that quick surveys of ordinary voters had yielded a much different analysis. In their eyes, Clinton had done much better than Lazio. One of her best moments had come in response to Russert's video display and question about her husband's scandal. Despite her inclination to keep her private life private, Hillary had talked about her own pain and how she "didn't know the truth" when she'd defended her husband. With this choice, she had faced a problem understood by every prominent woman. A man who shows restraint in the face of personal pain earns respect. A woman who does the same can be deemed icy and unnatural. But a woman who goes too far in the other direction risks being criticized for posing as a hysterical victim. In this case, Hillary struck just the right balance as she acknowledged the betrayal and its effect, but kept her poise.

Two days after Buffalo, *New York Times* columnist Gail Collins observed that Lazio had turned himself from a clean-cut, wholesome figure into "Darth Vader with dimples" by "invading her space." At the *Daily News,* columnist Lars-Erik Nelson noted that while Clinton had talked about what she would do for the state, Lazio had devoted himself to "telling us what a bad person Hillary Rodham Clinton is" and "blaming a wronged wife for being humiliated by her husband."[20]

Nelson was correct. Polls had already shown that about 45 percent of voters had decided, before the debate, that they didn't like Hillary Clinton. Lazio didn't need to do anything to win their support. An equal number had already decided they would vote for her. Among the rest of the voters were very few who would be persuaded by a stunt like Lazio's "Sign it right now!" Lazio was stuck in a trap that captured many Republicans outside regions where they had guaranteed majorities. In New York, no one could win a statewide race without appealing to moderates, but moderates were turned off by the kind of red-meat rhetoric that would get loyalists to leave their homes and cast their ballots come Election Day.

After the debate, Lazio's supporters doubled their bets on misogyny with a TV ad that used the children's board game Operation to suggest Hillary was a castrating woman. New York Republican Party chairman Bill Powers sent out a fund-raising letter imploring donors to write checks to "stop this ambitious, ruthless, scheming, calculating, manipulating woman." A new outside group calling itself the Emergency Committee to Stop Hillary Rodham Clinton raised more than $1 million to run additional TV ads against her.[21]

The attacks didn't work. Clinton maintained her lead in the polls all the way to Election Day, when Lazio failed even to capture all the votes of New Yorkers who had started off with a negative impression of Hillary Clinton. Her 55–43 percent win was decisive. Lazio kept all the votes of those who said they disliked Clinton but won very few more. Exit surveys found that minority voters and women who worked were Clinton's most enthusiastic supporters. She got 90 percent of the black vote and half the votes of white women. The only group she lost, by a narrow margin, was white men.[22]

Clinton took Lazio's concession call and proceeded directly to the hall at the Grand Hyatt Hotel, where her supporters were awaiting the

results. As Lazio finished thanking his own supporters and Rudy Giuliani embraced him on the stage of a ballroom across town, Clinton
appeared at her victory party wearing the same outfit—an aqua-blue
suit—that she had worn at the Buffalo debate. For the first time in
her life, an election-night celebration was about her achievement and
not her husband's. She stood center stage, a few steps in front of Senators Chuck Schumer and Daniel Patrick Moynihan, whom she would
replace; her daughter, Chelsea; and her husband, the president of the
United States. With the crowd chanting her name, she walked to her
right and touched Chelsea to get her attention in the sea of noise. As
Schumer stepped to the podium, the senator-elect's husband sidled over
to her and put a hand on her shoulder. In introducing her, Schumer
stumbled over the choice between "First Lady" and "senator-elect" and
then finally decided to call her "Hillary."

True to tradition, Hillary kept her speech short and vague, pledging
to "work my heart out for the next six years" and thanking everyone
she could name, including, at the end of her remarks, her daughter and
her husband. At the end of the speech, as the dignitaries assembled in a
row to raise their clasped hands, Hillary carefully placed herself between
her daughter and Senator Schumer. Positioned there, she would not be
overshadowed by her husband. His immediate future would require
adjusting to the life of a *former* president. He would turn to writing,
building a presidential library in Little Rock, and developing his charitable foundation. Hillary, having emerged from his shadow, would be the
most famous member of the United States Senate and one of a handful
of political figures known to the entire country. She was likely the only
newcomer to the Senate who would leave a 2000 victory rally to meet
with reporters and hear, almost immediately, a question that put a political target on her back:

"Are you going to go for the White House next time?"

"No," she replied, "I'm going to serve my six years as the junior
senator from New York."[23]

# 9

# Overcoming

Although she had overcome decades of mockery, innuendo, and conspiracy theories that blamed her for all sorts of crimes, including murder, Hillary Clinton's victory in the Senate election could not erase all that had come before. Reduced to a stereotype by those who couldn't tolerate the rise of women in any realm and vilified by opportunists in politics and the mass media, she had been held to impossible and conflicting standards that were decorated with vicious insults. Anyone subject to this kind of treatment would have felt both abused and angry. Certainly many in her camp would note the way she had been treated and marvel at her equanimity. If she was angry, she didn't show it.

Having chosen to maintain her marriage to one of two presidents who had ever been impeached (but not convicted), she would forever carry the special burden and benefits of this relationship. Would she have reached the Senate without the Clinton name?

Consider the talent and intelligence Hillary Clinton had shown before she ever met Bill Clinton. Her Wellesley commencement speech and acceptance at Yale Law School had made her more remarkable than him. Now add the resilience she exhibited during the long effort to assassinate her character. Millions of dollars had been poured into this effort by Richard Mellon Scaife and others, and thousands of hours had been devoted to it by the likes of David Bossie and Floyd Brown. Would this unprecedented hostility have been directed against Hillary Rodham if she had developed her own political career unrelated to a husband? None of the five women elected to the Senate in 1992 had been vilified in this way, so it would be fair to conclude that she had been as much hurt as helped by her marriage.

In the future, personal attacks of the sort suffered by the Clintons would become commoner, and polarization would increase as Americans, driven in part by the rise of extreme media such as Fox News, became more hardened in their partisan attitudes. Party affiliation would become a more powerful factor in a typical citizen's identity, with more people embracing us-versus-them sentiments that left little room for compromise and cooperation. By 2016, divisions were so great that more than half of Americans said they hoped their children would marry within their political party.[1]

For Hillary Clinton, who was both a national figure and a newcomer to the Senate, the changing dynamic meant that as she tried to learn the ways of the Senate, like every other incoming freshman, she would also be subject to an extraordinary and growing level of ill will. Among the ten other new senators who took the oath of office in 2001 were half a dozen former members of the House and a governor, but none came with the baggage of a spouse who was leaving the Oval Office. Indeed, for almost three weeks Hillary Clinton was both a senator and First Lady. The dual roles highlighted her status as a trailblazer but added to the irritation felt by those who had decided they hated her and her husband. She wasn't helped by the fact that as he left office, her husband pardoned billionaire tax felon Marc Rich, whose wife had made big donations to her Senate campaign. An act former president Jimmy Carter termed "disgraceful," the pardon prompted a rebuke from the editorial board of The New York Times, which called it an "outrageous abuse" of power.

In the Senate, Clinton fashioned herself an eager student (for her, a most comfortable role) and made anyone who was willing into a mentor. Soon enough, Republicans like Senator James Inhofe of Oklahoma and Democrat curmudgeons, including Robert Byrd of West Virginia, were calling her a friend. Senator Sam Brownback of Kansas asked her to forgive him for having hated her. Many senators had met her when she was First Lady, but in those days they were more interested in her husband's attention than hers. As a colleague, she possessed one of just one hundred votes in the chamber and was powerful in her own right.

Clinton's celebrity, magnified by the Secret Service agents who accompanied her everywhere, was a burden in a body where every member considered attention—from the press, voters, donors, and others—essential to survival. Paradoxically, many in this exclusive club were themselves taken with her celebrity. (When ninety-eight-year-old Strom Thurmond greeted her after her swearing in, he almost couldn't stop hugging and kissing her.) Hillary compensated by deferring to senior senators whenever possible and undertaking lots of boring but essential work on unglamorous issues like unemployment compensation, funding for firehouses, and legislation to help local police departments beef up their anti-terrorism capabilities. This last item was an extension of her response to the attacks of September 11, 2001, which occurred less than ten months after she assumed her duties as junior senator from New York.[2]

In New York City, jetliners hijacked by Al Queda terrorists crashed into the twin towers of the World Trade Center, causing them to collapse. More than 2,700 people died in New York. Separate hijackings resulted in a crash at the Pentagon, which killed 184, and the crash of a jet in rural Pennsylvania, which claimed 40 victims. (In all three cases the hijackers also died.) Hillary Clinton was on the scene in Lower Manhattan the day after the attack and offered encouragement to firefighters and rescue workers. As the recovery continued and Bush administration officials declared the site safe for workers, Clinton called attention to the hazardous conditions caused by the ash, chemicals, pulverized glass, and asbestos that blanketed the area around the collapsed towers. In the aftermath, she became a steadfast advocate for the New York firefighters, whose union had backed Rick Lazio, and she stayed in touch with victims who had survived. In the Senate, she pushed legislation that created medical testing programs for workers and residents exposed to the contaminants. She also supported Bush's plan to respond by invading Iraq (a decision she came to regret).[3]

The September 11 attacks were followed by a cooling period in national politics. Both Clintons addressed the 2004 Democratic National Convention, but the gathering would be remembered most for Barack Obama's debut as a national figure. Then a state senator from Illinois seeking a vacant U.S. Senate seat, he issued a rousing call for unity that included two lines that would be repeated in the press across the country: "There is not a liberal America and a conservative America— there is the United States of America. There is not a black America and a white America and Latino America and Asian America—there's the United States of America." This theme appealed to voters who were weary of partisan rancor. Coming from a young politician whose limited background gave him the advantage of a slender record to attack, it contrasted with older and better-known politicians like Hillary Clinton, who bore scars acquired over decades of debate and criticism.

Away from Capitol Hill, the campaign to assassinate her character was renewed by a young right-wing Christian lawyer who refashioned old tales of Clinton evil into a new attack that imagined that "liberalism dovetails with misogyny" and joined Hillary to a series of old accusations made against her husband. In a passage written, it seems, without much self-awareness or understanding of the difference between correlation and causation, author Candice E. Jackson allowed that both the Right and the Left failed to see what she alone had divined.

Born into a family of conservative Christian entertainers, Jackson was a recent graduate of Pepperdine University's law school, where Kenneth Starr became dean in 2004. As an undergraduate, she had transferred from community college to Stanford, where she wrote for a student paper funded by libertarian activist and billionaire Peter Thiel. One of her articles described supposed antiwhite bias in programs benefiting minority students, and another argued that women needn't organize to pursue equal treatment, because they already enjoyed equal opportunity. In the time between leaving Stanford and publishing her book, Jackson coauthored a sweeping criticism of federal criminal laws, and criticized the prosecutions of bond fraud by Michael Milken and insider trading by Martha Stewart under laws that penalized what they called "non-violent, nonpredatory behavior." The writers noted that Milken was pursued by the U.S. attorney in Manhattan, Rudy Giuliani, and Stewart by James Comey. "Instead of being reviled for his malicious prosecution of Stewart," complained the writers, "Comey recently was promoted to deputy U.S. attorney general, the second-highest post at the Justice Department."[4]

Jackson's book-length attempt to damn Hillary Clinton with her husband's sins was titled *Their Lives: The Women Targeted by the Clinton Machine* and was organized around the stories of seven women who had been sexually involved, or allegedly involved, with Bill Clinton. For readers who didn't catch on to the fact that the title referenced the former president's memoir, the publisher added a banner to the cover that read, "The Missing Chapters from Bill Clinton's *My Life*." The book's most pointed argument about Hillary targeted her loyalty to her husband. However, this criticism, which could have been made in a brief essay, was overwhelmed by hundreds of pages that created cartoons of the people in the text in service to a tormented political argument. It was issued by a fringe publisher whose other big title of 2005 was a picture book called *Help! Mom! There Are Liberals Under My Bed.*

*Their Lives* put Candice E. Jackson onto a path to more anti-Clinton activism and brief infamy for public statements about how "90 percent" of sexual assault complaints made on college campuses are lodged by women who regretted consensual sex. However, the book did not generate much interest, even in the right-wing political book market, where it was swamped by a gleefully salacious and catty work of alleged nonfiction by a writer whose career trajectory had taken him from the top spot at the *New York Times* Sunday magazine to gossip columnist for a Sunday newspaper insert called *Parade* to four books about the Kennedy family. With *The Truth About Hillary Clinton,* Edward Klein completed his descent into what conservative critic Kathleen Parker called "prurient tabloiding."[5]

In the run-up to its release, Klein's book got a promotional boost from longtime Clinton antagonist Richard Mellon Scaife, who funded a website devoted to promoting the book. It was featured on Newsmax

.com, which Scaife started with Christopher Ruddy of the Arkansas Project and by Regnery's Conservative Book Club. A Republican Party internet site, GOPUSA.com, sent half a million emails encouraging people to buy it, and the publisher, a division of Penguin devoted to right-wing opinion, announced that "publishing insiders say the book and its revelations could destroy her bid to run for the presidency in 2008." The catalog copy written to entice orders from booksellers said the book could hurt Hillary the way the so-called Swift Boat Veterans for Truth had harmed 2004 presidential candidate John Kerry. A combat hero who commanded a small attack boat in Vietnam, Kerry was smeared by false allegations of misconduct developed and disseminated with the aid of Republican donors and a consultant, Merrie Spaeth, who had previously worked for President Reagan and as a volunteer for Kenneth Starr during his pursuit of the Clintons as special prosecutor.[6]

Although the term *swiftboating* had become a pejorative, Klein's audience would be the readers who occupied the alternative universe of right-wing media outlets, where the service of a combat veteran like Kerry, who had been awarded a Silver Star for gallantry in action, could be turned against him. Alerted to the juicy gossip it contained, these readers ordered enough copies in advance to send *The Truth About Hillary Clinton* to the number-two spot on *The Times'* bestseller list. However, as negative reviews piled one upon another, sales declined. The scathing reactions came from left, right, and center. Conservative John Podhoretz wrote, "Thirty pages into it, I wanted to take a shower. Sixty pages into it, I wanted to be decontaminated. And 200 pages into it, I wanted someone to drive stakes through my eyes so I wouldn't have to suffer through another word." Peggy Noonan, who was herself part of the attack-Hillary squad, pronounced it "poorly written, poorly thought, poorly sourced." The sources for Klein's juiciest bits generally spoke on condition of anonymity, and those who would be quoted by name tended to be people with little or no connection to the subject. Worse were the straining efforts to infer, for example, that Hillary was a lesbian, a lousy mother (no "mothering instincts"), and a generally bitter woman. Klein wrote that though the supposedly lesbian Hillary suffered from "sexual frigidity," she had also carried on an affair with

Vince Foster. Chelsea had been conceived, according to the book, when Bill Clinton raped Hillary.[7]

Much of what Klein delivered to the scandal-hungry masses depended on his imagination to supply details he could not have known. Although he never spoke to Monica Lewinsky, he was able to report her "eyes filled with tears" when she attended an event where the president was present and that she was afraid to "defy" the First Lady. He relied on a conservative political operative as a source of Hillary calling her husband a "miserable cocksucker" and simply stated that she had herself appointed people to federal offices when she never possessed the power to do so. Klein was so negligent when it came to facts that he assigned White House jobs to people who never worked there and named one of Hillary's classmates at Wellesley as her lover even though the woman was the long-married mother of three and had publicly refuted the story.[8] Worse than Klein's abuse of the journalistic conventions of fact-checking, honest sourcing, and thorough reporting was his anachronistic view of humanity. He made so many negative comments about gays and lesbians—these words appear fifty times in his text—that the bigotry and prurience were distracting. Born in 1937, Klein came of age in an era when his prejudice would have been widely shared, but anyone who had been even moderately well informed about human rights progress would have known that sneering references to gays and lesbians advertised a writer's ignorance and moral limitations. By 2005, polls showed more Americans were accepting of homosexual relationships than rejecting of them. California had laws protecting legal rights of same-sex partners, and both Vermont and Massachusetts permitted same-sex marriages. As Klein attempted to use Hillary's friendships and collegial relationships with gay women as a smear, he was little different from those who used race to divide people long after the practice became shameful. The bigotry that had always been wrong became so unacceptable that only the most prejudiced or tone-deaf people continued to express it. Betraying more of his own sexual preoccupation, he even called Clinton advisor Susan Thomases a "dominatrix."

In Klein's case, the cringeworthy awfulness included his habit of describing women he didn't like in the most negative and sexist terms.

Thus he was the only observer ever to claim Hillary Clinton was a remarkably violent youngster whose adult nickname was "the Big Girl." He wrote that she was "homely . . . squat and lumpy from the waist down, with wide hips and thick calves and ankles." As a young woman, Klein reported, Clinton had neglected "personal grooming" and "dressed badly so that she would not have to compete with more attractive women in a contest she could not possibly win." She dressed in "spinster lady fashion." Klein somehow determined that Monica Lewinsky felt "conspicuous" due to weight gain and noted that a woman Hillary invited to dinner sported a "butch cut" hairstyle. White House staffer Evelyn Lieberman was "short, a little overweight, with grayish hair . . . prissy."[9]

Men whom Klein detested were not treated with the same consistent cruelty, although he did render Harold Ickes as a "seedy-looking man." As Klein otherwise spared one less-than-handsome man after another, it became obvious that he had a problem with women, especially those who dared to express themselves in any assertive way. Powerful women have always been subject to this and other double standards. No one examines a man's ankles to determine his worth or criticizes him for lacking fatherly instincts. However, a woman in the public eye can be denigrated for her appearance if she seems too powerfully intelligent or for her supposed lack of smarts if she's powerfully beautiful.

*The Truth About Hillary* was crafted to fuel the hatred of Hillary Clinton, which had been inflamed first in Arkansas by the likes of TV interviewer Jack Hill, who found it suspicious that she didn't have children, didn't use her husband's name, and dared to pursue her own career. More than twenty-five years later, Klein stimulated the outrage in his audience by focusing on her way of being a human being, which was somehow wrong, because she did it in a way that was different from what they preferred. On the plus side, Klein's book did provide an occasion for some of the more memorable reviews published in 2005. Humorist Joe Queenan noted that Klein's failures included falling short of the truly execrable prose that would have made it more amusing. "Klein has written a very bad book," noted Queenan, "but not anywhere near as bad a book as some of us would have liked—what could the author have done to ensure his enshrinement in the pantheon of the despicable? Personally, I would have preferred fewer footnotes like 'interview with a member of the Clintons' personal White House staff, who wished to remain anonymous' and more citations reading, 'Interview with friend who wished to remain anonymous for fear that Hillary Clinton's lesbian friends would hire commie gangsters associated with mobbed-up trade unions to whack her.'" In *The New Republic,* writer Keelin McDonell quoted one of Klein's strangest paragraphs at length to note its all-around offensiveness. The passage finds college classmates describing how she looked playing sports—the commentary covered many aspects of her physique to offer readers "smut, pure and simple."[10]

The smut was supplied in the service of a higher purpose—namely, the destruction of Clinton's political future. This job would require a qualified and competent Republican to run against her, and this was where the anti-Hillary movement fell apart. Although the published and broadcast attacks found audiences numbering in the millions across the country, New York voters, especially those in its larger cities, were not generally receptive to this propaganda, and the political environment required candidates to be both clever and skilled.

The early GOP front-runner, former Westchester County prosecutor Jeanine F. Pirro, was a relative moderate with wide name recognition and some charisma. (In 1997, *People* magazine included her in its annual "50 Most Beautiful People" feature.) As she announced her candidacy, Pirro noted that Hillary Clinton was likely to be distracted from work as a senator by a run for president and was treating New York State as "a doormat to the White House." It was a snappy quip, but it was overshadowed by Pirro's struggle to deliver her announcement speech. The tenth page of her text was somehow missing from the papers she brought to the podium, and when she discovered it was missing she spent thirty seconds looking for it before asking an aide, "Could I have page 10?"[11]

In addition to the missing page of her speech, Pirro was burdened by her husband's public record, which included fathering a child out of wedlock when they were married and a felony conviction for tax evasion. Her campaign spokesperson refused to say whether Pirro would turn down contributions from people with criminal pasts, which is common practice, and analysts talked about how Pirro was such a long shot that she must also be positioning herself for some future post, either in politics or as a host on Fox News. Abysmal fund-raising efforts (her campaign actually sent Hillary Clinton a plea for money) brought her just $400,000 in the first stage of a campaign that was expected to cost ten times that amount. Her bumbling on the stump sent the state GOP into such a panic that leaders began calling for her to withdraw. When she finally did withdraw, Pirro left the field to the former mayor of Yonkers John Spencer. Clinton won reelection with 67 percent of the vote, which put her even with Moynihan at the height of his popularity. Her victory was so complete that it included majorities in big cities from New York to Buffalo and in rural regions like Saint Lawrence and Franklin Counties. This broad success would be credited to her diligent work on behalf of rural voters and the value of repeatedly visiting every corner of the state. She was, to them, not the cartoon of a feminist/elitist drawn by her critics but a hardworking woman who showed in her loyalty to them, and her family, that she was not so different from people like themselves.

Clinton also won, at least in part, *because* New Yorkers understood she was likely to run for president and, Jeanine Pirro notwithstanding, they didn't mind the idea at all. Most well-informed New Yorkers understood that Clinton had been aiming for the presidency for a very long time. George W. Bush had made the idea easier to imagine by showing that Americans were not completely resistant to political family dynasties. At the same time, he had drained much of the country's enthusiasm for Republican presidents, opening the door for a Democrat. The conditions explained a glutted field of potential candidates, including previous nominees Al Gore and John Kerry as well as Senators Joe Biden of Delaware and John Edwards of North Carolina. Young and formidable as a speaker and fund-raiser, Edwards would eventually commit political suicide via sex scandal. (It would first be revealed by the *National Enquirer*, which would eventually function as an organ of the Donald Trump presidential campaign.) Some of the others were burdened with previous failed attempts that made them less appealing when compared with Hillary Clinton, whose celebrity and gender could work to her advantage. However, these factors also posed some peril.

As every well-known figure understands, intense examination by the press can magnify existing flaws and reveal or even create new ones. Also, as a former First Lady and the first woman with a good chance of becoming president, Hillary would have to confront the politics of gender in all its forms. For some, she would be too strong in her commitment to feminist ideals. Others would consider her too weak. She would be judged too cold or too emotional, too concerned about appearance or too frumpy. No man would have to deal with these concerns, in addition to all the usual political issues. Clinton could have expected to benefit at least a little from the fact that she would be the first person with minority status to make such a powerful bid, except for the blinding star power of Barack Obama.

Having burst onto the national political scene with his famous speech at the 2004 Democratic Party convention, Obama had been the subject of intense speculation ever since. Little interested in the role of vice president and disinclined, at first, to seek the Oval Office, he spent the better part of two years insisting he wasn't going to run for any higher office. He considered Hillary Clinton his role model for functioning as a senator while a celebrity, but he was not comfortable with the slow pace of life inside the world's most exclusive club. By the start of 2006, he had ordered that his schedule include trips to key places where he could assess his support and test out themes for a presidential campaign. He soon got encouragement from other Democratic senators who thought Hillary Clinton's vote authorizing the war in Iraq was a handicap. (This was one of those rare occasions when she was fairly critiqued for something she actually did.) In late October, Obama told *Meet the Press* host Tim Russert he was no longer set against running.

Obama's top advisor, David Axelrod, believed the country was readier for Obama than it was for another Clinton. Yes, the Bush family had opened the door for modern presidential dynasties, but he believed the second President Bush, whose Iraq War was launched on false claims about weapons of mass destruction and that country's links to terrorism, had soured voters on well-known leaders. Voters wanted a bigger change than Clinton represented, and, Axelrod believed, any effort she made to fit herself to the times would open her to charges of opportunism. All politicians are opportunists, but those with long records brought their previously established positions to every new contest. Add the wounds inflicted by the Clinton-hating media industry and Clinton was a less formidable favorite than national polls suggested. In September 2006, she led a fictional Democratic field while Rudy Giuliani and Senator John McCain of Arizona topped the Republicans. But then a survey released by CNN on November 1 showed she had actually lost support since September. Most of the defectors seemed to have been captured by Obama, who wasn't even on the previous poll but was suddenly in second place.[12]

Obama saw his candidacy as the pursuit of a personal ambition and an opportunity to prove something about America. If the country elected a black man with his name—Barack Hussein Obama—it would show the world that the promise of America was real and alter the way "millions of kids—black kids, Hispanic kids" looked at themselves. The senator stole the march on Clinton by announcing he would form an official "exploratory" committee days before she revealed "I'm in. And I'm in to win" in an email message to supporters. Weeks later, when he shifted from exploring to actually running, he did so before an estimated ten thousand people gathered before the old state capitol building in Springfield, Illinois, where Abraham Lincoln had begun his political career. On a cloudless but frigid Saturday, he electrified the home-state crowd with the cadences of a preacher and a message of generational change. The waves of cheers suggested the historical tide that seemed to be lifting him toward the presidency. Clinton, on the other hand, seemed like a candidate whose long and sincere preparation had drained her campaign of the easy excitement that attended Obama's events.[13]

Although huge crowds turned out to see Obama as he visited Iowa, New Hampshire, and other states that would play key roles in selecting the 2008 nominee, Hillary Clinton remained the front-runner. On paper, she was more qualified than Obama, and her connections to the donors and operatives who could support a campaign were more extensive. Like a football team protecting a fourth-quarter lead, her campaign seemed to adopt a just-don't-fumble strategy. The problem with this attitude is that it looks very much like the team with the lead feels entitled to a victory. Caution drains spontaneity, and moves that should come naturally suddenly become difficult. In an early dispatch from the campaign trail, Mark Leibovich of *The New York Times* noted Clinton's effort to present the country with "Mrs. Clinton—Version 08, Nurturing Warrior, Presidential Candidate Model." Leibovich couldn't resist the easy tropes used against many assertive women. He wrote that Clinton spoke in the "high, insistent pitch of a fed-up mom" and that she sometimes worried "aloud about gaining weight."

Clinton called herself "the most famous person you don't really know" and then labored to reassure people that she was not the caricature drawn by her many critics. She had been the target of so many attacks from conspiracy theorists, polemicists, and hype artists that her actual flaws—she could be stubborn, suspicious, overly calculating, and brusque—were almost charming in comparison with their claims. The negative hype seemed to establish a ceiling on her popularity, as Clinton never hit the 50 percent mark in preprimary polls. In the meantime, the number of people who had a firmly negative opinion about her rarely receded from the 42 percent figure reported in June 2007.[14]

Women were more receptive to her, but Clinton's gender did not guarantee her a huge advantage because, unlike African-American voters, they did not vote as a bloc. As journalist Melinda Henneberger discovered after the 2004 election, women voters had become deeply ambivalent about Hillary Clinton. Not one of the many women she interviewed said that Clinton was "the right one" to break the presidential gender barrier. "I like Hillary, but I'm afraid she'd be the only one who could keep the Democrats from winning," said one typical supporter. "She'd draw so many people out to vote against her that wouldn't come out otherwise." Another voter told Henneberger, "What turns me off about Hillary is I don't feel the realness from her."[15]

Again and again, Henneberger heard women say that something about Hillary Clinton made them unsure. She seemed competent and strong, but not authentic. In some cases, the critique seemed to suggest that she wasn't performing well *as a woman,* because she didn't display the right kind or level of emotion. Reserve was interpreted as coldness. A laugh became a cackle. Too warm and she was insincere. Too tough and she was a bitch. All of this was known to Clinton and those around her, which meant they often struggled to calibrate her tone in addition to her positions on issues, which also presented her with problems. The key example was her 2002 vote in support of the Iraq War. By 2007, most Americans had come to regret the invasion as a product of lies presented as "intelligence." Many other senators who cast the same vote had announced they were wrong to do so, but Clinton prevaricated by suggesting the vote wasn't exactly for the authorization of a war. This was the claim of a too-proud politician, not a human being, and coming from one who had already been painted as untrustworthy, it was a significant mistake.[16]

Obama's campaign seized on Clinton's evasion and, with seven words, offered in a campaign ad, made it into an effective weapon. "She will say anything," intoned the announcer on the commercial, "and change nothing."

"Say anything" was unfair, although Clinton would have fared better if she had said the vote was wrong and just taken her lumps. "Change nothing" was ridiculous. Just as Obama's election would change how millions of black and Hispanic kids might view America and themselves, Clinton's election would inspire millions of women and girls with the similarly new vision of an American president. However, as a real estate market collapse began the Great Recession, Americans turned more decisively against President Bush—his approval rating dropped below 30 percent—and the political establishment, which included Hillary Clinton. Team Obama correctly recognized that the country didn't want a little change; it wanted a major shift. Blessed with charisma and a once-in-a-generation gift for oratory, he presented Americans with a chance to repudiate centuries of racism and join a movement. By the January 3, 2008, Iowa caucuses, when the Democratic Party began choosing its candidate, Clinton was on the defensive. Obama defeated her, and the Democratic Party began the process of actually choosing its candidate.

When Obama prevailed in Iowa, a state with almost no black residents, he showed he could win almost anywhere, and Clinton was widely regarded as finished. Once 20 percentage points, her lead over

Obama in New Hampshire had been receding for weeks. Then, days after Iowa, pollsters found he had caught her and then raced past her. On the day before the primary, RealClearPolitics.com reported that Obama was preferred by New Hampshire Democrats by a margin of 38 to 30 percent. For the Clinton team, the situation was reminiscent of 1992, when polls showed Bill Clinton suffered a similar rapid decline after a losing effort in the Iowa caucuses. He embarked on a frenzied effort highlighted by frequent recitations of a stump speech, which Hillary Clinton called "the Fight Like Hell" speech. He also accepted a local politician's advice to stop giving press conferences and "go to the mall and shake hands." The effort worked as Clinton halved his deficit, finished second to a senator from neighboring Massachusetts, and reestablished himself as a viable contender.[17]

In 2008, Hillary was determined to replicate the effort that won her husband the nickname "the Comeback Kid." She drank beer with reporters, raced to New York to appear on *Late Show with David Letterman,* and visited every corner of New Hampshire to give her own version of a comeback speech. As she matched her husband's effort in 1992, she also had to put up with a kind of negative response that never plagued him. At one event in Nashua, she was heckled by young men shouting a sexist "Iron my shirt!" and at a debate in Manchester, she was peppered with questions about her personality. Was she courageous? Was she tough? Was she likable? The likability issue was raised by a moderator who cited a University of New Hampshire study that found voters believed she had the most experience of the candidates and would be more likely to win a general election. He wanted to know what she would tell those "who see a résumé and like it but are hesitating on the likability issue, where they seem to like Barack Obama more."

Clinton smiled broadly and joked, "Well, that hurts my feelings!" She paused as some in the audience laughed and applauded. She then added, "But I'll try to go on." With a glance toward Obama, she said, "He's very likable. I agree with that. I don't think I'm that bad."

"You're likable enough, Hillary," replied Obama.

"Thank you so much," she then said. "I appreciate that." Then she steered the talk back to the business at hand: the election of a president.

If Obama didn't know it in the moment, he learned soon enough that the patronizing "likable enough" quip, offered in a snide tone, was a self-inflicted wound similar to the injury Rick Lazio suffered when he chose to leave his debate lectern and demand Clinton sign a letter of agreement on campaign financing back in the 2000 election. In these instances, Clinton's gender actually worked in her favor, as many voters, but most especially women, heard condescension in Obama's remark.

On the day before the election, she gave a talk and took questions at a breakfast/lunch spot called Café Espresso, which is squeezed between a paint store and a copy shop in the coastal city of Portsmouth. There a sixty-four-year-old woman named Marianne Pernold, who had immigrated to America as a nine-year-old, decided to ask a question. Pernold had attended an Obama rally a week earlier and was favorably impressed. She wanted to support Hillary, but like many American women, her feelings about her were mixed. As she would later explain, she wanted to "know her as a woman." With this in mind, she asked what she might ask of a friend.

"How do you do it?"

When laughter greeted the question, she reframed it.

"How do you keep upbeat, and so wonderful?"

Clinton, dressed in a royal-blue jacket and holding a microphone with both hands, started to speak, saying, "I think," but then stopped to consider the question with more care. In the silence, a woman seated nearby broke the tension by saying, "Who does your hair?" The candidate smiled and said, "Luckily, on special days, I do have help. If you look at some of the websites and listen to the commentators, you'll see they manage to find me on the days when I didn't have help."

Clinton then turned toward Pernold and confessed, "It's not easy. It's not easy. I couldn't do it if I didn't just passionately believe it was the right thing to do. I have so many opportunities from this country, and I just don't want to see us fall backwards." With her eyes filling up and her voice catching in her throat, Clinton managed to say the word *no* and then stopped and shook her head. After a bit of applause gave her a moment to compose herself, she added that her candidacy was "personal, for me, not just political, and it's not just public. I see what's

happening. It's about our country, it's about our kids' futures, it's really about all of us together."

The Q&A at Café Espresso allowed Clinton to show she was not the stilted and inauthentic creature her critics described. Decades of microscopic inspection and critique had caused her to be guarded and defensive, but she was still a human being. However, the long effort to brand her as, to put it bluntly, a cold bitch had worked to such an extent that TV reporters who had attended the kaffeeklatsch rushed to broadcast her exchange with Marianne Pernold as if evidence of Hillary Clinton's humanity were urgent news. Within hours, the story was beamed to the entire nation on TV news channels and online, and opposing candidates tried to flip the script.

In Laconia, near New Hampshire's Lake Winnipesaukee, candidate John Edwards invoked one side of the she's-too-soft/she's-too-tough double standard to suggest that Clinton needed to learn how to fight like a man. "I think what we need in a commander in chief is strength and resolve," said Edwards. "Presidential campaigns are tough business, but being president of the United States is also a very tough business. And the president of the United States is faced with very, very difficult challenges every single day and difficult judgments every single day. What I know is that I'm prepared for that." (Within weeks, as reporters chased the story of a mistress's pregnancy, Edwards would withdraw from the race.) In the Obama camp, spokesman David Axelrod posed as a detached observer to paint a picture of Clinton as a manipulator, without taking responsibility for the thought. "People all over this country are watching this moment, and a fair number of them will say she was doing it for the cameras."[18] No one can know what had been in Clinton's heart and mind, but when voters were asked about her interaction with the women at the café, they told the press that it seemed like a spontaneous and sincere exchange. When they went to the polls, they gave her a victory of nearly 3 percentage points, which represented a swing of nearly 10 percent in about a week's time. In a field with three big-name competitors and several lesser ones, this was a significant win, which Clinton followed with more disciplined efforts at traditional re-

tail politics. In state after state, she shook thousands of hands, made speech after speech, and solicited donations and endorsements.

Prior to the Pennsylvania primary, Clinton visited the Pittsburgh *Tribune-Review,* a newspaper owned by Richard Mellon Scaife, the financier of the bizarre Arkansas Project and other propaganda efforts that blamed the Clintons for an endless number of crimes that were never prosecuted. When afflicted with Clinton paranoia, Scaife had warned that Bill Clinton could "order people done away with at his will. He's got the entire federal government behind him." However, in recent years, after being introduced to the president, Scaife had developed such a respect for him that he had made substantial donations to the Clinton Foundation, which did charitable work around the world. After attending the session with Clinton, Scaife decided the paper would endorse her in the primary. The editorial he published noted she was far more experienced in government—as an engaged First Lady to a governor and a president, as a second-term senator in her own right. "She has a real voting record on key issues. Agree with her or not, you at least know where she stands instead of being forced to wonder."

The strange-bedfellows endorsement was based, in part, on Hillary Clinton's willingness to meet with an antagonist (Mellon said she showed "courage") and in part on the fact that her positions on key issues were more moderate than Obama's. She won in Pennsylvania, which kept her essentially tied with him in the count of delegates who would make the final selection at the party's convention. But with a superior online effort and Americans intrigued by the promise of a more radical shift, Obama surged in the final primaries and won the nomination. His victory represented an epochal change as remarkable as any that could have been imagined in 2006. It defied the early expectations of Democrats, many of whom considered Clinton a sure thing, and of Republicans, who had spent years gearing up to battle her in a general election.

With Clinton in mind, a right-wing organization called Citizens United set to work turning decades of lies and distortions about her into a ninety-minute video called *Hillary: The Movie.* Citizens United was run by longtime anti-Clinton operative David Bossie. The former partner of the man who created the racist Willie Horton ad of 1988, Bossie had begun his anti-Clinton crusade hounding friends and family of a woman whose suicide supposedly had something to do with then governor Bill Clinton. Although the George H. W. Bush campaign called this episode "despicable" and "filthy," Bossie had later been hired by Representative Dan Burton to chase down allegations about the Clintons. Burton, who had fathered a child with a mistress and called Bill Clinton a "scumbag," had famously shot a watermelon in his backyard to demonstrate something about Vince Foster's death. Under his sponsorship, Bossie ran amok to such a degree—he even doctored audiotape evidence—that Speaker of the House Newt Gingrich, hardly a friend of the Clintons, demanded Bossie leave the committee staff. Bossie complied but didn't suffer for lack of employment. He joined Citizens United, wrote loony books about Al Gore and John Kerry, and then took up the Hillary Clinton video project.

Bossie's main trick involved devising flimsy accusations against Democrats and feeding them to reporters who were either credulous or willing to ignore the usual standards to get an attention-grabbing story broadcast or published. This practice was first noticed in 1994 by the *Columbia Journalism Review*, which noted that Bossie's claims were often presented without reference to the fact that they came from a partisan organization that spent $2 million per year trying to bring down the Clintons. "Of course, journalists get leads and documents from all kinds of sources, savory and otherwise," wrote author Trudy Lieberman. "Then the good journalist goes on to corroborate, amplify, and analyze the facts, and judge whether Fact A really does connect to Fact B. Those elements were missing from most of the pieces we examined." Instead, the material Bossie distributed was augmented with vague references to the Clintons' character and "scandalous odors" attributed to no source in particular.[19]

Fourteen years after Bossie was revealed to be an unreliable and ruthless partisan, the recycled propaganda that was *Hillary: The Movie* ran into trouble with the Federal Election Commission, which restricted its distribution and advertisement. The FEC acted under the provisions of the McCain-Feingold Act. Devised to address potential influence-buying by deep-pocketed contributors, the act regulated political campaign donations and spending. Bossie's film, which was essentially a ninety-minute anti–Hillary Clinton political advertisement, violated the law. Over the long term, Bossie would work with star lawyer Theodore B. Olson, whose deceased wife had authored one of the early book-length works of anti-Hillary propaganda—*Hell to Pay*—to challenge the McCain-Feingold law. With an annual budget in the millions, Bossie's organization, Citizens United, was ready for a long, expensive battle.[20]

If Bossie's intent as a film producer had been to stop the Democrats from seizing the White House, he targeted the wrong candidate. As Obama won the Democratic Party nomination, the Clintons pledged their support, making sure there would be no family squabble at the convention. Then, in a speech that was perhaps the best address she had given to date, she warned of the dangers posed by world adversaries like Vladimir Putin and by domestic problems represented by "jobs lost, houses gone, falling wages, rising prices. The Supreme Court in a right-wing headlock and our government in partisan gridlock."

Clinton campaigned for Obama through the fall, and with his general election victory she became the immediate front-runner for the post of secretary of state. Her main obstacle appeared to be her husband's record, which included his avid pursuit of donations for the Clinton Foundation, which netted tens of millions of dollars from autocratic rulers of Arab oil states as well as corporations and powerful individuals. The money provided health care, education, disaster relief, and economic development assistance. However, many of the donors would have business with the State Department, which could pose conflict of interest concerns for Secretary Clinton. The issue was raised in her confirmation hearing but did not delay the Senate's approval, which came on a 94–2 vote the day after Obama was sworn in.

As in the past, the secretary of state's top priorities would include America's relationship with Russia, which was filled with tension. Under the leadership of Vladimir Putin, Russia had sought to rebuild its military and extend its influence, often in conflict with American interests. Although term limits had forced Putin to give way to President Dmitry

Medvedev in 2008, he had simultaneously assumed a coequal status as prime minister and was generally regarded as the most powerful figure in Russia. A veteran of the Cold War intelligence service, Putin spoke and acted like a man who wanted to restore the superpower status of the old Soviet regime under the new Russian flag. He viewed the United States as a military, economic, and moral threat and recoiled at the advance of liberal Western cultural norms, especially equality for homosexuals.

Putin gained power by offering ordinary Russians a mix of machismo, orthodox Christianity, and superpatriotic nationalism. (Photos of a buff, shirtless Putin became staples in his propaganda campaign.) His opponents would be harassed and intimidated by government agencies and murderous thugs. When American businessman Bill Browder called world attention to corruption in Moscow, his lawyer, Sergei Magnitsky, was arrested and brought to a prison where he died after four years of brutal treatment. Browder had the resources to publicize Magnitsky's death and lobbied Western governments until they imposed sanctions as a response. (The U.S. law that cracked down on Russia was named for Magnitsky.) In general, the violent and suspicious deaths of most journalists and politicians who criticized Putin were not so widely reported. However, an outcry did accompany the murder of Alexander Litvinenko after he was poisoned in London by agents sent from Russia.[21]

American support for independence movements in the former Soviet republics of Georgia, Ukraine, and Kyrgyzstan had put pressure on Putin. He also saw ominous portents in Barack Obama's support for the so-called Arab Spring protests and in U.S. actions in the Russian client state of Libya, which ended with dictator Muammar Gaddafi's death at hands of American-backed militiamen. In the third year of Hillary Clinton's tenure at the State Department, mass protests arose in dozens of Russian cities as voters suspected that his United Russia party—mocked as the Party of Crooks and Thieves—had achieved a fraudulent victory in parliamentary elections. Independent observers had reported ballot stuffing, manipulation of voter lists, and hacking of election observers' websites.[22]

Clinton was already on record as a critic of Russian meddling in Ukraine's election, when a pro-Putin candidate relied on American consultant Paul Manafort's tactics to smear his opponent, whom he eventually put in prison. Days after the Russian election debacle, Clinton used a visit to Lithuania to call attention to the signs of fraud in the Russian election. "The Russian people, like people everywhere, deserve the right to have their voices heard and their votes counted," she said. "And that means they deserve fair, free, transparent elections and leaders who are accountable to them." She called for a "full investigation of electoral fraud and manipulation." In the audience at the event was Russian foreign minister Sergey Lavrov, who days later attended a meeting convened by Putin, where he blamed Hillary Clinton for the protests.

"She set the tone for certain actors inside the country; she gave the signal," Putin told Russian officials gathered around a huge conference room table. "They heard this signal and, with the support of the U.S. State Department, started actively doing their work." Putin alleged that hundreds of millions of dollars had been secretly supplied to protest organizers by Americans who sought financial gain through political disruption. "We are all grown-ups here," added the cynical Putin. "We all understand the organizers are acting according to a well-known scenario and in their own mercenary political interests."[23]

As an autocrat who had long labored to bend Russians' reality to his purpose, Putin was so well versed in the methods of manipulating people on a mass scale—through misinformation campaigns and covert action—that he might have found it hard to believe there *wasn't* a hidden hand involved. Some Russians may have drawn inspiration from what they knew of the American revolutionary period or the values of the Declaration of Independence, but Putin could offer no evidence to support the idea that the United States had aided the organization or actions of the protesters. Nevertheless, Hillary Clinton would serve as a convenient focus for Putin's anger, which she inflamed as she continued to call into question the election results. With her backing, Congress would approve the Magnitsky Act, which would punish many of Putin's rich friends by barring them from the United States and restricting their access to global banking systems.[24]

For Putin, who tended to believe that events were orchestrated by a scheming elite and not a matter of historical forces, the postelection protests and Magnitsky Act sanctions represented personal offenses. The person most responsible was the woman whom some in the Kremlin called "a lady with balls." It was a term of both derision and admiration, as Clinton had shown herself to be a tough diplomatic player. Putin saw little difference between his own persona and the nation, and he viewed Clinton as an enemy to himself personally and to the Russian state. To be sure, Putin resented President Obama, who frequently contrasted the Russian and American political models, but Clinton spoke more forcefully, and as a woman she presented an affront to his ego.

As a man who arranged for himself to be photographed and filmed riding horses shirtless and performing athletic feats, Putin had defined himself in cartoonish, macho terms. Any challenge made by a woman was sure to register as not just opposition but an existential threat to a masculine identity that was so fragile that its maintenance required constant publicity and admiration. Conveniently, America was full of fragile, mediocre men with whom he could find common cause in hating Hillary Rodham Clinton. And while plenty of women had learned to hate her, too, these men would make all the difference.[25]

# 10

# We Create Our Own Reality

D id you know that Hillary Clinton is the Antichrist?
During the campaign that put him in Congress, Republican
Ryan Zinke said she was, in fact, the evil figure of Bible prophecy who
would appear to deceive the world before the battle of Armageddon and
second coming of Jesus. "We need to focus on the real enemy," Zinke
told a crowd in Montana, and that meant Clinton, whom he called the
"anti-Christ."[1]

Zinke was a bit more flamboyant than most Republicans in Congress. A retired army vet who handed out bullets to supporters, he lik-
ened the federal government to corrupt regimes in Afghanistan and Iraq.
However, his ideas were not far from the GOP mainstream. By 2014, the
party that had created the Environmental Protection Agency had come
to embrace conspiracy theories and paranoia about the bogeymen of
government. Senator Ted Cruz of Texas warned of a United Nations
scheme to "abolish" golf courses and paved roads. Representative Jody
Hice of Georgia blamed "kicking God out of the public square" for
mass shootings and suggested that lunar eclipses could portend "world
changing, shaking type events."[2]

According to many in the GOP, one of the most earthshaking issues of the twenty-first century involved Hillary Clinton's response to an attack on an American government compound in the Mediterranean city of Benghazi, Libya. With more than one million people in its metropolitan area, Benghazi had lived uneasily under Muammar Gaddafi and was a center of the movement that led to his fall in 2011. (As President Obama ordered American forces to aid the rebellion, the United States earned wide appreciation.) A year later, as various factions fought for control of the country, more than one hundred fighters from an Islamist militia called Ansar al-Sharia descended on a U.S. State Department compound and, later, a Central Intelligence Agency facility. The firefights and mortar attacks killed the American ambassador to Libya, Christopher Stevens, foreign service officer Sean Smith, and two CIA guards.

The assaults were launched on the tenth anniversary of the September 11 attacks that had killed thousands in the United States and touched off the so-called war on terror. They also occurred just hours after officials at the U.S. embassy in Cairo condemned an inflammatory anti-Muslim video—*Innocence of Muslims*—produced by American-based right-wing Christian extremists. Media outlets friendly to former strongman ruler Hosni Mubarak, who was awaiting trial on murder and corruption charges, had inflamed public outrage, which had led to mass protests around the Muslim world, including one at the American embassy in Cairo. Taking place after the ambassador condemned *Innocence of Muslims,* the Cairo protest saw the wall surrounding the embassy breached and the American flag hauled down and replaced with an Islamist banner.[3]

Occurring without injury, the incident at the Cairo embassy was hardly noteworthy compared with what happened at Benghazi, where Islamists capitalized on outrage over the film and attacked with a ferocity that overwhelmed security officers. The two diplomats were killed, but CIA contractors arrived to evacuate others under fire. These events transpired from around 9:40 p.m. to 11:30 p.m. A second attack at 5:15 a.m. left two of the security contractors dead before friendly Libyan forces finally arrived at 6:00 a.m. and provided the remaining Americans safe passage to the airport, where they were flown out of the country.[4]

Journalists who later investigated the attacks found that two days before the assaults militia leaders had told diplomats that Benghazi was becoming unsafe. (Earlier in the year, locals had twice tossed a type of small explosive device used by fishermen to stun their prey into the diplomatic compound.) However, in the same meeting, they had also expressed gratitude for U.S. aid and asked for more American involvement in the city's recovery from the civil conflict. The CIA team for the U.S. facilities had not considered Ansar al-Sharia a threat and had not mentioned the group when they briefed Stevens on security on September 10. In August, Ambassador Stevens had signed a cable to Washington titled *The Guns of August,* which described a region where militias and opportunists carried out killings, kidnappings, and crime. However, a force of twenty well-armed CIA defenders housed nearby seemed sufficient for the State Department mission in Benghazi.

When the attack came, it was as if the chaos of the civil war had spilled into the compound and exploded. The original militiamen, who had apparently planned and started the assault, were joined by others angered by *Innocence of Muslims,* misled by false rumors of Americans killing a Libyan, or simply excited to join a fight. Given the number of men firing into the two facilities, the loss of life was remarkably small. Nevertheless, it was the worst loss of Americans at a U.S. mission in more than twenty years. (Several attacks on American civilians outside of government facilities had been deadlier.) And as soon as it occurred, Republicans sought to exploit it for partisan purposes.[5]

Breaking a pledge to suspend campaign attacks on the anniversary of 9/11, GOP presidential nominee Mitt Romney used the Benghazi assault to criticize the Obama administration. "It's disgraceful that the Obama administration's first response was not to condemn the attacks on our diplomatic missions but to sympathize with those who waged the attacks." Coming before the Americans who escaped had been evacuated, and prior to any announcement of casualties, Romney's statement was ill conceived, ill timed, and ill informed. It was, in its conception, the politicization of a murderous attack on Americans. The timing put Romney in the position of opposing the U.S. government even as diplomats were pursued by their attackers. The argument was based on a misunderstanding, if not a deliberate distortion, of the administration's

response. The expression of sympathy had been made by the ambassador in Cairo hours *before* the Benghazi attack. Also, Hillary Clinton had
condemned the attacks before Romney made his statement, sending
a dispatch to the Associated Press: "I condemn in the strongest terms
the attack on our mission in Benghazi today," Clinton said in a written
statement received by the AP at 10:08 p.m. "As we work to secure our
personnel and facilities, we have confirmed that one of our State Department officers was killed. We are heartbroken by this terrible loss."

Romney's second-day attempt at clarification was similarly flawed.
He said that the Cairo embassy "put out a statement after their grounds
had been breached. Protesters were inside the grounds. They reiterated
that statement after the breach." Again, the ambassador's statement was
issued *prior* to the protesters climbing over the wall. The part about the
reiteration was true, as far as it went. Romney failed to offer the full
story, which would have included the fact that the reiteration, expressed
in a brief social media tweet, was quickly withdrawn.[6]

Appearing at the White House with Hillary Clinton, President
Obama spoke first about the attacks a little before 11:00 a.m. on the
morning after they occurred. He condemned the killings, praised the
deceased, and said, "No acts of terror will ever shake the resolve of this
great nation, alter that character, or eclipse the light of the values that we
stand for. Today we mourn four more Americans who represent the very
best of the United States of America. We will not waver in our commitment to see that justice is done for this terrible act. And make no mistake,
justice will be done."[7]

For all the moral clarity it expressed, the administration did stumble
when it sent United Nations ambassador Susan Rice out to speak to
the press about the attacks days later. Typical of her remarks was the assessment she offered ABC News, which began with a caveat about the
early stages of the U.S. investigation and continued with her saying, "But
our current best assessment, based on the information that we have at
present, is that, in fact, what this began as, it was a spontaneous—not a
premeditated—response to what had transpired in Cairo." Rice spoke
after receiving so-called talking points that had been labored over for
days by a variety of agencies and finally approved by CIA director David

Petraeus. However, by the time they finished their work, it was quite clear that events in Cairo had nothing to do with the Benghazi attacks. Days afterward, Obama noted the offensive film but said, "Extremists and terrorists used this as an excuse to attack a variety of our embassies, including the consulate in Libya." Clinton and others in the administration would call it an act of terrorism, but others' claims that it was linked to Al Queda, which carried out the original 9/11 attacks, proved inaccurate; Ansar al-Sharia was sympathetic to Al Queda but not affiliated with it. As a militia, it was not labeled as a terrorist organization at the time of the Benghazi assaults, but it would be designated as one in 2014. In the same year, its leader would be captured by U.S. forces and brought to stand trial in Washington, where he would be convicted on terrorism charges and sentenced to a twenty-two-year prison term.[8]

Coming with two months left in the 2012 election campaign, the Benghazi attack gave Mitt Romney a chance to argue that Obama and Clinton had been negligent in their response to terrorism, even though Al Queda founder Osama bin Laden and many of his immediate subordinates had been killed or captured during the Obama presidency. Romney's claims were picked up by Fox News commentators and by Republican members of Congress, who believed that the administration, or rather, more specifically, Susan Rice, had purposely misrepresented events by stressing that they were related to the protest against *Innocence of Muslims,* which occurred in neighboring Egypt. A fair review of events would conclude that her statements reflected the fact that all the hands involved in preparing the memo that informed her had produced a flawed report that she'd echoed in interviews. Corrections followed, but her statements would allow partisans to complain for years to come.

In the meantime, reviews of the State Department's handling of security at the facilities in Benghazi raised legitimate questions. As the U.S. ambassador in Tripoli, Christopher Stevens had requested more guards for Benghazi, but none were supplied. But as with everything about this case, the facts were difficult to follow. Although many, including the president, called the State Department outpost in Benghazi a "consulate," it was, in fact, a temporary office and residence, with the CIA annex located one mile away. This status had placed the outpost in a kind of bureaucratic limbo outside the system that funded security upgrades. A government review of this problem would also reveal that "Embassy Tripoli did not demonstrate *strong and sustained advocacy* with Washington for increased security for Special Mission Benghazi" (emphasis added). And in fact, Ambassador Stevens's requests for greater security related primarily to the American facilities in the capital, not Benghazi.[9]

Stevens had believed he understood the dynamics of the competing militias that jockeyed for power in Libya. Most of the militia leaders considered him a friend and ally. However, Ahmed Abu Khattala of Ansar al-Sharia disagreed with those who were grateful for America's help in the fight against Gaddafi. Devoted to a more extreme religious ideology, he led a group of men who shared his anger about Western morals and blamed American political interference for the problems of the Muslim world. They were eager fighters who quickly gained access to the compound, ransacked the buildings, and lit the fire that killed Stevens and Smith. The nearby CIA contractors arrived too late to save them, and no U.S. military forces were close enough to help.[10]

In the weeks after the attacks, Mitt Romney and Republicans in Congress made what happened in Benghazi a frequent element of the campaign to defeat Obama at the polls. (This was, obviously, a repeat of the effort that was made to attack President Clinton through then First Lady Hillary.) As secretary of state, Hillary Clinton publicly accepted responsibility for security at the Benghazi compound even though decisions were made at levels of the bureaucracy far below hers. "I'm in charge of the state department's sixty-thousand-plus people all over the world [at] 275 posts," she said in one TV interview. "I don't think we want to get into any blame game. I think what we want to do is get to the bottom of what happened, figure out what we're going to do to protect people and prevent it from happening again, and then track down whoever did it and bring them to justice."[11]

Public opinion polls showed that Benghazi was not front of mind with voters, who were far more concerned with the economy, health care, and the federal budget. Those who did care about international relations, which was where Benghazi might fit as an issue, actually preferred Obama over Romney. The Republican candidate's team likely knew what voters were thinking before public polls revealed it. Romney stopped talking about Benghazi a couple of weeks before the voters cast their ballots, choosing to emphasize traditional GOP policies like tax cuts, raising the age of Social Security eligibility, and repealing regulations adopted by Congress after the Great Recession of 2007–2009. Others continued to talk about the attacks as if the administration had failed on a grand scale and was seeking to cover up embarrassing facts. Much of this talk occurred on right-wing radio programs and on Fox News and involved rumormongering and misrepresentations. A typical example was offered by former Speaker of the House of Representatives Newt Gingrich, one week before the election, on a program hosted by Greta Van Susteren.

A careful listener would have heard Gingrich preface his remarks with the fact that they were based on a rumor, shared with him by a lawmaker who had heard that two news organizations had obtained documents proving that the White House had ordered the military to ignore calls for aid on the night of the attacks. This made Gingrich's source as reliable as kids playing a game of telephone, but he went ahead anyway. "They were a group in real-time trying to mobilize marines and C-130s and the fighter aircraft, and they were told explicitly by the White House stand down and do nothing. This is not a terrorist action," said Gingrich. "If that is true, and I've been told this by a fairly reliable U.S. senator, if that is true and comes out, I think it raises enormous questions about the president's role, and Tom Donilon, the national security advisor's role, the secretary of defense Leon Panetta, who has taken it on his own shoulders, that he said don't go. And that is, I think, very dubious, given that the president said he had instructions they are supposed to do everything they could to secure American personnel."

No evidence ever arose to support Gingrich's claim, and the most reliable facts would not be reported until an FBI team led by Director Robert Mueller and a State Department accountability review board (ARB) completed their work. Without a scandal to divert them, voters considered Romney's GOP policy orthodoxy and rejected it in favor of giving Obama four more years in the White House. With his victory, Obama became the first candidate since Eisenhower to capture more than 51 percent of the vote for president, twice. The 2012 victory would mark the end of Obama's own pursuit of public office. Secretary Clinton was, in many eyes, the person most likely to represent the Democratic Party in the presidential race of 2016. House Republicans seemed to consider her the most formidable figure in the opposition party and someone they needed to take down. California congressman Kevin McCarthy, the third-most-powerful Republican leader, would eventually explain, "Everybody thought Hillary Clinton was unbeatable, right? But we put together a Benghazi special committee, a select committee. What are her numbers today? Her numbers are dropping."[12]

The "numbers" that bothered Republicans when they examined Hillary Clinton after the 2012 election included the results of public opinion polls that saw her popularity rising steadily ever since she became secretary of state. By the time of the 2012 election, more Americans held a favorable view of her than of President Obama. By the start of 2013, 67 percent of all Americans viewed her positively, and in February, she was judged to be the single most popular political figure in the country. Even among Republicans, Clinton enjoyed rather high support, as 37 percent said she was doing a good job and 32 percent said they held intensely negative views about her.[13]

When the ARB issued its report on Benghazi, it gave Clinton's critics some facts to work with. First, it confirmed that no local protests related to *Innocence of Muslims* had preceded the attack. Although it noted the State Department's security successes, it also described "systemic failures and leadership and management deficiencies at senior levels within two bureaus of the State Department (the 'Department') resulted in a Special Mission security posture that was inadequate for Benghazi and grossly inadequate to deal with the attack that took place." The mission was found to be too reliant on locals to reinforce American guards posted on assignments of such limited duration—forty days or less—that they were not as effective as they could have been. The ARB reported that Ambassador Stevens had not considered Benghazi to be especially unsafe and that his expertise caused Washington to give "unusual deference" to his opinion. Twenty incidents of violence or attempted violence involving diplomats had occurred in the six months prior to September 12, which, the board suggested, should have focused greater attention on the mission's security needs in all. One hundred people were interviewed by the ARB, which found "management deficiencies at senior levels within two bureaus" led to inadequate security at the U.S. facilities.[14]

According to the State Department's 2012 organizational chart, the bureaus responsible for the forces used to defend American outposts functioned four levels below the secretary's office. Although Clinton had assumed responsibility for their functions, this was a matter of management principle and not practicality. No one could make every key decision affecting the work of a global entity tasked with highly sensitive work in every imaginable setting. However, mature leaders accept the burden of tragedies that occur in their organizations because they are in charge of the management scheme. When the inevitable errors and unexpected events arise, the best response includes reviews like the report from the ARB. In political or legal settings, the reaction often also includes a battle for partisan advantage or compensation awarded in a courtroom.

In the case of Benghazi, which was a faraway place with a name that sounded strange to American ears, critics tried their best to make the name of the city synonymous with dereliction of duty and turned every element of the attacks and the aftermath into an indictment of Hillary Clinton. A useful example of this process arose when the release of the ARB report coincided with a health crisis for the secretary of state. Clinton had contracted a stomach virus and then, unsteady due to dehydration, fell and suffered a concussion. No mystery attended this development. Clinton's illness had been announced by officials prior to her fall, and the concussion was acknowledged by two different physicians.

As a sixty-five-year-old woman, Clinton was of an age when a stomach bug can be especially debilitating, so dehydration, light-headedness, and a fall that caused a concussion hardly constituted a shocking set of events. Add Clinton's workload, which would be enough to exhaust someone half her age, and it was surprising that she hadn't suffered a setback earlier. During her four years at the State Department, Clinton had logged more than two thousand hours of flight time during more than four hundred days of travel covering almost one million miles. In 2012 alone, when she was preparing to step down and hand the post to her successor, John Kerry, Clinton visited seventy-one countries.

Clinton's illness and injury came as the Senate Committee on Foreign Relations was preparing to conduct a hearing on the Benghazi attacks. Noting the timing, Fox News host Megyn Kelly speculated about it being an "excuse" Clinton might use to avoid testifying at a Senate hearing. The network's commentator John Bolton talked of a "diplomatic illness" that strikes those who "don't want to go to a meeting, or conference, or event." The issue was seized by another Fox talker, Andrea Tantaros, who decided Clinton was "being a professional victim," and the New York Post—which, like Fox, was owned by Rupert Murdoch—ran the headline HILLARY CLINTON'S HEAD FAKE. (The article mocked her with a quote about a malingering kid plucked from the poem "Sick" by Shel Silverstein.)[15]

The fake was so well conceived that after the Post slammed her for one of "the most transparent dodges in the history of diplomacy," Clinton's body joined in the conspiracy by forming a blood clot in a vein behind her ear, which was discovered in a post-concussion doctor's visit. Two days in the hospital, where she received medicine to dissolve the clot, ended the scare, but the paranoid response to Benghazi was only beginning. Two weeks after returning to work, Clinton appeared before the Senate Committee on Foreign Relations. Republicans on the committee pressed Clinton on the security deficiencies confirmed by the review board, and while Clinton accepted general responsibility, she explained that she never saw specific requests for more protection at the Benghazi sites and did not participate in the department's response to them. Republican senator James Risch questioned Clinton about Susan Rice's press statements. When he asked if Clinton had selected Rice to speak for the administration, she said she had not and agreed with his description of the events in Benghazi. "You are right, it was a terrorist attack," she said. "I called it an attack by heavily armed militants." Risch, a lawyer whose career in government included serving as governor of Idaho, seemed satisfied. "Well done," he said.

If Risch had acted as an experienced political leader who understood moments of crisis, Republican Ron Johnson revealed himself to be a more extreme partisan whose lifetime in the plastics industry had not prepared him for the very first office he ever held—U.S. senator—which he had captured by spending $9 million of his own money. At the hearing, Johnson returned to the question of initial reports on the attacks but was not satisfied with Clinton's answers. The result was the kind of back-and-forth rarely seen in the Senate:[16]

> JOHNSON: The point I am making is a very simple phone call to these individuals I think would have ascertained immediately that there was no protest prior to this. I mean, this attack started at 9:40 p.m. Benghazi time, and it was an assault. And I appreciate the fact that you called it an assault. But, I mean, I am going back to then ambassador Rice five days later going on the Sunday shows and what I would say purposefully misleading the American public.
>
> CLINTON: Well, Senator—yes.
>
> JOHNSON: Why was that not known? And again, I appreciate the fact of the transparency of this hearing, but why were we not transparent to that point in time?
>
> CLINTON: Well, first of all, Senator, I would say that once the assault happened and once we got our people rescued and out, our most immediate concern was, number one, taking care of their injuries. As I said, I still have a DS [diplomatic security] agent at Walter Reed seriously injured. Getting them into Frankfurt, Ramstein, to get taken care of, the FBI going over immediately to start talking to them. We did not think it was appropriate for us to talk to them before the FBI conducted their interviews . . .
>
> JOHNSON: But, Madam Secretary, do you disagree with me that a simple phone call to those evacuees to determine what happened would have ascertained immediately that there was no protest? I mean, that was a piece of information that could have been easily, easily obtained.
>
> CLINTON: Well, but, Senator, again—

JOHNSON: Within hours if not days.

CLINTON: Senator, you know, when you are in these positions, the last thing you want to do is interfere with any other process that is going on, number one.

JOHNSON: I realize that is a good excuse.

CLINTON: Number two—well, no, it is the fact. Number two, I would recommend highly you read both what the ARB said about it and the classified ARB because even today, there are questions being raised. Now, we have no doubt they were terrorists. They were militants. They attacked us. They killed our people. But what was going on and why they were doing what they were doing is still—

JOHNSON: No, no, no. Again, we were misled that there were supposedly protests and then something sprang out of that, and assaults sprang out of that. And that was easily ascertained that that was not the fact. And the American people could have known that within days, and they did not know that.

Coming after his crack about Clinton's "good excuse," Johnson's interruption, which began with "No, no, no. Again, we were misled" seemed to push the secretary of state past the limit of her patience. Her voice became louder, and she raised her hands to emphasize the point she was about to make.

CLINTON: And with all due respect, the fact is we had four dead Americans.

JOHNSON: I understand.

CLINTON: Was it because of a protest or was it because of guys out for a walk one night who decided they would go kill some Americans? What difference, at this point, does it make? It is our job to figure out what happened and do everything we can to prevent it from ever happening again, Senator. Now, honestly, I will do my best to answer your questions about this. But the fact is that people were trying in real time to get to the best information. The IC [intelligence community] has a process, I understand, going with the other committees to explain how these talking points came out. But, you know, to be clear, it is, from my perspective, less important today looking backward as to why these militants decided they did it than to find them and bring them to justice. And then maybe we will figure out what was going on in the meantime.[17]

In fact, the different agencies tasked with analyzing the attacks, which occurred in a city without a formal government or a regular police force, had struggled to piece together an accurate account of the events. No evidence had been raised to show that reports on the attacks were purposely misleading. And as the top official to sign off on the information given to Susan Rice, CIA director Petraeus was hardly the type to participate in a scheme to misrepresent events in Benghazi. He was a four-star general who once described himself as a Republican but had stopped to emphasize his commitment to apolitical public service. The idea that in the days after the Benghazi attacks he and others conspired to manipulate Congress and the American public for some uncertain purpose was, for Clinton, beyond the pale.[18]

After spending the morning with the Senate Committee on Foreign Relations, the secretary of state devoted the afternoon, right up to 5:00 p.m., answering similar questions posed by the House Foreign Affairs Committee, where her answers to Senator Johnson were already being distorted into a partisan complaint. According to Representative Jeffrey Duncan of South Carolina, "Americans" were already upset about her morning testimony when, after answering him twice, she gave Senator Johnson a testy reply to his questions about Susan Rice's early comments on the assaults. (Johnson would eventually brag about being "the guy that got under her skin.") Duncan didn't say how many Americans were upset, or just how, in a matter of hours, their outrage could have developed. What was readily apparent was the plan to turn the word *Benghazi* into a weapon that would be used to attack Clinton and diminish her prior to the 2016 presidential election.[19]

As usual, the partisan effort would be aided by the right-wing media, where Clinton, long identified as an enemy, was mocked for choking up while discussing her meeting with the families of the Americans killed in Benghazi. On Fox News, she was accused of "lip-synching" emotion and expressing how she felt in a way that was "staged." It was certain that if Clinton had failed to show any emotion, she would have been derided as cold and unfeeling, and any man who showed similar emotion would have been credited with possessing a genuine heart. Clinton, whose emotional expressions had been dissected for decades, was not eligible for such generosity. However, when it came to the issues raised at the hearings, she was generally thought to have prevailed. And even Brit Hume of Fox News noted how she had managed to "dominate" the proceedings.[20]

Although the first examinations of Benghazi failed to establish that Clinton was personally responsible for the deaths that occurred there, five different GOP-controlled congressional committees would continue looking into the attacks under the supervision of Speaker of the House John Boehner, who would admit that the purpose was to apply some sort of pressure on his political opponents. (Two Senate committees continued reviews, but in a less partisan fashion.) As House committee aides collected documents and conducted interviews, two main themes emerged. One held that for some reason, high-level officials had withheld the military aid—namely, attack aircraft—that would have destroyed the force assaulting the Americans.

The idea that the men in Benghazi were denied adequate military support as they fought for their lives evoked images of men dying as they fought valiantly against a superior force. If anyone failed to imagine this horror, Senator Rand Paul reminded them of it in an essay in which he cited the 1993 battle in Mogadishu, Somalia, that became the basis for a book and then a movie called Black Hawk Down. The Somalia tragedy, in which nineteen soldiers were killed and eighty were wounded, was different from Benghazi in ways too numerous to recount. Mogadishu did not involve an attack on U.S. facilities or a defensive struggle for survival. There the fight lasted for days. In Benghazi, the struggle lasted hours. In Somalia, American forces had tried to conduct a lightning raid to capture a militia leader. More than one thousand militia fighters responded. Hundreds of them died as the Americans' superior weapons and methods compensated for the Somalis' greater numbers. Afterward, the secretary of defense resigned.

*Black Hawk Down,* with its grueling battle that left no doubt about the desperate fight waged by the U.S. side, established in American culture a firm and frightening sense of what a fight with radical militias might be like. This is undoubtedly why Paul compared the two, urging Americans to view Benghazi as the equivalent of what they saw in *Black Hawk Down* (he even mentioned the film by name) and agree, with him, that "Mrs. Clinton should never hold high office again."[21]

As many witnesses would confirm, and Paul had to know, the United States had no appropriate forces to send to Benghazi to effect a rescue or reinforce those under attack. No aircraft could have reached the city in time to help. However, this didn't deter members of Congress from repeatedly raising the issue of an inadequate military response. The same kind of stubborn insistence on false assertions was part of the second major line of criticism, which followed a document trail to suggest that Secretary Clinton had personally refused to supply more security forces requested by diplomats in Libya before the attacks. This idea was put forth by Representative Darrell Issa, chairman of the House Committee on Oversight and Reform. "The secretary of state was just wrong," announced Issa in the spring of 2013. "She said she did not participate in this, and yet only a few months before the attack, she outright denied security in her signature in a cable."

The cables were, in fact, group emails. And the "signature" was actually just the secretary's name, which clerks affix to the bottom of every communication sent from Washington to any diplomatic outpost in the world. This action is taken thousands of times every month, whether the secretary sees an outgoing message or not, and even when he or she is abroad. Similarly, messages sent to Washington almost always include the secretary among the recipients. This is a matter of form, not function, as the vast majority of communiqués are distributed to lower-level officials authorized to take action. As R. Nicholas Burns, a diplomat who served in the George W. Bush administration, explained, "A very small fraction would be seen by the secretary of state."[22]

As Burns made his point, he also highlighted the overarching problem of the era—namely, that for many in the Republican Party, facts no longer mattered. From Benghazi to the science of climate change, these politicians operated as if truth were an anachronism that had been replaced by a level of sloganeering and doublespeak that made Newt Gingrich's rhetoric seem quaint. This was not a fringe attitude. In 2004, an aide in the Bush White House told *The New York Times* that the administration presided over a post-reality world in which the administration could determine public perception of the truth separate from established facts. Others who dwelled in the "reality-based community" didn't understand their understanding of truth had been eclipsed. "When we act," said the aide, "we create our own reality." This Orwellian cast of mind allowed for the Bush team to respond to the September 11 attacks, which were carried out by a Saudi-dominated Al Queda based in Afghanistan, with a massive war in Iraq. The pretexts, including claims that Iraq was in on the attacks and possessed weapons of mass destruction (WMDs), were false, but even as American soldiers died and Iraq was decimated, President Bush never seemed to adjust to the truth. He even joked about looking for WMDs in the White House and failing to discover them.

Bush had shown how policy could be pursued outside of reality and demonstrated that the public could be diverted by repeated distortions, like the unsubstantiated claim that Iraq had something to do with 9/11, even at the cost of many lives and hundreds of billions of dollars. By the time Issa took up the Benghazi issue, the distortion process had become a reflex. He organized a committee hearing under the title "Benghazi: Exposing Failure and Recognizing Courage," and his allies announced it would reveal blockbuster evidence that Hillary Clinton had neglected her duties and covered up the truth. "If you link Watergate and Iran-Contra together and multiply it times maybe ten or so, you're going to get in the zone where Benghazi is," explained Representative Steve King of Iowa.

The gigantic scandal King promised did not emerge; however, witnesses did recall the anguish of seeking aid when no military force with the necessary capabilities was close enough to help. Also, one State Department official who had been in Tripoli at the time of the attacks,

Gregory Hicks, said he was initially discouraged from helping Republicans in their investigation and that he had been demoted for raising questions about the response to the attacks. These points supported congressional critics' complaints that the administration had not been sufficiently cooperative with House investigation.

In the run-up to the House hearing, Hicks was represented by a lawyer who said he was a whistleblower who would reveal significant corruption at the State Department. The attorney, Victoria Toensing, had been a widely quoted critic of Bill Clinton during his presidency. In the Clinton years, she and her lawyer husband, Joseph diGenova, appeared in the press hundreds of times, mainly in support of special prosecutor Kenneth Starr. The effort helped them build a thriving business, but with the end of the Clinton presidency, they had faded from the media landscape. Benghazi helped make them relevant again, but only for a moment, as the Hicks story turned out to be less compelling than it had first seemed. When he finally appeared Hicks qualified his testimony by explaining that he was cautioned about responding to congressional inquiries without having a lawyer present, as was department policy. He also said he had been able to share what he knew with both Congress and the ARB. Hicks also said that Secretary Clinton had called him as the attacks were still going on to ask for information. This recollection conflicted with the idea that she had not been actively involved in responding to the attacks as they occurred.[23]

Try as they did, the committee didn't present a simple story of failure and courage or a compelling narrative similar to *Black Hawk Down*. This was, obviously, because the Benghazi tragedy had multiple causes, including the quick withdrawal of American and allied forces from Libya shortly after Gaddafi's ouster. This choice had created a power vacuum more dangerous than even Ambassador Stevens, an expert, seemed to recognize. In the aftermath of his murder, his decision to visit Benghazi was called into question by those who deemed it too dangerous. Islamic militants had been seizing property in the region ever since Gaddafi's death, and locals who had promised to protect American diplomats were weak and unreliable.[24]

After the committee did its work and the press reported the results, opinion pollsters found that Clinton's views on the attacks were favored over those of Republicans in Congress by 48–38 percent. Among GOP loyalists, however, 41 percent thought that Benghazi was "the biggest scandal in U.S. history" and thus more consequential than Iran-Contra, Watergate, and Teapot Dome. The intensity of this feeling suggested that the respondents were influenced more by the hyper-partisanship of the times and the demonization of Hillary Clinton than by the attacks and events surrounding them. Indeed, the poll-takers discovered nearly 40 percent of those who were certain Clinton was in the wrong couldn't locate Benghazi on a map. Some guessed it was in Cuba. Others put the city in North Korea. This ignorance was consistent with a 2012 study that had found that people who got their news from Fox News, where Benghazi was most frequently touted as a scandal, were less well informed than people who reported no regular consumption of news from any source. (Later studies would show that Fox had a powerful effect on voting patterns, influencing viewers to support Republicans in elections.)[25]

Fox News both amplified and augmented GOP positions, and its method involved reducing issues to relatively simple conflicts between recognizable good guys and bad guys. When the matter of Susan Rice's statements on Benghazi failed to inspire palpable outrage, congressional Republicans and Fox began alleging that the president and secretary of state had been disengaged on the night of the attack. As committees once again convened and questioned witnesses, it turned out that Obama had been briefed soon after the start of the crisis and that the response had been led by Clinton and the national security advisor Thomas Donilon throughout the night. Although these facts were known, the idea that the attacks were all but ignored persisted. The disinformation effort reached a ridiculous level in May 2013 when, as hosts of the morning show *Fox & Friends* wondered aloud about Donilon's whereabouts on the night of September 11, 2012, a photo flashed on the screen showing him meeting with the president to discuss the attack moments after word of it reached Washington.[26]

With the demands of providing programs all day every day, and hosts who sometimes fell short of fulfilling their assignments, Fox occasionally suffered the kind of live-television miscue that spoiled its message. Political consultant Karl Rove, whose Crossroads GPS organization specialized in political attacks, was not subject to the same pressures. As the Benghazi case unfolded, he took snippets of testimony and joined them with slick graphics designed to evoke military technology to create the first TV advertisement of the 2016 election, which was still three and a half years away. The spot opened with a map, which helped the ill informed locate Benghazi, and the words AL QAEDA OPERATIVES TOOK PART IN BENGHAZI ATTACK. This assertion was false, but it allowed Rove to put the terrorist group Americans feared the most into the viewers' minds. He used out-of-context quotes to support the question, "Was she part of a cover-up?" Viewers were left with the undeniable impression that of course she was.[27]

Karl Rove, who had poured more than $100 million into the 2012 congressional elections, wasn't the only one watching the Benghazi issue with an eye for drama. Political groups and media outlets followed the investigations closely, ever alert for a new element that would make the story more accessible to the public. In September 2013, the mother of Sean Smith, one of the two diplomats killed in Benghazi, spoke to the committee of her heartbreak and said that she had not been kept informed of government investigations into her son's death. She also expressed anger about being told that the Benghazi attack that caused her thirty-four-year-old son's death was linked to the *Innocence of Muslims* video.[28]

Patricia Smith heard about the video and received condolences when she met with Clinton and President Obama at Joint Base Andrews outside of Washington as her son's body arrived in the United States. The meeting occurred three days after the attacks, when officials still believed *Innocence of Muslims* had something to do with them. In the months that followed, Smith came to believe that she had been purposely misled and became a steadily more outspoken critic of Secretary Clinton and the State Department. As the mother of one of the attack's victims, Patricia Smith's expression of emotion was riveting, and her symbolic status placed her beyond reproach by anyone in the administration. However, her recollections of events at Joint Base Andrews did not align with the recollections of others who had been present. Jan Stevens, father of the murdered ambassador, recalled that "nothing whatsoever" had been said about the film. Smith's complaint about receiving too little follow-up on the investigation of the attacks may not have taken into account the government policy of contacting only those closest to the deceased. For those who are married, and Sean Smith was married, the contact would be made with a spouse. Like so much about Benghazi, these complexities were not easy to explain, and the process of laying out all the facts brought with it the risk of more confusion. In the case of Patricia Smith, in 2013, Clinton chose to avoid a public debate with a grieving mother.[29]

Grief, suspicion, partisanship, and the limits of human memory made it possible for anyone so inclined to find scandal in the Benghazi tragedy. The committees that conducted hearings heard public testimony that could be useful in providing material for political campaign ads, but their reports did not reach damning conclusions. The last one issued by the committee that Patricia Smith addressed in May 2013 noted suspected flaws in the State Department's review of what happened in Benghazi, but nothing to support the idea that Hillary Clinton or anyone else lied about the events or that the Americans who were attacked were denied aid. Nevertheless, the theory that Clinton and others not only failed to act but interfered with rescuers who may have saved lives bounced around right-wing media with remarkable resilience. These ideas were energized by commentary from people who weren't witnesses to the events or informed by accurate information, but still spread the notion that rescuers were ready and able to act but orders to "stand down" blocked them.[30]

The idea that someone told eager fighters to stand down fit neatly into a narrative that would have noncombatants heedlessly block the actions of valiant military men and women. It was advanced by Jason Chaffetz, a Republican member of Congress from Utah, who seized upon a report that some reinforcements were kept in the Libyan capital of Tripoli when others boarded a plane that delivered them to Benghazi minutes before the second attack. Those who remained in Tripoli were supposed to care for the evacuees when they arrived. Chaffetz went on Fox News to say, "We had people that were getting killed, we had people who are willing to risk their lives to save them, and somebody told them to stand down."

In fact, the victims of the attack on the diplomatic post were already dead when responders were mustered. The closest aircraft that were armed to fight the attackers were at a base in the Horn of Africa, two thousand air miles from Benghazi. The small group of fighters who did arrive helped repel the second assault. Survivors and the bodies of the dead were evacuated within twelve hours of the first shots fired. The officer who was supposedly told his troops should stand down told the House Armed Services Committee that the incident never happened. This evidence led the committee to publish a statement debunking the idea. This didn't deter media and political figures who continued to talk about the stand-down order as if it had actually been issued. It was a tale that would appeal to anyone who admired the military and believed its capabilities were comparable to what they saw at the movies, where fighters and machines could accomplish almost anything if only the bureaucrats got out of the way. As such, the stand-down myth was a bit of political propaganda that took on a life of its own. Advanced by Fox News more than eight times, it took hold as truth in certain corners of the internet, where it affirmed the belief that Hillary Clinton was untrustworthy, incompetent, and perhaps even anti-American in every way imaginable.[31]

Smearing Hillary Clinton was, for too many, the whole point of deploying seven committees to investigate Benghazi. Those in the Senate who followed a more thoughtful approach found ample evidence that the State Department had been warned of growing danger and did not improve security. However, the senators also noted that Ambassador Stevens had taken great a risk in visiting Benghazi when he did. A detailed inventory of the forces available to aid the Americans who were attacked showed that while every effort was made to mount a response, no one could have reached Benghazi in time. The committee found no evidence that anyone had been told to stand down. Similarly, it pointed out that at the time Susan Rice talked about protests sparking the attacks, CIA officials were saying this was true. Only later did it emerge that this was not true. Overall, the deaths in Benghazi were deemed "preventable," but the security failures were mainly attributed to a bureaucracy overwhelmed by the challenges it faced. Hillary Clinton was not found to be especially culpable in any way.[32]

From the perspective of a Republican political warrior, the Senate's effort on Benghazi was an abject failure because it did not damage Hillary Clinton's prospects for 2016. Others, most notably a conservative organization called Judicial Watch, continued to promote the idea that officials should continue to dig for scandal. Judicial Watch was founded at the start of the Clinton presidency by a notoriously litigious lawyer named Larry Klayman who had, by his own count, filed about eighty lawsuits against the Clintons, including one by Gennifer Flowers. Klayman left Judicial Watch to mount a failed bid for the United States Senate in 2004. When Barack Obama was elected president, Klayman became a prominent "birther" who said the president was secretly a Muslim who was not American-born and was thus not eligible for the office he won in 2008.

Financed largely by foundations established by wealthy conservative activists such as Richard Scaife, by 2014 Judicial Watch had grown into a big operation with a budget in excess of $20 million. By 2016, the budget would balloon to $45 million. The source of this money would be obscure, as changes in reporting requirements allowed Judicial Watch to keep secret its donors. What the public did know was that during its twenty years, Judicial Watch had been engaged with every Clinton controversy and a host of pseudo-controversies that never made it out of the right-wing fever swamp. This record made the organization a perfect partner for newcomers who saw an opportunity for power and profit in joining the crowd of activists, propagandists, and conservative media that made Hillary Clinton and Barack Obama the enemies who would reliably energize readers, viewers, and donors. In the internet age, those with the right connections could get visibility with a minimal investment of time and money.

In 2012, funding from a small number of wealthy donors and links to Judicial Watch and a right-wing internet site called Breitbart News enabled a nationalist named Steve Bannon to create an "institute" devoted to the anti-Clinton cause. Long part of the financial and media elite,

Bannon was a millionaire who told a story about his father's stock market losses to explain his pose as a crusader on behalf of people who had been left behind by the global economy. Likely apocryphal, the tale would be offered as justification for a long campaign that would find him making common cause with racists, anti-Semites, and misogynists. Bannon had collaborated with David Bossie of Citizens United on a movie titled *Border War: The Battle over Illegal Immigration* and was involved in myriad political media projects. These were accomplished with money provided by both nonprofit entities and profit-making ones, and often outside the actual mass media business, where success depended on whether people actually bought what was on offer.[33]

Bannon's Government Accountability Institute was a good example of this activity. It had a substantial internet presence but was actually quite small in real life, with no address other than a post office box. It declared, in capital letters on tax forms, that its mission was to "INVESTIGATE AND EXPOSE CRONY CAPITALISM, MISUSE OF TAXPAYER MONIES, AND OTHER GOVERNMENTAL CORRUPTION OR MALFEASANCE." However, most of its activities seemed concerned with supporting the work of its president, Peter Schweizer, who was paid more than $200,000 per year.

Schweizer's résumé included his work as a consultant for the George W. Bush White House and a $100,000 gig as an advisor to failed vice presidential candidate Sarah Palin. At the beginning of his career, he worked for a political group called Young America's Foundation that got $10 million from billionaires Richard and Helen DeVos. (Among those YAF had aided over the years were Ann Coulter, future attorney general Jeff Sessions, and future White House aide Stephen Miller.) The Government Accountability Institute's other paid employees included Bannon himself; Stuart Christmas, a local lawyer whose address was the same as the institute's; and Wynton Hall, who also worked for Breitbart and promoted himself as a "celebrity ghostwriter." According to charity tax records, each of these men was paid more than $100,000 in 2014. Bannon somehow logged thirty hours per week working for the institute, even as he ran Breitbart and other businesses. Much of the money for these salaries came from a foundation controlled by the family of hedge fund billionaire Robert Mercer.[34]

Mercer, who held a $10 million stake in Breitbart, was a conserva-
tive Christian who owned a large machine gun collection, which was
symbolic of his assertive approach to life. He refused to acknowledge
the scientific evidence of man-made climate change and considered the
political elite in America generally corrupt. A relative newcomer to the
game of high-stakes influence, he engaged Bannon as an advisor and
began donating millions to conservative candidates and such organizations as Citizens United, the Government Accountability Institute, and
Young America's Foundation. Between 2010 and 2014, *all three* of these
nonprofits made payments to Bannon. Combined they exceeded $1.1
million.[35]

The Government Accountability Institute was able to do more with less
by relying on information found in the press, which it used to create
its own "investigations," and by working with material from organizations like Judicial Watch. Both raised false alarms about terrorism that
strained common sense. The institute would try and generally fail to get
attention for a claim that terrorism was funded by food stamps. Judicial
Watch made more headway with claims that a terrorist training camp
existed in Mexico, near the U.S. border, where fighters were poised to
cross into the United States. No law enforcement agency confirmed this
claim, the Mexican government refuted it, and it was judged untrue or
highly unlikely by reputable fact-checkers. However, it would be taken
up and repeated by prominent politicians, including Republican member of Congress Trent Franks of Arizona, who said, in 2014, "It is true
that we know that ISIS is present in Ciudad Juárez [Mexico]." Juárez
shares a twenty-mile border with El Paso, Texas, which meant that if
what Franks said were true, the United States faced a serious threat.[36]

In a Congress where a member in good standing actually promoted
a terrifying and seemingly false theory about terrorists poised on the
border, it was difficult for anyone to tamp down speculation about Benghazi, especially when partisans were prepared to believe almost anything about Clinton and Obama. In 2014, Speaker Boehner created a
"select committee" devoted only to the Benghazi attacks and gave it

the task of making one last investigation. Days after he announced this move, the National Republican Congressional Committee, which organized the party's election efforts for the House of Representatives, sent out a fund-raising appeal offering recipients the chance to become "a Benghazi watchdog right now." This could be achieved with a donation sent to the committee. To his credit, the chairman of the new panel, a former federal prosecutor named Trey Gowdy of South Carolina, criticized the fund-raising message as a matter of seeking cash "on the backs of four murdered Americans." He promised that he would never seek campaign funds by citing the Benghazi issue.[37]

Eventually, the most important product of the Benghazi investigations would be the discovery that—like previous secretaries of state—Hillary Clinton had used a private email account and that some sensitive messages had moved through this account and through a server that was maintained in her private home and under her control. (The private server had been installed to handle former president Bill Clinton's email.) This practice allowed Clinton to continue using a BlackBerry phone and a familiar email address as secretary of state. It would also frame the most significant controversy of her political life.

In the meantime, despite six investigations that concluded no serious scandal had occurred, the select committee on Benghazi maintained the idea that something remained to be discovered about the attacks. When four months passed before the committee conducted its first public hearings, and key interviews of State Department officials would be delayed until February 2015, it became apparent that the work would be done at a pace that would keep Benghazi in the news until well into the 2016 presidential campaign season. This schedule would burden Hillary Clinton at a time when she would be expected to focus more fully on presidential politics and keep the sense of outrage among GOP voters, who already hated her, at a high pitch. Republicans who controlled the committee signaled their purpose with press releases that called Democrats "Dishonest Dems" and recycled debunked claims about officials who callously refused to order a rescue. They also used committee staff to critique *The New York Times'* coverage of the Benghazi issue. Much of this material was written by an aide named Matt Wolking, who after graduating from a Christian college had started his career producing Laura Ingraham's radio show. His efforts on behalf of the committee created a feedback loop that provided official statements for Ingraham and others in right-wing media—Breitbart, Fox News, and others—to cite to make the partisan attacks that were the basic ingredients of their products.[38]

For all the committee's complaints about *The New York Times,* the paper and other mainstream media actually picked up on the email controversy and investigated it assertively. Beginning in early 2015, *The Times* began devoting significant space—more than one hundred articles in twelve months—to the story and reactions to it. Clinton turned the server she used over to the FBI and gave tens of thousands of email records to the State Department, which then gave them to the House committee. Amid all this activity, Clinton made the inevitable official when she announced she would seek her party's nomination, and every one of sixteen Republicans eyeing the GOP nod used the issue to attack her politically. (Donald Trump staked out the most extreme view, calling her a "criminal.")[39]

The email controversy was complicated by the fact that it involved technology many people didn't understand and by the public pronouncements of those like Trump who announced their conclusions long before the facts were known. Hence, the one-hundred-plus articles in *The Times.* When she left office in 2013, long before the issue became an issue, Clinton had ordered a review of tens of thousands of archived messages to determine which were personal and which related to government business and belonged to the State Department. Roughly fifty-five thousand were judged to be official and given to the government. A year later, as news of the private account circulated, a technician for a company hired to do the review and delete personal emails realized he had mistakenly left them intact. (He would describe this as an "oh shit moment.") On his own initiative, he went back into the files and erased thousands of personal ones using a program called BleachBit.[40]

An ordinary utility for removing data, BleachBit was free for anyone to use and less effective than expensive technology that left no trace of deleted files. However, its name suggested a process that was as tough on data as a caustic cleaner might be on germs and grime. Clinton's antagonists came to say she "bleached" or "acid-washed" computer equipment, which anyone would rightly imagine involved something like dropping a hard drive in a bucket of chemicals. This was a powerful image but wrong on many counts. There had been no buckets, and the software left data that would allow for the emails to be recovered.

BleachBit and every other detail of Clinton's email management would become public in a slow process that seemed as if she was trying to control political damage while Republicans were seeking to maximize it. Clinton may well have been acting defensively, but in the context of a presidential campaign, the complexity of the problem made any effort to manage it futile. For example, at the start of the publicity about the private account and server, she said, "I want the public to see my email. I asked State to release them. They said they will review them for release as soon as possible." On the surface, this seemed a reasonable statement, but the review took months, which delayed the release and fueled her critics.[41]

Mistakes were evident on all sides. As Clinton and the House Select Committee on Benghazi prepared for a public hearing, which would be her last on the topic, chairman Trey Gowdy announced he had received additional emails from Clinton and in the process made public the name of a secret CIA source. Another key Republican, Kevin McCarthy, made his infamous remarks about using Benghazi to ruin Clinton politically and immediately dropped out of contention to succeed John Boehner as Speaker of the House.[42]

On the day when Gowdy and Clinton would face each other in public for the last time, Clinton arrived at the Rayburn House Office Building wearing a blue pantsuit and modest gold jewelry. She walked into the hearing room of the House Committee on Ways and Means, which was used for the session, flanked by police officers who towered over her and blocked reporters who asked, "Madam Secretary, are you prepared?" She smiled, offered a "Good morning," and continued to stride. The ornate hearing room, designed in the colonial revival style, is decorated with columns, carved eagles, gold drapery, and emerald-green carpet. Past committee chairmen stare down from portraits on the walls. Clinton sat alone at a desk equipped with a microphone and faced members of the committee, who sat in two semicircular rows, one at floor level and one raised. Behind her sat aides armed with files.

At 10:00 a.m., Gowdy began the day with a promise of fairness. This was followed by an eleven-hour marathon (with breaks totaling seventy-five minutes), which would see the lone witness defuse the controversy with a remarkable command of the facts and a consistently cogent argument. Occasionally, a representative's question or stunt—one ripped up papers to demonstrate how he imagined her neglect of duty—broke her concentration. By 7:15 in the evening, when a committee member pressed her to amplify her recollection of being alone on the night of the attacks—"Were you alone *all* night?"—Clinton actually laughed out loud. But these moments were few, as Clinton recalled events in the same way she had before, but in greater detail. She accepted responsibility for many key decisions, but not those related to specific requests for security measures. Committee members made several attempts to suggest that Ambassador Stevens had asked her own office for greater protection, but she refuted this notion.

> *He did not raise security with the members of my staff. He raised security with the security professionals. I know that's not the answer you want to hear. But those are the facts. If he had raised it with me, I would be here telling you he had.*

As various representatives tried to bait her, Clinton generally, but not always, resisted the urge to parry. However, she occasionally gave in. When Republican Peter Roskam of Illinois asked, sarcastically, "Should I wait while you take notes from your staff?" Clinton replied, "No, I can do more than one thing at a time."

When it was over, Gowdy told the press that no significant new information had been obtained, and Clinton left behind the impression of a woman who was poised, well informed, and resilient. With the exception of a coughing fit that occurred late in the evening, she remained alert and composed. When asked about her email, Clinton shifted to remarks about her job at the State Department, where, she said, very little was communicated electronically and the most sensitive information arrived in her office in a locked case, which she returned to a waiting courier after reviewing its contents.

Clinton's stamina, which was widely noted, contradicted recent efforts to suggest that she was too old and too infirm to be trusted with the presidency. Matt Drudge, the original king troll of the internet, had recently suggested that a magazine cover photo of Clinton showed her leaning on a "walker" that was actually a chair. He had also published a picture, purported to be of a haggard and startlingly aged Clinton, that was created with photo-editing software. Just who altered the photo was never revealed, but it made her appear to be in her nineties. The Hillary Clinton who testified was a few days shy of sixty-nine years old and bore the crow's-feet to prove it, but she wasn't the decrepit figure of Drudge's imagination on the Drudge site. Those who may have been surprised to see someone younger looking than they expected, but still longed for a reason to mistrust her, could have turned to the reliably hateful Edward Klein's latest anti-Hillary compilation, *Unlikeable: The Problem with Hillary Clinton*.

Published a month before the hearing, this book said that Clinton's appearance was an issue not because she looked too old but because she looked too young. This was because she had arranged for plastic surgery to be done in her home, over the course of several operations, on her eyes, neck, cheeks, and forehead. How this had been done while Clinton remained almost continually in the public eye as she campaigned for president was not explained. The story, like much of Klein's writing, was credited to an anonymous source. He also seemed to presume that readers would see something awful in the idea that she had work done.[43]

The seventy-seven-year-old Klein's breathless reporting of a rumor about Clinton and surgery said more about his age than Clinton's. He may have reached adulthood at a time when only movie stars and the wealthy went under the knife, but by 2015, things had changed. Cosmetic surgery had become so accepted and common that it was available on the installment plan in every city of any size. Of course, clinkers like the surgery anecdote wouldn't diminish sales of the book. Among the millions who had been conditioned to hate Hillary Clinton were many who would enjoy getting riled up by a book that assured them they were right to detest her. These same Americans would regard the record established by all the different Benghazi investigations, including those controlled by Republicans, and conclude that despite all this effort, some dark truth about the secretary of state remained unexposed.

Immediately after the House select committee hearing, pollsters found that by a 48–42 margin, most Americans didn't consider the email issue important. When asked if the Benghazi investigations had been unfair, the yeses outnumbered the noes 40–27. But while 55 percent viewed Clinton as knowledgeable and experienced enough to be president, only 45 percent deemed her trustworthy. Discovered so early in the 2016 presidential campaign, while Republican candidates were still focused mainly on one another, this number was not good news for Clinton. It indicated that the decades of assaults on her character had taken a toll and pointed to the tactic that would be used against her should she win her party's nomination.[44]

Although even middle-of-the-road *Time* magazine declared that Clinton had prevailed at the hearing—HOW HILLARY CLINTON WON THE BENGHAZI HEARING read the headline—the verdict of the reporting in the mainstream press was not decisive in the way it would have been in the past. Like Clinton, journalists had been subject to decades of demonization by conservative activists. By 2015, many conservatives were unwilling to trust what information was reported outside their own partisan channels, like Fox News and Breitbart, even though those outlets had been shown, again and again, to be the least reliable. Inside this echo chamber, one could barely hear contrary information, and the original melodies of the attacks against Clinton were about to become a loud and complex symphony.[45]

# 11

# Chaos

Alexandra Krylova and Anna Vladislavovna Bogacheva learned about purple states, which sometimes vote for the "red" GOP and sometimes go for "blue" Democrats, on a coast-to-coast tour of America in the spring of 2014. For two young Russians with eager minds, this business trip must have been the adventure of a lifetime. They visited nine states, from California to New York, recording and absorbing all they could about American politics. Before they flew home, they dumped the burner phones they had bought for secret communication.

After they returned to Saint Petersburg, Krylova and Bogacheva reported to their office at the Internet Research Agency, which occupied a blocky four-story building at 55 Savushkina Street. The IRA, which employees also called the Factory, was established by an ally of Vladimir Putin named Yevgeny V. Prigozhin. Once imprisoned for robbery and prostitution, Prigozhin had grown immensely wealthy thanks to government contracts awarded to his main businesses, Concord Management and Consulting and Concord Catering. These entities oversaw the Factory, which was staffed by bright young Russians who were paid well for work that depended on their creative skills. The purpose of this work, which involved flooding YouTube, Facebook, Instagram, and

Twitter with posts, wasn't always obvious, but the perspective was clear from the start. As one writer named Alexei would recall, he was hired after he was asked to write a persuasive essay about a conspiracy theory, first described in a novel, that imagined an American-led Cold War campaign to destroy Soviet society. This dark fantasy had been revived after the collapse of the Soviet Union and was so widely known that anyone with skill could spin a story about it on command.[1]

Dozens of Alexeis awaited Krylova and Bogacheva, who spilled out the knowledge they had acquired and began to organize a big new initiative called Project Translator. Eventually staffed by ninety people, the goal, according to an internal memo, was to disrupt American politics by spreading "distrust toward the candidates and the political system in general." Soon, the place was humming, twenty-four hours a day, with the production of blog posts, video, tweets, and commentaries. Project Translator writers worked under thousands of false American identities and created online groups with names such as "secured borders" and "Blacktivist" and "Army of Jesus." Others at the Internet Research Agency focused on Russian society, building up Vladimir Putin and stoking outrage about the United States. One typical domestic post invented the "news" that Americans were obsessed with a new video game with a slavery theme. This narrative would have been familiar to anyone who knew about the propaganda produced by the KGB during the Soviet era. Racism in America was a favorite topic for the Soviets, who used it to counter criticism of their country's suppression of civil rights.[2]

Although creating general political mayhem was its original purpose, Project Translator soon calibrated its efforts to damage Hillary Clinton's chance in the 2016 elections. Some fake influencers like Blacktivist were tuned to discourage those who might support Clinton from getting involved in her campaign or even voting. "No Lives Matter To Hillary Clinton. Only Votes Matter To Hillary Clinton," announced one Blacktivist post. Others boosted her main rival for the Democratic Party's nomination, Vermont senator Bernie Sanders. However, the biggest volume of material was designed to spread false information about Clinton in a way that would sway fence-sitting voters against and amplify the antagonism of those who already detested her. A Russian poster called

Being Patriotic wrote, for example, "Hillary Clinton is the co-author of Obama's anti-police and anti-Constitutional propaganda!"

Functionally equivalent to an online marketing campaign for a political candidate or party, Project Translator used corny graphics and flawed grammar to mimic the kind of messages that might be posted by motivated American citizens. This fake authenticity, projected by thousands of fake personalities, would prompt more than thirty million people to share the dispatches from the Factory with their online friends. The Russians also seized on new issues as they arose, sending out posts that boosted the efforts of the many well-funded and freelance antagonists who had made it their mission to attack Hillary Clinton. Books like the prolific Ed Klein's latest harangue, *Unlikeable,* proliferated as various writers and their financial backers sought to create a thematic foundation for other forms of media—like the Mercer-funded CNS News, Fox News, and Breitbart, as well as conservative newcomers like the website the Independent Journal Review. Typical of IJR.com was an item titled "13 Extremely Vulgar Comments That Came Out of the Mouth of Hillary Clinton," which included material from discredited sources in arguing that Hillary Clinton was a profane shrew. Its author, Kyle Becker, has studied Russian and Russian literature and was an alumnus of the right-wing Heritage Foundation's youth leadership program. He would eventually be suspended for fabricating a conspiracy theory story about Barack Obama but would move on to Fox News, where he would work as a producer.[3]

Many new online operations like IJR.com, which sprang to life as the election neared, functioned without the old-fashioned regard for the fact-checking and fairness that were still practiced by the mainstream media. This was natural given that many were created by political activists and not journalists. The fact that they rejected the old rules was what lent them greater credibility among readers and viewers who had been persuaded that the mainstream media—often expressed as "the MSM"—where fact-checkers and lawyers were employed to keep journalists honest, was corrupt and unreliable. The key to their success was providing reinforcement of preexisting bias—in this case, "Hillary Clinton is awful"—with provocative snippets that kept people coming back for more. This clickbait produced revenue from advertisers who paid every time someone opened a new web page.[4]

The publication of a book was a news event in and of itself, especially if it offered juicy bits that could be flung at eager readers and viewers like chicken feed scattered in a yard. The fact that these items came packaged in hardcovers lent them extra respectability, and if the anecdotes, quotes, and arguments were especially provocative, editors and producers clamored to pay for excerpts or to trade lavish displays on their websites or programs. Authors received advertising that leveraged whatever goodwill came under the banner of a Breitbart or Fox. Viewers, readers, and listeners whose appetites were whetted by a promise of what a book might reveal were more likely to part with the $29.99, the going rate for a hardcover, to get more.

No one had profited more from Hillary hating than Edward Klein, and he would publish a second book on Hillary Clinton, *Guilty as Sin,* to capitalize on the 2016 election. However, by the time this compilation of mostly recycled, anonymously sourced material hit bookstores, he faced stiff competition from a host of younger writers with greater energy and nerve. No one could beat Roger Stone in the nerve department. A professional political extremist, Stone had founded an anti-Hillary Clinton group called Citizens United Not Timid for no apparent reason other than to have its initials used as an acronym. He was a longtime advisor to then candidate Donald Trump and a proud political dirty trickster who sported a tattoo of Richard Nixon. Stone's coauthor for the book *The Clintons' War on Women* matched his recklessness and exceeded him in his paranoia. Robert Morrow said that both Lyndon Johnson and George H. W. Bush had participated in a conspiracy that led to the assassination of John F. Kennedy and that in the Reagan years child sex trafficking had occurred at "the elite levels of the Republican party." Where Hillary Clinton was concerned, Morrow's record was replete with commentary about her sexuality—he said she was a lesbian and promiscuous with men—and longing for her death.[5]

In *The Clintons' War on Women,* Morrow and Stone combined previously made claims and a smattering of new allegations to depict Bill Clinton as a serial rapist and Hillary as an enabler who covered up and even facilitated his crimes. Among the oldies rehashed in this book were claims that Clinton had fathered a black son, whom he ignored, and that Hillary conceived Chelsea Clinton during an affair. In a preface, Kathleen Willey, who had offered conflicting accounts of an unwanted sexual encounter, said the former president had raped her and that people hired by Hillary Clinton had subjected her to many forms of harassment, even killing her cat. During his publicity efforts for the book, Stone alleged that Hillary was guilty of "the degradation and psychological rape of women" and that in addition to Kathleen Willey's cat, the Clintons had been responsible for the deaths of more than forty people.[6]

The lurid claims and the authors' track records worked against Stone and Morrow, whose book got no serious attention from reviewers and was overshadowed by *Crisis of Character* by Gary Byrne. Formerly a uniformed secret service officer, Byrne presented a laundry list of incidents that supposedly proved that both Bill and Hillary Clinton were despicable people unworthy of trust. The book reached the top of bestseller lists but failed to gain much notice outside the right wing because much of what it reported had been debunked or originated with the *National Enquirer* and other sources that lacked credibility. Byrne's credibility was at issue, too, since, as an officer in uniform, he would not have had contact with the Clintons in the private settings where he could have witnessed unguarded moments of the sort he described. This point was made to *The Washington Post* by the president of the Association of Former Agents of the United States Secret Service. Byrne's claims were also diminished by the fact that in at least one instance, he had previously testified, under oath, to facts that completely contradicted one of the most shocking stories in the book.[7]

The most effective anti-Clinton book of the campaign season was *Clinton Cash* by Peter Schweizer. Years of effort and $1.7 million of Mercer family money went into the book, which was published by HarperCollins, which was owned by longtime Clinton antagonist Rupert Murdoch. In its tone, reporting, and writing quality, *Clinton Cash* would not have passed muster with many editors, but HarperCollins released it as if it were a worthy work. After complaints were lodged, the publisher acknowledged that the book contained errors that required "seven or eight passages" be corrected and retailer Amazon.com  contacted its customers to tell them "significant revisions have been made" and they could access the new version of the electronic book for free. Though an embarrassment for HarperCollins, these troubles didn't change the fact that a book bearing the imprimatur of a mainstream publisher could be cited by those who needed arguments to use against Hillary Clinton.

*Clinton Cash* argued that as secretary of state, Hillary Clinton had secretly encouraged powerful foreigners and others to make donations to the Clinton Foundation and to pay six-figure speaking fees to her husband. In exchange, Schweizer implied, she used her office, in one way or another, to benefit the donors. (Engaged in health, education, and economic development around the world, the foundation earned top ratings from charity analysts.)[8]

Much of Schweizer's argument involved inference based on the timing of events that only seemed suspect to a researcher who failed to complete an investigation. For example, Schweizer made much of a U.S. funding paid to an Irish company that worked in Haiti after the devastating 2010 earthquake. Bill Clinton was invited to speak in Ireland by the firm's owner. Schweizer presumed he had been paid handsomely. He had, in fact, earned nothing personally, as the host made a donation to the Clinton Foundation. Schweizer made a different kind of error when it came to his claim that some sort of funny business had transpired when TD Bank began selling shares of a pipeline project after it paid Bill Clinton for speeches. In fact, the share sale announcement, which Schweizer used as a source, was a fake. No such divestment had occurred.[9]

The TD Bank and Irish speech tales were stricken from the electronic version of his book soon after it was published, but the most widely reported claim in the book remained. This bit focused on the sale of a Canadian-based company called Uranium One. The firm owned some uranium mines in Wyoming, which meant that federal approval was required when it was acquired in 2010 by a state-owned company in Russia. Schweizer's supposed smoking gun was the fact that the Clinton

Foundation had received more than $130 million in donations from a major Uranium One investor named Frank Giustra. The problem, for Schweizer, was that Giustra sold his interest in Uranium One three years *before* the Russian deal. Also, Schweizer's *Clinton Cash* claim that Hillary Clinton either approved or could have stopped the sale was simply false. The State Department did have a vote on the committee that considered the sale, but eight other agencies had equal say. Finally, *Clinton Cash* asserted that control of 20 percent of U.S. uranium, a metal essential to energy production and the manufacture of nuclear weapons, was transferred to Russia in the sale. In fact, the Wyoming facilities had the potential to produce 20 percent of U.S. uranium, but experts said this shouldn't be considered a measure of its actual share. Besides, 90 percent of the uranium used in the United States came from abroad.[10]

Despite the flaws in his argument, Schweizer received invaluable press attention for his book as its release approached. From those who were reliably anti-Hillary Clinton, he got breathless excitement. Skeptics like George Stephanopoulos of ABC News (who had worked in the Clinton White House) were much less friendly. When Schweizer sat for a prepublication interview, Stephanopoulos outlined the problems in the Uranium One story and listened as Schweizer offered the circular argument that the issue "deserves further scrutiny" because of the claims in his book. Stephanopoulos then asked, "But based on what? Based on what?"

Schweizer struggled to reply, saying, "Well, I think based on her . . ."

As Schweizer's voice faltered, Stephanopoulos asked, "Do you have any evidence that she actually intervened in this issue?"

"No, we don't have direct evidence," confessed Schweizer. "But it warrants further investigation because, again, George, this is part of the broader pattern. You either have to come to the conclusion that these are all coincidences or something else is afoot."[11]

The "pattern" Schweizer referenced was to be found in his book, but so many of his examples would be discredited that the notion that something nefarious could be concluded fell apart. However, even a casual survey of Schweizer's background would uncover an actual pattern of flawed reporting and misrepresentations in his previous work:

- In 1993, claims in Schweizer's debut book, *Friendly Spies,* were debunked by reporters for *The Times of London,* who found "checkable facts do not check out" and "individuals credited for supplying information do not exist or cannot be tracked down." Years later, the book did not appear on Schweizer's website, where other books were listed.[12]

- In 2005, comedian Al Franken caught Schweizer's erroneous claim that he had neglected minorities by hiring just 1 black worker out of 112 people he had employed over the years. Schweizer was wrong when it came to Franken's hiring authority (he never had the chance to employ so many folks) and wrong about the number of minority candidates he hired when he could make the choice.[13]

- In 2007, *USA Today* editors corrected a Schweizer claim that, despite his concern for the environment, Al Gore was collecting royalties on a zinc mine. The mine had been closed for years.[14]

- In 2011, Schweizer retracted a claim that Senator Sheldon Whitehouse of Rhode Island used "insider information" he learned as a public official to profit in the stock market.[15]

- In 2011, Schweizer also made false claims of insider trading against Representative Jim McDermott. The claim didn't match either the facts of the stock trading or the timing of government action.[16]

- In 2013, Schweizer falsely claimed that as president, Barack Obama had only met once with the Health and Human Services secretary Kathleen Sebelius. As *Time* debunked this claim, it documented numerous meetings and explained that in using White House public logs and presidential calendars as his sources, Schweizer overlooked the fact that visits with cabinet secretaries are often not included in these reports.[17]

By the time *Clinton Cash* was published in 2015, Schweizer had been caught in so many distortions of fact that no reputable newspaper would have employed him as a cub reporter. His employment history, his benefactors, and the fact that the victims of his acts were all Democrats left little doubt about his agenda. However, just as the schemers behind the Arkansas Project had enticed mainstream reporters to take up the nonissue of Whitewater, with the aid of Bannon's Breitbart, Fox News, and his Murdoch-owned publisher HarperCollins, Schweizer seeded the press with tantalizing hints of what *Clinton Cash* revealed. Long before its publication, *The New York Times, The Washington Post,* and Fox News committed to reporting on the book in exchange for early access to its contents.[18]

Some mainstream outlets presented the claims in *Clinton Cash* with many caveats and dashes of skepticism. The editorial board of *The New York Times,* for example, followed the paper's report on the Uranium One tale with a piece that noted its complexity and that "there is no indication that Mrs. Clinton played a role in the uranium deal's eventual approval by a cabinet-level committee." The same editorial observed that Hillary Clinton had resigned from the Clinton Foundation board to prevent conflicts of interest, and the foundation had begun to reveal more data about its operations than required by law. Nevertheless, the editorial board wrote, "the foundation's role in the lives of the Clintons is inevitably becoming a subject of political concern."[19]

Separate from the editorial, *The Times's* Schweizer-inspired news report on Uranium One, which bore the headline CASH FLOWED TO CLINTON FOUNDATION AMID RUSSIAN URANIUM DEAL, explained, "Whether the donations played any role in the approval of the uranium deal is unknown." However, the overall thrust of the article made it clear that something suspicious and perhaps dangerous had occurred. The piece noted that Uranium One lands held 20 percent of U.S. uranium reserve but not that the law barred the sale of American uranium abroad. Under the subheading "The Power to Say No," the article explained that a Committee on Foreign Investment in the United States, which included a representative of the Department of State, could have stopped the Uranium One sale. Actually, the committee could only make a recommendation to the president, who had the power to say no. Although the committee's work was generally kept confidential, the department's man on the panel said he had never been contacted by Hillary Clinton to discuss *any* matter under consideration. Finally, the writers described donations to the Clinton Foundation as a matter of Hillary Clinton's husband "collecting millions in donations from people associated with Uranium One." It was, of course, the charity that "collected" the donation, and as oversight groups had documented, more than 86 percent of the money the Clinton Foundation raised was spent on programs, with less than 11 percent going to administration.[20]

When the nonpartisan PolitiFact website looked into Uranium One, it concluded that the secretary of state was not authorized to stop the deal and that "there is no evidence that donations to the Clinton Foundation from people with ties to Uranium One or Bill Clinton's speaking fee influenced Hillary Clinton's official actions." PolitiFact was one of many mainstream news operations that were both derided and courted by the Right. When its findings were supportive, archconservatives deemed PolitiFact authoritative. When they were not, they said that the fact-checkers were unfair.

Unfortunately for Clinton, the online fact-checkers worked in a slow and piecemeal fashion, and even when they reached conclusions, they couldn't match the effect of the coverage the issue, and *Clinton Cash,* received in the early days of the 2016 campaign. The key was the tactic Schweizer's Breitbart colleague Wynton Hall termed *anchor left, pivot right.* This meant enticing one big mainstream media outlet like *The Times* to legitimize a narrative and then using that imprimatur to expand its effectiveness. (Former Arkansas Project conspirator David Brock offered a variation on this idea, suggesting that Schweizer needed a "host body" to nourish his claims long enough for them to gain strength.)[21]

As ideal host bodies, *The Times* and *The Post* energized the arguments in *Clinton Cash* and disseminated them to other outlets, where they were reprinted. Their distillations of Schweizer became fodder for broadcasters, including the New York public radio station WNYC, which devoted more than half an hour to a conversation with one of the authors of its first big news report about Uranium One and the Clinton Foundation. From this point forward, those who would defend Schweizer and his book could point to the paper of record and note that it had seemingly certified that a genuine controversy had been revealed. Eventually, the weaknesses in the book, and the press accounts about the Uranium One story, would be revealed by many journalists, including Shepard Smith of Fox News, who would spark outrage among viewers by declaring that Hillary Clinton had not approved the sale of the mines and that the owner's donations preceded the deal by three years.[22]

Shepard Smith wouldn't reach his conclusion about the Clinton Foundation until a year *after* the 2016 election. The lag between fiction and fact was something that Steve Bannon and his chosen candidate, Republican front-runner Donald Trump, had always planned to exploit. Both men were first-rate propagandists with deep experience manipulating both the press and public perception. Trump had first peddled his fake biography—young real estate mogul—to *The New York Times* in 1976. The result was a lengthy profile that announced that a trust fund baby who had never begun, let alone finished, a project was a visionary with movie star looks who was worth $200 million. The most prestigious media source in the country even let his father declare, as if a proud papa's evaluation meant anything, that "Donald is the smartest person I know."

When compared with Trump, Bannon was late to the game of manipulating the public. In the 1980s and 1990s, he had worked in many fields, including as an investment banker at Goldman Sachs and in movie production. His artistic taste ran toward the Nazi impresario Leni Riefenstahl, whom he admired for her ability to manipulate audiences through fear. Work on a hagiographic documentary about Ronald Reagan—a *New York Post* critic called it "very much like Soviet propaganda"—allowed him to meet David Bossie, the lifelong Clintonhater and head of Citizens United. The two would work together on films that demonized migrants and boosted President George W. Bush.

In 2005, while Trump was starring in the reality TV show *The Apprentice,* Bannon leaped from the world of on-screen fantasies into the business of selling imaginary goods to computer gamers. Played by tens of millions of people, the online games involved live competition between teams and individuals anywhere in the world. Some were oriented around playful adventures, but virtual killing and plunder were the main activities in many of the most popular ones. A participant inhabited the perspective of an avatar and experienced rising levels of excitement as he (they were mostly males) moved through suspenseful scenarios that climaxed when he either killed enough competing avatars or died. Victories earned rewards such as virtual gold, which could be cashed in for weapons, armor, or magical powers.

Much like living in a movie, the games allowed players to be strong, agile warriors in a land populated by fantasy figures, including females who were generally young, buxom, and scantily clad. (In some games, including a version of *Grand Theft Auto*, players could virtually rape those characters.) The gaming environment encouraged an us-versus-them mentality and a level of individual achievement worthy of a conservative political fantasy. It contrasted sharply with a real world where it was increasingly difficult for young men to earn a living with meaningful work that allowed them to be independent. Bannon's company paid extremely low wages to workers in Asia—known as gold farmers—who won prizes in the gaming universe that were then sold for actual dollars. The purchases allowed customers to cheat the game, which infuriated other players. Bannon and his colleagues were able to talk investors, including bankers at his old employer Goldman Sachs, into putting $60 million into the company. It soon went into decline and would sell much of its business at a discount.[23]

Bannon returned to media in a big way after Barack Obama was elected, joining Breitbart, becoming an occasional guest on Fox News, and appearing at rallies for the so-called Tea Party movement of angry conservatives. After Andrew Breitbart's death in 2012, Bannon became the top official at the site, which, *Time* magazine noted, "pushed racist, sexist, xenophobic and anti-Semitic material." As he published white nationalists such as Milo Yiannopoulos, he made Breitbart into what he called "the platform for the alt-right," a movement known for its virulent anti-immigrant, anti-Muslim, anti-feminist ideology. The alt-right was populated in part by gamers and former gamers, whose alienation and rage against "normies" were expressed in increasingly angry postings in web communities, where they claimed special understanding of the hypocrisy and evils of powerful institutions and individuals like Hillary Clinton. They practiced both trolling, which involved sending provocative messages to people they dislike, and "doxing," which added real-world elements to the trolling phenomenon by making a target's phone number, street address, and other sensitive information public. The word derives from the term *docs,* which refers to documents.[24]

A wealthy former investment banker who knew the resentments and technologies of the alt-right, Bannon had arranged the funding for his friend Schweizer's *Clinton Cash,* watched the host bodies of the mainstream media embrace part of it, and then used Breitbart to expand on the initial wave of publicity the book generated. Before and during his time as Trump's campaign manager, Bannon considered the mainstream press—*The New York Times,* CNN, *Time,* ABC News, *The Washington Post,* and others—his enemy. These outlets had long been responsible for fact-checking the politicians and others who would try to sell the American people on an idea or a product, and their determinations helped shape what was accepted as true about everything from climate change to candidates for office. With Breitbart and books and films and now in the 2016 campaign, he would overwhelm journalists with so many claims and accusations about Hillary Clinton that they would be too busy, and too distracted, to focus on the usual work of vetting his man. When he talked about this, he borrowed a football term—*flooding the zone*—that described sending so many players into a part of the field that defenders couldn't track them all. "The real opposition is the media," he would famously tell the writer Michael Lewis. "And the way to deal with them is to flood the zone with shit."[25]

As Bannon flooded the zone, Trump presaged his candidacy with sexist attacks that included forwarding on Twitter the timeworn slogan, "If Hillary can't satisfy her husband what makes her think she can satisfy America?" On Twitter and Facebook, where the audience was counted in "followers" or "friends," Trump tried to game the system by counting millions who were no more real than the gold Steve Bannon used to sell to gamers. As insiders knew, a fake social media audience could be purchased from companies that offered everything from simple dummy followers to sophisticated bots that were programmed to automatically reply in terms that made readers think a real person had tapped out a message. During the 2016 election, one tech firm that tracked such things estimated that only 21 percent of his Twitter followers were real. What was the point of this deception? Besides the satisfaction he may have gained by cheating to win, the fake followers could be used to support his claim to massive popularity.[26]

No matter how many actual people received his supremely lacerating tweets, the trolling style and frequent sexism worked for Trump in the netherworld of the alt-right and among his most avid fans at campaign rallies. These followers thrilled to his borrowing a Yiddish term for penis to say she was "schlonged" in her 2008 race against Barack Obama and cheered every time he called her a liar or a criminal. At times during the election season, a similar casual misogyny seemed to arise among supporters of Clinton's rival for the 2016 Democratic nomination, Bernie Sanders. Some of this behavior occurred in the open and was documented as Clinton and Sanders competed to win delegates to the nominating convention. However, much of what occurred online was created by bots and imposters using false social media accounts to masquerade as Sanders supporters.[27]

Sanders's campaign team noticed the messages and traced many of them to sites and accounts in Russia and former Soviet republics. During the New Hampshire primary, these countries were responsible for making the words *bitch* and *vagina* and *rapist* some of the most commonly used terms in social media posts about Hillary Clinton. Much of this material was coming from Veles, Macedonia, where at least one hundred websites published pro-Trump, pro-Sanders, and anti-Clinton articles that were then promoted as "news" on Facebook and Twitter.

A city of fifty-five thousand, Veles was so poor it couldn't support a single movie theater and so polluted by Communist-era industry that when Macedonia was part of Yugoslavia it was declared the second-most-despoiled place in the country. Jobs were scarce, and young adults filled their time playing the same online games that occupied their peers in America and searching for ways to make money. For years, the tech-savvy operated websites linked to advertisers through search engines and Facebook. Some made money offering information on consumer goods, sports, health, and diet, but those who shifted to American politics with posts that offered wild attacks on Hillary Clinton hit it big.

They didn't even have to work at creating authentic-seeming content, because American and British propagandists would do it for them.

The most productive source for American political items was a group called Liberty Writers. It was owned by young propagandists named Paris Wade and Ben Goldman. Working with other Americans, including established conspiracy-monger Alicia Powe, Wade and Goldman were responsible for hundreds of items that appeared on Macedonian sites, including USA Politics Today, which had been created in 2015 by a local lawyer named Trajche Arsov. A self-identified libertarian who considered Republican senators Rand Paul and Ted Cruz his idols, Arsov was a pioneer in an industry that soon operated hundreds of anti-Clinton sites. His website recycled many old smears such as "HUGE Scandal. Chelsea isn't Bill Clinton's Daughter?" According to Arsov, "No one, literally no one, in Veles created his own articles."[28]

Macedonians found that the greatest success, and therefore highest revenues, came from pages that told readers the most outrageous and frightening lies about Hillary Clinton. Links to these would circulate like wildfire among Americans, who added Macedonians to their Facebook friends lists. In a country where the average income was about $370 per month, Macedonians earned ten times as much publishing fictions about Clinton's imminent arrest or Pope Francis's endorsement of Trump. (The income from millions of visitors rivaled the money made by local drug dealers.) For a while, business was so good that people with almost no tech training were brought into the business. Arsov would recall that among them was a pig farmer who made much more money in front of a screen than he did tending animals.

Good as things were in Macedonia, they were even better for the most active political deceivers in the United States. A California man named Jestin Coler earned $30,000 per month by baiting readers with outlandish lies about Clinton. Coler's method began with coining names like *Denver Guardian* that echoed the authenticity of an established media company. (Here he operated like the *Independent Journal Review,* but with no big investor.) Pages at these sites were loaded with real news taken from an actual publisher and then supplemented with inflammatory fake stories written to seem true. As Coler would explain, the pieces that attracted the highest readership, and thus the most revenue, were "any sort of a gun-grabbing story, pro-abortion, anti-Obama, or anti-Hillary, anti-Muslim, anything anti-Mexican, anti-immigrant, just kind of this Right-wing red meat."

Although he imagined himself a satirist, Coler's articles were not especially humorous, and only the most careful visitors to his websites would find any indication that they were intentionally deceiving. And those who read the stories as they were repurposed by Russians or Macedonians wouldn't have any access to the disclaimer. Coler's justification for his deceptions reverberated with the frustration of countless men of his generation, including denizens of the alt-right, who struggled in an economy where, for decades, the rich and superrich gained and the rest saw little improvement. Expenses like housing and health care skyrocketed, and women, many entering the workforce out of necessity, became competitors with men who struggled to attain the identity of "provider." For them, life presented frustration at a level their fathers and grandfathers didn't know. If the solution involved disrupting and deceiving, so be it.

"People do worse things for money," Coler told writer Zachary Crockett. "I didn't do anything illegal. . . . I live in a very affluent part of the country, and buying a house was always unattainable. Not anymore. It afforded a better life for me and my family." And so it was that he used sites that appeared authoritative to push ideas that would alarm and enrage and inflame hatred with headlines that included:

CITY IN MICHIGAN FIRST TO FULLY IMPLEMENT SHARIA LAW

COLORADO POT SHOP TO PROVIDE FREE MARIJUANA TO SYRIAN REFUGEES

HILLARY CLINTON PROMISES TO CONFISCATE "THREE TIMES AS MANY" GUNS AS OBAMA DID

WHITE HOUSE PLANS TO RECRUIT ILLEGALS TO GUARD NATION'S BORDER![29]

Coler was not alone in his effort to exploit the internet for profit at Hillary Clinton's expense. In Maryland, a twenty-three-year-old man named Cameron Harris created a website that mimicked in its name and appearance a Christian news site and began offering articles that said, among other things, that Hillary Clinton had filed court papers seeking a divorce and that she blamed racism for the death of a gorilla in an Ohio zoo. Race, always a reliable subject for those who would inflame, was one of Harris's favorite topics. In one of his stories, he spread the lie that protesters had killed a black Trump supporter. However, anything that riled Trump's supporters by accusing Clinton of something heinous produced clicks that brought Harris revenue. One article, inspired by the candidate's claim that the election would be "rigged," reported that ballots marked for Clinton had been found in an Ohio warehouse. This "report" circulated to six million people on Facebook, where it was widely accepted as truth. Others that were widely shared accused Bill Clinton of pedophilia and alleged that pro-Clinton activists had killed a homeless military veteran. The election would be over before anyone made public that the site and its contents were fraudulent and that Harris, who estimated his site had earned him $100,000 in just a few months, was an aide to a Republican state legislator.[30]

While Harris, Coler, and the Macedonians manipulated voters for profit, the Russians spent millions to campaign against Clinton and in favor of her Republican opponent in the general election, Donald Trump. The Internet Research Agency continued to troll Americans with political messages, many written to appeal to conservative Christian prejudices, and it began to spend money on Facebook to get its messages before a wider audience. A memo circulated to staff described the campaign as an attempted to disrupt the U.S. election and urged workers to "use any opportunity to criticize Hillary and the rest (except Sanders and Trump—we support them)." The agency also began stressing messages that exploited racial sensitivities. One typical message read, "You know, a great number of black people support us saying that #HillaryClintonIsNotMyPresident." Others aligned with the Trump/GOP arguments that Clinton was opposed to private firearm ownership, weak on terrorism, and worthy of criminal prosecution.[31]

In the meantime, the Russian Federal Security Service (FSB) and Main Intelligence Directorate (GRU) launched attacks on the Democratic National Committee and the Clinton campaign. Through methods like "spearfishing," emails that entice recipients to open attachments that let intruders steal information, the Russian agencies took emails, documents, and even donor information from both organizations. In May 2016, James Clapper, the U.S. director of national intelligence, revealed that American authorities were aware of the attacks. At about the same time, at a London bar called the Kensington Wine Rooms, a young Trump campaign advisor named George Papadopoulos spent much of a night drinking with Alexander Downer, Australia's ambassador to Britain, informing him that Russia had dirt on Hillary Clinton.[32]

If a twenty-eight-year-old with less than a year's worth of experience in politics knew that the Russians had negative information about Clinton *and he was talking about it in a London bar,* the hacks perpetrated by the GRU and FSB were not going to stay secret very long. Moving to get ahead of any news about the document theft, the Russians concocted a fake internet provocateur named Guccifer 2.0 and would use him to claim responsibility for the hacking. The ruse depended on the fact that a real Romanian hacker who went by the name Guccifer had been caught and prosecuted for stealing the data of various celebrities and governments. Just prior to the document thefts' being made public, a prominent Moscow businessman, who knew both Putin and Trump, notified the campaign that a Russian lawyer possessed Clinton secrets to share. On June 9, 2016, Natalia Veselnitskaya met with Donald Trump Jr., presidential campaign manager Paul Manafort, and the candidate's son-in-law, Jared Kushner, at Trump Tower in New York City. On June 15, a cybersecurity company hired by the Democrats announced that their computer systems had been breached by Russian organizations code-named Cozy Bear and Fancy Bear. The next day, Guccifer 2.0 announced he was the culprit, not the Russians.[33]

With hackers tunneling into campaign computers, thousands of trolls attacking from Russia, Eastern Europe, and the United States, and dishonest new sites generating wave after wave of malicious content, Hillary Clinton faced an unprecedented onslaught. Eventually, investigators would be deployed to determine if foreign actors actively coordinated with elements of the Trump team, but no active cooperation would have been necessary. No central authority was required for people to seize upon existing themes and phrases and then use them for their own purposes. A remarkable number of people—including Clinton supporters—made and sold merchandise that demonized her. T-shirts emblazoned with HILLARY FOR PRISON did well, but the sexist and sexualized stuff—buttons that read HILLARY WILL GO DOWN FASTER THAN BILL'S PANTS or GOOD LUCK HILLARY—DON'T BLOW IT!—flew off the virtual shelves at online selling sites such as Etsy and eBay. Amy Doughty, who worked as a school nurse and supported Clinton enthusiastically, made good money selling a button that bore a photo of Monica Lewinsky and the message I GOT THE "JOB" DONE WHEN HILLARY COULDN'T.

Doughty felt a twinge of guilt over being a woman who profited from appealing to misogyny, and she marveled at the power of hate in the marketplace. "The meaner they are, the more people buy them," she told *Time*. "These buttons are completely sexist." Indeed, what she was doing was the rough equivalent of a black person selling Sambo merchandise during the civil rights movement, and she admitted it made her "nervous." She was delighted that Hillary Clinton had demonstrated for her daughter "that she can be anything she wants to be." However, her father had taught her that "when it comes to money and business, you be bipartisan," which meant selling LIFE'S A BITCH, DON'T ELECT ONE baseball caps. And when her daughter asked her what a blow job was, she told her, "Mommy just made $2."[34]

In another political season, the degrading messages sold by Amy Doughty and many others would have been purchased as novelty items by fringe supporters of an ordinary candidate like John McCain or Mitt Romney, who would not have tolerated racist material directed at their opponent, who was the first black major-party candidate. However, Hillary Clinton was running against Donald Trump, who had made sexism part of his identity and described as "beautiful" the emotions expressed by followers who chanted, "Hang the bitch," "Kill her," and "Cunt." His campaign events were places where people felt uninhibited about expressing hate or rage toward Clinton, Democrats, and the news media, whom Trump demonized in terms Bannon surely appreciated. As he called the press "dishonest" and "scum" and purveyors of "fake news," his supporters began to heckle and threaten reporters who covered the election. This rhetoric challenged the notion that news reports were ever fair or accurate and eroded the idea that anything could be understood to be true.[35]

Attacks on legitimate journalism and the role reporters played sorting fact from fiction helped Trump promote claims that were false but resonated with anyone who had been exposed to books like *Clinton Cash* or the various Benghazi investigations. Heads nodded as Trump said Ambassador Stevens "was left helpless to die as Hillary Clinton soundly slept in her bed" or Clinton "illegally deleted" thirty-three thousand emails she should have turned over to FBI investigators. Trump would cry, "Crooked Hillary!" and his followers chanted, "Lock her up!" in a kind of call-and-response that would have seemed unimaginable before 2016.

The accusations Trump flung in the form of slogans were all distortions, but they came at such a rate that it was impossible for anyone in politics or the press to counter them. Besides, the facts were often so nuanced that following them required more time than most people could devote to the task. For example, when the FBI investigated Clinton's State Department email practices, it found that other secretaries of state had followed similar practices, and no relevant emails had been withheld by Clinton. On the other side of the ledger, agents documented sloppiness and a small number of instances where sensitive information had been inadvertently shared. This was concerning, but not worthy of further action. When he announced the finding, FBI director James Comey said, "Although there is evidence of potential violations of the statutes regarding the handling of classified information, our judgment is that no reasonable prosecutor would bring such a case."[36]

Many Americans saw Comey for the first time when they watched news reports of his announcement. Extremely tall (he was six foot eight), straight-backed, and stridently confident in his moral compass, the fifty-five-year-old Comey presented himself as the antithesis of the man once regarded as the personification of the bureau, J. Edgar Hoover. Dictatorial and corrupt, Hoover had used FBI agents to gather information on politicians, civil rights leaders, athletes, and entertainers and tried to tip the scales in the 1948 presidential election in favor of Thomas Dewey. By the end of his thirty-seven years atop the FBI, he was as much reviled as admired. Comey, in contrast, was outspoken about the limits the law

imposes on public officials and agencies like the FBI. Comey was determined to show he was not motivated primarily by politics. Throughout
his career, he had consistently signaled that he considered himself a nonpartisan public official because, as he once said, the Justice Department
must "be seen as the good guys, and not as either this administration or
that administration."

The FBI director's long-running effort to stand above the fray of
power politics was, in itself, a source of power, which he had amplified
by seeking just enough positive press attention to establish a shiny public profile. For example, in 2014 he brought the TV news program *60
Minutes* into a top-secret agency command center and was rewarded
with a glowing profile titled "The Director," which portrayed him as
strong, resolute, and humble. "I believe that Americans should be deeply
skeptical of government power," he said, referencing himself along with
other officials. "You cannot trust people in power." When interviewer
Scott Pelley asked if his loyalty belonged to the president, Comey replied, "No, my responsibility, I took an oath to support and defend the
Constitution of the United States."

This kind of statement was well tuned to an age of skepticism when
public relations experts coached leaders to counteract mistrust and suspicion by presenting themselves as open, ethical, and self-aware. As he
guided the TV crew into a room formerly kept secret, Comey demonstrated his openness, and with his pledge to be loyal to the nation's
founding document, he staked out the public service high ground. He
was, like corruption fighter Eliot Ness, a clean-cut lawman whose integrity could function as a weapon.[37]

Conscientious as he may have been, Comey was not immune to
politics. His statement clearing Clinton of the threat of criminal charges
had been influenced by Attorney General Loretta Lynch's firm suggestion that he refer to an FBI "matter" and not an "investigation." The politics built into Comey's action became evident immediately. Democrats
said Comey cleared Clinton and put to rest the email issue. Republicans stressed a passage that said her team had been "extremely careless
in their handling of very sensitive, highly classified information." Polls
showed that Trump briefly gained some ground on Clinton following

this first Comey statement, but voters soon returned to their previous preferences.

While Comey ruled out a prosecution of Clinton, the investigations by House Republicans and the FBI probe that occasioned the director's remarks contributed to a general sense that she must have done something bad. In the meantime, no public mention was made of the fact that American officials were tracking Russian efforts to tear down the woman who had vexed Vladimir Putin in the past and elevate a man who seemed happy to work with Moscow despite its record of human rights abuses. Alerted by the Australian diplomat, who had listened to George Papadopoulos talk about Russians at the Kensington Wine Rooms, the bureau was stepping carefully so as to avoid the appearance of meddling in the campaign.

As much as the FBI sought to steer clear of the election, Julian Assange was determined to influence the outcome. As founder of WikiLeaks, the global organization devoted to divulging stolen secrets, Assange argued that hacks that obtained the secrets of the powerful, which could then be publicized, constituted a justifiable form of "information warfare" against his enemies. He had long criticized American influence in the world, and this made the former secretary of state a natural foe. However, his animus toward Western powers was made more personal after WikiLeaks revealed U.S. military secrets and then Swedish authorities charged him with sexual assault. In 2014, a besieged Assange claimed asylum in Ecuador's embassy in London. With the United States and Clinton as common enemies, Assange and Vladimir Putin would be natural allies. Assange briefly hosted a show on the state-controlled RT television network (formerly called Russia Today), and WikiLeaks had taken pro-Russia stances in world affairs when WikiLeaks made public thousands of documents hacked from the Democrats by Russia. Given the context, it was apparent to experts that Wikileaks was acting as a fence for the goods stolen by Russians.[38]


Coming days before the Democrats opened their national convention, the dump by WikiLeaks included some real emails, some fake ones, and many that embarrassed Clinton and the party. Emails that showed that Democratic National Committee officials, who were supposed to be neutral, favored Clinton over her rival Bernie Sanders outraged his followers and led to acrimony at the convention. Donald Trump used a press conference to gleefully declare, "Russia, if you're listening, I hope you're able to find the 30,000 emails that are missing."[39]

As Trump crowed and the press scrambled to inform the public about the contents of the emails, Trump's friend and longtime political ally Roger Stone heard from a right-wing activist named Jerome Corsi. According to press accounts made later, Stone had asked Corsi to go to London to pick up documents from Assange. Corsi had not gone himself but sent a contact in London to the Ecuadoran embassy. On August 2, he wrote to Stone to say, "Word is friend in embassy plans 2 more dumps. One shortly after I'm back. 2nd in Oct. Impact planned to be very damaging." Stone then talked to others about having dinner with Assange and said that WikiLeaks planned more revelations. He published an article at Breitbart.com supporting the Russian Guccifer 2.0 fiction, and he predicted, specifically, that emails damaging to Clinton campaign manager John Podesta would be published soon. Stone also heard from a WikiLeaks source that it planned to spread false claims about Hillary's health. Within days, Fox News and the *National Enquirer* were distributing innuendoes about her condition, and within weeks, Trump was speculating about it in his speeches.

WikiLeaks could get a hearing for its claims because as of 2016, the organization—and Assange—enjoyed a reputation for spilling authentic documents that revealed the powerful in ways that sparked worldwide outrage. Although others were targeted, WikiLeaks' major releases involved U.S. government files, and the pattern suggested an anti-U.S. and pro-Russia bias. The State Department under Hillary Clinton was subject to frequent WikiLeaks document dumps, and Julian Assange made no secret of his hatred for her. This made him a natural ally for the Trump campaign. In September, WikiLeaks privately contacted Donald Trump Jr., who had previously welcomed Russians to meet at Trump

Tower, with news about a new anti-Trump website "about to launch." The message said, "We have guessed the password. It is 'putintrump.' See 'About' for who is behind it. Any comments?" Trump Jr. replied, "Off the record I don't know who that is, but I'll ask around."

Weeks later, Assange would offer Trump Jr. help with the issue of his father's tax returns, which had been kept secret despite a long tradition of candidates making returns public. Here Assange seemed to be looking for a way to cover his efforts to defeat Clinton. "If we publish them," he told Trump Jr., "it will dramatically improve the perception of our impartiality."

The tax returns were never revealed, but Assange's motivations were evident for all to see as he turned WikiLeaks' Twitter account into a kind of *Pravda* for Trump's benefit. He dredged up the long-settled matter of Vince Foster's suicide to claim, "FBI interview with Hillary Clinton over death of White House aid have gone 'missing' from the US National Archives," and offered a truly bizarre claim about John Podesta. "The Podestas' 'Spirit Cooking' dinner? It's not what you think. It's blood, sperm and breastmilk. But mostly blood." These and other comments were the rantings of a man who by the fall of 2016 had spent more than four years holed up in Ecuador's London embassy, deprived of the usual interactions that are part of a stable human existence. He considered himself to be at war, and in this battle, truth was not a constraint.[40]

No concerted effort would be required to determine that Assange and the Trump campaign sought the same goal—namely, the political destruction of Hillary Clinton—and were not constrained in their pursuit by ordinary morality. Taking up a deranged conspiracy theory spread first by Roger Stone, Assange promoted the idea that a young man named Seth Rich, who had worked for the Democratic Party, was murdered for something having to do with WikiLeaks. (Supposedly, the Clinton campaign believed Rich had given Assange the documents that were hacked.) Rich was in fact killed as part of a robbery. Nevertheless, Assange and right-wing media, including Breitbart.com, continued to promote the idea that somehow his death was connected to Clinton. A week after Assange stepped into the issue, Donald Trump hired Steve

Bannon to serve as chief executive officer of his campaign. He called him a "street fighter." He would work in tandem with new campaign manager Kellyanne Conway, whose husband, George T. Conway III, had led the anti-Clinton group of lawyers who called themselves the Elves as they worked on the Paula Jones lawsuit against then president Bill Clinton.

Kellyanne Conway's biography made her the scrappy sort that Bannon seemed to believe himself to be. The granddaughter of alleged Philadelphia mobster Jimmy "the Brute" DiNatale (*The Brute* was carved on his grave marker), Conway was raised by her single mother after her parents were divorced when she was three. As a high schooler, she worked on a farm. She attended a Catholic college and law school but passed up a career in the law to work in politics. She was one of a small group of young women in Washington whose social lives attracted almost as much attention as their work lives. Conway dated senator and future insurance company pitchman Fred Thompson. She married her husband in 2001 and had met Trump when she was on the board of a condominium building where she lived. Prior to the 2016 election, Bannon had made her part of an informal "cabal" he had organized to make illegal immigration a political issue that could anger and motivate white voters. After peaking during the George W. Bush administration, the number of unauthorized immigrants in the United States had actually declined steadily, but Trump consistently spoke of a supposed crisis involving people from Mexico who entered the country and committed violent crimes. Although these immigrants actually committed fewer crimes than others, by scapegoating them Trump attached them to every resentment and frustration of his supporters and rallied them to his side.[41]

If anything besides anti-immigrant fervor bonded the likes of Conway, Bannon, and others who backed Trump, it was hostility toward Hillary Clinton, which was an energizing force so powerful that it spanned continents and moved the afflicted to extreme measures. In Russia, the bosses at the Internet Research Agency ordered up a video game that showed Clinton bombing innocent people and implored the social media trolls who were targeting the U.S. election to keep up the pace of their efforts. One "account specialist" was criticized for a "low number of posts dedicated to criticizing Hillary Clinton." Groups organized to discourage minority voters from supporting Clinton began to urge them to support a Green Party gadfly candidate whose campaign had included attacks on Clinton as a mother. In late 2015, Jill Stein had sat at a table with Putin at a dinner in Moscow, where Trump's chief intelligence advisor, retired army general Michael Flynn, had occupied the chair to Putin's right. Flynn was going around the country leading cheers of "Lock her up!" about Clinton. Stein was, like Trump, spouting pro-Russia views that ran counter to both Republican and Democratic orthodoxy. Stein questioned the validity of the NATO defense organization, and Trump repeatedly expressed his admiration for Putin.[42]

Although they may not have known it, the Russians' effort was augmented by a truly innovative and effective social media campaign by elements of Trump's own election team, led by digital consultant Brad Parscale and a British-based contractor called Cambridge Analytica. Founded by Bannon and Mercer, Cambridge had access to between four and five thousand bits of information about every American on Facebook. Many of these people had relied on news recommended by online friends to stay informed. This data could be used to bombard voters with messages that were tailored to appeal to their prejudices. For example, voters who were avid gun owners could be sent a stream of notices about how Clinton wanted to take away their right to arms. With their Facebook friends receiving similar messages and then sharing them spontaneously, the ideas pushed out by both Parscale and Cambridge Analytica were amplified.

Combined, the pro-Trump bot army outnumbered Clinton's by five to one. And though Parscale would question its effectiveness, the programming done by Cambridge was informed by a theory of psychological manipulation that made it unique. It was paired with online weapons that allowed Trump's workers to take over pro-Clinton social media communities, and all this activity was calibrated, based on feedback, to move voters one by one. Trump's campaign schedule and themes were adjusted to take advantage of the insights gained in this process, to change not only minds but also the flow of information online. Thus what one expert termed an "emotional leash" was placed around a voter's mind.[43]

Cambridge Analytica and Parscale's group worked out of view and with methods so esoteric that few would have understood what was going on even if they had been informed. The press *had* reported that Russia had been making attempts to influence the election, but the issue was not widely understood. Nevertheless, Trump was irked by the suggestion that he was getting aid from a country that was opposed to American interests all over the world. He used the first of his debates with Clinton to deny the Russians' involvement and suggest that almost anyone, including "somebody sitting on their bed that weighs four hundred pounds," could have hacked into his opponent's computers. In this same debate, he said he doubted Clinton possessed the "stamina" to be president, echoing a conspiracy theory that held that she was somehow hiding a health problem. Immediately after the debate, Roger Stone declared that a Secret Service agent had told him Clinton suffered from "some advanced form of epilepsy." Having proved her stamina as both secretary of state and a campaigner, Clinton was a noticeably fit woman who suffered from no significant health problems, but in the blizzard of lies that swirled in the final weeks of the campaign, these were just additional flakes.[44]

On October 7, two days before the second debate, *The Washington Post* published news that Trump had been caught on videotape bragging that because he was a celebrity, he could sexually assault women—"grab 'em by the pussy" was how he put it—and get away with it. Coming after more than a dozen women had accused him of similar behavior, the report, posted online with the actual video from the program called *Access Hollywood,* would have ruined the chances of any other candidate in any other presidential election. But in this one, Trump's ally Assange immediately answered by making public thousands of emails stolen from Clinton campaign manager John Podesta. The release of the emails had been foreshadowed by Roger Stone in a Twitter post that included the words "@HillaryClinton is done. #Wikileaks." The noteworthy emails revealed the private complaints shared by Podesta and others in the campaign and facts about how Hillary Clinton had changed her positions on certain issues. No scandal emerged, but the mere act of making the emails available to the world altered the political conversation. Sure, the *Access Hollywood* recording and allegations of sexual abuse were bad, but what about the WikiLeaks revelations? Emails! Hillary Clinton! Surely something terrible had been revealed.[45]

At the second debate, Trump invited three women who had accused Bill Clinton of sexual improprieties—Juanita Broaddrick, Paula Jones, Kathleen Willey—to be part of his entourage and thereby shake his rival's composure. The stunt was contained by debate organizers, who nevertheless allowed the women to sit in the audience, where they would serve as a distraction for the press, TV broadcasters, and the debaters. Trump used the presence of his guests to argue that Bill Clinton was a sexual predator and his opponent had aided his offenses. "Bill Clinton was abusive to women," he said. "Hillary Clinton attacked those same women and attacked them viciously." The authoritative PolitiFact.com judged these claims to be "mostly false," but the tactic was useful. After the debate, a satisfied Trump ally, Rudy Giuliani, expressed regret only that elements of the plan had been blocked. "We were going to put the four women in the VIP box," Giuliani told *The Washington Post*. "We had it all set. We wanted to have them shake hands with Bill, to see if Bill would shake hands with them."[46]

Giuliani, who was enjoying his time in the spotlight as a spokesman for Trump, was in regular contact with former FBI agents who told him there was "a revolution going on inside the FBI" over Hillary Clinton. (One of Giuliani's close friends, retired FBI official James Kallstrom, considered the Clintons equivalent to a "crime family" and said that FBI agents were "furious" about the way Comey had handled the investigation into Clinton's emails.) On October 26, Giuliani couldn't contain himself and told an interviewer on Fox News to expect "some pretty big surprises."

At the FBI, Comey was considering the "revolution" that Giuliani described. At issue was a case in New York that was tangentially connected to Clinton and evidence that had not yet been fully assessed. Some people in the powerful New York office were clamoring about newly discovered documents and fuming over the fact that nothing was being done. Comey thought about "the standard" governing FBI public statements. Written policy and tradition hold that "if you can avoid it, you take no action that might have an impact on an election." In this case, people were already casting ballots in states that permitted early voting. Two Saturdays prior to the actual date of the election, Comey felt himself to be caught between long-standing policy and the dissension in the ranks.

"I'm sitting there, on the morning of October 27, and I can't see a door that's labeled, 'No action here.' I can only see two doors, and they're both actions. One says, 'Speak,' the other says, 'Conceal.'" Of course, Comey had a third option, which would mean waiting. No one at the FBI had actually *read* the documents in question. Comey couldn't say whether they were any more important than pages torn from a telephone book found blowing around a landfill.

Comey would later say that he couldn't see the third option. Two days after Giuliani's warning, and just eleven days before the election, he announced that because of new evidence, he was reopening the previously closed investigation of Clinton's mishandling of official emails. The announcement was made in a 160-word letter to Congress:[47]

> In previous congressional testimony, I referred to the fact that the Federal Bureau of Investigation (FBI) had completed its investigation of former Secretary Clinton's personal email server. I am writing to supplement my previous testimony.
>
> In connection with an unrelated case, the FBI has learned of the existence of emails that appear to be pertinent to the investigation. I am writing to inform you that the investigative team briefed me on this yesterday, and I agree that the FBI should take appropriate investigative steps designed to allow investigators to review these emails to determine whether they contain classified information, as well as to assess their importance to our investigation.
>
> Although the FBI cannot yet assess whether or not this material may be significant, and I cannot predict how long it will take us to complete the additional work, I believe it is important to update your Committees about our efforts in light of my previous testimony.

This was, by all appearances, the surprise Rudy Giuliani had predicted. The pertinent emails had been found in a laptop belonging to a former member of Congress, Anthony Weiner of New York City, who was under investigation for sending sexually explicit texts and photos to a minor. Weiner had been involved in two previous sexting scandals with adult women, which had ruined his political career. This third case involved a minor and constituted criminal activity, for which he would serve prison time. The Clinton-related emails had found their way onto the laptop's memory because Weiner was married to longtime Clinton aide Huma Abedin, who had used the computer at home.

No one outside of her family had worked with Clinton more closely, for a longer period of time, and with greater loyalty than Abedin. This collaboration began when Abedin had been a college-age intern at the White House in 1996. As a Muslim American, she had been targeted for conspiracy theory smears advanced by a handful of GOP members of Congress, and the paranoid corners of the internet teemed with suggestions that she was somehow supportive of terrorists. Her husband's scandals had been excruciating. The one that resulted in Comey's letter took that pain to a new level. Joining Abedin with Weiner in the context of the FBI's investigation of Clinton created a toxic trifecta of innuendo—terrorism, sex crime, and mishandled emails—that had an immediate effect. Pollsters discovered that the number of supporters who said they felt "enthusiastic" about voting for Clinton dropped to 43 percent of her supporters, compared with 53 percent for Trump. In the same time period, Trump was found to be leading not just in key states but overall. For Clinton, Comey's announcement meant that once again the sexual behavior of a man who should have known better, and supposedly wanted her to succeed, had created a crisis for her.[48]

Hours and then days passed with FBI agents and analysts feverishly working to review the emails and Clinton's adversaries speaking as if the verdict were in. Paul Ryan, the Republican Speaker of the House of Representatives, said that Clinton should not be trusted with the national security briefings routinely offered to major-party candidates for president. Donald Trump lauded Comey for his "guts" and cited a string of false claims about Clinton to conclude "this is bigger than

Watergate." Aides to Clinton refuted the suggestion that Comey had described something damning, which, in fact, he had not. However, they couldn't erase the effect of the announcement, which was exceptionally powerful because of its source. Polls that had shown her leading consistently narrowed, and in some swing states Trump surpassed her. At a rally in New Hampshire, he said, "Hillary Clinton's corruption is on a scale we've never seen before. We must not let her take her criminal scheme into the Oval Office."[49]

Comey did not say how long the FBI would need to examine the new emails, so it came as a shock to many when, eight days later, he made this final assessment public. "Based on our review," he said in a *third* letter to Congress, "we have not changed our conclusion that we expressed in July with respect to Secretary Clinton."

Huma Abedin hadn't divulged state secrets. Anthony Weiner hadn't shared classified information along with pictures of his penis. Indeed, the laptop held only copies of emails previously obtained by investigators, and nothing to justify the "revolution" that Giuliani said was occurring within the ranks at the FBI.

Arriving on a Sunday, when Americans were far more likely to tune their televisions to football than the news, Comey's final word was unlikely to reach voters in time to make an impact. With Trump issuing public statements of gratitude—"Thank you, Huma. Thank you, Anthony Weiner"—at his rallies, the damage to Clinton had been done. Incredibly, the most boorish mainstream-party nominee of the modern age, a man with no record of previous public service, was poised to defeat a candidate whose entire adult life had been devoted to the kind of work—lawyer, First Lady, U.S. senator, secretary of state—that made her one of the most qualified persons ever to seek the presidency.[50]

Clinton had made mistakes. The email controversy would not have happened if she had given up her BlackBerry phone, adapted to the State Department's communication regime, and separated her personal and diplomatic emails. She didn't understand the depth of middle-class anxieties about the economy and social change, and she committed gaffes, including an outrageous reference—a "basket of deplorables"—to Trump zealots. Her campaign neglected rural voters and parts of the industrial Midwest even as union organizers and farm country Democrats begged for attention.[51]

Even with her errors, Clinton won nearly three million more votes than Donald Trump. Of course, winning the most votes does not guarantee a presidential candidate election. American presidential elections ultimately depend on an Electoral College, which is comprised of "electors" from each state. The system is weighted to favor less populous states, which are allotted more of these representatives per capita. Thus all the effort that Trump's campaign, Russians, Cambridge Analytica, Macedonians, pop-up "news" outlets, right-wing media, and others made to push and pull voters toward him yielded an extraordinary result. In Michigan, Democratic voters who stayed home and fifty-one thousand who turned out for Jill Stein allowed Trump to win by a little more than ten thousand votes. The same dynamic gave Trump narrow victories in Wisconsin and Pennsylvania. Altogether, a crowd that wouldn't even fill the Rose Bowl determined who would be president.

It would strain credulity to believe that the targeted efforts of all the internet-based propagandists didn't motivate the number of voters Trump needed to prevail in the handful of purple states responsible for making him president. If the case for this argument isn't persuasive, add the impact of James Comey's extraordinary actions, induced by FBI agents and retirees who seemed to favor Trump, and the scales were sufficiently weighted to wipe out Hillary Clinton's lifelong service and preparation for the presidency. As pollster Nate Silver noted after the election, Clinton's support dropped sharply the day that Comey announced he was reopening the investigation into her emails. The impact was greatest in the three swing states of Michigan, Wisconsin, and Pennsylvania, and when voters were asked about when they made up their minds, the late-deciders went for Trump and against Clinton.[52]

# Afterword

Exit polls showed that the 2016 election had pitted one America against another. The one that voted for Hillary Clinton was more female (by 12 percentage points), more Hispanic (44 points), and vastly more black. Trump voters were older, whiter, and far more likely to live in rural areas. Demographically speaking, Clinton's voters represented the future and Trump's looked like the America of the past. The camps were also separated on the matter of truth. Trump's innuendo and accusations against Clinton, his embrace of conspiracy theories about Barack Obama, and his lies about immigrants all felt like truth to voters accustomed to decades of GOP rhetoric amplified by right-wing media. Clinton's references to serious policies and higher ideals failed to resonate outside of her base of support.[1]

The conflict between the two Americas was evident in the protests that followed Donald Trump's election. On the weekend of his inauguration, millions of people attended events that ranged from a march that filled Pennsylvania Avenue in Washington, D.C., for many blocks to a rally that attracted ten people to the westernmost community in the Aleutian Islands.

Organized primarily as women's marches, the protests were energized by anger over the misogyny that had been directed at Hillary Clinton, disappointment over the narrow defeat of the first woman to be nominated for president by a major party, outrage over Russia's assault on the electoral system, and fear of Donald Trump. In the first two years of his presidency, he would do nothing to allay this fear. Riven by chaos, his administration saw record numbers of firings and resignations. Even Steve Bannon failed to satisfy the president and resigned after serving just months in the White House.

Trump's firing of FBI director James Comey triggered the appointment of a special counsel (former FBI director Robert Mueller), who embarked on an investigation that began to reveal the extent of Russian efforts to help Trump and hurt Clinton and exposed a host of legal problems for the president. Mueller, the special counsel, reported broad evidence of the Trump team's contacts with Russians and a dozen or more instances where the president attempted to obstruct justice. But for federal rules barring prosecution of a sitting chief executive of the United States, Trump would have been charged. Among the other details Mueller made public was Trump's failed effort to have Hillary Clinton prosecuted for using a private email system when she was secretary of state and his ongoing interest in seeing her imprisoned.

In addition to producing his report, Mueller indicted, won convictions or negotiated guilty pleas with thirty-four individuals charged with more than one hundred crimes. Despite this record, Trump and his allies continued to summon Hillary Clinton as the bogeywoman responsible for all that might be wrong in America. The president maintained his call for her to be prosecuted, and Republicans in Congress called for public hearings to explore controversies that had long since been put to rest. The fixation on Clinton, who was a private citizen with no political plans, was so much a part of the GOP's identity that it seemed like an addiction.

In the meantime, scandals enveloped many of those who had aided Trump in business and politics. A handful wouldn't live to see the ultimate flowering of their work in Trump's Washington. Others who had participated in the long-running distortion of American politics would renew their efforts, publishing more books, appearing on Fox News, and enjoying the favor of the new administration.[2]

### Roger Ailes

The once-all-powerful head of Fox News was forced to resign amid sexual harassment allegations, which his employer had secretly settled at a cost of many millions of dollars. Within a year, he would die of complications from a fall. (He had hemophilia.) He was replaced at Fox by executive Bill Shine, who would be named in lawsuits as an abettor of sexual harassment. Shine would leave Fox for the Trump White House and then political consulting.[3]

### Julian Assange

The WikiLeaks provocateur who did all he could to defeat Hillary Clinton in the 2016 campaign remained in Ecuador's embassy in London, safe from extradition, until April 2019, when police were suddenly admitted to the embassy, where they arrested him. A gaunt figure with a huge white beard, he was half carried and half dragged to a waiting police van. Ecuador's president explained that he had revoked Assange's asylum protection due to numerous violations of protocols and problems with his living habits. Officials also reported that Assange had taken to smearing feces on embassy walls. When asked about his arrest, Clinton said, "The bottom line is that he has to answer for what he has done."[4]

### Steve Bannon

After guiding Trump to victory in 2016, Bannon worked for eight months at "chief strategist" for the Trump White House. In that time, he appeared on the cover of *Time,* which called him "the Great Manipulator" and speculated about his status as the second-most-powerful person in the world. Bannon frequently clashed with other administration officials and maintained regular private contact with journalists. He was widely blamed for letting writer Michael Wolff prowl the West Wing. Wolff's book *Fire and the Fury: Inside the Trump White House* revealed an administration riven by internal conflicts and too chaotic to govern well. After leaving the White House, Bannon took his ethno-nationalist message to countries around the world, delivering speeches and consulting with like-minded politicians and attacking, among others, Pope Francis.[5]

### Todd Blodgett
Former publisher of *Slick Times* and onetime distributor of hatecore neo-Nazi music, Blodgett had a change of heart that led him to advise the Federal Bureau of Investigation on right-wing extremism. In an interview published in 2000 by the Southern Poverty Law Center, a hate-group watchdog organization, he said he has been an opportunist but was "not a hateful person."

### David Bossie
Through three decades of Clinton hating, Bossie turned himself into a well-to-do agitator, earning roughly $500,000 per year from Citizens United and related organizations. He also controlled a fund that made donations to Republican candidates. After Trump's election, he served as a champion in the media and, in an astounding display of chutzpah, bemoaned the "politics of personal destruction" in Washington. Bossie joined Fox News as a commentator and was suspended, for two weeks, when he told a black panelist he was out of his "cotton-picking" mind.[6]

### Jestin Coler
The creator of a "satirical" website that churned out anti-Clinton propaganda eventually revealed his methods to the national news media and explained that he sought a pro-Trump audience because his supporters were more open to clicking on his fantastical items. He abandoned the fake news business and began giving speeches on the danger of online deception. However, a statement he published as he announced this decision suggested a limited grasp of the dynamic he had exploited. Ignoring the decades-long vilification of journalists by right-wing politicians, he blamed the mainstream media for the public's willingness to believe his fake reports.[7]

## George Conway

One of the Elves who had quietly aided Kenneth Starr and Paula Jones, Conway married Republican pollster and future Trump White House counselor Kellyanne Conway. (The two were introduced by Ann Coulter.) He built a successful law practice and withdrew from public life until he became an outspoken critic of President Trump. Conway repeatedly called out Trump's lies—"Summa Cum Liar" was one of his constructions—and openly speculated about the president's mental condition. As Trump publicly excoriated him, and his wife stood firmly for her boss, Conway became a cult hero for anti-Trump citizens.[8]

## Matt Drudge

Although he would rarely be as influential as he was during the Clinton presidency, Drudge would retain enough power that GOP candidates would seek to stay in his favor. When he became the subject of reporting on his sex life, he denied the reports about him and became even more private in his personal behavior. Drudge supported Donald Trump's 2016 campaign, but after Trump was elected, Drudge occasionally expressed misgivings about the president. In March 2019, the Drudge Report was ranked forty-fifth among U.S. websites, a bit ahead of *The New York Times* but well behind the likes of Fox News and CNN.[9]

## Gennifer Flowers

True to the times, she would devote her life to turning her fame into cash. She played herself on-screen, appeared in a stage show called *Boobs! The Musical,* and pursued a failed lawsuit against former Clinton aides. She earned money selling books and recordings of her music and giving speeches. According to her website, her speaking topics include, "The M years—Surviving menopause mania."[10]

## Michael Flynn

Having led the cheers of "Lock her up!" at Trump rallies, the former general was named the new president's national security advisor. Before he even took office, Flynn spoke with Russian officials and, in a possible seeming violation of the law, apparently signaled there would be changes in U.S. policy under Trump. He left the administration after he apparently lied about this contact and would confess to breaking the law and become a cooperating witness in federal prosecutions. In 2019, he would become the subject of wild conjecture among fans of a conspiracy theory called Q Anon, which holds that world affairs are being controlled by a cabal of the wealthy and powerful.[11]

### Newt Gingrich

Forced to resign after his own scandals and election failures, he became a political entrepreneur, selling books, speeches, video productions, and advice. (He received as much a $75,000 for a single speech.) He dabbled with presidential bids and became an advisor to the Donald Trump campaign. In 2017, Gingrich joined the crowd that promoted a conspiracy theory about the death of a Democratic Party activist named Seth Rich. Trump appointed Gingrich's third wife, Callista, ambassador to the Vatican, and Gingrich began spending much of his time in Rome.

### Lucianne Goldberg

Called to testify in a Maryland court, Goldberg said she mistakenly advised Linda Tripp to tape phone calls with Monica Lewinsky. Dogged by critics on the Left, Goldberg initially sounded a defiant tone but then admitted their scrutiny had taken a toll. She became a regular contributor to a website called Free Republic but stepped away from the site when she believed it had been taken over by "gun-nut, Jew-baiting crazies." Her son Jonah, heir to her provocative nature, authored a number of hysterical political books, including *Suicide of the West* and *Liberal Fascism,* which was decorated with a smiley face wearing a Hitler mustache.

### Rudy Giuliani

Having failed in his Senate campaign, the former New York mayor briefly ran for president in 2008 but garnered little support. He worked as a lawyer and security consultant and then, in 2016, leveraged his longstanding relationship with Donald Trump to become a key campaign figure. After Trump's election, he became one of the president's many private attorneys, concerning himself mainly with advocating for him on television. In 2018, his third wife, Judith Nathan, sought to divorce him. Giuliani was reportedly involved with a Republican fund-raiser who is eighteen years his junior. He also worked diligently to promote conspiracy theories that blamed Ukraine and not Russia for foreign interference in the 2016 campaign.

### Karin Immergut

The lawyer who asked the most personal questions of Monica Lewinsky—"Did he bring you to orgasm?"—was appointed U.S. attorney by George W. Bush. In 2018, President Trump nominated her to become a federal judge. Her nomination was temporarily blocked, but Trump renewed the nomination in 2019.[12]

### Michael Isikoff

After rising to national prominence by dint of his reporting on the Lewinsky affair, Isikoff became one of the best-known reporters in America and a frequent presence on national television. For four years, he was a correspondent for NBC News. He authored several books, including the most recent *Russian Roulette: The Inside Story of Putin's War on America and the Election of Donald Trump,* which he published with cowriter David Corn. He would once say that Linda Tripp offered him possession of the famous soiled dress owned by Monica Lewinsky but that he rebuffed the offer.

### Brett Kavanaugh

The member of Kenneth Starr's team who revived the investigation of Vince Foster's death was nominated to the District of Columbia federal appeals court by George W. Bush, whom he had served as staff secretary. He was confirmed by the Senate and sat until he was nominated to the Supreme Court by Trump in 2018. As his Senate hearing approached, several women who knew him during high school and college accused him of sexual assault or misconduct. The nomination divided the country, and Kavanaugh's emotional testimony included admissions of excessive drinking and angry replies to questions posed by senators. He was narrowly confirmed.[13]

### Matt Lauer

The host of *Today* who grilled Hillary Clinton about her husband's behavior became one of the leading figures in television and commanded
at the peak of his career an annual salary of $25 million. In 2016, he
conducted live interviews with Trump and Clinton. It was widely noted
that he was more pointed in his approach to Clinton and went easy on
Trump. In 2017, investigative reporters for *The New York Times* and *Variety* began asking NBC about complaints of sexual harassment lodged
against him. The complaints dated back to 2000. After conducting its
own investigation, NBC fired Lauer. He retreated from public life and
made no public statements after a brief and qualified apology for his
past behavior.[14]

### Monica Lewinsky

In the controversy that made her a public figure, Monica Lewinsky was
regarded, variously, as a naïf, a seductress, a fool, and a destroyer. In 2002,
she answered audience questions during a TV program, and in 2004, she
began to note that Clinton had failed to apologize to her. She earned
a master's degree at the London School of Economics and Political
Science and gradually developed a following as an advocate for women
and as an anti-harassment advocate. She devoted particular attention to
the problem of the public shaming of women.[15]

### Rush Limbaugh

The king of partisan radio maintained his national audience despite
multiple scandals and controversies, including treatment for drug addiction and claims that actor Michael J. Fox had faked symptoms of
Parkinson's disease as he promoted stem cell research. He issued a rare
apology when advertisers stopped sponsoring his program after he called
a young woman a "slut" and a "prostitute" because she advocated for
insurers to pay for contraception. Like others in right-wing media, he
suggested there might be truth to conspiracy theories, and he lambasted
those who protested against Donald Trump. However, in a media environment that included Fox News and countless imitators, he no longer
wielded the influence he enjoyed during the Clinton presidency.

## Christopher Ruddy

After attacking the Clintons on behalf of Richard Scaife, Ruddy transformed the billionaire's $25,000 investment in a new website called Newsmax into a media empire that included both publishing and broadcasting. Newsmax targeted affluent middle-aged and older conservatives and was influential in Republican politics. Ruddy and his benefactor, Scaife, moderated in their views toward the Clintons. Ruddy would eventually extol Clinton's presidency and declare that his friend Scaife agreed that Clinton had been effective.[16]

## Richard Mellon Scaife

Thanks to an introduction from Ruddy, Scaife met Bill Clinton, and the two established a kind of friendship. He subsequently met with Hillary Clinton and decided that he agreed with many of her positions on policy. Scaife contributed to the Clinton Global Initiative and wrote an editorial boosting Hillary's candidacy for the Democratic Party's presidential nomination. When he died, Bill Clinton spoke at his memorial service.[17]

## Peter Smith

The financier who backed David Brock and other participants in the Arkansas Project continued to pursue the Clintons long after the project ended. He wrote checks to support the work of Newt Gingrich, other candidates, and the Republican Party. Although he had nearly exhausted his considerable fortune, in 2016 he backed a fruitless scheme to acquire emails belonging to Hillary Clinton. In May of 2017, he committed suicide in a Minnesota hotel room, leaving a note explaining that he was acting before the expiration of a $5 million life insurance policy. News outlets reported that in fact the policy would have been valid for eight more years.[18]

## Kenneth Starr

As the author of the famously prurient Starr report on the Clinton-Lewinsky scandal, Kenneth Starr became synonymous with an excessive moralism that suggested a preoccupation with sex. After the Clinton presidency, he taught law at various schools and represented clients including Blackwater, which functioned as a kind of army for hire around the world, and anti–gay marriage activists in California. He became president of Baylor University in 2010 and was in charge when half a dozen women alleged sexual abuse by football players. After reviewing Starr's response to the complaints, the school's regents removed him from the presidency. In 2018, Starr published *Contempt: A Memoir of the Clinton Investigation*. In his review of the book, Princeton historian Sean Wilentz wrote that Starr had revealed his prosecution team's contempt and "prosecutorial fury" for Hillary Clinton, who Starr complained showed an "in your face" attitude. Starr also wrote that while the president had been amiable, Hillary "made no effort to be cordial."[19]

### Roger Stone

The author of *The Clintons' War on Women* and founder of Citizens United Not Timid spent his postelection years denying he had conspired with WikiLeaks or Russian operatives to aid the Trump campaign. He appeared frequently on the Infowars internet video channel operated by Alex Jones. (A notorious conspiracy theorist, Jones would actually say that a "form of psychosis" had caused him to promote bizarre ideas including the notion that a mass killing at an elementary school in Newtown, Connecticut, had been a hoax.) Stone regularly condemned those investigating the 2016 election and was suspended by the social media site Twitter for inflammatory postings about journalists. In January 2019, his home was raided by FBI agents, who arrested him and then searched for evidence on orders from special counsel Robert Mueller. He was charged with making false statements to law enforcement officials, witness tampering, and obstruction.[20]

### Donald Trump

After assuming the presidency, Donald Trump continued his diatribes about Hillary Clinton while also pursuing an agenda of anti-immigration action, tax cuts for the rich, outreach to authoritarian leaders, and criticism of American allies. Trump pandered to Russian president Vladimir Putin and attacked Robert Mueller hundreds of times. Incapable of bringing the country together, he had approval ratings that never rose much above 40 percent.

Whenever Trump felt pressure from prosecutors or Democrats, he repeated his calls for legal action against his 2016 opponent. Many Republicans in Congress joined him, insisting that long after the election she should still be subject to investigation and prosecution. Trump also scapegoated FBI agents and the Justice Department. He was joined in this by the likes of Rudy Giuliani, who went on television to say agents had committed criminal offenses in their investigations of Trump and his campaign.

As president, Donald Trump rarely visited states where he had not won in 2016 and communicated mainly through emotion-laden social media posts and campaign rally speeches that resembled stream-of-consciousness rants. Laced with profanity and name-calling, these performances included lies about migrants, wild claims about his "ratings," and attacks on deceased senator John McCain. (Trump was humiliated when McCain's family barred him from attending the senator's funeral.)

In 2019, press revelations and congressional investigations unearthed a scheme by which Trump and his lawyer Rudy Giuliani attempted to extort the government of Ukraine in order to help the president's reelection campaign. After Giuliani orchestrated the removal of the career diplomat who was the American ambassador to Kyiv, Trump conditioned military aid on an announcement, by the Ukrainian president, that his government was investigating allegations against former vice president Joe Biden and indications that Ukraine and not Russia interfered with the 2016 election. (Biden was leading the field of Democrats seeking to oppose Trump in the 2020 presidential election.) Ukraine needed the aid to fight an ongoing war with Russia; however, no credible information justified such an announcement.

After the Ukrainian shakedown was revealed the war funding was sent and congressional committees set in motion the process that led to Trump's impeachment by the House of Representatives. Partisan votes in the Senate blocked his conviction, but Trump would enter the 2020 general election as only the third president ever impeached by the House. The others had been Andrew Johnson and Bill Clinton.

## United States

In the wake of the 2016 election, Americans opposed to Trump's methods, policies, and style rallied against him at thousands of public gatherings and mobilized to block his more egregious actions. Lawsuits halted his sweeping ban on Muslim visitors to the United States, and the appointment of special counsel Robert Mueller ensured that Trump couldn't evade accountability by firing FBI director James Comey. A Republican-controlled Congress rejected Trump's effort to "repeal and replace" Obamacare, and people inside his administration undercut their colleagues in continuous leaks to the press.

A true team of vipers, the Trump administration was racked by the incompetence of many appointees and the departure of the best, including defense secretary James Mattis, chief of staff John Kelly, and economic advisor Gary Cohn. Numerous appointees fled Washington amid complaints that they abused public funds, and various Trump family members and entities were subject to local, state, and federal investigations. So many scandals afflicted the president, his allies, and his government that news outlets regularly published charts to help people keep track.

In 2017, Alabama voters broke a twenty-five-year-long streak to send a Democrat, Doug Jones, to the United States Senate. Jones prevailed despite Trump's active effort in Republican Roy Moore's behalf, including a rally speech made days before voting.

The 2017 results in Alabama foreshadowed the 2018 midterms, when Democrats gained forty seats in the House of Representatives. This was the biggest gain for the party since Watergate, and it gave the Democrats a majority and thus control of committees that would embark on numerous investigations of the Trump administration. The election also brought a remarkable shift in the composition of Congress. A record number of women—102—were elected to the House, and this included the first Muslim woman and first Native American woman ever to serve.

The political shift, which imperiled Donald Trump, was not Hillary Clinton's doing. However, it did indicate that the majority she had won in 2016 wasn't going away. And when an eight-year-old girl wrote to tell her she lost a class election to a boy, Clinton offered her an encouraging reply that conflicted with Donald Trump's winning-is-everything mantra. "The most important thing is that you fought for what you believe in," she told Martha Morales, "and that is always worth it."

# Acknowledgments

In the everlasting argument about opportunity and equality, the haves often say the have-nots are fully responsible for their condition. In this analysis, extraordinary individuals are cited as inspiring examples. Dave Thomas, an orphan, founded the Wendy's restaurant chain; Sandra Day O'Connor went from a farm on a dirt road to the Supreme Court; Barack Obama, a black kid abandoned by his father, became president of the United States.

The exceptions are supposed to make it obvious that the individual's fate is up to her. Of course, the fact that they are *exceptions,* notable because they run counter to the norm, negates the argument. We marvel at Thomas, O'Connor, and Obama because we know the odds are stacked against them. We resist acknowledging this truth because doing so requires acknowledging that the sexism and misogyny that exist at the foundation of American life make life harder for 50.8 percent of the population. The facts also confront those who are advantaged—namely, white males like me—with the plain truth that we have the inside lane in every race.

As with every form of bigotry, the assumptions that penalize girls and women can be so insidious that they seem to represent a kind of natural order. So it is that we who benefit prefer to believe that our status is deserved and our achievements are merited. Able-bodied white heterosexual men who dominate business, politics, science, the arts, and religion would rather not consider the powerful cultural assumption that success in America comes with a white male face. Doing so casts doubt on countless achievements—scholarships, degrees, promotions, awards, and even book contracts—and the pride that they confer.

The shadow cast by prejudice makes beneficiaries uncomfortable. Some react with anger. Others express self-pity. They complain about "political correctness" and bias against white men. These diversions prevent an empathetic reckoning with both the damage done to women and the many ways in which society is deprived when they are denied the equal opportunity to create and contribute.

My own understanding of the continual and vast effects of sexism grew mainly out of my relationship with my wife, Toni, whose success as a psychotherapist, writer, artist, and academic always required what seemed, to me, to be extra effort. My daughters, Elizabeth and Amy, have lived with the same reality, which forces them to consider, again and again, whether they truly understand the context of their lives. The reflexive ways in which women's voices are ignored and their ideas are rejected aren't openly announced. In fact, those who discount women are often unaware of their preexisting assumptions. They just feel a certain way, and act accordingly.

The credit my wife and daughters deserve doesn't make them responsible for the ways I still conform to ancient stereotypes. Nevertheless, without their help I wouldn't have even taken up the topic of this book. (The irony of a man's name on the cover page is also not lost on us.) On a political and philosophical level, I must also acknowledge many influential writers whose work contributed to this project. Among the modern ones are Susan Faludi, Roxane Gay, Germaine Greer, Eve Ensler, Betty Friedan, Gloria Steinem, Margaret Atwood, Maya Angelou, Andrea Dworkin, Toni Morrison, and Adrienne Rich. Many more could be credited, along with a host of writers who exposed other forms of bigotry, from racism to anti-Semitism to ableism. My mentors in the study of prejudice have included Reginald Wells, Les Payne, and Karine Jean-Pierre, to name just three.

More aid to my effort in these pages was provided by the extraordinary copy editor Sara Ensey. Carl Bernstein and Joe Conason, whose books about Hillary Clinton inform mine, offered keen insights. John Gartner's acute understanding of Bill Clinton demonstrated to me that history, biography, and psychology can be joined in pursuit of a deeper analysis of a major public figure. Peter Eisner, Richard Galant, and Susan Berg helped with ongoing conversations about all the issues presented in this book and my approach to them on a professional and personal level. Further encouragement came from Eleanor Smeal and Katherine Spillar, who answered some very basic questions with patience and sincerity. As researchers, Diane Herbst and Lydia Carey contributed both facts and context. As an attorney, Elisa Rivlin proved to be a literary whiz. As editors, Thomas Dunne and Stephen S. Power offered faith, wisdom, and correction.

# Notes

## Introduction

1. Trump Twitter Archive, accessed March 30, 2019. Matt Stieb, "Lindsey Graham Blocks House Vote to Make Mueller Report Public," *New York,* March 14, 2019.
2. Kathryn Lundstrom, "Texas Education Board Moves to Reinsert Hillary Clinton, Helen Keller into Curriculum," *Texas Tribune,* November 14, 2018. Larry Buchanan and Karen Yourish, "Trump Has Publicly Attacked the Russia Investigation More Than 1,100 Times," *New York Times,* February 19, 2019.
3. Michael Sebastian, "29 Times Donald Trump Has Been Completely Insulting to Women," *Cosmopolitan,* October 21, 2016, www.cosmopolitan.com/politics/news/a44629/donald-trump-insults-women/. Tyler G. Okimoto and Victoria L. Brescoll, "The Price of Power: Power Seeking and Backlash Against Female Politicians," *Personality and Social Psychology Bulletin* 36, no. 7 (2010): 923–936.
4. "1978 Speech by Gingrich," PBS, www.pbs.org/wgbh/pages/frontline/newt/newt78speech.html. Nicole Hemmer and Brent Cebul, "They Were Made for Each Other: How Newt Gingrich Laid the Groundwork for Donald Trump's Rise," *New Republic,* July 11, 2016. David Corn and Tim Murphy, "A Very Long List of Dumb and Awful Things Newt Gingrich Has Said and Done. Still, He May Have a Prominent Role in the Trump Administration," *Mother Jones,* November 15, 2016. Karen Dewitt, "The 104th Congress: The Speaker's Mother; Quick Indignation After CBS Interview," *New York Times,* January 5, 1995.
5. James Salzer, "Gingrich's Language Set New Course," *Atlanta Journal-Constitution,* January 29, 2012. Adam Berinsky, "The Birthers Are Back," YouGov, July 11, 20112.

Tom Jensen, "Trump Remains Unpopular; Voters Prefer Obama on SCOTUS Pick," Public Policy Polling, December 9, 2016. Asawin Suebsaeng and Dave Gilson, "Chart: Almost Every Obama Conspiracy Theory Ever," *Mother Jones,* November 2, 2012.

6. Rick Perlstein, "The Long Con," *Baffler,* November 21, 2012. "Robertson Letter Attacks Feminists," *New York Times,* August 26, 1992. David Osborne, "The Swinging Days of Newt Gingrich," *Mother Jones,* November 1, 1984.

7. Nathan Kalmoe and Lilliana Mason, "Lethal Mass Partisanship," presented at National Capital Area Political Science Association meeting, January 2019.

8. Catherine Thompson, "Donald Trump Spreads the Message That 'Hillary Clinton Can't Satisfy Her Husband,'" *Business Insider,* April 17, 2015. Sophie Tatum, "Trump: Clinton 'Doesn't Have the Stamina' to Be President," CNN, September 27, 2016.

9. Mahita Gajinan, "Donald Trump Just Called Hillary Clinton the Devil and Threatened to Prosecute Her," *Fortune,* October 10, 2016.

10. Shanto Iyangar and Masha Krupenkin, "The Strengthening of Partisan Affect, Symposium on Partisanship," *Political Psychology,* February 13, 2018.

11. Jonathan Allen and Amie Parnes, *Shattered: Inside Hillary Clinton's Doomed Campaign* (New York: Crown, 2017), 380–388.

12. Clare Malone, "From 1937 to Hillary Clinton: How Americans Have Felt About a Woman President," *Five Thirty Eight,* June 9, 2016, https://fivethirtyeight.com/features /from-1937-to-hillary-clinton-how-americans-have-felt-about-a-female-president/.

13. Michael McFaul, "Why Putin Wants a Trump Victory (So Much He Might Even Be Trying to Help Him)," *Washington Post,* August 17, 2016. Gideon Resnick, "How Pro-Trump Twitter Bots Spread Fake News," *Daily Beast,* November 17, 2016, www.thedailybeast.com/how-pro-trump-twitter-bots-spread-fake-news. John McCormack, "The Election Came Down to 77,744 Votes in Pennsylvania, Wisconsin, and Michigan," *Weekly Standard,* November 10, 2016, www.weeklystandard .com/the-election-came-down-to-77744-votes-in-pennsylvania-wisconsin-and -michigan-updated/article/2005323.

14. "1978 Speech," PBS. Hemmer and Cebul, "Made for Each Other." Corn and Murphy, "A Very Long List." Dewitt, "104th Congress."

15. Perlstein, "The Long Con." "Robertson Letter Attacks Feminists." Osborne, "Swinging Days."

16. William Frey, "The U.S. Will Become Minority White in 2045," Brookings, March 14, 2018. Diana C. Mutz, "Status Threat, Not Economic Hardship, Explains the 2016 Presidential Vote," *Proceedings of the National Academy of Sciences,* May 8, 2018. Marc Hooghe and Ruth Dassonneville, "Explaining the Trump Vote: The Effect of Racist Resentment and Anti-Immigrant Sentiments," *PS: Political Science & Politics* 51, no. 3 (2018): 528–534.

17. Mutz, "Status Threat." Daniel Cox, Rachel Lienesch, and Robert P. Jones, "Beyond Economics: Fears of Cultural Displacement Pushed the White Working Class to Trump," Public Religion Research Institute, May 9, 2017. Jen Wieczner, "Hillary Clinton Is the First to Say 'I'm Sorry' in a Presidential Concession Speech," *Fortune,* November 14, 2016, www.fortune.com/2016/11/14/hillary-clinton-concession -speech-sorry-hallelujah/.

## 1. What's in a Name?

1. Richard Hofstadter, *Anti-Intellectualism in American Life* (New York: Knopf, 1963). "Bill Clinton's 1978 Governor's Victory Speech," YouTube video, 2:17, posted by Talk Business & Politics, May 19, 2014, https://www.youtube.com/watch?v=CX4kv67HpeE. Andrew Kaczynski, Ilan Ben-Meir, and Dorsey Shaw, "Watch This Rare, Long-Forgotten Interview with Young Hillary Clinton," *Buzzfeed,* May 15, 2015, www.buzzfeed.com/andrewkaczynski/hillary-clinton-1979?utm_term=.ehx3Qp2agq#.ccG728x90O.
2. Richard Nixon, "Presidential Nomination Acceptance Speech," 4President.org, www.4president.org/speeches/nixon1968acceptance.htm.
3. Daniel Walker, *Rights in Conflict: The Violent Confrontation of Demonstrators and Police in the Parks and Streets of Chicago During the Week of the Democratic National Convention of 1968* (New York: New American Library, 1968).
4. Bruce A. Ragsdale, "The Chicago Seven: 1960s Radicalism in the Federal Courts," Federal Judicial Center, 2008.
5. John D. Gartner, *In Search of Bill Clinton* (New York: St. Martin's Press, 2008), 107.
6. Hillary Clinton, *Living History* (New York: Scribner, 2004), 475.
7. J. Anthony Lukas, "Why the Watergate Break-In?," *New York Times,* November 30, 1987, www.nytimes.com/1987/11/30/opinion/why-the-watergate-break-in.html.
8. "John N. Mitchell Dies at 75; Major Figure in Watergate," *New York Times,* November 10, 1988.
9. Carl Bernstein and Bob Woodward, "FBI Finds Nixon Aides Sabotaged Democrats," *Washington Post,* October 10, 1972, www.washingtonpost.com/politics/fbi-finds-nixon-aides-sabotaged-democrats/2012/06/06/gJQAoHIJJV_story.html?utm_term=.0bbfe90eb5bd. Hillary Clinton, "Student Commencement Speech," Wellesley, www.wellesley.edu/events/commencement/archives/1969commencement/studentspeech#MaMBmRgcWuO4trm4.99.
10. Tim Weiner, "Transcripts of Nixon Tapes Show the Path to Watergate," *New York Times,* October 31, 1997, www.nytimes.com/1997/10/31/us/transcripts-of-nixon-tapes-show-the-path-to-watergate.html. Evan Thomas, "The Untapped Secrets of the Nixon Tapes," *Atlantic,* July 29, 2014.
11. Carroll Doherty, Jocelyn Kiley, Alec Tyson, and Bridget Jameson, *Beyond Distrust: How Americans View Their Government* (Washington, DC: Pew Research Center, 2015), www.pewresearch.org/wp-content/uploads/sites/4/2015/11/11-23-2015-Governance-release.pdf.
12. Peter Applebome, "Orval Faubus, Segregation's Champion, Dies at 84," *New York Times,* December 15, 1994.
13. Roy Reed, "Fulbright: The Scholar in Foreign Affairs," *New York Times,* June 2, 1974.
14. Gartner, *In Search of Bill Clinton,* 43–51.
15. Claire Cain Mille and Derek Willis, "Maiden Names, on the Rise Again," *New York Times,* June 27, 2015, www.nytimes.com/2015/06/28/upshot/maiden-names-on-the-rise-again.html.
16. Virginia Clinton Kelley, *Leading with My Heart* (New York: Pocket Books, 1994), 88.

17. Mille and Willis, "Maiden Names." Claudia Goldin and Maria Shim, "Making a Name: Women's Surnames at Marriage and Beyond," *Journal of Economic Perspectives* 18, no. 2 (Spring 2004): 143–160.

18. Scott Manningham, "Legal Issues of Rape Discussed at Workshop," *Northwest Arkansas Times,* March 3, 1976. Sally Carter, "In Parenthesis," *Northwest Arkansas Times,* April 4, 1976.

19. Rochelle Semmel Albin, "Psychological Studies of Rape," *Signs* 3, no. 2 (1977): 423–435. Peggy Frizell, "Best-Selling Author Speaks on Rape," *Northwest Arkansas Times,* March 2, 1976.

20. "News Brief," *Hope Star,* October 25, 1977.

21. Bill Simmons, "Clinton," *Blytheville Courier News,* November 8, 1978.

22. Adrienne Rich, *On Lies, Secrets, and Silence* (New York: W. W. Norton, 1978).

23. Carl Bernstein, *A Woman in Charge: The Life of Hillary Rodham Clinton* (New York: Vintage, 2008), 176–178.

24. Bill Clinton, *My Life* (New York: Knopf, 2004), 284, 291.

25. "Who's Fooling Whom?," *Blytheville Courier News,* April 5, 1982.

## 2. She's Ambitious

1. Julie Coffman and Bill Neuenfeldt, "Frontline Managers Are Key to Women's Career Aspirations," Bain & Company, June 17, 2014. Ethan Michelson, Indiana University Law School, "Women in the Legal Profession, 1970–2010: A Study of the Global Supply of Lawyers" *Indiana Journal of Global Legal Studies* 20, no. 2 (Summer 2013), www.repository.law.indiana.edu/cgi/viewcontent.cgi?article =1531&context=ijgls.

2. Michelson, "Women in the Legal Profession." John M. Broder, "Clintons' Tax Returns Show Big Losses, Gains: Presidency: White House Releases 1977–79 Records in Response to Questions About Whitewater Deal," *Los Angeles Times,* March 26, 1994.

3. Erving Goffman, "The Arrangement Between the Sexes," *Theory and Society* 4, no. 3 (Autumn 1977): 301–331.

4. Phyllis Schlafly, *The Power of the Positive Woman* (New York: Jove, 1977).

5. Bruce Stokes, "Business Forum: High Mortgage? Look at Prices of Land," *New York Times,* December 13, 1981.

6. Jeff Greenfield, "Remembering Dale Bumpers 1925–2016," *Politico,* December 31, 2016, www.politico.com/magazine/story/2016/12/senator-dale-bumpers-arkansas -obituary-214568. Dale Bumpers, "June 11, 1982, Entry in Bumpers' Diary," Special Collections, University of Arkansas Libraries, Fayetteville, Arkansas.

7. Kevin Merida, "It's Come to This: A Nickname That's Proven Hard to Slip," *Washington Post,* December 20, 1998. Paul Greenberg, "Slick Willie's Back," *Blytheville Courier News,* September 1984.

8. Stokes, "Business Forum: High Mortgage?"

9. Kern Alexander, *Alexander Report* (Gainesville, FL: Education Finance and Research Institute, 1978).

10. David Brock, *The Seduction of Hillary Rodham* (New York: Free Press, 1997), 154. "Hillary Got None of PSC Fee, Firm Says," *Northwest Arkansas Times,* September 20, 1986.

## 3. Woman Trouble

1. Garry Clifford and Peter Carlson, "Gary Hart: George McGovern's Whiz Kid Has Grown Up, and Now He Wants a Chance to Be President Too," *People,* August 22, 1983.
2. Jim McGee, Tom Fiedler, and James Savage, "The Gary Hart Story: How It Happened," *Miami Herald,* May 10, 1987. Eleanor Randolph, "The Press and the Candidate," *Washington Post,* May 1987. Kyle Munzenrieder, "How Bickering South Florida Models Brought Down a Presidential Campaign," *Miami New Times,* September 22, 2014.
3. Jim McGee and Tom Fiedler, "Miami Woman Linked to Hart: Candidate Denies Any Impropriety," *Miami Herald,* May 3, 1987.
4. Matt Bai, *The Truth Is Out* (New York: Vintage, 2014), 88–90.
5. Gail Sheehy, "A Matter of Hart," *Vanity Fair,* September 2014.
6. Rick Perlstein, "Exclusive: Lee Atwater's Infamous 1981 Interview on the Southern Strategy," *Nation,* November 13, 2012.
7. "Transcript: Boogie Man: The Lee Atwater Story," *Frontline,* PBS, www.pbs.org /wgbh/pages/frontline/atwater/etc/script.html. James Fallows, "Was Gary Hart Set Up?," *Atlantic,* November 2018.
8. "Floyd Brown Exposed," YouTube video, 5:32, posted by "sallystipend," June 11, 2008, www.youtube.com/watch?v=7PnfpefgI5c.
9. David Brock, *The Seduction of Hillary Rodham* (New York: Free Press, 1997), 257.
10. Candice E. Jackson, *Their Lives: The Women Targeted by the Clinton Machine* (Washington, DC: World Ahead Publishing, 2005), 67–68.
11. Carl Bernstein, *A Woman in Charge: The Life of Hillary Rodham Clinton* (New York: Vintage, 2008), 98.
12. Caitlin Flanagan, "Jackie and the Girls: Mrs. Kennedy's JFK Problem—and Ours," *Atlantic,* July/August 2012.
13. Bernstein, *Woman in Charge,* 176–178. Greg Mitchell, *Tricky Dick and the Pink Lady: Richard Nixon vs. Helen Gahagan Douglas—Sexual Politics and the Red Scare, 1950* (New York: Random House, 1998), *New York Times* excerpt, www.nytimes.com /books/first/m/mitchell-tricky.html?mcubz=1.
14. Meredith L. Oakley, *On the Make: The Rise of Bill Clinton* (Washington, DC: Regnery, 1994), 498. Joe Conason and Gene Lyons, *The Hunting of the President: The Ten-Year Campaign to Destroy Bill and Hillary Clinton* (New York: Thomas Dunne, 2000), 16–18.
15. Conason and Lyons, *Hunting,* 13–17.
16. Elisabeth Bumiller, "Lee Hart," *Washington Post,* March 27, 1984, www .washingtonpost.com/archive/lifestyle/1984/03/27/lee-hart/16f71328-5755-4cb2 -b89c-11b6e5447bfd/?utm_term=.722bc91e18bf.

17. Steven D. Solomon and Lorie J. Teagno, "Frequently Asked Questions About Infidelity," *Divorce Magazine,* August 17, 2018, www.divorcemag.com/articles/frequently-asked-questions-about-infidelity/.

18. Ted Van Dyk, "Clinton's Middle Class Hang-Up," *New York Times,* January 30, 1992. William Safire, "Essay: The Hillary Problem," *New York Times,* March 26, 1992.

19. Steven A. Holmes, "The 1992 Campaign: Republicans; Buchanan's Run Exposes Fissures in the Right," *New York Times,* February 4, 1992. Newsweek Staff, "Is Pat Buchanan Anti-Semitic?," *Newsweek,* December 22, 1991, www.newsweek.com/pat-buchanan-anti-semitic-201176. William F. Buckley, *In Search of Anti-Semitism* (New York: National Review, 1991). Clarence Page, "Talk like a Newt with the Gingrich Diatribe Dictionary," *Chicago Tribune,* September 19, 1990.

20. Robin Toner, "The 1992 Campaign: Political Memo: This Year It's the Democrats Who Run on G.O.P. Tactics," *New York Times,* August 9, 1992.

21. Jonathan Merritt, "Pat Robertson, Christianity's Crazy Uncle," *Week,* October 17, 2016, http://theweek.com/articles/654452/pat-robertson-christianitys-crazy-uncle.

22. Norman Mailer, "By Heaven Inspired," *New Republic,* October 12, 1992.

23. Jon Meacham, *Destiny and Power: The American Odyssey of George Herbert Walker Bush* (New York: Random House, 2015), 511.

24. Marilyn Tucker Quayle, "1992 Republican National Convention Remarks," Iowa State University Archives of Women's Political Communication, https://awpc.cattcenter.iastate.edu/2017/03/21/remarks-at-the-1992-rnc-aug-19-1992-2/.

25. Robin Toner, "The 1992 Campaign: Political Memo: Backlash for Hillary Clinton Puts Negative Image to Rout," *New York Times,* September 24, 1992. Tamar Lewin, "The 1992 Campaign: Issues: Women and Families: Legal Scholars See Distortion in Attacks on Hillary Clinton," *New York Times,* August 24, 1992. Adam Nagourney "'Cultural War' of 1992 Moves In from the Fringe," *New York Times,* August 29, 2012. Judith Warner, "Hillary Clinton: The Inside Story, Families & Children," On-TheIssues, August 1, 1993, www.ontheissues.org/Archive/Inside_Story_Families_+_Children.htm. Andrew Rosenthal, "The 1992 Campaign: Issues—'Family Values': Bush Tries to Recoup from Harsh Tone on 'Values,'" *New York Times,* September 21, 1992. Bradford Plumer, "The Two-Income Trap," *Mother Jones,* November 8, 2004.

26. Gail Sheehy, "What Hillary Wants," *Vanity Fair,* May 1992.

27. For Limbaugh's comments about Chelsea Clinton, see: Eric Hananokia and Ben Dimiero, "FLASHBACK: When Rush Limbaugh's Hate Was Televised," Media Matters for America, March 15, 2012, www.mediamatters.org/blog/2012/03/15/flashback-when-rush-limbaughs-hate-was-televised/184523.

### 4. Caricature

1. Michael Kelly, "The Inauguration: The First Couple: A Union of Mind and Ambition," *New York Times,* January 20, 1993.

2. Thomas L. Friedman, "Hillary Clinton to Head Panel on Health Care," *New York Times,* January 26, 1993. Bureau of the Census, *Health Insurance Coverage—1993*

(Washington, DC: U.S. Department of Commerce Economics and Statistics Administration, 1994), www.census.gov/prod/1/statbrief/sb94_28.pdf.

3. "Remarks by the President in 'Town Meeting with Bill Clinton,'" White House, February 10, 1993, https://clintonwhitehouse6.archives.gov/1993/02/1993-02-10-transcript-of-town-hall-meeting-detroit.html.

4. James Hoggan, "Chamber of Commerce: A Long History of Killing Clean Energy Policy," *Huffington Post,* March 18, 2010. M. Teresa Cardador, Anna R. Hazan, and Stanton A. Glantz, "Tobacco Industry Smokers' Rights Publications: A Content Analysis," *American Journal of Public Health,* September 1996.

5. Maureen Dowd, "White House Memo: Hillary Clinton's Debut Dashes Doubts on Clout," *New York Times,* February 8, 1993.

6. Carl Brown, "Then and Now First Ladies," Roper Center, https://ropercenter.cornell.edu/then-and-now-first-ladies/. "Hillary Clinton Favorability Timeline," Pew Research Center, May 19, 2015, www.people-press.org/2015/05/19/hillary-clinton-approval-timeline/. "Presidential Approval Ratings—Bill Clinton," Gallup, June 4, 1999, http://news.gallup.com/poll/116584/presidential-approval-ratings-bill-clinton.aspx.

7. Thomas B. Edsall, "What Motivates Voters More Than Loyalty? Loathing," *New York Times,* March 1, 2018. Shanto Iyengar and Masha Krupenkin, "The Strengthening of Partisan Affect," *Political Psychology,* February 13, 2018. Alan I. Abramowitz and Steven W. Webster, "Negative Partisanship: Why Americans Dislike Parties but Behave Like Rabid Partisans," *Political Psychology,* February 2018. Conor M. Dowling and Amber Wichowsky, "Attacks Without Consequences? Candidates, Parties, Groups, and the Changing Face of Negative Advertising," *American Journal of Political Science* 59, no. 1 (2014).

8. Mark Gillespie, "Hillary Clinton Remains Polarizing Figure," Gallup, June 6, 2003, https://news.gallup.com/poll/8572/hillary-clinton-remains-polarizing-figure.aspx. Hillary Clinton, "Remarks by First Lady Hillary Rodham Clinton," White House, April 7, 1993, https://clintonwhitehouse3.archives.gov/WH/EOP/First_Lady/html/generalspeeches/1993/19930407.html.

9. Jesselyn Cook and Andy Campbell, "Congressional Candidate in Virginia Admits He's a Pedophile," *Huffington Post,* May 31, 2018, https://www.huffingtonpost.com.mx/entry/nathan-larson-congressional-candidate-pedophile_us_5b10916de4b0d5e89e1e4824?ec_carp=1686725770713260082.

10. Rory O'Connor, "Laura Ingraham: Right-Wing Radio's High Priestess of Hate," *Huffington Post,* May 25, 2012, www.huffingtonpost.com/rory-oconnor/laura-ingraham-right-wing_b_106034.html.

11. James Reston, "Washington: Kennedy and Bork," *New York Times,* July 5, 1987.

12. "Thomas Accuser Angela Wright Sticks to Claims," National Public Radio, October 9, 2007, www.npr.org/templates/story/story.php?storyId=15113601. Howard Kurtz, "A Revisionist's Nightmare," *Washington Post,* June 10, 1993. Frank Rich, "Journal: David Brock's Women," *New York Times,* January 6, 1994.

13. Don Van Natta Jr. and Jill Abramson, "Quietly, Team of Lawyers Who Disliked Clinton Kept Jones Case Alive," *New York Times,* January 24, 1999.

14. David Brock, *Blinded by the Right* (New York: Three Rivers Press, 2003), 151–155.

15. Stephen Marche, "Guns Are Beautiful: To Stop Gun Violence, We Need to Stop Fetishizing Guns," *Esquire,* February 12, 2013, http://www.esquire.com/news -politics/a19335/guns-are-beautiful-0313/.

16. David Brock, "His Cheatin' Heart," *American Spectator,* January 1994. Howard Kurtz, "Journalist in the Crossfire," *Washington Post,* January 13, 1994, www.Washingtonpost .Com/Archive/Lifestyle/1994/01/13/Journalist-In-The-Crossfire/A418cc6d-aee7- 43db-ae46-9187ca46d57f/?utm_term=.5aea3a18e0c3.

17. William C. Rempel and Douglas Frantz, "Troopers Say Clinton Sought Silence on Personal Affairs: Arkansas: The White House Calls Their Allegations About the President's Private Life 'Ridiculous,'" *Los Angeles Times,* December 21, 1993.

18. Brock, *Blinded,* 61–62.

19. "Koppel Covers for Limbaugh's Rumor-Mongering," Fairness & Accuracy in Reporting, July 1, 1994, http://fair.org/extra/koppel-covers-for-limbaughs-rumor-mongering/.

20. Eric Kleefeld, "Great Moments in Dan Burton History," *Talking Points Memo,* January 31, 2012, https://talkingpointsmemo.com/election2012/great-moments-in-dan -burton-history.

21. David Osborne, "The Swinging Days of Newt Gingrich," *Mother Jones,* November 1, 1984. David Beers, "Master of Disaster," *Mother Jones,* October 1989. David Corn and Tim Murphy, "A Very Long List of Dumb and Awful Things Newt Gingrich Has Said and Done. Still, He May Have a Prominent Role in the Trump Administration," *Mother Jones,* November 15, 2016.

22. Brock, *Blinded,* 219.

23. Stephen Labaton, "No Whitewater Charges Seen from First Phase of Inquiry," *New York Times,* June 30, 1994.

24. Michael Powell, "Sen. Faircloth: The Man D.C. Loved to Hate," *Washington Post,* November 5, 1998.

25. David Johnson, "Appointment in Whitewater Turns into a Partisan Battle," *New York Times,* August 13, 1994.

26. Margaret Carlson, "Looking Back at Hillary's First 100 Days as First Lady," *Vanity Fair,* June 1993.

27. Paul Starr, "The Hillarycare Mythology," *American Prospect,* September 13, 2007.

28. Elizabeth Kolbert, "The Ad Campaign: Playing on Uncertainties About the Health Plan," *New York Times,* October 21, 1993. "Ben Goddard Oral History, Co-founder, Goddard-Claussen," University of Virginia Miller Center, April 30, 2008, https:// millercenter.org/the-presidency/presidential-oral-histories/ben-goddard-oral -history-co-founder-goddard-claussen.

29. William Kristol, "Defeating President Clinton's Health Care," Project for a Republican Future, December 2, 1993.

30. Clarence Page, "Talk like a Newt with the Gingrich Diatribe Dictionary," *Chicago Tribune,* September 19, 1990.

31. "Whitewater Timeline," *Washington Post,* 1998, www.washingtonpost.com/wp -srv/politics/special/whitewater/timeline.htm. Stephen Ansolabehere and Shanto Iyengar, *Going Negative: How Political Ads Shrink and Polarize the Electorate* (New York: Free Press, 1996).

## 5. A Multifront Assault

1. Paul Johnson, "A World Without Leaders," *Commentary,* July 1994.
2. "Biography of Paul Johnson," Paul Johnson Archives, http://pauljohnsonarchives.org /?page_id=4.
3. Susan Schmidt, "Partial Support Offered on Whitewater Allegation," *Washington Post,* October 20, 1994. Howard Kurtz, "Muckrakers and the Mudslinger," *Washington Post,* April 19, 1994. Trudy Lieberman, "Churning Whitewater," *Columbia Journalism Review,* May–June 1994.
4. William Safire, "Foster's Ghost," *New York Times,* January 6, 1994. William Safire, "What's the Charge?," *New York Times,* January 13, 1994. William Safire, "Essay: Why No Firestorm?," *New York Times,* December 11, 1995.
5. Associated Press, "Now It's Gingrich's Mom at the Center of a Storm," *Chicago Tribune,* January 5, 1995. "Gingrich Clan Completes Private White House Tour," *Asbury Park Press,* January 14, 1995.
6. Mark Hosenball, "Whitewater's Sleuth: Who Is Jean Lewis?," *Newsweek,* March 22, 1994.
7. Jeff Gerth and Stephen Engelberg, "U.S. Investigating Clinton's Links to Arkansas S.& L.," *New York Times,* November 2, 1993. Kevin Merida, "Whitewater Tape Played," *Washington Post,* August 10, 1995, www.washingtonpost.com/archive /politics/1995/08/10/whitewater-tape-played/37139eca-3c93-4d2c-92b0 -fd21895c145a/?utm_term=.18ef86d93e84. Jeff Gerth, "Whitewater Prosecutor Agrees on Plea Bargain," *New York Times,* March 21, 1994. James Leach, Congressional Record, March 24, 1994.
8. David E. Rosenbaum, "The Whitewater Inquiry: Clinton's Account of Deal Is Questioned," *New York Times,* March 25, 1994. Gene Lyons, *Fools for Scandal: How the Media Invented Whitewater* (New York: Franklin Square Press, 2010), 95–101. Joe Conason and Gene Lyons, *The Hunting of the President: The Ten-Year Campaign to Destroy Bill and Hillary Clinton* (New York: Thomas Dunne, 2000), 197. Richard Cohen, "A Dead Letter Lives Again," *Washington Post,* December 5, 1995.
9. "Whitewater Investigation Part 3," C-SPAN video, 1:46:18, November 29, 1995, www.c-span.org/video/?68642-1/whitewater-investigation-part-3.c-span.
10. Hillary Clinton, *Living History* (New York: Scribner, 2004), 296–297.
11. For a complete recounting of the Starr investigation, see: Ken Gormley, *The Death of American Virtue: Clinton v. Starr* (New York: Crown, 2010). Ewing's presentation appears on pages 478–483.
12. Robert O'Harrow Jr. and Michael Kranish, "After Investigating Clinton White House and Vincent Foster's Death, Brett Kavanaugh Had a Change of Heart," *Washington Post,* August 2, 2018. Sean Wilentz, "Why Was Kavanaugh Obsessed with Vince Foster?," *New York Times,* September 5, 2018.
13. Conason and Lyons, *Hunting,* 87–90.
14. Gerth, "Whitewater Prosecutor Agrees."
15. Conason and Lyons, *Hunting,* 162. "Deputy Independent Counsel Says He Wrote 'Rough Draft Indictment' of Hillary Clinton," CNN, March 18, 1999, http://edition

.cnn.com/ALLPOLITICS/stories/1999/03/18/mcdougal/. Clinton, *Living History*, 328. Conason and Lyons, *Hunting,* 163. Stephen Labaton, "Whitewater Counsel Wants to Reduce One Man's Sentence," *New York Times,* March 26, 1997.

16. William Safire, "Essay: Blizzard of Lies," *New York Times,* January 8, 1996.

17. Toni Locy and Susan Schmidt, "First Lady Testifies for Four Hours," *Washington Post,* January 27, 1996. Robin D. Givhan, "Her True Colors," *Washington Post,* February 4, 1996.

18. David Johnston, "Special Counsel Linked to Suit Against Clinton," *New York Times,* August 12, 1994. Don Van Natta Jr. and Jill Abramson, "The President's Trial: The Lawsuit: Quietly, a Team of Lawyers Kept Paula Jones's Case Alive," *New York Times,* January 24, 1999. Gormley, *American Virtue,* 590.

19. "Woman Says Clinton Made Advance in '91," *New York Times,* February 12, 1994.

20. Lloyd Grove, "It Isn't Easy Being Right," *Washington Post,* February 14, 1994. Jonathan Marshall, "The Right's Long War on Media," *Consortium News,* July 20, 2017, https://consortiumnews.com/2017/07/20/the-rights-long-war-on-media/. Tim Golden, "Salvador Skeletons Confirm Reports of Massacre in 1981," *New York Times,* October 22, 1992. David Segal, "The Pied Piper of Racism," *Washington Post,* January 12, 2000.

21. For Starr, see: Bill Clinton, *My Life* (New York: Knopf, 2004), 709.

22. Van Natta and Abramson, "President's Trial." Joe Conason, "Drudge's Mystery Source? It's Wachtell's Conway," *New York Observer,* February 16, 1998. David Brock, *Blinded by the Right* (New York: Three Rivers Press, 2003), 201. George T. Conway III, "'No Man in This Country . . . Is Above the Law': Clinton: The Threat of a Flood of Suits Is Contrived to Save Him Embarrassment," *Los Angeles Times,* June 24, 1994.

23. Neil A. Lewis, "Sex Harassment Suit Based on 1860's Law," *New York Times,* May 7, 1994.

24. Conason and Lyons, *Hunting,* 269. Newsweek Staff, "Paula Jones's Credibility Gap," *Newsweek,* May 22, 1994, www.newsweek.com/paula-joness-credibility-gap -188742.

25. Murray Waas, "The Falwell Connection," *Salon,* March 11, 1998, www.salon.com /1998/03/11/cov_11news/.

26. Imus's song reported on *60 Minutes* broadcast, CBS, March 31, 1996. "60 MINUTES {THE LETTER; IMUS} (TV)," Paley Center for Media, www.paleycenter.org /collection/item/?q=cbs&p=19&item=T:63178.

27. Mary Jacoby, "Ex-FBI Agent's Book Has Many Hidden Authors," *Chicago Tribune,* July 3, 1996. Gary Aldrich, *Unlimited Access: An FBI Agent Inside the Clinton White House* (Washington, DC: Regnery, 1996), 70. "Southeastern Legal Foundation," SourceWatch, www.sourcewatch.org/index.php/Southeastern_Legal_Foundation.

28. Ithiel de Sola Pool and Manfred Kochen, "Contacts and Influence," *Social Networks* 1, no. 1 (1978–1979): 42.

29. Jason Vest, "The Spooky World of Linda Thompson," *Washington Post,* May 11, 1995.

30. "The Way Things Aren't: Rush Limbaugh Debates Reality," Fairness & Accuracy in Reporting, March 8, 1992, http://fair.org/extra/the-way-things-arent/.

31. Molly Ivins, "Lyin' Bully," *Mother Jones,* May–June 1995, www.motherjones.com

/politics/1995/05/lyin-bully/. For a thorough explication of the economic change pressuring Americans, see: Charles H. Ferguson, *Predator Nation: Corporate Criminals, Political Corruption, and the Hijacking of America* (New York: Crown, 2012).

32. Walter Newell, "The Crisis of Manliness," *Weekly Standard,* August 3, 1998.

33. Gabriel Sherman, *The Loudest Voice in the Room* (New York: Random House, 2017), 160–168, 200–202. Tim Alberta, "John Boehner Unchained," *Politico,* November– December 2017, www.politico.com/magazine/story/2017/10/29/john-boehner -trump-house-republican-party-retirement-profile-feature-215741. Lawrie Mifflin, "Fox Presents Its Lineup for News Channel," *New York Times,* September 5, 1996.

34. Brock, *Blinded,* 111.

35. David Brock, "Roger Ailes Is Mad as Hell," *New York,* November 17, 1997.

36. Reuters, "Drudge Bites Back," *Wired,* June 2, 1998, www.wired.com/1998/06 /drudge-bites-back/. "Clinton Aide Settles with Matt Drudge," *New York Times,* May 4, 2001.

### 6. "I Love Dish!"

1. Lucianne Goldberg and Jeannie Sakol, "Two Members of Pussycat League Attack Women's Liberation," *Montreal Gazette,* October 30, 1971. J. Anthony Lukas, *Nightmare: The Underside of the Nixon Campaign* (New York: Viking, 1976). "Talk of the Town," *New Yorker,* February 2, 1998. John Cloud, "Clinton's Crisis: Lucianne Goldberg: In Pursuit of Clinton," *Time,* February 2, 1998.

2. For Aldrich, see: Newsweek Staff, "Clinton and the Intern," *Newsweek,* February 1, 1998, www.newsweek.com/clinton-and-intern-169918. "Magazine: Tripp Tried to Write a Clinton 'Tell-All' Book," CNN, January 25, 1998, www.cnn.com /ALLPOLITICS/1998/01/25/tripp.goldberg/. For rat pack, see: Gabriel Sherman, *The Loudest Voice in the Room* (New York: Random House, 2017), 230. "Ink," *New Yorker,* December 28, 1998.

3. Goldberg/Tripp conversations from record of Clinton impeachment proceedings: S. Doc. No. 106-3 (1999), "Factual Record: Transcripts of Two Telephone Conversations Between Linda Tripp and Lucianne Goldeberg," www.gpo.gov/fdsys/pkg /GPO-CDOC-106sdoc3/pdf/GPO-CDOC-106sdoc3-14-7.pdf.

4. For $500,000, see: Michael Isikoff, *Uncovering Clinton: A Reporter's Story* (New York: Crown, 1999).

5. Art Moore, "Kathleen Willey Suspects Clinton Murdered Husband," *World Net Daily,* November 5, 2011, www.wnd.com/2007/11/44397/.

6. Jeff Leen, "The Other Woman in the Jones Case," *Washington Post,* January 29, 1998, www.washingtonpost.com/wp-srv/politics/special/clinton/stories/willey012998 .htm.

7. Philip M. Seib, *Going Live: Getting the News Right in a Real-Time, Online World* (New York: Rowman and Littlefield, 2001), 146. Michelangelo Signorile, "David Brock's Out, and Sorry," Strauss Media, April 2, 2002.

8. Jeffrey Toobin, *A Vast Conspiracy: The Real Story of the Sex Scandal That Nearly Brought Down a President* (New York: Random House, 2000), 219–225. Isikoff, *Uncovering Clinton,* 250–268. "Excerpts from News Conference: 'It Was a Mistake,'" *New York Times,* February 22, 1997.

9. Adam Clymer, "House, in a 395–28 Vote, Reprimands Gingrich," *New York Times,* January 22, 1997. Juli Weiner, "An Unabridged Guide to All of Newt Gingrich's Wives," *Vanity Fair,* August 10, 2010. Howard Kurtz, "Report of Hyde Affair Stirs Anger," *Washington Post,* September 17, 1998. Beth Berselli and Paul Farhi, "How and What Newt Told Marianne," *Washington Post,* August 14, 1999.

10. Steven Brill, "Pressgate," *Brill's Content,* August 1998. Joe Conason, "Drudge's Mystery Source? It's Wachtell's Conway," *Observer,* February 16, 1998, https://observer .com/1998/02/drudges-mystery-source-its-wachtells-conway/.

11. Ken Gormley, *The Death of American Virtue: Clinton v. Starr* (New York: Crown, 2010), 377–392.

12. Ibid., 413.

13. Libby Torres, "How America Failed to Learn Its Lesson from the Clinton-Lewinsky Scandal," *Daily Beast,* October 28, 2018, www.thedailybeast.com/how-america -failed-to-learn-its-lesson-from-the-clinton-lewinsky-scandal.

## 7. Almost Numb to It

1. Pamela Engle, "How Vladimir Putin Became One of the Most Feared Leaders in the World," *Business Insider,* February 14, 2017, https://www.businessinsider.com/how -vladimir-putin-rose-to-power-2017-2. "Putin's Revenge—Transcript," *Frontline,* PBS, October 25 and November 1, 2017, www.pbs.org/wgbh/frontline/film/putins -revenge/transcript/.

2. "Transcript of Clinton's 1997 State of the Union," CNN, February 1, 2005, http:// edition.cnn.com/2005/ALLPOLITICS/01/31/sotu.clinton1997/.

3. David Brock, "I Knew Brett Kavanaugh During His Years as a Republican Operative. Don't Let Him Sit on the Supreme Court," NBC, September 7, 2018, www.nbcnews.com/think/opinion/i-knew-brett-kavanaugh-during-his-years -republican-operative-don-ncna907391.

4. David Usborne, "The Peacock Patriarchy," *Esquire,* August 5, 2018.

5. "Today: Tuesday," C-SPAN video, 18:00, January 27, 1998, www.c-span.org/video /?99377-1/today-tuesday.

6. The Birch Society veteran was John Rees of the Maldon Institute. See: Kris Hermes, *Crashing the Party: Legacies and Lessons from the RNC 2000* (Oakland, CA: PM Press, 2015). "Information on Judicial Watch's lawsuits against Clinton Administration," Wikipedia, https://en.wikipedia.org/wiki/Judicial_Watch#Clinton_Administration. Aggregated Grants from the Scaife Family Foundation, Carthage Foundation, Allegheny Foundation, and the Sarah Scaife Foundation. Daniel Moritz-Rabson, "Former Trump Campaign Manager Admits There Was, in Fact, a 'Vast Right-Wing Conspiracy' to Undermine the Clintons," *Newsweek,* November 25, 2018.

7. Florence Graves and Jacqueline E. Sharkey, "Starr and Willey: The Untold Story," *Nation,* May 12, 1999.

8. Diane Blair Papers, University of Arkansas Libraries, Fayetteville, Arkansas.

9. Bill Clinton, Clinton's Grand Jury Testimony, Starr report, September 11, 1998.

10. James Pitkin, "Judgment Call: Gordon Smith's Choice for a Plum Federal Court Job May Be in Trouble. Hint: It Has More Than a Little to Do with Monica Lewinsky," *Willamette Week,* January 16, 2008.

11. Hannah Cooper, Lisa Moore, Sofia Gruskin, and Nancy Krieger, "Characterizing Perceived Police Violence: Implications for Public Health," *Journal of Public Health,* July 2004. "Mission Failure: Civilian Review of Policing in New York City, 1996–2004," New York Civil Liberties Union, www.nyclu.org/en/mission-failure-civilian-review -policing-new-york-city-summary-findings. Janny Scott, "Now, Conflicting Views from Women Who Supported Clinton," *New York Times,* August 28, 1998. Barbara Kellerman, "The Clinton Presidency on Crisis," *Presidential Studies Quarterly,* Fall 1998.

12. David Talbot, "This Hypocrite Broke Up My Family," *Salon,* September 17, 1998, www.salon.com/1998/09/17/cov_16newsb/.

13. Melinda Henneberger, "Impeachment: The First Lady: Clinton's Top Defender Rallies Troops at Front," *New York Times,* December 20, 1998.

14. Ken Gormley, *The Death of American Virtue: Clinton v. Starr* (New York: Crown, 2010), 675. "Report of the Special Master on Rule 6 e Inquiry," submitted by Hon. John W. Kern III, United States District Court for the District of Columbia, released August 23, 2018, www.archives.gov/files/foia/docid-70105464.pdf.

15. "Starr's Tenure as Independent Counsel Marked by Strongly Unfavorable Public Opinion," Gallup, October 19, 1999. Amelia Thomson-DeVeaux, "How Mueller's First Year Compares to Watergate, Iran-Contra and Whitewater," *FiveThirtyEight,* May 17, 2018, https://fivethirtyeight.com/features/how-muellers-first-year-compares -to-watergate-iran-contra-and-whitewater/.

## 8. Unstoppable

1. Ron Rosenbaum, "Who Puts the Words in the President's Mouth?," *Esquire,* December 1995.

2. Peggy Noonan, *The Case Against Hillary Clinton* (New York: Regan Books, 2000), 74–92, 180. Rosenbaum, "Who Puts the Words?"

3. Garnett Stackelberg, "Media Mighties Laud Author's Story of Hillary," *Palm Beach Daily News,* September 28, 1999. Roxanne Roberts, "Commitments," *Washington Post,* September 4, 1995.

4. Eric Alterman et al., *What Liberal Media?: The Truth About Bias and the News* (New York: Hachette, 2003), 2–4. Andrea Ahles, "Hell to Pay a Rehash on Hillary, Not Original Research," *Lincoln Journal Star,* April 23, 2000.

5. Charles H. Quick, "Check Out Hillary's Past," *Press & Sun Bulletin,* January 27, 2000.

6. Barbara Olson, *Hell to Pay* (Washington, DC: Regnery, 2001), for jihad: 123; secret police: 305; attention: 265; services: 308; scandal: 301–304.

7. Debbie M. Price, "Hair Care Reform Could Take Press off Health Car Makeover," *Cincinnati Enquirer,* June 9, 1993.

8. Lucinda Franks, "The Intimate Hillary," *Talk,* September 1999, 166.

9. Deborah Orin, "Bill's OK with First Lady's 'Abuse'-Excuse Theory," *New York Post,* August 3, 1999. John Podhoretz, "The Myth of Hillary's Brilliance," *New York Post,* August 5, 1999. Howard Kurtz, "Did Not! Did Too! Wanna Bet?," *Washington Post,* August 5, 1999. Richard Brookhiser, "First Lady Reminds Us of Mess We Left Behind," *Observer,* August 16, 1999. Christopher Caldwell, "Hillary Clinton, Psycho-analyst," *Weekly Standard,* August 16, 1999.

10. Michael Tomasky, *Hillary's Turn* (New York: Free Press, 2001), 41.

11. Michael Tomasky, "The Mystery of Rudy Giuliani's Moral Decline Isn't Such a Mystery at All," *New York,* December 9, 2016, www.nymag.com/intelligencer/2016 /12/rudy-giulianis-moral-decline-isnt-such-a-mystery-at-all.html. Wayne Barrett, *Rudy!* (New York: Basic Books, 2000), 460. For Giuliani's smear of police shoot-ing victim Patrick Dorismond, see: Barrett, *Rudy!,* 335–338. Dan Barry, "Political Memo: Mayor Tries to Make It a Sharpton-Clinton Slate," *New York Times,* March 27, 2000. Kevin Baker, "Is Rudy Giuliani Losing His Mind?," *Politico,* September 4, 2016, www.politico.com/magazine/story/2016/09/rudy-giuliani-donald-trump -2016-214207.

12. Radley Balko, "More on the Time Rudy Giuliani Helped Incite a Riot of Rac-ist Cops," *Washington Post,* November 16, 2016. Nat Hentoff and Nick Hentoff, "Rudy's Racist Rants: An NYPD History Lesson," Cato Institute, July 14, 2016, www.cato.org/publications/commentary/rudys-racist-rants-nypd-history-lesson. Michael Grunwald, "Trial Puts Giuliani, NYPD on Defensive," *Washington Post,* March 30, 1999.

13. Richard Pérez-Peña, "As '08 Candidate, Giuliani Strikes a New Tone on Guns," *New York Times,* March 23, 2007. Barrett, *Rudy!,* 460.

14. Peter Beinart, "Hillary Clinton and the Tragic Politics of Crime: The Criminal-Justice Policies She Now Denounces Once Helped Her Husband Capture the White House," *Atlantic,* May 1, 2015, www.theatlantic.com/politics/archive/2015 /05/the-tragic-politics-of-crime/392114/.

15. Anne-Marie O'Neill, "Giuliani and Judith Nathan Started Their Marriage by Ending Another," *People,* April 4, 2018. Elisabeth Bumiller, "The Mayor's Separation: The Over-view: Giuliani and His Wife of 16 Years Are Separating," *New York Times,* May 11, 2000.

16. Mike Allen, "Lazio Fundraising Letter Slams Clinton," *Washington Post,* July 2, 2000. Joel Siegel, "Lazio's Poison Pen Letter," *Daily News,* July 6, 2000. Craig Horo-witz, "Rudy's Choice," *New York,* May 29, 2000, http://nymag.com/nymetro/news /politics/newyork/features/3261/.

17. Michael Tomasky, *Hillary's Turn* (New York: Free Press, 2001), 190–194.

18. Charlotte Templin, "Hillary Clinton as Threat to Gender Norms: Cartoon Images of the First Lady," *Journal of Communication Inquiry* 23, no. 1 (1999): 231–236. D. Burgess and E. Burgida, "Who Women Are, Who Women Should Be," *Psychology Public Policy and Law* 5, no. 3 (1999): 665–696, https://psycnet.apa.org/record/2000-03912-006.

Joan L. Connors, "Barack vs. Hillary: Race, Gender and Political Cartoon Imagery of the 2008 Presidential Primaries," *American Behavioral Scientist* 54, no. 3 (2010).

19. "Most Admired Man and Woman," Gallup, 2019, www.news.gallup.com/poll/1678/most-admired-man-woman.aspxo.

20. Jane Gross, "Cautious Assessments Favor the Performance of Mrs. Clinton," *New York Times,* September 14, 2000. Gail Collins, "Winging It in Buffalo," *New York Times,* September 15, 2000. Lars-Erik Nelson, "First Lady Talks Issues as Lazio Gets Personal," *Daily News,* September 14, 2000.

21. Maureen Dowd, "A Man and a Woman," *New York Times,* September 20, 2000.

22. "Exit Poll Shows Lazio Support Little More Than Anti-Hillary Vote," *Rochester Democrat and Chronicle,* November 8, 2000.

23. "Excerpted Comments of the Senator-Elect," *New York Times,* November 9, 2000.

## 9. Overcoming

1. "Presidential Approval Ratings—Bill Clinton, Report," Gallup, www.news.gallup.com/poll/116584/presidential-approval-ratings-bill-clinton.aspx. "Congress and the Public," Gallup, www.news.gallup.com/poll/1600/congress-public.aspx. Gary C. Jacobson, "Public Opinion and the Impeachment of Bill Clinton," *British Elections & Parties Review* 10, no. 1 (2000): 1–31, doi: 10.1080/13689880008413034.

2. Michael Tomasky, "Cool on the Hill," *New York,* February 3, 2003.

3. Shawn Zeller, "As a Senator, Hillary Clinton Got Along with the GOP. Could She Do So as President?," *Roll Call,* September 26, 2016. Ed Pilkington, "9/11 Tapes Reveal Raw and Emotional Hillary Clinton," *Guardian,* September 9, 2016.

4. Marykate Jasper, "Betsy Devos' Pick to Head Civil Rights Office Once Complained about Anti-White Discrimination," *Mary Sue,* April 15, 2017, www.themarysue.com/betsy-devos-civil-rights-reverse-racism/. William Anderson and Candice E. Jackson, "Washington's Biggest Crime Problem: The Federal Government's Ever-Expanding Criminal Code Is an Affront to Justice and the Constitution," *Reason,* April 2004.

5. Erica Green and Sheryl Gay Stolberg, "Campus Rape Policies Get a New Look as the Accused Get DeVos's Ear," *New York Times,* July 12, 2017. Kathleen Parker, "There's Something (Else) About Hillary," *Chicago Tribune,* June 20, 2005.

6. Raymond Hernandez, "Conservatives Promoting Anti-Clinton Book," *New York Times,* June 17, 2005. Brian Cogan and Tony Kelso, *Encyclopedia of Politics, the Media, and Popular Culture* (Santa Barbara, CA: ABC-CLIO, 2009), 155, 187, 335, https://en.wikipedia.org/wiki/Swift_Vets_and_POWs_for_Truth#cite_note-Cogan2-20. John Colapinto, "A Star Is Born, Lost, and Found," *New Yorker,* April 3, 2012.

7. John Podhoretz, "Smear for Profit—New Hillary 'Bio' Is Just Trash," *New York Post,* June 22, 2005. John Swaine, "Edward Klein: The Difference Between the Truth and a Lie," *Guardian,* July 14, 2014. Edward Klein, *The Truth About Hillary* (New York: Sentinel, 2005), for mothering: 92; bitter: 53; frigid: 64; Foster affair: 22; rape: 90; references to lesbianism throughout.

8. Klein, *Truth,* for Lewinsky: 1–2; cocksucker: 15; appointments: 64. Eric Kriss, "CNY Native Appalled by Book on Hillary Clinton (Denies Lesbianism, Cites 'Bunker Mentality')," *Free Republic,* June 15, 2005, www.freerepublic.com/focus/f-news /1423171/posts.

9. Klein, *Truth,* for dominatrix: 235; violent: 49; Big Girl: 11; physical: 24–25; Monica: 3; butch: 65; Lieberman: 108.

10. Joe Queenan, "'The Truth About Hillary': Many a Dubious Revelation," *New York Times,* July 31, 2005. Keelin McDonell, "Defense Mechanism," *New Republic,* July 4, 2005.

11. Patrick D. Healy, "Pirro Begins Her Senate Campaign by Assailing Clinton," *New York Times,* August 10, 2005.

12. For Axelrod and Obama in run-up to 2008, see: David Axelrod, *Believer: My Forty Years in Politics* (New York: Penguin, 2015). "Poll: Obama Now Trails Only Clinton on '08 List," CNN, November 2, 2006, http://edition.cnn.com/2006/POLITICS /11/01/poll.2008/.

13. Axelrod, *Believer,* 199.

14. Mark Leibovich, "Clinton Shapes Her Image for '08 Race," *New York Times,* March 6, 2007. "Nationwide Opinion Polling for the 2008 Democratic Party Presidential Primaries," Wikipedia, https://en.wikipedia.org/wiki/Nationwide_opinion_polling _for_the_2008_Democratic_Party_presidential_primaries. Dalia Sussman, "The Caucus: Poll," *New York Times,* June 5, 2007.

15. Melinda Henneberger, *If They Only Listened to Us: What Women Voters Want Politicians to Hear* (New York: Simon & Schuster, 2007), 48.

16. "Hillary Clinton Defends 2002 Iraq War Vote on Meet the Press," *Huffington Post,* March 28, 2008, www.huffingtonpost.com/2008/01/13/hillary-clinton-defends-2 _n_81261.html.

17. Patrick Healy, "Resurrection: How New Hampshire Saved the 1992 Clinton Campaign," *New York Times,* February 8, 2016.

18. Anne E. Kornblut, "It's Not Easy, an Emotional Clinton Says," *Washington Post,* January 8, 2008. "The Woman Who Elicited Clinton's Emotion," CBS, January 8, 2008, www.cbsnews.com/news/the-woman-who-elicited-clintons-emotion/. Maureen Dowd, "Can Hillary Cry Her Way Back into the White House?," *New York Times,* January 9, 2008. Michael Kruse, "The Woman Who Made Hillary Cry," *Politico,* April 20, 2015, www.politico.com/story/2015/04/the-woman-who-made-hillary -clinton-cry-117171.

19. Trudy Lieberman, "Churning Whitewater," *Columbia Journalism Review,* May–June 1994. "Floyd Brown Exposed," YouTube video, 5:32, posted by "sallystipend," June 11, 2008, www.youtube.com/watch?v=7PnfpefgI5c. Russ Baker, "Portrait of a Political 'Pit Bull,'" *Salon,* December 22, 1998, www.salon.com/1998/12/22 /newsa950556369/. Eric Schmidt, "A Top Aide Resigns," *New York Times,* May 10, 1998. Eric Boehlert, "You Can't Teach an Old Attack Dog New Tricks," *Salon,* July 20, 2004, www.salon.com/2004/07/20/david_bossie/.

20. Robert Barnes, "'Hillary: The Movie' to Get Supreme Court Screening," *Washington Post,* March 15, 2009.

21. John Schindler, "Why Vladimir Putin Hates Us," *Observer,* November 22, 2016. Simon Schuster, "One Rich American vs. Moscow: The Question of William Browder," *Time,* December 3, 2011. Jeremy Wilson, "Here's a List of Putin Critics Who've Ended Up Dead," *Buisness Insider,* March 11, 2016, www.businessinsider .com/list-of-people-putin-is-suspected-of-assassinating-2016-3.

22. Michael Schwirtz and David M. Herszenhorn, "Voters Watch Polls in Russia, and Fraud Is What They See," *New York Times,* December 5, 2011.

23. Hillary Clinton, secretary of state remarks, LitExpo Conference Center, Vilnius, Lithuania, December 6, 2011. Simon Schuster, "All the Wrong Moves: Putin Plots His Strategy Against the Protesters," *Time,* December 9, 2001. Simon Schuster, "Occupy Kremlin: Russia's Elections Lets Loose Public Rage," *Time,* December 5, 2011. Luke Harding, "Former Trump Aide Approved Black Ops to Help Ukrainian President," *Guardian,* April 5, 2018. Lally Weymouth, "Yulia Tymoshenko and the Fight for Ukraine: 'We Cannot Accept Peace on Putin's Terms,'" *Washington Post,* September 19, 2018. For Putin quote, see: Michael Isikoff and David Corn, *Russian Roulette: The Inside Story of Putin's War on America and the Election of Donald Trump* (New York: Hachette, 2017), 36.

24. Angela Stent, "U.S.-Russia Relations in the Second Obama Administration," Brookings, December 31, 2012, www.brookings.edu/articles/u-s-russia-relations-in-the -second-obama-administration/.

25. Michael Crowley and Julia Ioffe, "Why Putin Hates Hillary," *Politico,* July 25, 2016, www.politico.com/story/2016/07/clinton-putin-226153. For Putin's view of Clinton, see: "Putin's Revenge—Transcript," *Frontline,* PBS, October 25 and November 1, 2017, www.pbs.org/wgbh/frontline/film/putins-revenge/transcript/.

## 10. We Create Our Own Reality

1. Caleb M. Soptelean, "Ryan Zinke Campaigns in Bigfork, Says Hillary Clinton Is the 'Anti-Christ,'" *Bigfork Eagle,* January 30, 2014.

2. Brian Tashman, "Five of the Craziest Conspiracy Theories That the Freshman Republican Class Will Bring to Congress," *Right Wing Watch,* November 5, 2014, www .rightwingwatch.org/post/five-of-the-craziest-conspiracy-theories-that-the -freshman-republican-class-will-bring-to-congress/. Ian Millhiser, "TX Sen Candidate Ted Cruz Spouts Paranoid Fantasy About United Nations / George Soros Conspiracy to Eliminate Golf," *ThinkProgress,* March 12, 2012, https://thinkprogress.org /tx-sen-candidate-ted-cruz-spouts-paranoid-fantasy-about-united-nations-george -soros-conspiracy-to-407d1f395556/. Miranda Blue, "7 Outrageous Rants from GOP House Candidate Jody Hice on Blood Moons, Sandy Hook, Women and 'Judicial Terrorists,'" *Right Wing Watch,* May 28, 2014, http://www.rightwingwatch.org /post/7-outrageous-rants-from-gop-house-candidate-jody-hice-on-blood-moons -sandy-hook-women-and-judicial-terrorists/.

3. Safa Sorour, "The US Embassy in Cairo Condemns 'Religious Incitement' to Produce an Offensive Film of the Prophet," *Egypt Independent,* September 11, 2012. Max

Fisher, "The Movie So Offensive That Egyptians Just Stormed the U.S. Embassy over It," *Atlantic,* September 11, 2012, www.theatlantic.com/international/archive /2012/09/the-movie-so-offensive-that-egyptians-just-stormed-the-us-embassy -over-it/262225/. Emad Mekay, "The Muhammad Movie: Look Who Fanned the Flames," *Columbia Journalism Review,* January 7, 2013. "US Embassy in Egypt 'Warned' of Violence over Anti-Islam Film," RT, September 18, 2012, www.rt.com /news/us-warned-film-violence-376/.

4. Zack Beauchamp, "9 Questions About Benghazi You Were Too Embarrassed to Ask," *Vox,* July 18, 2016, www.vox.com/2015/10/12/9489389/benghazi-explained.

5. David D. Kirkpatrick, "A Deadly Mix in Benghazi," *New York Times,* December 28, 2013.

6. "Fact-Checking Romney's Statements on Libya Attacks," *San Jose Mercury News,* September 14, 2012.

7. Barack Obama, "Remarks by the President on the Deaths of U.S. Embassy Staff in Libya," White House, September 12, 2012, www.obamawhitehouse.archives.gov /the-press-office/2012/09/12/remarks-president-deaths-us-embassy-staff-libya.

8. "'This Week' Transcript: U.S. Ambassador to the United Nations Susan Rice," ABC, September 16, 2012, www.abcnews.go.com/Politics/week-transcript-us-ambassador -united-nations-susan-rice/story?id=17240933. Eugene Kiely, "Benghazi Timeline," FactCheck.org, June 29, 2016, https://www.factcheck.org/2012/10/benghazi -timeline/. Glenn Kessler, "Is Hillary Clinton a 'Liar' on Benghazi?," *Washington Post,* October 30, 2015.

9. Glenn Kessler, "Barbara Boxer's Claim That GOP Budgets Hampered Benghazi Security," *Washington Post,* May 16, 2013.

10. John H. Cushman Jr., "Added Security in Libya Was Rejected, G.O.P. Says," *New York Times,* October 2, 2012. Fred Burton and Samuel M. Katz, "Forty Minutes in Benghazi," *Vanity Fair,* August 2013. Zeke Miller and Alex Rogers, "Timeline: The Benghazi E-Mails: How the Obama Administration Created the Benghazi Talking Points," *Time,* May 16, 2013. Eric Schmitt and Mark Landler, "Focus Was on Tripoli in Requests for Security in Libya," *New York Times,* October 12, 2012. Michael R. Gordon and Eric Schmitt, "Libya Attack Shows Pentagon's Limits in Region," *New York Times,* November 3, 2012. Adam Goldman and Greg Miller, "Former CIA Officer in Benghazi Challenges Michael Bay's '13 Hours,'" *Chicago Tribune,* January 15, 2016.

11. "Hillary Clinton Takes Responsibility for Libya US Deaths," BBC, October 16, 2012, www.bbc.com/news/av/world-us-canada-19958802/hillary-clinton-takes -blame-for-us-deaths-in-libya.

12. Jeff Poor, "Gingrich: Senator Told Me Networks May Have White House Emails Commanding Counterterrorism Group to Stand Down on Benghazi Rescue," *Daily Caller,* October 31, 2012, https://dailycaller.com/2012/10/31/gingrich-rumor -says-networks-have-white-house-emails-telling-counterterrorism-group-to-stand -down-on-benghazi-rescue/. Sarah Kliff, Dylan Mathews, and Brad Plumer, "The 2012 Election in Charts," *Washington Post,* November 7, 2012. E. J. Dionne, "Kevin McCarthy's Truthful Gaffe on Benghazi," *Washington Post,* September 30, 2015.

13. Jon Cohen and Aaron Blake, "Hillary Clinton Reaches New Heights of Political

Popularity," *Washington Post,* January 23, 2013. "Hillary Clinton Is Most Popular National Figure, Quinnipiac University National Poll Finds; Obama Approval Sinks After Reelection," Quinnipiac University, February 8, 2013, https://poll.qu.edu /national/release-detail?ReleaseID=1849.

14. "Accountability Review Board (ARB) Report [Benghazi Report of December 19, 2012]," Homeland Security Digital Library, December 19, 2012, https://www.hsdl .org/?abstract&did=727502.

15. Megan Garber, "Hillary Clinton Traveled 956,733 Miles During Her Time as Secretary of State," *Atlantic,* January 29, 2013, https://www.theatlantic.com/politics /archive/2013/01/hillary-clinton-traveled-956-733-miles-during-her-time-as -secretary-of-state/272656/. David Brock, Ari Rabin-Havt, and Media Matters for America, *The Benghazi Hoax* (North Charleston, SC: Createspace, 2013), 43–44. Post Staff, "Hillary Clinton's Head Fake," *New York Post,* December 18, 2012, https://nypost.com/2012/12/18/hillary-clintons-head-fake/.

16. Elise Labott, "Hillary Clinton Hospitalized After Doctors Discover Blood Clot," CNN, December 31, 2012, https://edition.cnn.com/2012/12/30/politics/hillary -clinton-hospitalized/index.html.

17. United States Senate Committee on Foreign Relations, *Benghazi: The Attacks and the Lessons Learned* (Washington, DC: U.S. Government Printing Office, 2013), https://www.govinfo.gov/content/pkg/CHRG-113shrg86780/pdf/CHRG -113shrg86780.pdf.

18. "David Petraeus," Wikipedia, https://en.wikipedia.org/wiki/David_Petraeus.

19. Linda Qiu, "What You Need to Know About Hillary Clinton's 'Infamous Response' to Benghazi Question," PolitiFact, July 19, 2016.

20. "Chairman Royce on Fox News 'Special Report with Bret Baier' on Sec Clinton Testimony on Benghazi," YouTube video, 8:44, posted by House Foreign Affairs Committee Republicans, January 23, 2013, https://www.youtube.com/watch?v =heqYBf-Lev0.

21. Rand Paul, "The Moment of Responsibility for Hillary Clinton," *Washington Times,* May 10, 2013.

22. Glenn Kessler, "Issa's Absurd Claim That Clinton's 'Signature' Means She Personally Approved It," *Washington Post,* April 26, 2013.

23. Ron Suskind, "Faith, Certainty and the Presidency of George W. Bush," *New York Times,* October 17, 2004. David Teather, "Bush Jokes About Search for WMD, but It's No Laughing Matter for Critics," *Guardian,* March 26, 2004. Jeremy W. Peters and Eric Schmitt, "State Dept. Official to Testify on Benghazi Attacks," *New York Times,* May 7, 2013. Mark Landler, "Benghazi Debate Focuses on Interpretation of Early E-Mail on Attackers," *New York Times,* May 8, 2013. Committee on Oversight and Government Reform, *Benghazi: Exposing Failure and Recognizing Courage* (Washington, DC: U.S. Government Printing Office, 2013), https://www.govinfo .gov/content/pkg/CHRG-113hhrg81563/pdf/CHRG-113hhrg81563.pdf. Victoria Toensing, "Administration Relying on Shoddy Benghazi Report to Absolve Itself of Blame," *Weekly Standard,* May 12, 2013. Howard Kurtz, "The Power Couple at Scandal's Vortex," *Washington Post,* February 27, 1998.

24. Ethan Chorin, "The Deeper Blame for Benghazi," *New York Times,* May 13, 2013.

25. "Americans Trust Clinton over GOP on Benghazi," Public Policy Polling, May 13, 2013, https://www.publicpolicypolling.com/wp-content/uploads/2017/09/PPP _Release_National_51313.pdf. Michael B. Kelley, "Study: Watching Only Fox News Makes You Less Informed Than Watching No News at All," *Business Insider,* May 22, 2012, https://www.businessinsider.com/study-watching-fox-news-makes-you -less-informed-than-watching-no-news-at-all-2012-5. Gregory J. Martin and Ali Yurukoglu, "Bias in Cable News: Persuasion and Polarization," *American Economic Review* 107, no. 9 (2017).

26. Brock, Rabin-Havt, and Media Matters, *Benghazi Hoax,* 51.

27. Kevin Cirilli, "Crossroads Hits Clinton on Benghazi," *Politico,* May 10, 2013, https:// www.politico.com/story/2013/05/crossroads-hillary-clinton-benghazi-091177.

28. Rove's spending from OpenSecrets.org record of American Crossroads GPS.

29. Josh Rogin, "Benghazi Victim's Widow Praises State Department Cooperation," *Foreign Policy,* October 16, 2012, https://foreignpolicy.com/2012/10/16/benghazi -victims-widow-praises-state-department-cooperation/. Bill Adair and Lauren Carroll, "Checking Patricia Smith's Claims About Clinton and Benghazi," PolitiFact, July 18, 2016, https://www.politifact.com/truth-o-meter/article/2016/jul/18 /checking-patricia-smiths-claims-about-clinton-and-/.

30. Committee on Oversight and Government Reform, *Benghazi Attacks: Investigative Update Interim Report on the Accountability Review Board,* September 16, 2013.

31. Becky Bowers, "Jason Chaffetz Says Americans Ready to Save Men 'Getting Killed' in Benghazi Were Told to Stand Down," PolitiFact, May 14, 2013, https://www .politifact.com/truth-o-meter/statements/2013/may/14/jason-chaffetz/rep-jason -chaffetz-says-special-forces-ready-save-/. Brock, Rabin-Havt, and Media Matters, *Benghazi Hoax,* 51.

32. U.S. Senate Select Committee on Intelligence, *Review of the Terrorist Attacks on U.S. Facilities in Benghazi, Libya, September 11–12, 2012 Together with Additional Views,* January 15, 2014.

33. Nicholas Lemann, "The Problem with Steve Bannon's Story About His Father," *New Yorker,* March 21, 2017. Ben Shapiro, "3 Thoughts on Steve Bannon as White House 'Chief Strategist,'" *Daily Wire,* November 14, 2016.

34. Shawn Boburg and Robert O'Harrow Jr., "How Bannon's Multimedia Machine Drove a Movement and Paid Him Millions," *Washington Post,* April 9, 2017. John Swaine, "Offshore Cash Helped Fund Steve Bannon's Attacks on Hillary Clinton," *Guardian,* November 9, 2017.

35. Hannah Groch-Begley, "Who Funds Peter Schweizer's Government Accountability Institute?," Media Matters for America, April 21, 2015, www.mediamatters.org/blog /2015/04/21/who-funds-peter-schweizers-government-accountability-institute /203355. Jane Mayer, "The Reclusive Hedge-Fund Tycoon Behind the Trump presidency," *New Yorker,* March 27, 2017. "Who Are the Mercers, the Wealthy Backers of Breitbart?," *Deutsche Welle,* January 1, 2018, https://www.dw.com/en/who-are -the-mercers-the-wealthy-backers-of-breitbart/a-42100407.

36. Associated Press, "Conservative Firebrand Klayman Seeks Senate Seat," *Boca Raton /*

*Delray Beach News,* October 10, 2003. "Larry Klayman," Southern Poverty Law Center, https://www.splcenter.org/fighting-hate/extremist-files/individual/larry-klayman. Lauren Carroll, "Is ISIS in Mexico and Planning to Cross the Border?," PolitiFact, September 17, 2014, https://www.politifact.com/truth-o-meter/statements/2014/sep/17/trent-franks/isis-mexico-and-planning-cross-border/. Andrew Hart, "The 9 Biggest Myths About ISIS Debunked," *Huffington Post,* December 6, 2017, https://www.huffingtonpost.com.mx/entry/isis-myths-debunked_n_5875050?ec_carp=4029134910645546197. "JW Exposes Clinton Cash Machine," *Judicial Watch,* April 24, 2015. Bryan Tashman, "Right-Wing Group Judicial Watch Says It Prevented a Terrorist Attack," Right Wing Watch, April 20, 2015, http://www.rightwingwatch.org/post/right-wing-group-judicial-watch-says-it-prevented-a-terrorist-attack/. "Is ISIS on the U.S.-Mexican Border?," Snopes, https://www.snopes.com/fact-check/tijuana-transfer/.

37. Jake Sherman, "NRCC Fundraising Off of Benghazi," *Politico,* May 7, 2014, https://www.politico.com/story/2014/05/nrcc-fundraising-benghazi-106444.

38. Michael S. Schmidt, "G.O.P.-Led Benghazi Panel Bolsters Administration Position," *New York Times,* November 22, 2014. Majority Staff, "#DishonestDems Invent Clinton Hashtag Conspiracy," Select Committee on Benghazi, June 29, 2016, https://archives-benghazi-republicans-oversight.house.gov/news/press-releases/dishonestdems-invent-clinton-hashtag-conspiracy. For Matt Wolking, see: "Matt Wolking," Patrick Henry College, September 2015, https://www.phc.edu/alumni-profiles/matt-wolking.

39. Ashley Parker, "Republicans Fault Hillary Clinton over Emails on Talk Shows," *New York Times,* July 26, 2015.

40. Eric Lichtblau and Adam Goldman, "F.B.I. Papers Offer Closer Look at Hillary Clinton Email Inquiry," *New York Times,* September 2, 2016.

41. Meghan Keneally, Liz Kreutz, and Shushannah Walshe, "A Timeline of Hillary Clinton's Email Saga," ABC, November 7, 2016.

42. Jennifer Steinhauer and Michael S. Schmidt, "Benghazi Panel's Leader Under Fire as He Prepares to Face Hillary Clinton," *New York Times,* October 21, 2015. Gail Collins, "Hillary and Benghazi," *New York Times,* October 21, 2015.

43. Catherine Thompson, "Drudge Suggests Hillary Is 'Holding a Walker' on People Magazine Cover," *Talking Points Memo,* June 4, 2014. Edward Klein, *Unlikeable: The Problem with Hillary Clinton* (Washington, DC: Regnery, 2015), 147–150.

44. Greg Sargent, "Morning Plum: Clinton May Be Changing Minds on Benghazi, E-Mails," *Washington Post,* November 3, 2015.

45. Sam Frizell, "How Hillary Clinton Won the Benghazi Hearing," *Time,* October 23, 2015.

## 11. Chaos

1. "Inside the Russian Troll Factory, Zombie Troops and a Breakneck Pace," *Singapore Straits Times,* February 19, 2018, https://www.straitstimes.com/world/united-states

/inside-the-russian-troll-factory-zombies-troops-and-a-breakneck-pace. Garrett M. Graff, "Inside the Mueller Indictment: A Russian Novel of Intrigue," *Wired,* February 20, 2018, https://www.wired.com/story/inside-the-mueller-indictment-a-russian-novel-of-intrigue/.

2. Jolie Myers, "Meet the Activist Who Uncovered the Russian Troll Factory Named in the Mueller Probe," NPR, March 15, 2018, https://www.npr.org/sections/parallels/2018/03/15/594062887/some-russians-see-u-s-investigation-into-russian-election-meddling-as-a-soap-ope. Oliver Carroll, "St Petersburg 'Troll Farm' Had 90 Dedicated Staff Working to Influence US Election Campaign," *Independent,* October 17, 2017. Aja Romano, "Twitter Released 9 Million Tweets from One Russian Troll Farm: Here's What We Learned," *Vox,* October 19, 2018, www.vox.com/2018/10/19/17990946/twitter-russian-trolls-bots-election-tampering.

3. Hadas Gold, "IJR Suspends Three over Obama Conspiracy Post," *Politico,* March 21, 2017, www.politico.com/blogs/on-media/2017/03/independent-review-journal-suspends-3-over-obama-conspiracy-236310. Carole Cadwalladr, "Robert Mercer: The Big Data Billionaire Waging War on Mainstream Media," *Guardian,* February 26, 2017, www.theguardian.com/politics/2017/feb/26/robert-mercer-breitbart-war-on-media-steve-bannon-donald-trump-nigel-farage.

4. Philip Howard, Bharash Gnesh, and Dimitra Liotsiou, "The IRA and Political Polarization in the United States," Oxford Internet Institute, December 17, 2018. Scott Shane, "These Are the Ads Russia Bought on Facebook in 2016," *New York Times,* November 1, 2017. Thomas Heath, "IJReview Gets $1.5 M Funding, Led by GOP Politico and Investor Pete Snyder," *Washington Post,* January 6, 2015.

5. "A Tour Through Robert Morrow's Conspiracy Library," *Washington Post* video, 3:10, https://www.washingtonpost.com/video/politics/a-tour-through-robert-morrows-conspiracy-library/2016/03/03/287f6b5c-e163-11e5-8c00-8aa03741dced_video.html?utm_term=.a91f8d8da88e. Christina Lopez, "These Are the Unhinged, Misogynist Co-Authors of the Book Trump Is Using to Attack Clinton's Marriage," Media Matters for America, October 1, 2016, https://www.mediamatters.org/research/2016/10/01/these-are-unhinged-misogynist-co-authors-book-trump-using-attack-clinton-s-marriage/213468.

6. David Corn, "Trump's No. 1 Booster Goes Real Dirty to Attack the Clintons," *Mother Jones,* September 18, 2015. Roger Stone, "Corporal in Clintons' War on Women Is Back," *Daily Caller,* July 14, 2015.

7. Callum Borchers, "This Clinton Tell-All Is an Instant Best-Seller. So Why Is the Media 'Ignoring' It?," *Washington Post,* June 29, 2016.

8. "Brent Budowsky, "'Clinton Cash' Author Owes Hillary Clinton an Apology," *The Hill,* May 14, 2015. Jill Abramson, "Robert Mercer Invested Offshore Dark Money to Sink Clinton. He Must Be Delighted," *Guardian,* November 8, 2017, www.theguardian.com/commentisfree/2017/nov/08/robert-mercer-offshore-dark-money-hillary-clinton-paradise-papers. Nathan Reiff, "Trump Donor Robert Mercer Funded Book on Clinton Cash Dealings," *Investopedia,* January 19, 2017, https://www.investopedia.com/news/trump-donor-robert-mercer-funded-book-clinton-cash-dealings/.

9. Gabriel Debenedetti, "Book Alleges India Cash Swayed Hillary's Nuclear Stance," *Politico,* April 29, 2015, https://www.politico.com/story/2015/04/clinton-cash-book-india-nuclear-stance-secretary-state-117492. Annie Karni, "Clinton Cash' Publisher Corrects '7 or 8' Inaccurate Passages," *Politico,* May 14, 2015, https://www.politico.com/story/2015/05/clinton-cash-publisher-corrects-7-or-8-inaccurate-passages-117946.

10. Paul Rosenzweig, "Unpacking Uranium One: Hype and Law," *Lawfare,* October 27, 2017. "Over 90% of Uranium Purchased by U.S. Commercial Reactors Is from Outside the U.S.," U.S. Energy Information Administration, July 11, 2011, https://www.eia.gov/todayinenergy/detail.php?id=2150.

11. "'This Week' Transcript: 'Clinton Cash' Author Peter Schweizer," ABC, April 26, 2015, www.abcnews.go.com/Politics/week-transcript-clinton-cash-author-peter-schweizer/story?id=30568766.

12. David Leppard and Nick Rufford, "The Spy Who Wasn't There," *Washington Post,* April 11, 1993.

13. NR Staff, "Franken Writes Back," *National Review,* September 5, 2006, https://www.nationalreview.com/2006/09/franken-writes-back/.

14. Peter Schweizer, "Gore Isn't Quite as Green as He's Led the World to Believe," *USA Today,* December 7, 2006.

15. "Author Retracts Whitehouse Angle," *Providence Journal,* November 19, 2011.

16. Kyung M. Song, "McDermott Defends Timing of Stock Trades," *Seattle Times,* December 11, 2011.

17. Kate Picket, "Fact Check: Did Obama and Sebelius Only Meet in Person Once?," *Time,* December 6, 2013.

18. Dylan Byers, "New York Times, Washington Post, Fox News Strike Deals for Anti-Clinton Research," *Politico,* April 20, 2015, https://www.politico.com/blogs/media/2015/04/new-york-times-washington-post-fox-news-strike-deals-for-anti-clinton-research-205791.

19. New York Times Editorial Board, "Candidate Clinton and the Foundation," *New York Times,* April 23, 2015.

20. Jo Becker and Mike McIntire, "Cash Flowed to Clinton Foundation amid Russian Uranium Deal," *New York Times,* April 23, 2015. "Information on Clinton Foundation," Charity Navigator, https://www.charitynavigator.org/index.cfm?bay=search.summary&orgid=16680.

21. Eugene Kiely, "The Facts on Uranium One," PolitiFact, October 26, 2017, www.factcheck.org/2017/10/facts-uranium-one/. Nancy LeTourneau, "How Steve Bannon Played the Mainstream Media," *Washington Monthly,* August 21, 2017.

22. Brian Lehrer Show, "Clintons' Cash Flow," WNYC, April 27, 2015, https://www.wnyc.org/story/hillary-clintons-cash-flows/. Steve Barbash, "Fox News's Shepard Smith Debunks His Network's Favorite Hillary Clinton 'Scandal,' Infuriates Viewers," *Washington Post,* November 15, 2017.

23. Connie Bruck, "How Hollywood Remembers Steve Bannon," *New Yorker,* May 1, 2017. Pin-Yun Tarng, Kuan-Ta Chen, and Polly Huang, "An Analysis of WoW Players' Game Hours," Netgames '08, Worcester, Massachusetts, October 21–22, 2008. Jean Oggins and Jeffrey Sammis, "Notions of Video Game Addiction and Their

Relation to Self-Reported Addiction Among Players of World of Warcraft," *International Journal of Mental Health and Addiction,* April 2012. Julian Dibbell, "The Decline and Fall of an Ultra Rich Online Gaming Empire," *Wired,* November 24, 2008.

24. Judy Klemesrud, "Donald Trump, Real Estate Promoter, Builds Image as He Buys Buildings," *New York Times,* November 1, 1976. Philip Elliott and Zeke J Miller, "Inside Donald Trump's Chaotic Transition," *Time,* November 17, 2016. Sarah Posner, "How Donald Trump's New Campaign Chief Created an Online Haven for White Nationalists," *Mother Jones,* August 22, 2016.

25. Michael Lewis, "Has Anyone Seen the President?," *Bloomberg,* February 9, 2018.

26. Nick Bolton, "Trump's Biggest Lies?," *Vanity Fair,* August 4, 2016.

27. Brenden Gallagher, "The Most Sexist Things Donald Trump Has Said About Hillary Clinton (So Far),"VH-1, September 27, 2016. Marie Solis, "Bernie Sanders Official Campaign Site Once Invited Supporters to Bern the Witch," *Mic,* https://mic.com /articles/137707/a-bern-the-witch-event-appeared-on-bernie-sanders-official-site -and-the-internet-is-mad.

28. Craig Silverman, Anthony Belford, J. Lester Feder, and Saska Cvetkovska, "The Macedonia Connection," *BuzzFeed,* July 18, 2018, www.buzzfeednews.com/article /craigsilverman/american-conservatives-fake-news-macedonia-paris-wade-libert.

29. Charlotte Alter, "Sexist Hillary Clinton Attacks Are Best Sellers," *Time,* June 6, 2016. Samantha Subramanian, "Inside the Macedonian Fake News Complex," *Wired,* February 15, 2017. Amy Mitchell, "Key Findings on the Traits and Habits of the Modern News Consumer," Pew Research Center, July 7, 2016, http://www.pewresearch .org/fact-tank/2016/07/07/modern-news-consumer/. Ilan Mochari, "The Fascinating Marketing Power of Fear," *Inc.,* February 13, 2014, https://www.inc.com /ilan-mochari/customer-loyalty-horror-movies.html. James M. Jasper, "Constructing Indignation: Anger Dynamics in Protest Movements," *Emotion Review,* July 2014. M. J. Young, L. Z. Tiedens, H. Jung, and M. H. Tsai, "Mad Enough to See the Other Side: Anger and the Search for Disconfirming Information," *Cognitive Emotion,* January 2011. Sasha Lechash, "Watch the 'Godfather' of Fake News Try to Explain Himself on Samantha Bee's Show," *Mashable,* December 7, 2016, https://mashable .com/2016/12/07/fake-news-npr-samantha-bee-jestin-coler/#R90TNpAlPkqH. Zachary Crockett, "How the 'King of Fake News' Built His Empire," *Hustle,* November 7, 2017, https://thehustle.co/fake-news-jestin-coler. For data on inequality, see: "Income Inequality in the United States," Inequality, https://inequality.org/facts /income-inequality/.

30. Kim Lacapria, "Hillary Clinton Blamed Racism for the Death of a Gorilla in a Cincinnati Zoo," Snopes, June 3, 2016, https://www.snopes.com/fact-check/hillary -clinton-blames-racism-for-cincinnati-gorillas-death/. Scott Shane, "From Headline to Photograph, a Fake News Masterpiece," *New York Times,* January 17, 2017.

31. "United States of America v. Internet Research Agency," U.S. Department of Justice, February 16, 2018, https://www.justice.gov/file/1035477/download.

32. Sharon LaFraniere, Mark Mazzetti, and Matt Apuzzo, "How the Russia Inquiry Began: A Campaign Aide, Drinks and Talk of Political Dirt," *New York Times,* December 30, 2017.

33. Dmitri Alperovitch, "Bears in the Midst: Intrusion into the Democratic National Committee," *CrowdStrike,* June 15, 2016, https://www.crowdstrike.com/blog/bears -midst-intrusion-democratic-national-committee/.

34. Alter, "Sexist Hillary Clinton Attacks Are Best Sellers." Desi Lydic, "Sexism Sells," *Daily Show,* November 6, 2016, www.cc.com/video-clips/096kl4/the-daily-show -with-trevor-noah-sexism-sells—building-a-brand-with-misogynistic-political -humor.

35. Tara Golshan, "The Self-Reinforcing Cycle of Sexism at Donald Trump Rallies," *Vox,* September 30, 2016, https://www.vox.com/policy-and-politics/2016/9/30 /13122110/cycle-of-sexism-donald-trump-rallies.

36. James Comey, "Statement by FBI Director James B. Comey on the Investigation of Secretary Hillary Clinton's Use of a Personal E-Mail System," FBI, July 5, 2016, https://www.fbi.gov/news/pressrel/press-releases/statement-by-fbi-director-james -b-comey-on-the-investigation-of-secretary-hillary-clinton2019s-use-of-a-personal -e-mail-system.

37. James B. Comey, transcript, Hearing of the Subcommittee on Commercial and Administrative Law, House Committee on the Judiciary, May 3, 2007. John Stuart and Athan G. Theoharis, *The Boss: J. Edgar Hoover and the Great American Inquisition* (Philadelphia: Temple University Press, 1988). "2014: An Interview with FBI Director James Comey," CBS, June 19, 2016, http://www.cbsnews.com/news/2014-an -interview-with-fbi-director-james-comey/.

38. Raffi Khatchadourian, "No Secrets: Julian Assange's Mission for Total Transparency," *New Yorker,* June 7, 2010. Jennifer Williams, "Why the UN Ruled Julian Assange Is Being 'Arbitrarily Detained' and Why It Matters," *Vox,* February 5, 2016, www.vox.com /2016/2/5/10924922/assange-un-ruling. Chris Zappone, "DNCLeak: Five Times WikiLeaks and Russia Have Crossed Paths," *Sydney Morning Herald,* July 28, 2016.

39. Michael Crowley and Tyler Pager, "Trump Urges Russia to Hack Clinton's Email," *Politico,* July 27, 2016, www.politico.com/story/2016/07/trump-putin-no -relationship-226282.

40. Luiz Romero, "Roger Stone's Indictment Hints at the Origin of the #HillaryHealth Conspiracy Theories," *Quartz,* January 25, 2019. Robert Mackey, "Julian Assange's Hatred of Hillary Clinton Was No Secret. His Advice to Donald Trump Was," *Intercept,* November 15, 2017, https://theintercept.com/2017/11/15/wikileaks-julian -assange-donald-trump-jr-hillary-clinton/. Anna Schecter, "Mueller Has Emails from Stone Pal Corsi About Wikileaks Dem Email Dump," NBC, November 28, 2018, www.nbcnews.com/politics/justice-department/mueller-has-emails-stone -pal-corsi-about-wikileaks-dem-email-n940611. Julia Ioffe, "The Secret Correspondence Between Donald Trump Jr. and WikiLeaks," *Atlantic,* November 13, 2017, www.theatlantic.com/politics/archive/2017/11/the-secret-correspondence -between-donald-trump-jr-and-wikileaks/545738/.

41. Tina Ngyuen, "The 8 Biggest Lies in Trump's Big Anti-Clinton Speech," *Vanity Fair,* June 22, 2016, https://www.vanityfair.com/news/2016/06/donald-trump -clinton-speech-fact-check. Richard O. Lempert, "Claims That Clinton Lied About Emails Dissolve Under Scrutiny," *American Prospect,* November 1, 2016. Josh Rogin,

"Trump Allies, WikiLeaks and Russia Are Pushing a Nonsensical Conspiracy Theory About the DNC Hacks," *Washington Post,* August 12, 2016. Molly Ball, "Kellyanne's Alternative Universe," *Atlantic,* April 2017, www.theatlantic.com/magazine/archive/2017/04/kellyannes-alternative-universe/517821/. Kevin Shelly, "Paying Respects: When the Mob Bid Farewell to Kellyanne Conway's Grandfather," *Philly Voice,* June 28, 2017. Jeffrey S. Passel, "D'vera Cohn, 5 Facts About Illegal Immigration in the U.S.," StateAG.org, November 28, 2018, https://www.stateag.org/policy-areas/immigrant-communities/immigrant-communities-resources/2016/11/25/5-facts-about-illegal-immigration-pew-research-center.

42. Kat Katz, "How Backing Jill Stein Creates a Win for Sexism," *Medium,* July 15, 2016, https://medium.com/how-jill-stein-has-created-a-win-for-sexism/how-jill-stein-has-created-a-win-for-sexism-173752daec93. Rachel Wolfe, "Donald Trump, Bernie Sanders, and Jill Stein All Appear to Have Been Helped by Russian Election Interference," *Vox,* February 16, 2018, https://www.vox.com/policy-and-politics/2018/2/16/17021248/russian-election-interference-sanders-stein-trump. "United States of America v. Internet Research Agency." Casey Michel, "The Pro-Kremlin Talking Points of Jill Stein," *ThinkProgress,* December 19, 2017, https://thinkprogress.org/jill-stein-campaign-russia-ecf424ac3b7e/. Jonathan Martin and Amy Chozik, "Donald Trump's Campaign Stands by Embrace of Putin," *New York Times,* September 8, 2016.

43. Sean Illing, "Cambridge Analytica, the Shady Data Firm That Might Be a Key Trump-Russia Link, Explained," *Vox,* April 4, 2018, www.vox.com/policy-and-politics/2017/10/16/15657512/cambridge-analytica-facebook-alexander-nix-christopher-wylie.

44. "Trump Adviser Roger Stone Claims Clinton Was Placed on an 'Oxygen Tank' Immediately After Presidential Debate," Media Matters for America, September 27, 2016, www.mediamatters.org/video/2016/09/27/trump-adviser-roger-stone-claims-clinton-was-placed-oxygen-tank-immediately-after-presidential/213346.

45. "18 Revelations from Wikileaks' Hacked Clinton Emails," BBC, October 27, 2016, www.bbc.com/news/world-us-canada-37639370.

46. Andrea Mitchell and Alastair Jamieson, "Trump Planned Debate Stunt, Invited Bill Clinton's Accusers to Rattle Hillary," NBC, October 10, 2016, https://www.nbcnews.com/storyline/2016-presidential-debates/trump-planned-debate-stunt-invited-bill-clinton-accusers-rattle-hillary-n663481. Jon Greenburg, "Trump Says Clinton Viciously Attacked Those Who Charged Abuse by Bill," PolitiFact, October 10, 2016, www.politifact.com/truth-o-meter/statements/2016/oct/10/donald-trump/donald-trump-says-hillary-clinton-viciously-attack/.

47. Matt Zapotosky, "Rudy Giuliani Is Claiming to Have Insider FBI Knowledge. Does He Really?," *Washington Post,* November 4, 2016. Harper Nedig, "Ex-FBI Official: Clintons Are a 'Crime Family,'" *Washington Examiner,* October 30, 2016. "'This Week' Transcript 4-15-18: James Comey Interview Clips, White House Press Secretary Sarah Sanders, Sen. Susan Collins and Rep. Adam Schiff," ABC, April 15, 2018, https://abcnews.go.com/beta-story-container/Politics/week-transcript-15-18-james-comey-interview-clips/story?id=54470491. Peter Elkind, "James Comey's Conspicuous Independence," *New Yorker,* May 11, 2017.

48. Dean Obeidallah, "Donald Trump's Despicable Anti-Muslim Huma Abedin Smear," *Daily Beast,* August 31, 2016, http://www.thedailybeast.com/articles/2016/08/31/donald-trump-s-despicable-anti-muslim-huma-abedin-smear.html. Emily Guskin and Scot Clement, "Post-ABC Tracking Poll: Trump 46, Clinton 45, as Democratic Enthusiasm Dips," *Washington Post,* November 1, 2016, www.washingtonpost.com/news/the-fix/wp/2016/11/01/post-abc-tracking-poll-clinton-falls-behind-trump-in-enthusiasm-but-has-edge-in-early-voting/?utm_term=.4cdc5dc39d6c.

49. "Statement by FBI Director James B. Comey on the Investigation of Secretary Hillary Clinton's Use of a Personal E-Mail System," FBI, July 5, 2016, www.fbi.gov/news/pressrel/press-releases/statement-by-fbi-director-james-b-comey-on-the-investigation-of-secretary-hillary-clinton2019s-use-of-a-personal-e-mail-system. Eugene Kiely, Lori Robertson, and D'Angelo Gore, "Spinning the FBI Letter," FactCheck, October 31, 2016, http://www.factcheck.org/2016/10/spinning-the-fbi-letter/. "FBI Director Comey Faces Fury for Cryptic Letter About Clinton Email Inquiry," *Guardian,* October 29, 2016, www.theguardian.com/us-news/2016/oct/29/fury-fbi-director-cryptic-letter-clinton-emails-response.

50. Matt Apuzzo, Adam Goldman, Michael S. Schmidt, and William K. Rashbaum, "Justice Dept. Strongly Discouraged Comey on Move in Clinton Email Case," *New York Times,* October 29, 2016.

51. Nathan J. Robinson, "The Clinton Comedy of Errors," *Current Affairs,* April 26, 2017.

52. Nate Silver, "The Comey Letter Probably Cost Clinton the Election," *FiveThirtyEight,* May 3, 2017, https://fivethirtyeight.com/features/the-comey-letter-probably-cost-clinton-the-election/.

## Afterword

1. Alec Tyson and Shiva Maniam, "Behind Trump's Victory: Divisions by Race, Gender, Education," Pew Research Center, November 9, 2016, www.pewresearch.org/fact-tank/2016/11/09/behind-trumps-victory-divisions-by-race-gender-education/. Benjamin Wittes, "Five Things I Learned from the Mueller Report: A Careful Reading of the Dense Document Delivers Some Urgent Insights," *Atlantic,* April 29, 2019. Ryan Teague Beckwith, "Here Are All of the Indictments, Guilty Pleas and Convictions from Robert Mueller's Investigation," *Time,* March 24, 2019. Michael S. Schmidt, "Mueller Report Reveals Trump's Fixation on Targeting Hillary Clinton," *New York Times,* April 24, 2019.

2. Tyson and Maniam, "Behind Trump's Victory." Wittes, "Five Things." Beckwith, "All of the Indictments." Schmidt, "Mueller Report."

3. Clyde Haberman, "Roger Ailes, Who Built Fox News into an Empire, Dies at 77," *New York Times,* May 18, 2017.

4. Lindsey Bever, "Assange Is the 'Only Foreigner' the Trump Administration Would Welcome to the U.S., Clinton Jokes," *Washington Post,* April 12, 2019.

5. Marc Townsend, "Steve Bannon 'Told Italy's Populist Leader: Pope Francis Is the Enemy,'" *Guardian,* April 13, 2019.

6. Brent D. Griffiths, "David Bossie Apologizes for 'Cotton-Picking Mind' Comment to Black Panelist," *Politico,* June 24, 2018.

7. "Jestin Coler," Nieman Foundation, https://nieman.harvard.edu/authors/jestin-coler/.

8. Dana Cancian, "George Conway Congratulates Trump on Surpassing 10,000 False Claims: 'No One but You Could Have Achieved This,'" *Newsweek,* April 29, 2019.

9. Jason Le Mier, "Drudge Turns on Trump over Fears His Threats Could Lead to 'Licensing of All Reporters,'" *Newsweek,* May 9, 2018.

10. Official Website of Gennifer Flowers, www.GenniferFlowers.com.

11. Peter Bergen, "The Mystery of Mike Flynn," CNN, December 18, 2018.

12. Mark Joseph Stern, "One of Monica Lewinsky's Most Notorious Interrogators Is About to Get a Seat on the Federal Bench," *Slate,* March 28, 2019.

13. Jess Row, "Why Is Being Held Accountable So Terrifying Under Patriarchy?," *New Yorker,* November 30, 2018.

14. David Usborne, "The Peacock Patriarchy," *Esquire,* August 5, 2018.

15. "Monica Lewinsky: Emerging from 'the House of Gaslight' in the Age of #MeToo," *Vanity Fair,* March 2018.

16. Matt Pearce, "Who Is Christopher Ruddy, and Why Does He Know What the President Is Thinking?," *Los Angeles Times,* June 17, 2017.

17. Kenneth Vogel, "Clinton Eulogizes Scaife," *Politico,* August 2, 2014.

18. Katherine Skiba, David Heinzzmann, and Todd Lighty, "Peter W. Smith, GOP Operative Who Sought Clinton's Emails from Russian Hackers, Committed Suicide, Records Show," *Chicago Tribune,* July 13, 2017. Thomas Lipscomb, "The Trouble with Peter Smith," RealClearPolitics.com, October 13, 2018.

19. Sean Wilentz, "Presumed Guilty," *New York Review of Books,* March 7, 2019. Associated Press, "Ken Starr Leaves Baylor After Complaints It Mishandled Sex Assault Inquiry," *New York Times,* August 19, 2016.

20. Darren Samuelsohn, Josh Gerstein, Marc Caputo, and Caitlin Oprysko, "Roger Stone Arrested in Mueller Investigation," *Politico,* January 25, 2019.

# Index